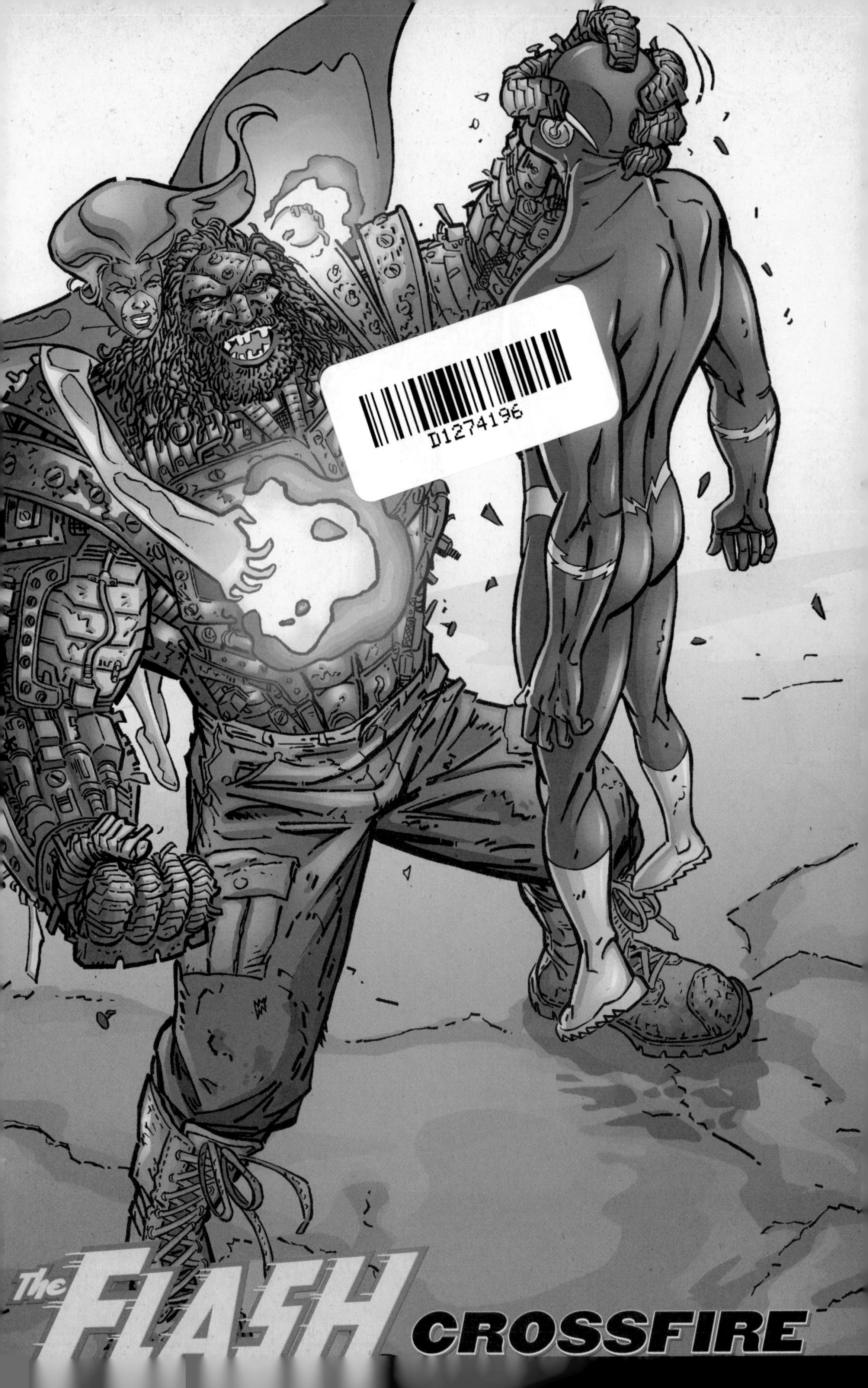
The FLASH
CROSSFIRE

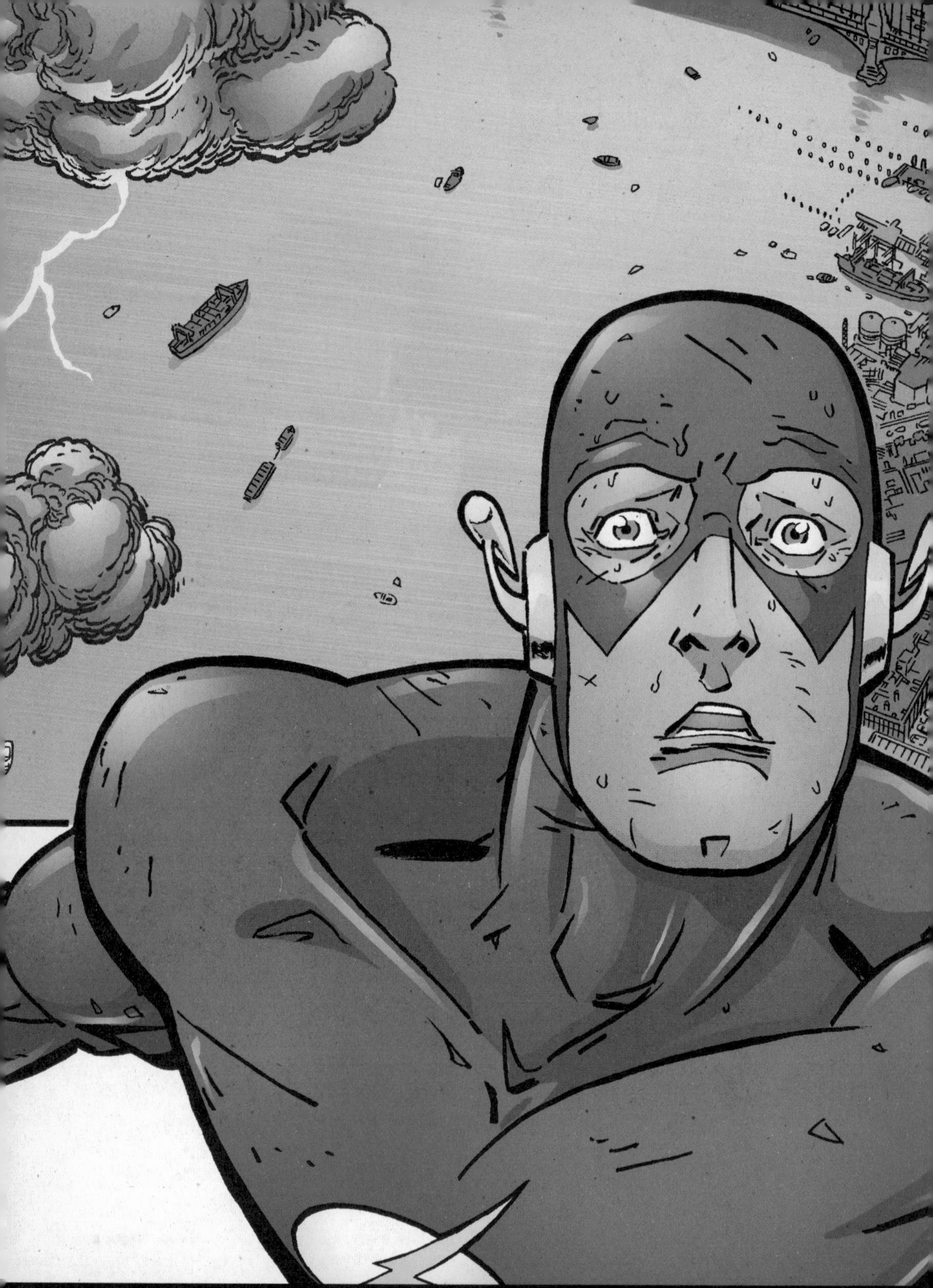

Dan DiDio VP-Editorial Joey Cavalieri Editor-original series Bob Greenberger Senior Editor-Collected Edition
Robbin Brosterman Senior Art Director Paul Levitz President & Publisher Georg Brewer VP-Design & Retail Product Development
Richard Bruning Senior VP-Creative Director Patrick Caldon Senior VP-Finance & Operations Chris Caramalis VP-Finance
Terri Cunningham VP-Managing Editor Alison Gill VP-Manufacturing Lillian Laserson Senior VP & General Counsel
Jim Lee Editorial Director-Wildstorm David McKillips VP- Advertising & Custom Publishing John Nee VP-Business Development
Cheryl Rubin VP-Brand Management Bob Wayne VP-Sales & Marketing

THE FLASH: CROSSFIRE

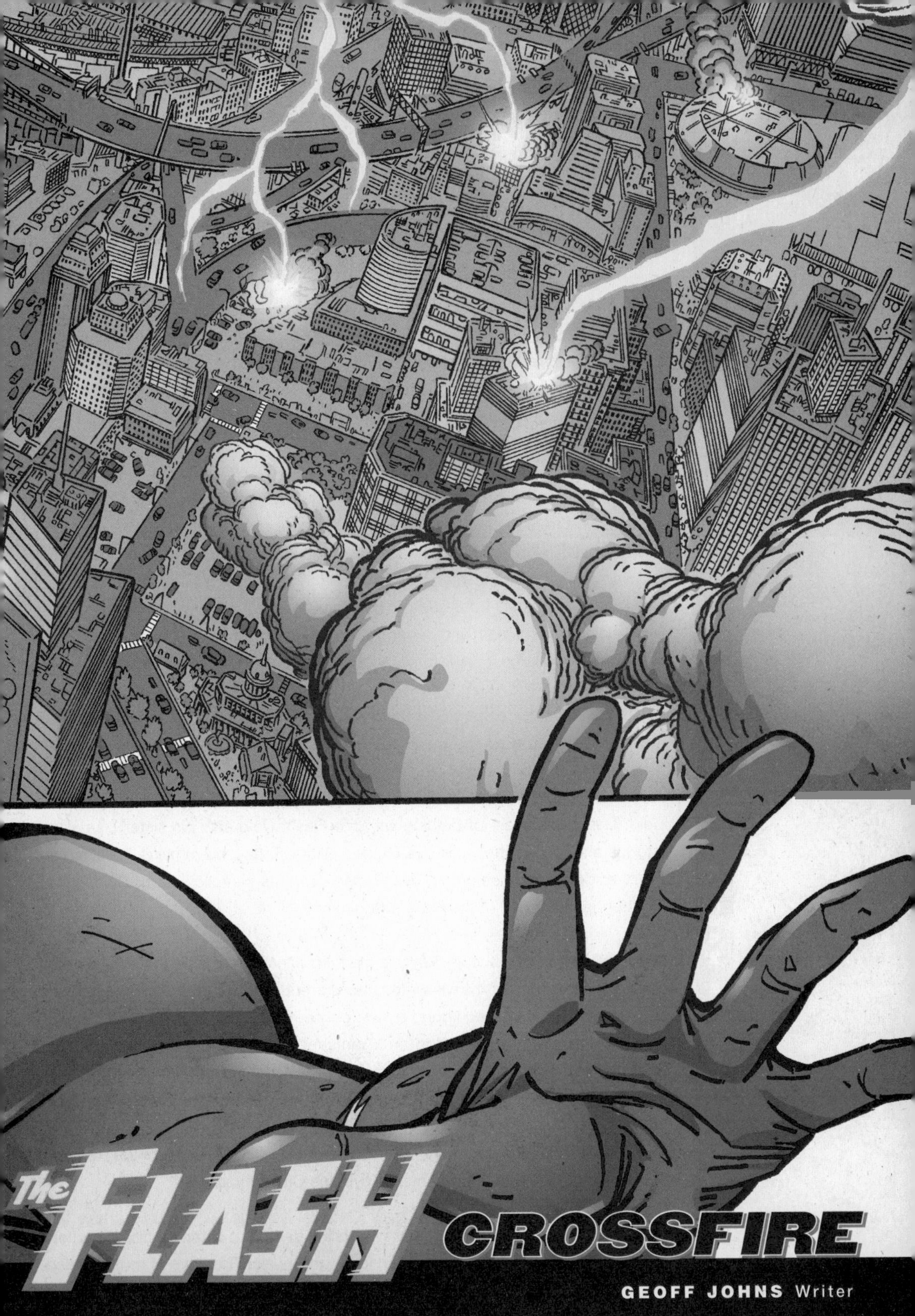

The FLASH CROSSFIRE

GEOFF JOHNS Writer

SCOTT KOLINS RICH BURCHETT JUSTINIANO Pencillers

DOUG HAZLEWOOD DAN PANOSIAN WALDEN WONG Inkers

JAMES SINCLAIR Colorist **GASPAR SALADINO BILL OAKLEY** Letterers

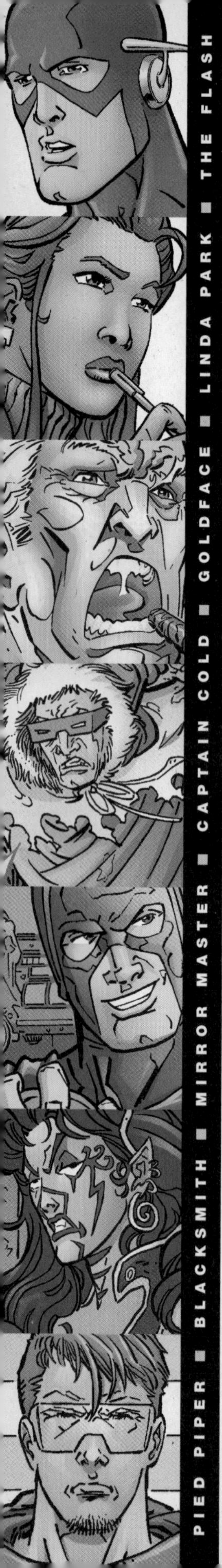
THE FLASH
LINDA PARK
GOLDFACE
CAPTAIN COLD
MIRROR MASTER
BLACKSMITH
PIED PIPER

C H A R A C T E R   B I O S

THE FLASH: Caught in a bizarre accident, teenager Wally West was struck by an erratic bolt of lightning and bestowed with the gift of incredible super-speed. After years of training as Kid Flash to Barry Allen's Flash, Wally inherited the mantle of the Scarlet Speedster following the death of his mentor. Now, protecting Keystone City, he carries on the legacy of the fastest man alive — Wally West is the Flash!

LINDA PARK: Linda Park originally thought Wally to be brash and arrogant — which he was. But Linda also saw something else in him, the spark of a better man. As their relationship developed, that spark turned into a flame of love that led them to marry. So strong is their bond that it has enabled Flash to find his way home, regardless of time, dimension, or location. Recently, Linda has enrolled at Central City Medical College.

GOLDFACE: Keith Kenyon was a simple chemist who discovered a powerful elixir derived from ancient gold. It altered Kenyon, giving him enhanced strength and a golden skin tone. He turned to crime to pay for his experiments and crossed paths first with Green Lantern, and then the Flash. While in Iron Heights, Kenyon's skin turned from flesh into organic metal. Upon his release, Kenyon followed his father's path and became a union leader, now the head of Union 242, Keystone City's largest work force.

CAPTAIN COLD: Leonard Snart was never more than a common thief until the day he was taken down by the Flash. In prison, Len promised himself he would face the Flash when he got out. The opportunity came after he stole an experimental cryogenic engine. Snart created a cold-gun and renamed himself Captain Cold. During his years of battling with the Flash, Cold saw his sister Lisa slide into his shadow as the villainous Golden Glider. Today, he remains guilt-ridden over her death and has grown even colder towards his fellow man. Cold is the most underestimated of the Flash's Rogues.

MIRROR MASTER: Just as Wally is the third generation Flash, there have been several incarnations of the Mirror Master. Currently wearing the costume is Evan McCulloch. Hired and equipped by the government as an enforcer, he quickly outgrew the need for direction and banished his superiors to a mirror world. He has used the reflecting ability of mirrors in ways that Sam Scudder, the original Mirror Master, never dreamt of. McCulloch will do anything for a price.

BLACKSMITH: Almost nothing is known about the female leader of the Rogues, save that she has been operating in Keystone City for years.

PIED PIPER: Hartley Rathaway was born deaf, but after modern medical science restored his hearing he fell in love with music. That love of music fueled an interest in sonics that ultimately led the wealthy youth to assume the costumed guise of the Pied Piper. Rathaway seemed more interested in challenging the second Flash than in committing crimes, and he ultimately turned away from that path. Today, as a friend to Wally West, he is a champion of civil and social rights across Keystone and Central City.

C H A R A C T E R   B I O S

WEATHER WIZARD: Mark Mardon was a small-time crook who either got lucky or was a murderer. A prison escapee, Mardon headed to his older brother's observatory for shelter, where he either found his brother dead (from a heart attack) or killed him. What is indisputable is that he took possession of his brother's invention, a "weather wand" capable of controlling weather. Using the wand, Mardon became the thief known as Weather Wizard. He has battled various incarnations of the Flash, improving his control over the wand's properties with experience.

MURMUR: Dr. Michael Christian Amar was a surgeon, well-respected throughout the twin cities of Keystone and Central. But Amar was also a costumed serial killer, nicknamed "Murmur" by the local papers for his constant muttering, a nervous tic he could not control. He was caught by Keystone Police, identified by his speech impediment. In order to insure he never incriminate himself again, Murmur cut out his own tongue. Murmur recently was the catalyst for a massive breakout in Iron Heights.

MAGENTA: Frances Kane's metahuman magnetic abilities manifested themselves at the worst time conceivable. While in the car with her father and brother, Kane's powers kicked in, causing a terrible accident that left both men dead. From then on, whenever Kane would use her magnetic abilities, a twisted side of her psyche, later dubbed Magenta, would emerge. Over the years, Magenta has switched sides between good and evil, most recently reemerging more in control of her powers and more focused on toying with her ex-lover, The Flash.

GIRDER: After steelworker Tony Woodward assaulted a young female at work, a riot ensued and he was thrown into a vat of molten steel by angry co-workers. No ordinary metal, it was, in fact, scrap from S.T.A.R. Labs that had undergone several mysterious experiments. Woodward rose up from the pit in the metallic form of Girder. Endowed with incredible strength, Girder's greatest enemy is rust, which painfully eats away more of his body each day.

PLUNDER: While trapped in a "mirror world" within his wife's diamond ring, the Flash was tracked by a bounty hunter calling himself Plunder. Realizing he was trapped in a reflection, which was destined to fade away, Plunder escaped "Wonderland" on the heels of the Flash. Plunder's true identity is unknown, but he is a "reflection" of somebody in the real world.

...and introducing a brand new **TRICKSTER.**

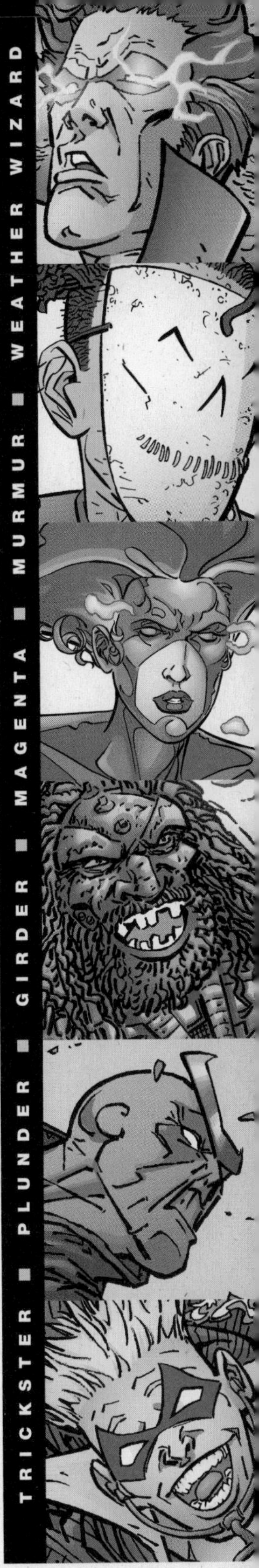
TRICKSTER ■ PLUNDER ■ GIRDER ■ MAGENTA ■ MURMUR ■ WEATHER WIZARD

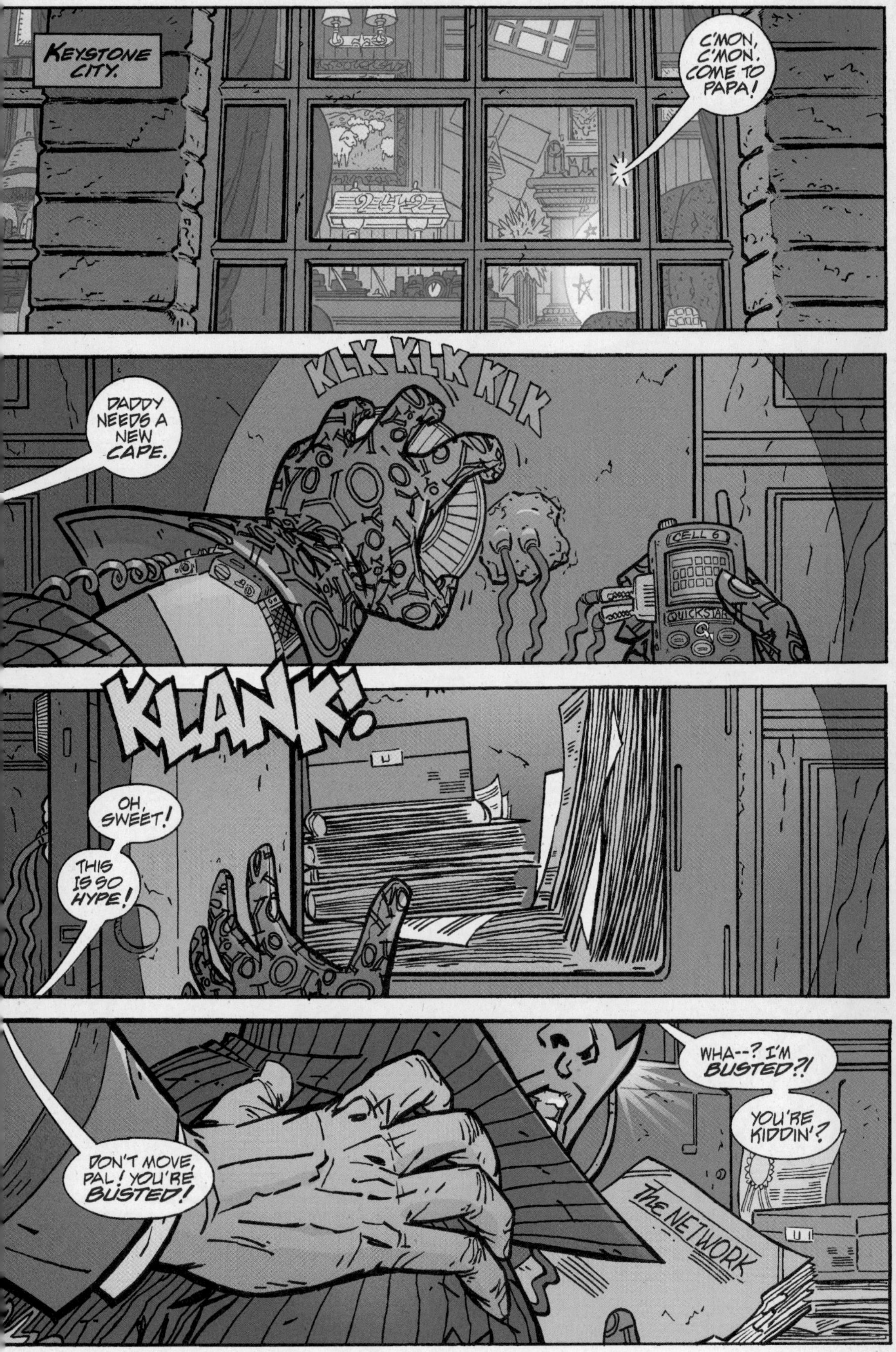
KEYSTONE CITY.
C'MON, C'MON. COME TO PAPA!
DADDY NEEDS A NEW CAPE.
KLK KLK KLK
CELL 6
QUICKSTAR
KLANK!
OH, SWEET!
THIS IS SO HYPE!
WHA--? I'M BUSTED?!
YOU'RE KIDDIN'?
DON'T MOVE, PAL! YOU'RE BUSTED!
The NETWORK

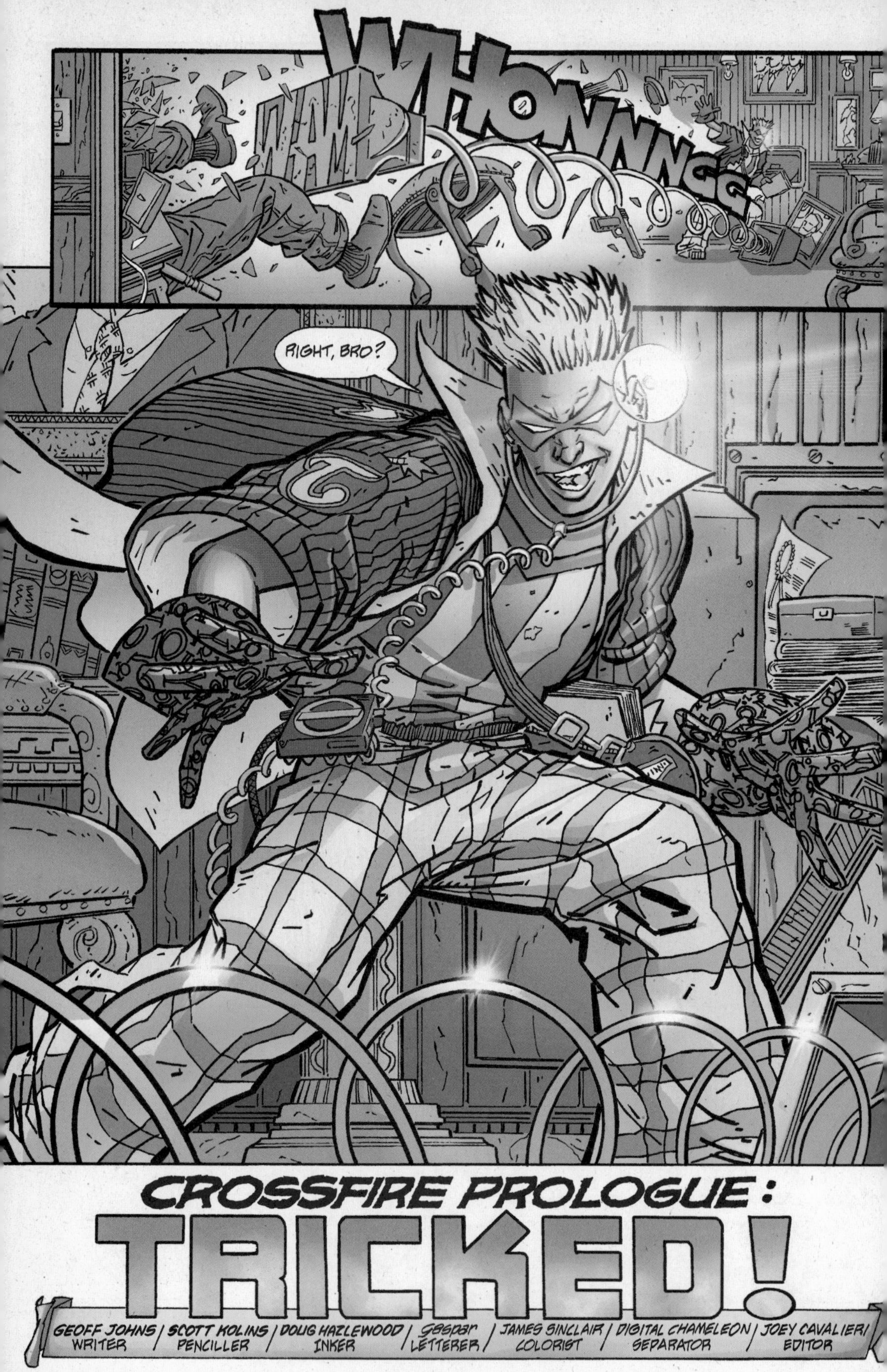
WHONNNGG
WAM
RIGHT, BRO?
CROSSFIRE PROLOGUE:
TRICKED!
GEOFF JOHNS WRITER / SCOTT KOLINS PENCILLER / DOUG HAZLEWOOD INKER / Gaspar LETTERER / JAMES SINCLAIR COLORIST / DIGITAL CHAMELEON SEPARATOR / JOEY CAVALIERI EDITOR

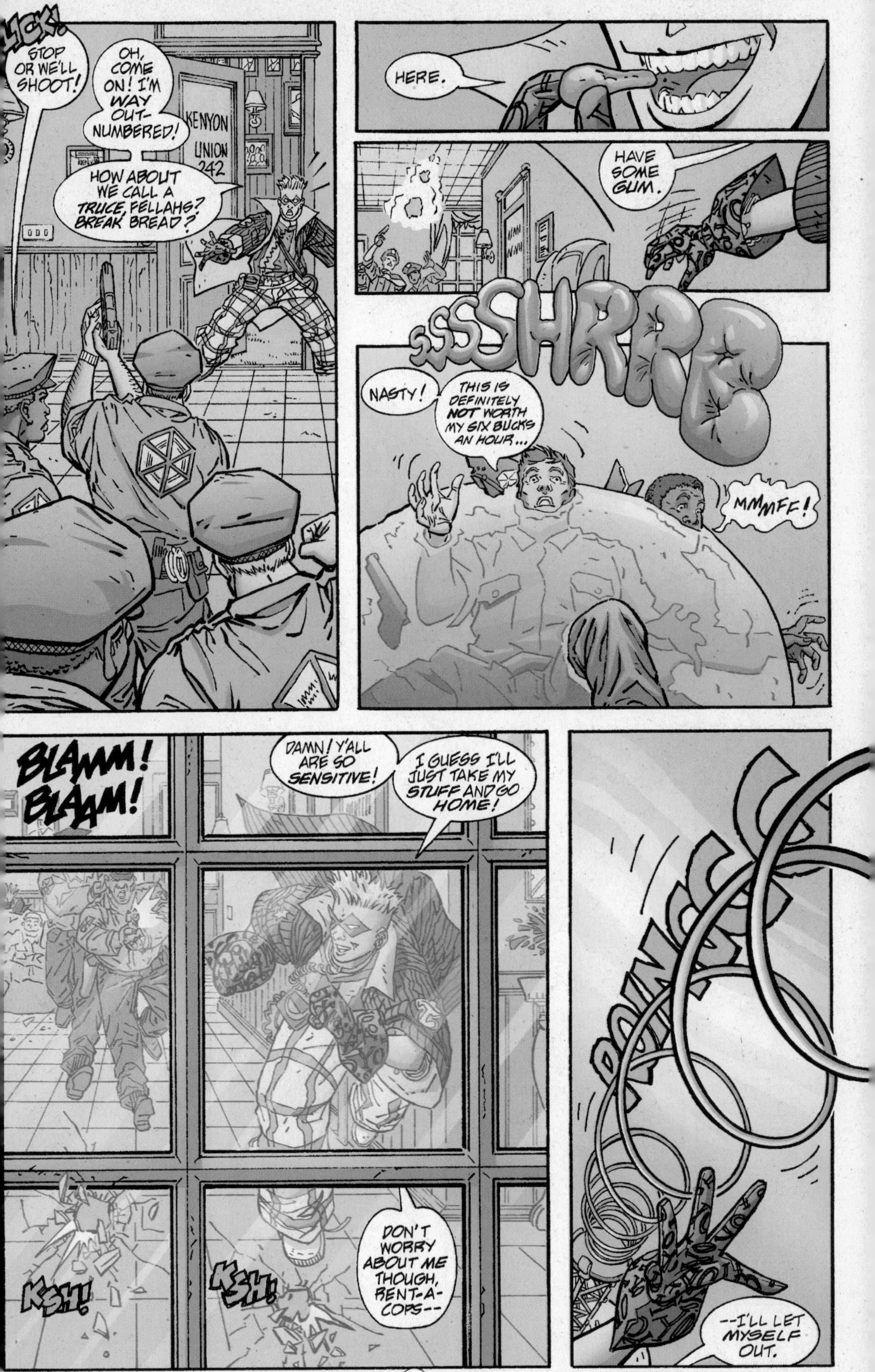
LICK!
STOP OR WE'LL SHOOT!
OH, COME ON! I'M WAY OUT-NUMBERED!
KENYON UNION 242
HOW ABOUT WE CALL A TRUCE, FELLAHS? BREAK BREAD?
HERE.
HAVE SOME GUM.
SSSSHRRP
NASTY!
THIS IS DEFINITELY NOT WORTH MY SIX BUCKS AN HOUR...
MMMFF!
BLAMM! BLAAM!
DAMN! Y'ALL ARE SO SENSITIVE!
I GUESS I'LL JUST TAKE MY STUFF AND GO HOME!
KSH!
KSH!
DON'T WORRY ABOUT ME THOUGH, RENT-A-COPS--
--I'LL LET MYSELF OUT.

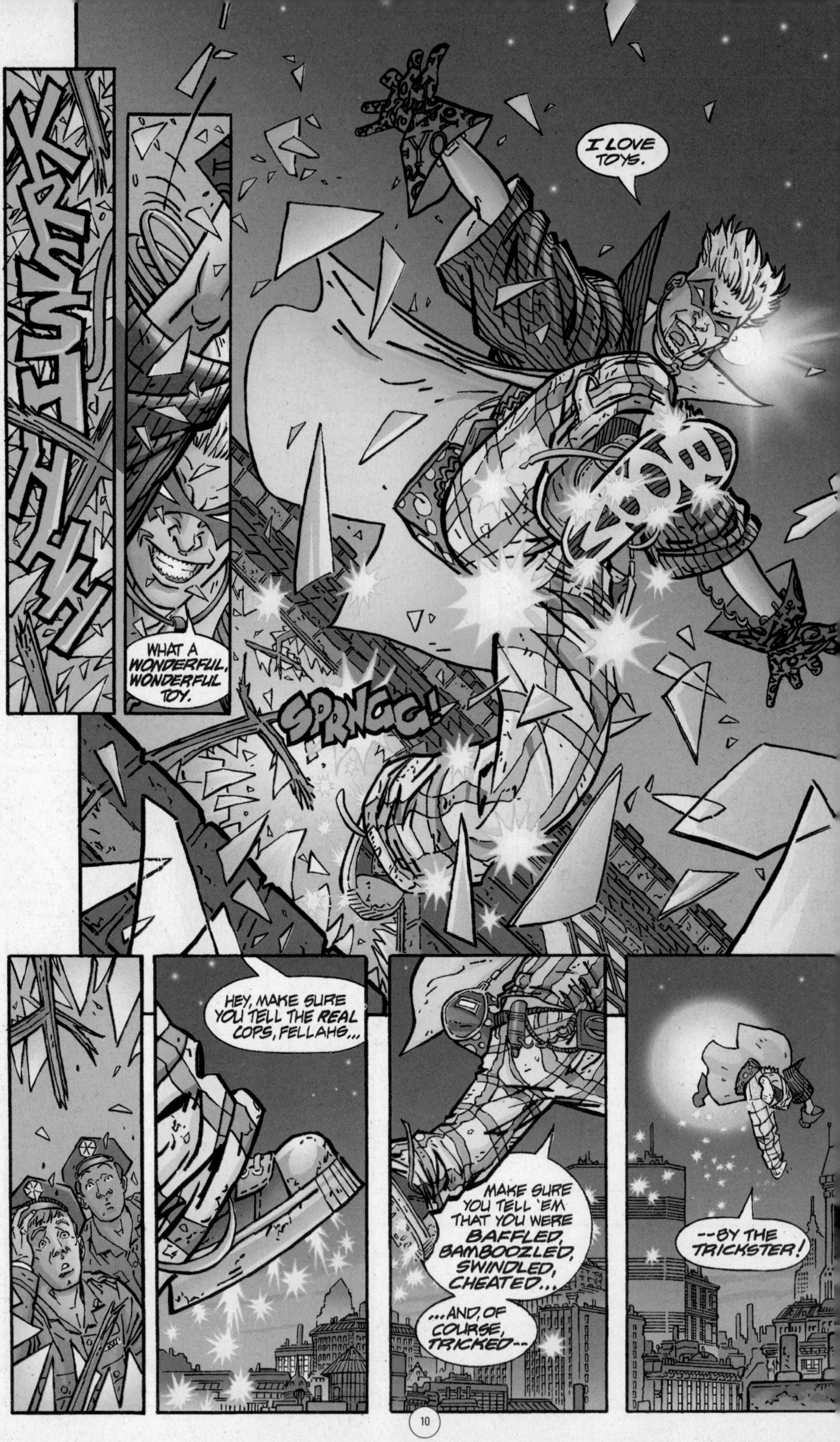

KRASHHH!
WHAT A WONDERFUL, WONDERFUL TOY.
I LOVE TOYS.
SPRNGG!
HEY, MAKE SURE YOU TELL THE REAL COPS, FELLAHS...
MAKE SURE YOU TELL 'EM THAT YOU WERE BAFFLED, BAMBOOZLED, SWINDLED, CHEATED...
...AND, OF COURSE, TRICKED--
--BY THE TRICKSTER!

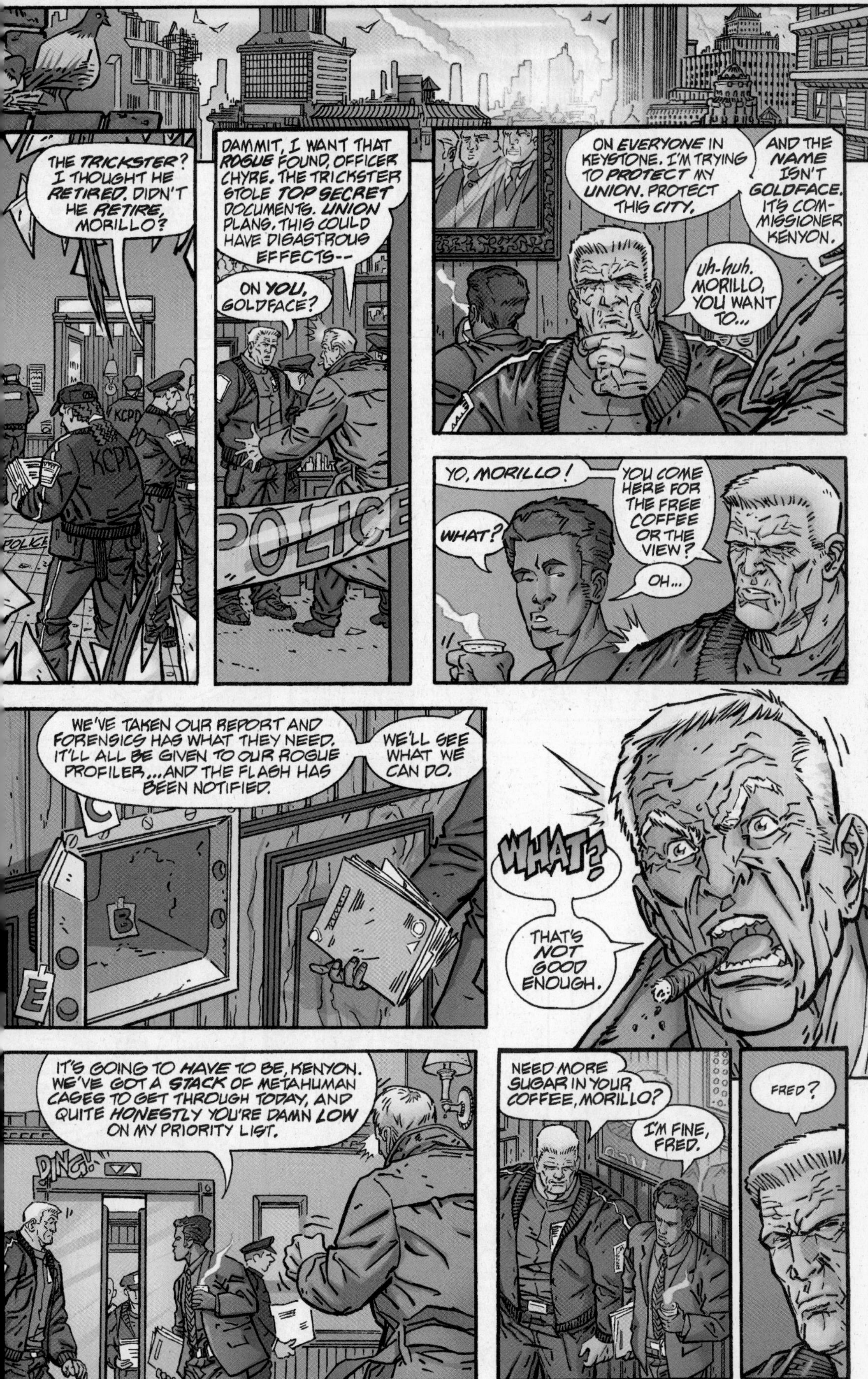

THE TRICKSTER? I THOUGHT HE RETIRED. DIDN'T HE RETIRE, MORILLO?
DAMMIT, I WANT THAT ROGUE FOUND, OFFICER CHYRE. THE TRICKSTER STOLE TOP SECRET DOCUMENTS. UNION PLANS. THIS COULD HAVE DISASTROUS EFFECTS--
ON YOU, GOLDFACE?
POLICE
ON EVERYONE IN KEYSTONE. I'M TRYING TO PROTECT MY UNION. PROTECT THIS CITY.
AND THE NAME ISN'T GOLDFACE. IT'S COMMISSIONER KENYON.
uh-huh. MORILLO, YOU WANT TO...
YO, MORILLO!
WHAT?
YOU COME HERE FOR THE FREE COFFEE OR THE VIEW?
OH...
WE'VE TAKEN OUR REPORT AND FORENSICS HAS WHAT THEY NEED. IT'LL ALL BE GIVEN TO OUR ROGUE PROFILER,...AND THE FLASH HAS BEEN NOTIFIED.
WE'LL SEE WHAT WE CAN DO.
WHAT?
THAT'S NOT GOOD ENOUGH.
IT'S GOING TO HAVE TO BE, KENYON. WE'VE GOT A STACK OF METAHUMAN CASES TO GET THROUGH TODAY, AND QUITE HONESTLY YOU'RE DAMN LOW ON MY PRIORITY LIST.
DING!
NEED MORE SUGAR IN YOUR COFFEE, MORILLO?
I'M FINE, FRED.
FRED?

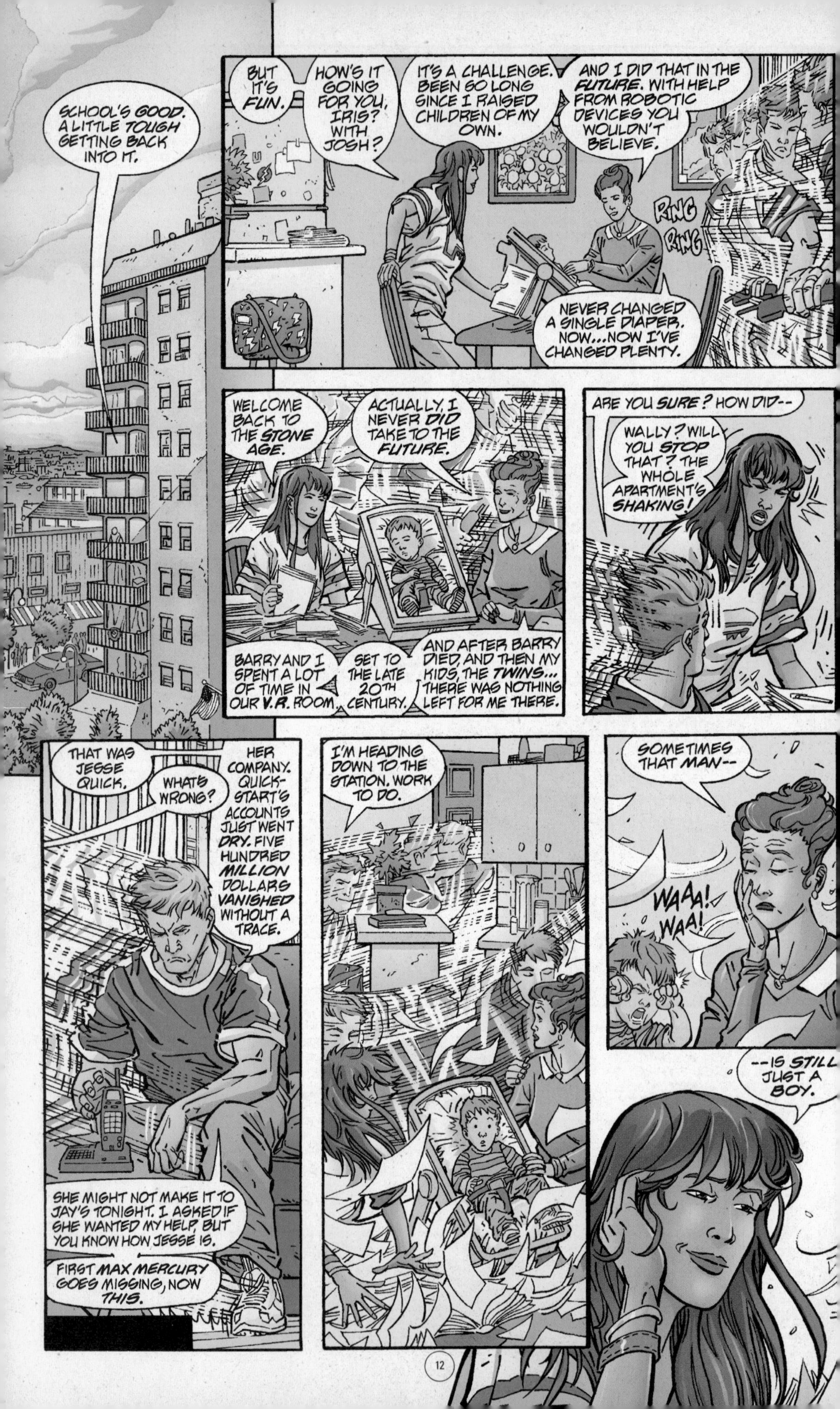

SCHOOL'S GOOD. A LITTLE TOUGH GETTING BACK INTO IT.
BUT IT'S FUN.
HOW'S IT GOING FOR YOU, IRIS? WITH JOSH?
IT'S A CHALLENGE. BEEN SO LONG SINCE I RAISED CHILDREN OF MY OWN.
AND I DID THAT IN THE FUTURE. WITH HELP FROM ROBOTIC DEVICES YOU WOULDN'T BELIEVE.
RING
RING
NEVER CHANGED A SINGLE DIAPER. NOW...NOW I'VE CHANGED PLENTY.
WELCOME BACK TO THE STONE AGE.
ACTUALLY, I NEVER DID TAKE TO THE FUTURE.
BARRY AND I SPENT A LOT OF TIME IN OUR V.R. ROOM,
SET TO THE LATE 20TH CENTURY.
AND AFTER BARRY DIED, AND THEN MY KIDS, THE TWINS... THERE WAS NOTHING LEFT FOR ME THERE.
ARE YOU SURE? HOW DID--
WALLY? WILL YOU STOP THAT? THE WHOLE APARTMENT'S SHAKING!
THAT WAS JESSE QUICK.
WHAT'S WRONG?
HER COMPANY. QUICK-START'S ACCOUNTS JUST WENT DRY. FIVE HUNDRED MILLION DOLLARS VANISHED WITHOUT A TRACE.
SHE MIGHT NOT MAKE IT TO JAY'S TONIGHT. I ASKED IF SHE WANTED MY HELP, BUT YOU KNOW HOW JESSE IS.
FIRST MAX MERCURY GOES MISSING, NOW THIS.
I'M HEADING DOWN TO THE STATION. WORK TO DO.
SOMETIMES THAT MAN--
WAAA!
WAA!
--IS STILL JUST A BOY.

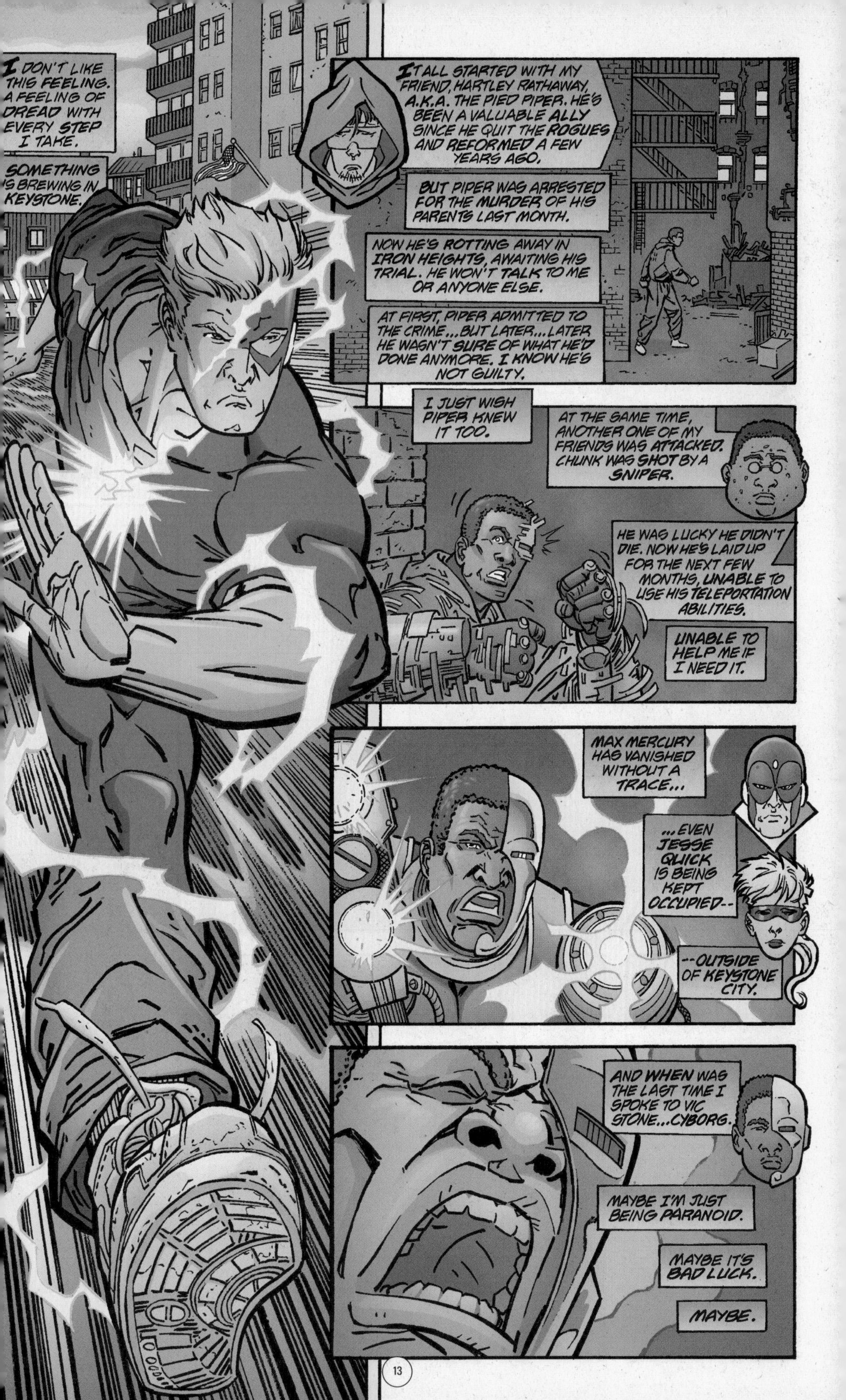

I DON'T LIKE THIS FEELING. A FEELING OF DREAD WITH EVERY STEP I TAKE.
SOMETHING IS BREWING IN KEYSTONE.
IT ALL STARTED WITH MY FRIEND, HARTLEY RATHAWAY, A.K.A. THE PIED PIPER. HE'S BEEN A VALUABLE ALLY SINCE HE QUIT THE ROGUES AND REFORMED A FEW YEARS AGO.
BUT PIPER WAS ARRESTED FOR THE MURDER OF HIS PARENTS LAST MONTH.
NOW HE'S ROTTING AWAY IN IRON HEIGHTS, AWAITING HIS TRIAL. HE WON'T TALK TO ME OR ANYONE ELSE.
AT FIRST, PIPER ADMITTED TO THE CRIME... BUT LATER... LATER HE WASN'T SURE OF WHAT HE'D DONE ANYMORE. I KNOW HE'S NOT GUILTY.
I JUST WISH PIPER KNEW IT TOO.
AT THE SAME TIME, ANOTHER ONE OF MY FRIENDS WAS ATTACKED. CHUNK WAS SHOT BY A SNIPER.
HE WAS LUCKY HE DIDN'T DIE. NOW HE'S LAID UP FOR THE NEXT FEW MONTHS, UNABLE TO USE HIS TELEPORTATION ABILITIES.
UNABLE TO HELP ME IF I NEED IT.
MAX MERCURY HAS VANISHED WITHOUT A TRACE...
...EVEN JESSE QUICK IS BEING KEPT OCCUPIED--
--OUTSIDE OF KEYSTONE CITY.
AND WHEN WAS THE LAST TIME I SPOKE TO VIC STONE...CYBORG.
MAYBE I'M JUST BEING PARANOID.
MAYBE IT'S BAD LUCK.
MAYBE.

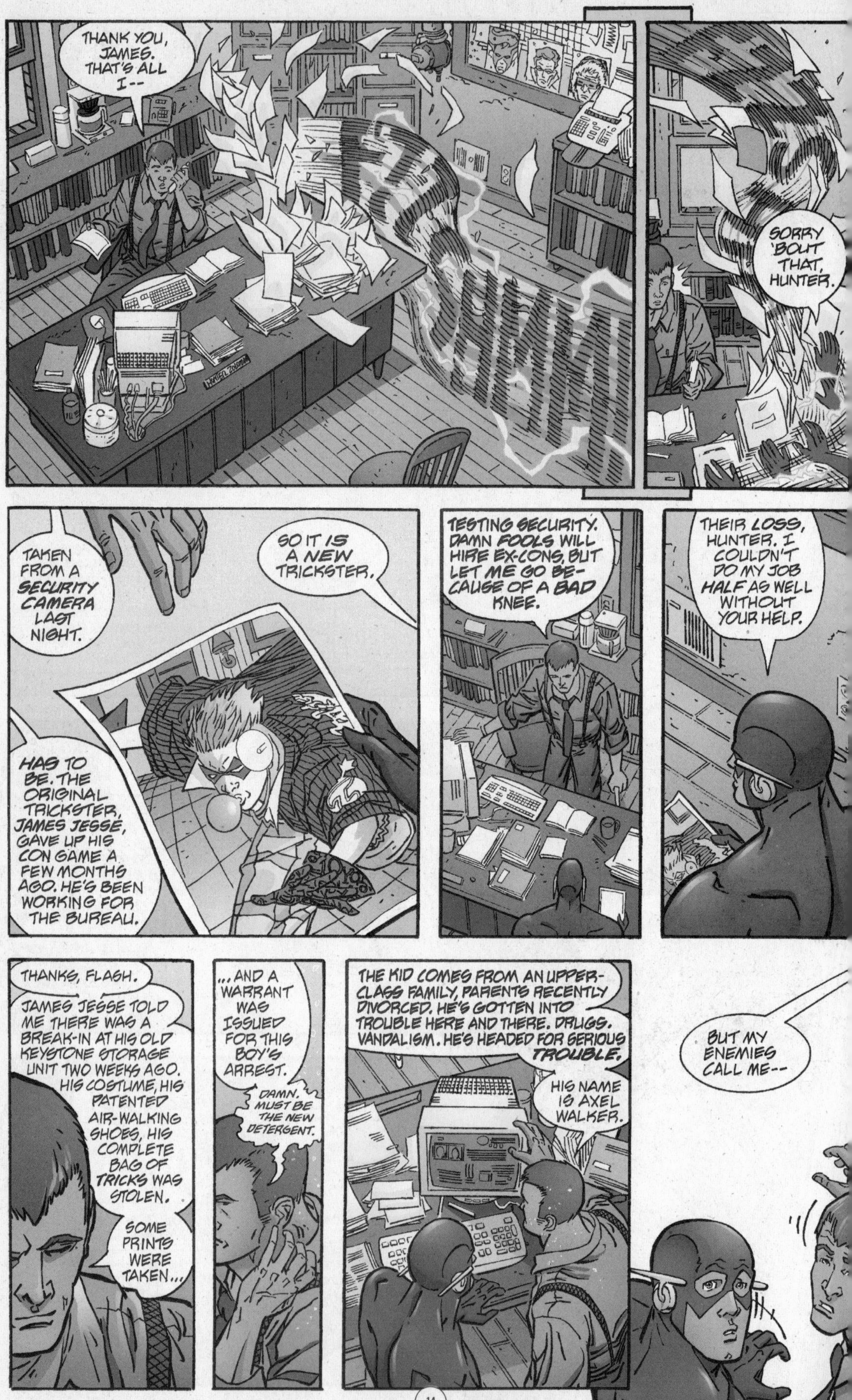
THANK YOU, JAMES. THAT'S ALL I--
SORRY 'BOUT THAT, HUNTER.
TAKEN FROM A SECURITY CAMERA LAST NIGHT.
SO IT IS A NEW TRICKSTER.
HAS TO BE. THE ORIGINAL TRICKSTER, JAMES JESSE, GAVE UP HIS CON GAME A FEW MONTHS AGO. HE'S BEEN WORKING FOR THE BUREAU.
TESTING SECURITY. DAMN FOOLS WILL HIRE EX-CONS, BUT LET ME GO BE-CAUSE OF A BAD KNEE.
THEIR LOSS, HUNTER. I COULDN'T DO MY JOB HALF AS WELL WITHOUT YOUR HELP.
THANKS, FLASH.
JAMES JESSE TOLD ME THERE WAS A BREAK-IN AT HIS OLD KEYSTONE STORAGE UNIT TWO WEEKS AGO. HIS COSTUME, HIS PATENTED AIR-WALKING SHOES, HIS COMPLETE BAG OF TRICKS WAS STOLEN.
SOME PRINTS WERE TAKEN...
...AND A WARRANT WAS ISSUED FOR THIS BOY'S ARREST.
DAMN. MUST BE THE NEW DETERGENT.
THE KID COMES FROM AN UPPER-CLASS FAMILY, PARENTS RECENTLY DIVORCED. HE'S GOTTEN INTO TROUBLE HERE AND THERE. DRUGS. VANDALISM. HE'S HEADED FOR SERIOUS TROUBLE.
HIS NAME IS AXEL WALKER.
BUT MY ENEMIES CALL ME--

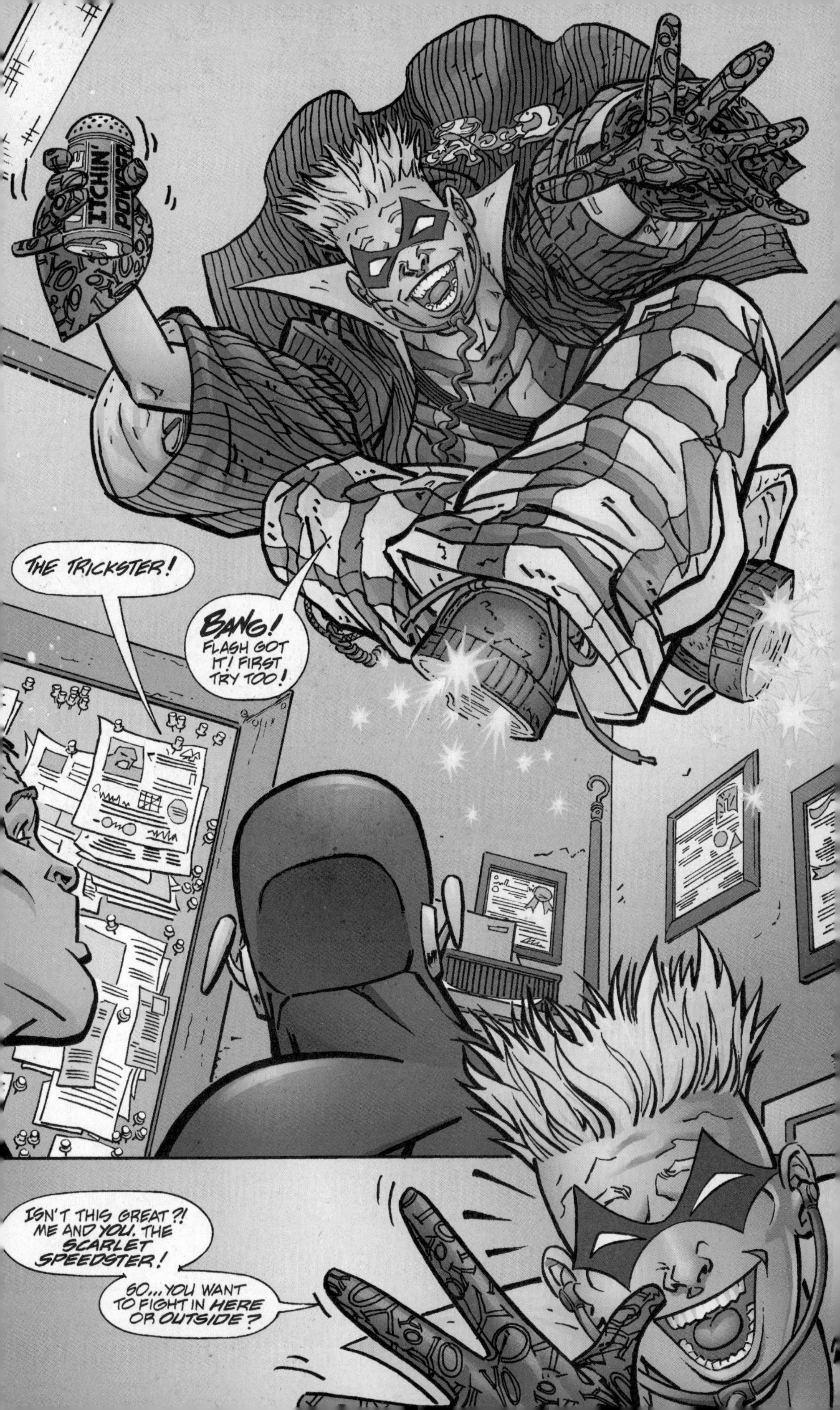
ITCHIN' POWDER
THE TRICKSTER!
BANG! FLASH GOT IT! FIRST TRY TOO!
ISN'T THIS GREAT?! ME AND YOU. THE SCARLET SPEEDSTER!
SO... YOU WANT TO FIGHT IN HERE OR OUTSIDE?

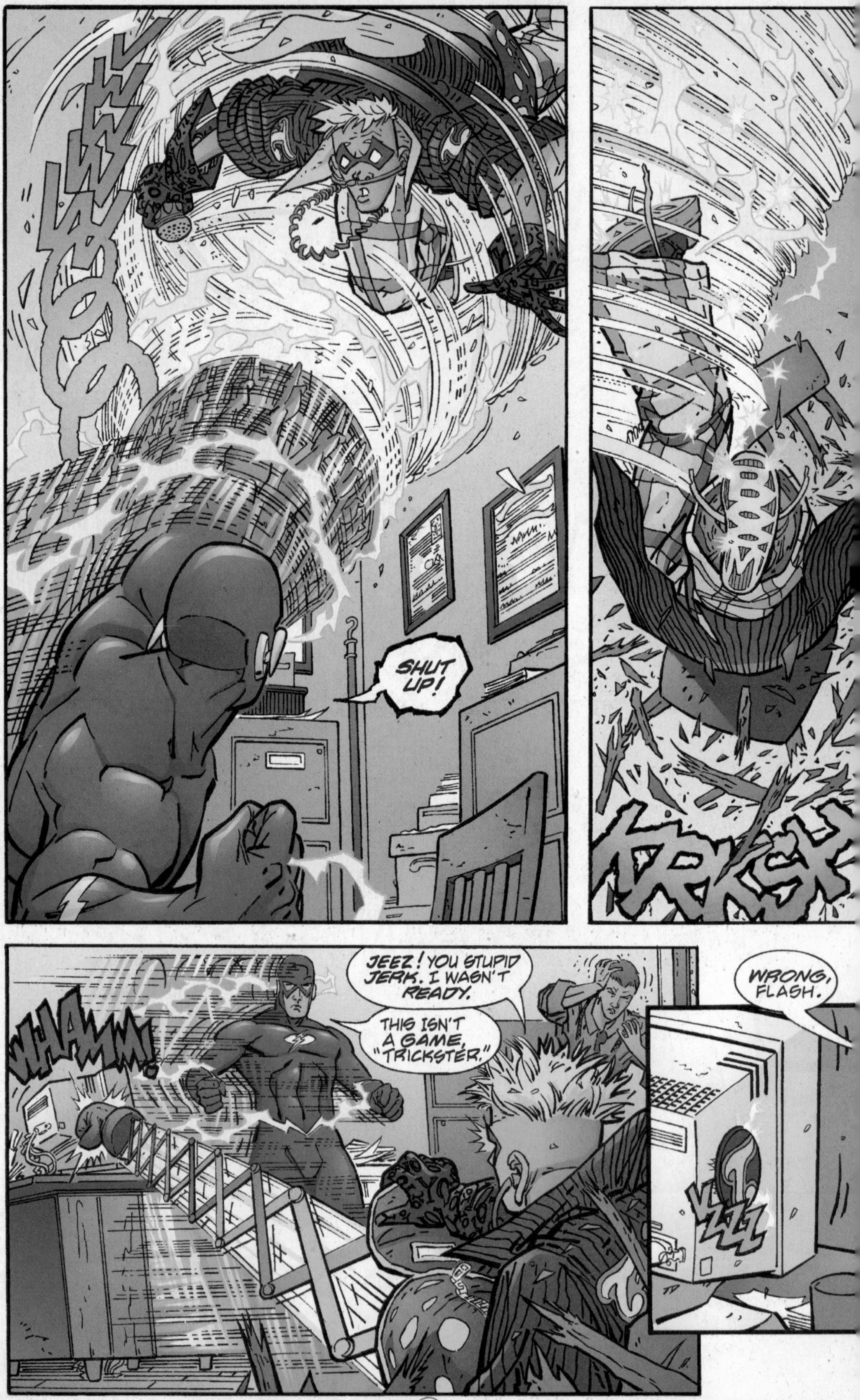
WHOOOOSH
SHUT UP!
KRRKSH
WHAMM!
JEEZ! YOU STUPID JERK. I WASN'T READY.
THIS ISN'T A GAME, "TRICKSTER."
WRONG, FLASH.
VZZZ

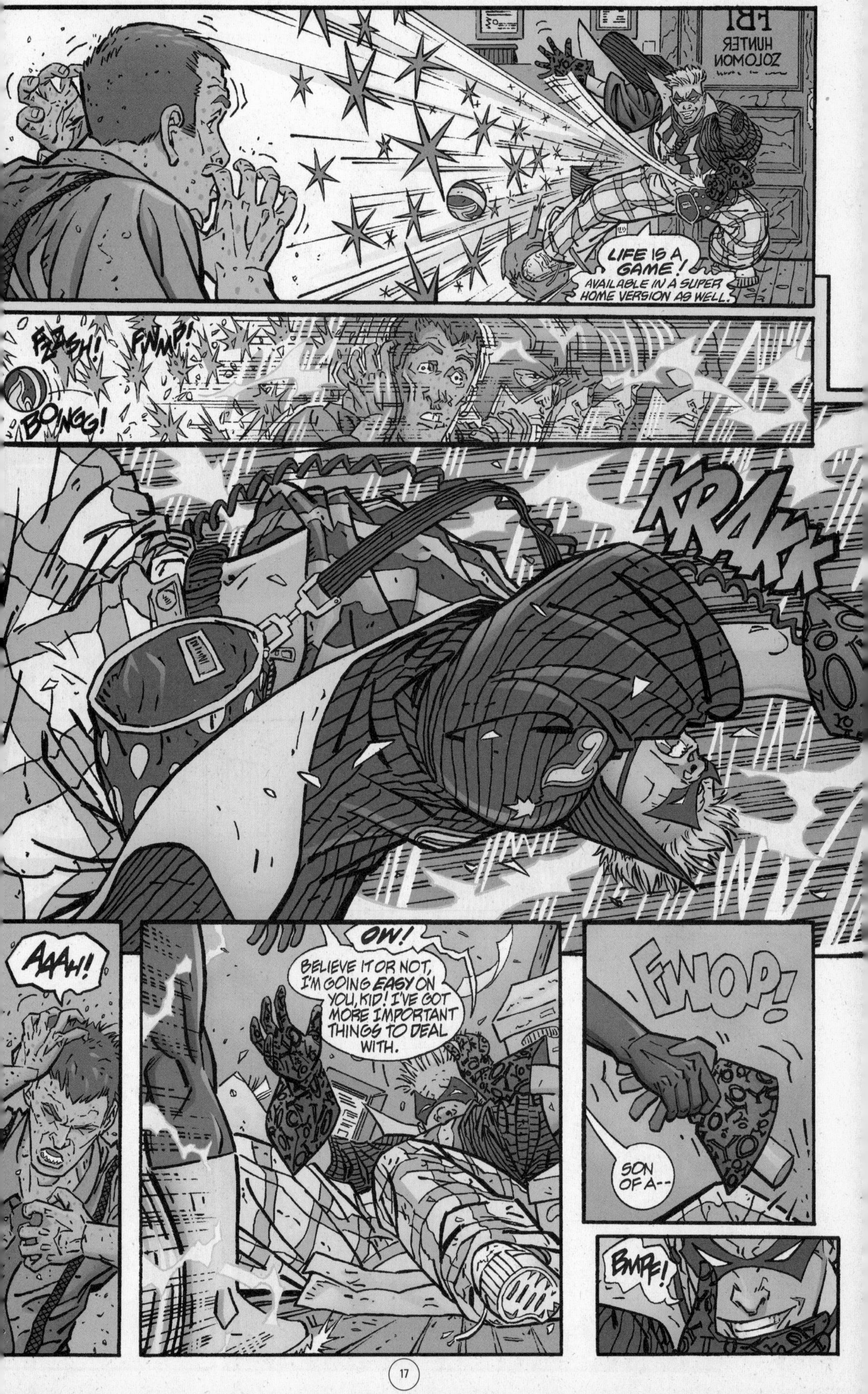
FBI
HUNTER
SOLOMON
LIFE IS A GAME! AVAILABLE IN A SUPER HOME VERSION AS WELL.
FLASH! FWMP!
BOINGG!
KRAKK
AAAH!
OW!
BELIEVE IT OR NOT, I'M GOING EASY ON YOU, KID! I'VE GOT MORE IMPORTANT THINGS TO DEAL WITH.
FWOP!
SON OF A--
BMPF!

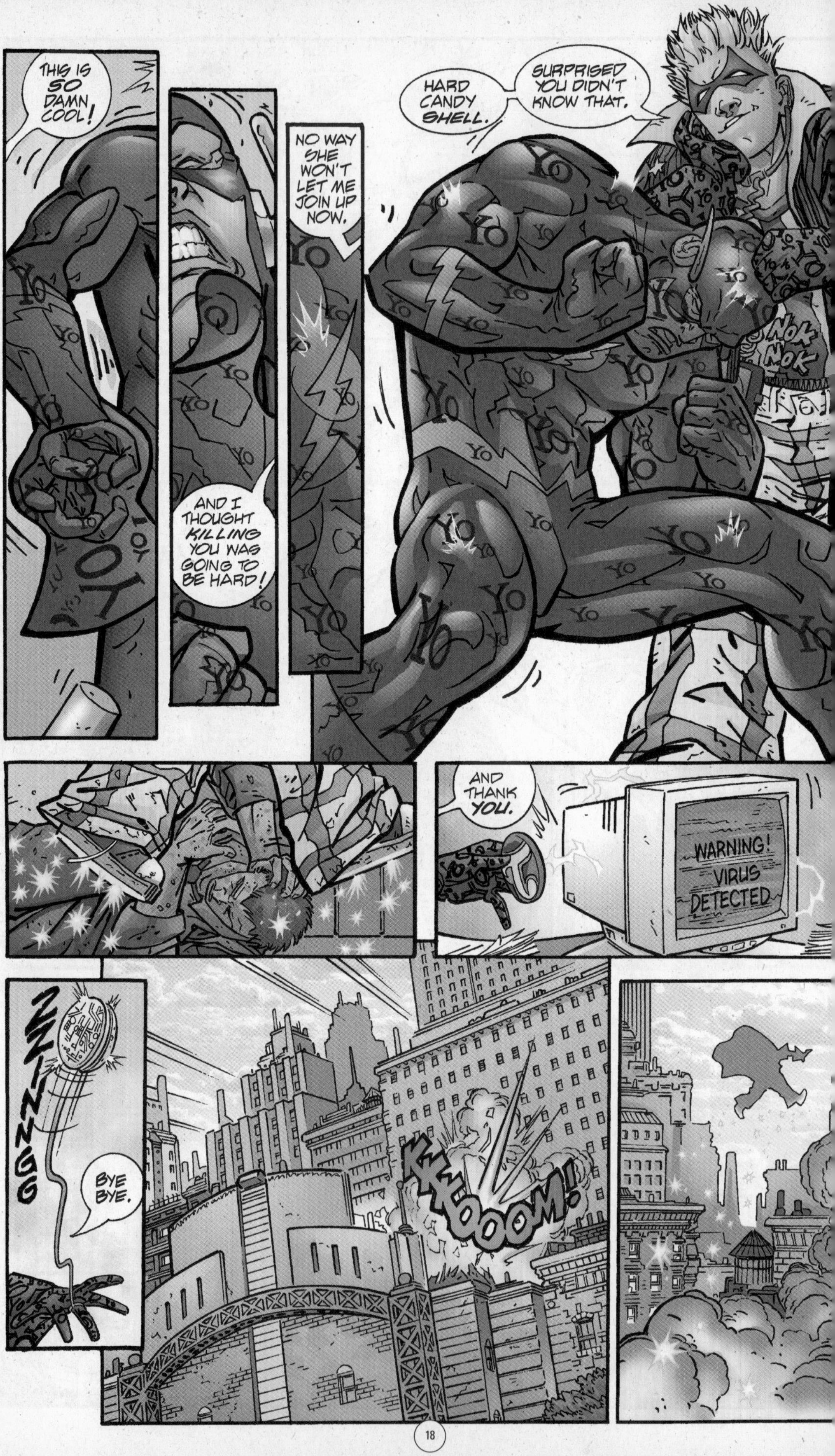
THIS IS SO DAMN COOL!
AND I THOUGHT KILLING YOU WAS GOING TO BE HARD!
NO WAY SHE WON'T LET ME JOIN UP NOW.
HARD CANDY SHELL.
SURPRISED YOU DIDN'T KNOW THAT.
NOK NOK
AND THANK YOU.
WARNING! VIRUS DETECTED
ZZZINNNGG
BYE BYE.
KKKBOOOM!

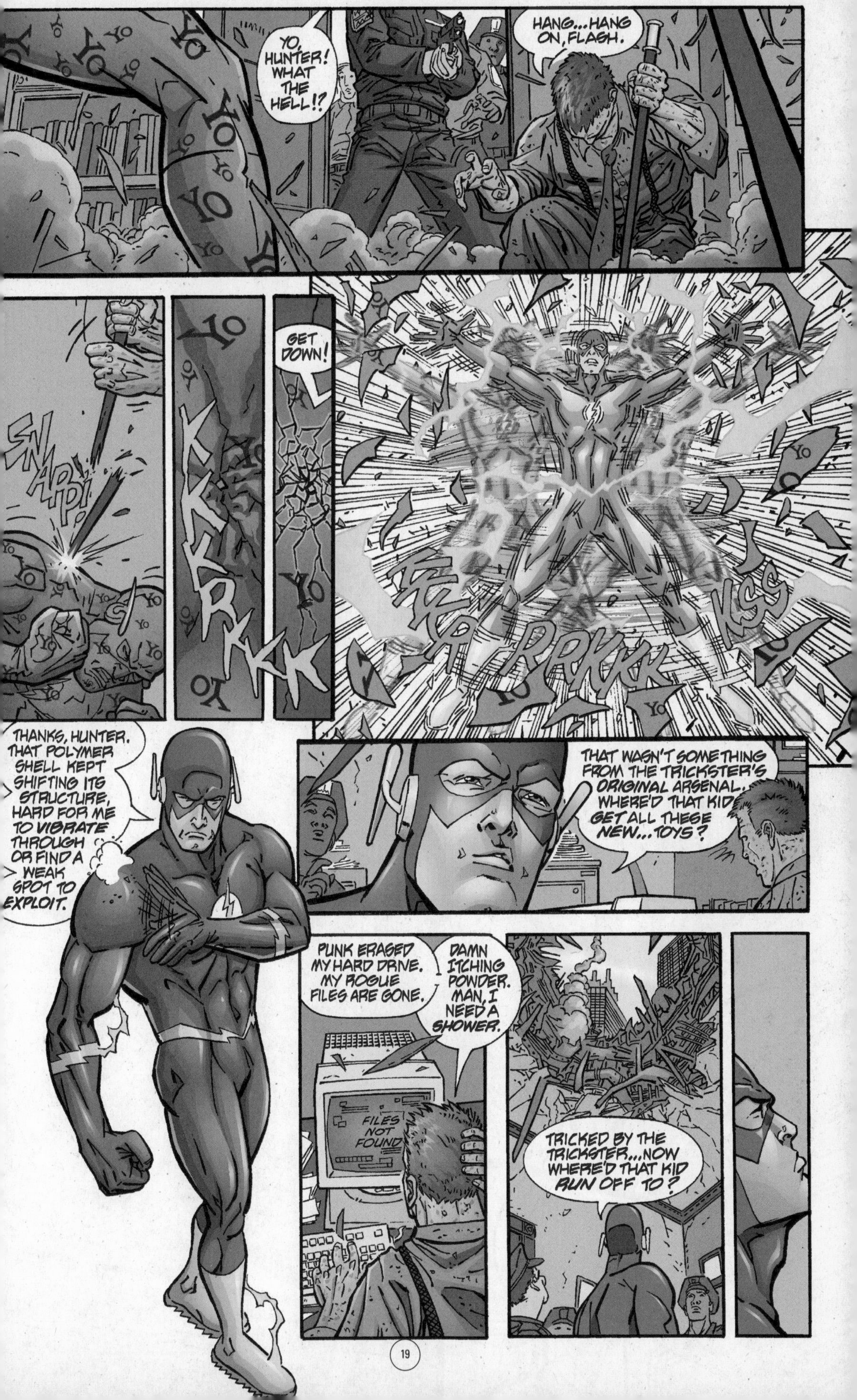

YO, HUNTER! WHAT THE HELL!?
HANG...HANG ON, FLASH.
SNAP!
KKKRKKK
GET DOWN!
KKRRRKKKK KSS
THANKS, HUNTER. THAT POLYMER SHELL KEPT SHIFTING ITS STRUCTURE, HARD FOR ME TO VIBRATE THROUGH OR FIND A WEAK SPOT TO EXPLOIT.
THAT WASN'T SOMETHING FROM THE TRICKSTER'S ORIGINAL ARSENAL. WHERE'D THAT KID GET ALL THESE NEW...TOYS?
PUNK ERASED MY HARD DRIVE. MY ROGUE FILES ARE GONE.
DAMN ITCHING POWDER. MAN, I NEED A SHOWER.
FILES NOT FOUND
TRICKED BY THE TRICKSTER...NOW WHERE'D THAT KID RUN OFF TO?

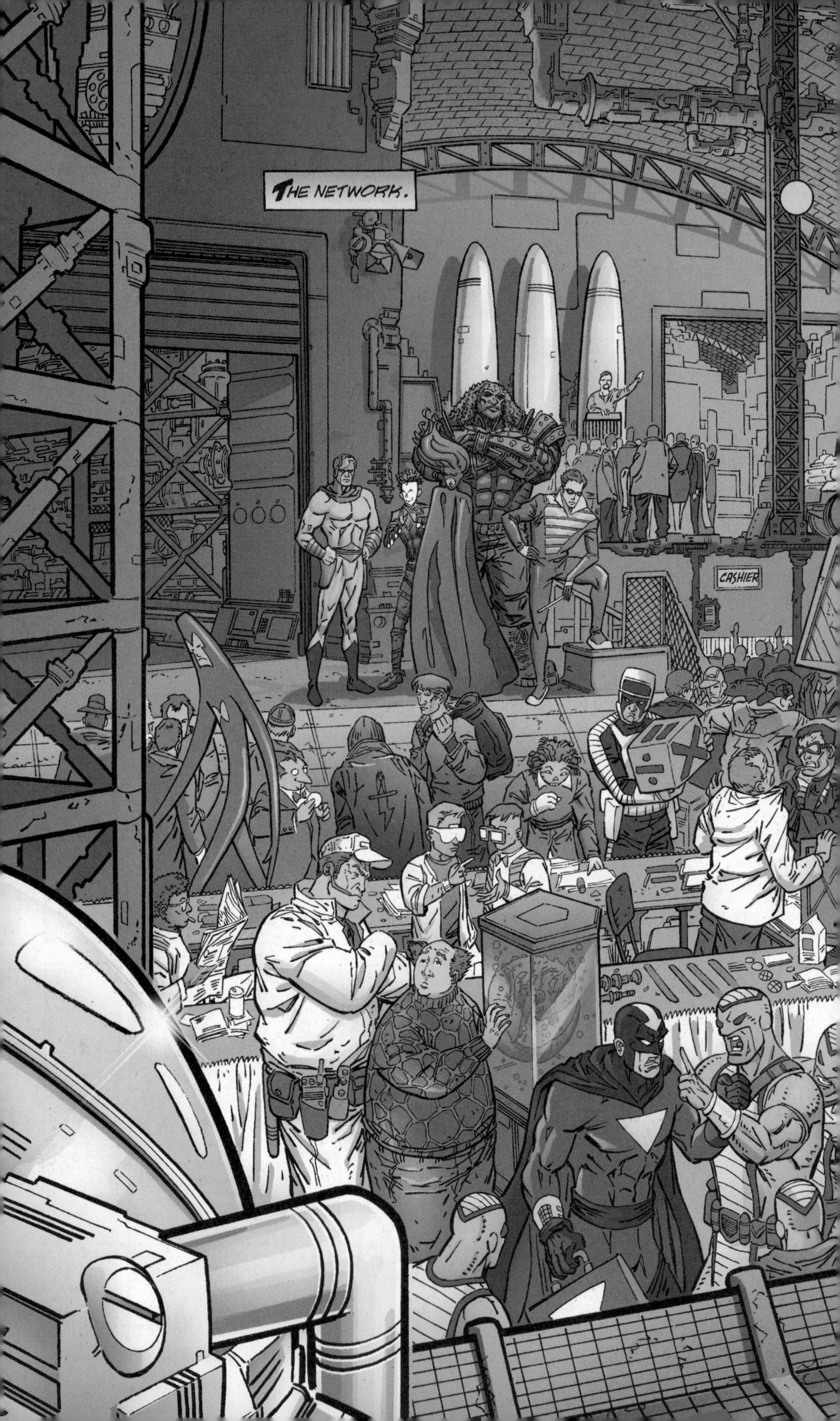
THE NETWORK.
CASHIER

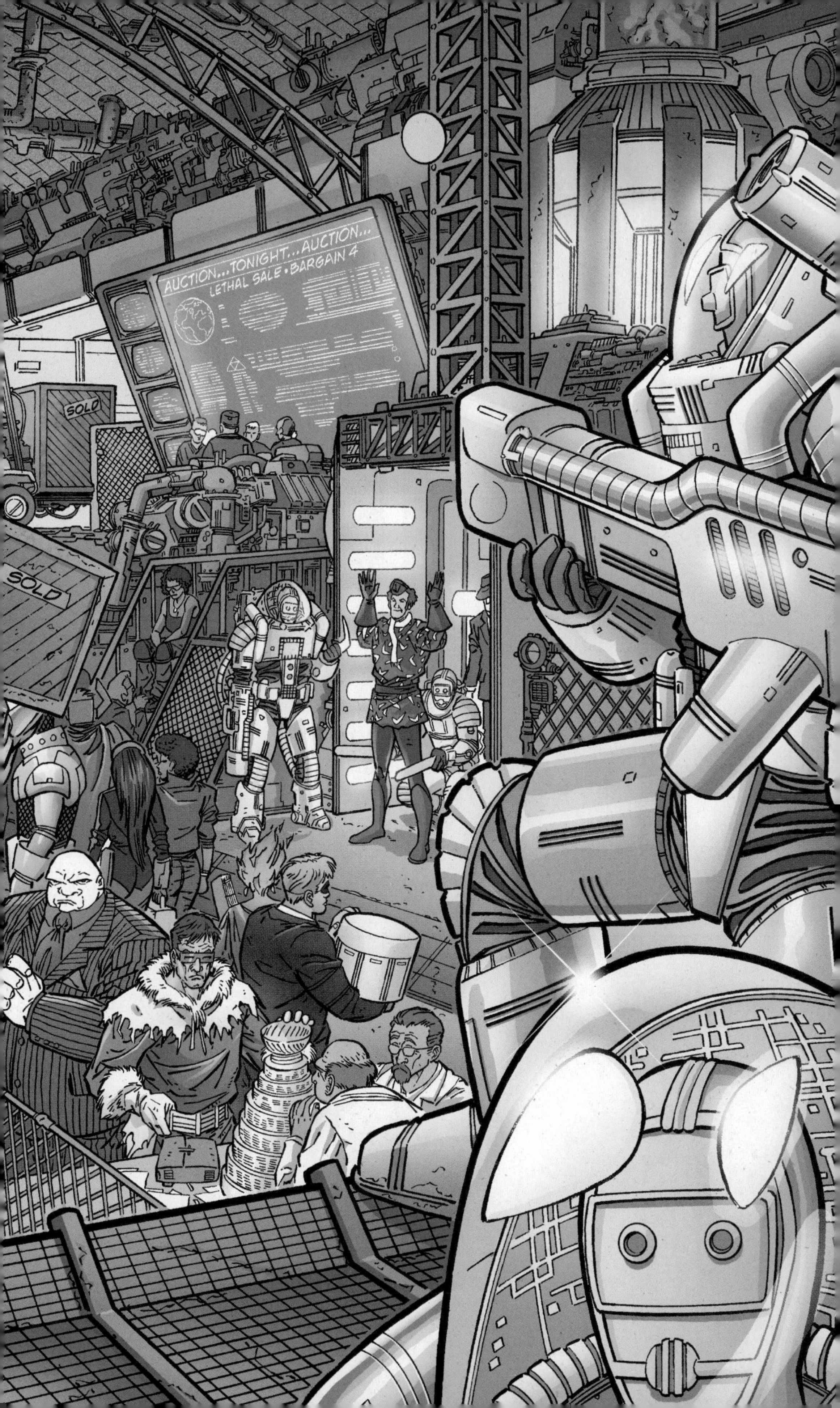
AUCTION...TONIGHT...AUCTION...
LETHAL SALE • BARGAIN 4
SOLD
SOLD

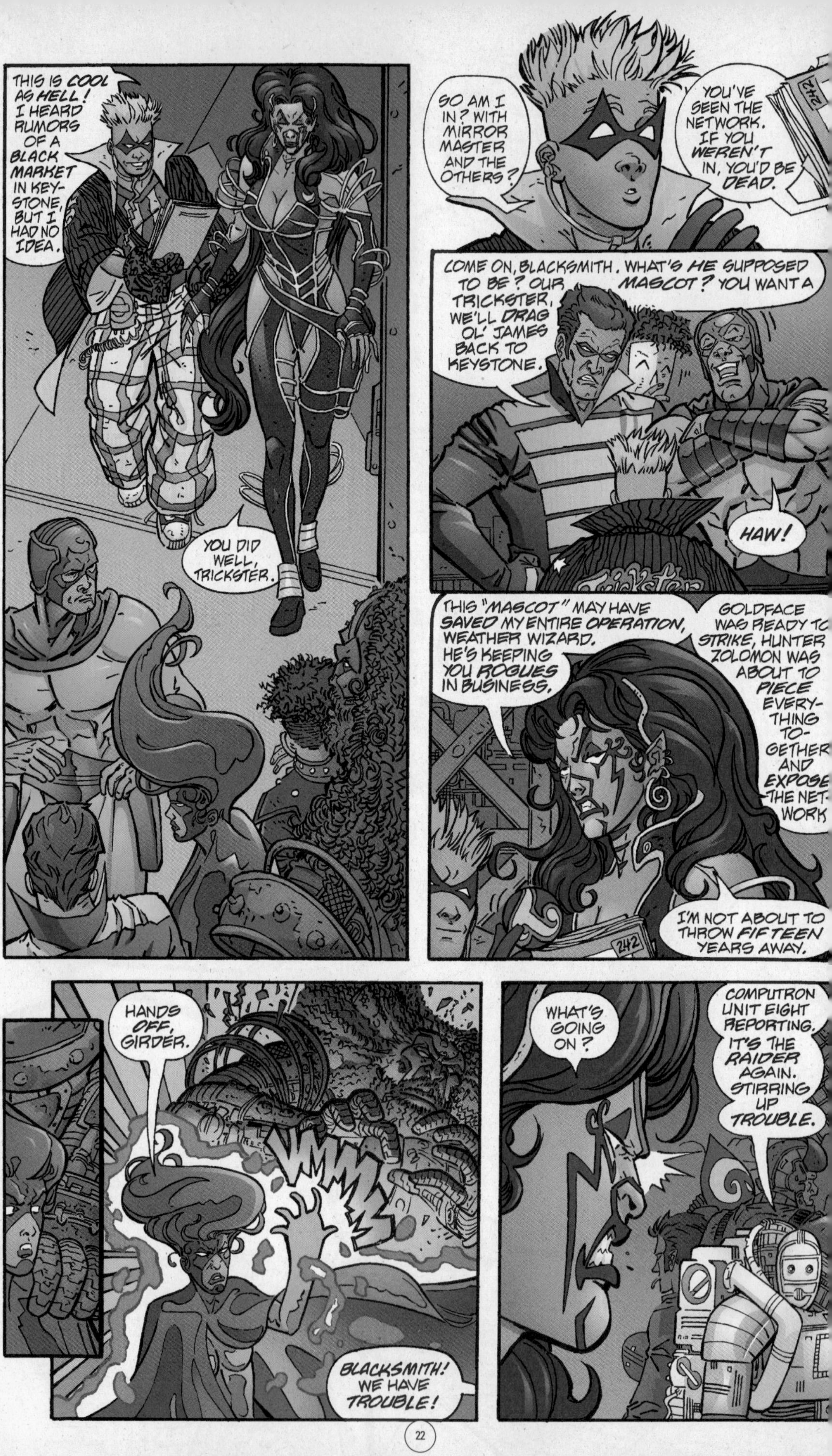

THIS IS COOL AS HELL! I HEARD RUMORS OF A BLACK MARKET IN KEY-STONE, BUT I HAD NO IDEA.
YOU DID WELL, TRICKSTER.
SO AM I IN? WITH MIRROR MASTER AND THE OTHERS?
YOU'VE SEEN THE NETWORK. IF YOU WEREN'T IN, YOU'D BE DEAD.
COME ON, BLACKSMITH. WHAT'S HE SUPPOSED TO BE? OUR MASCOT? YOU WANT A TRICKSTER, WE'LL DRAG OL' JAMES BACK TO KEYSTONE.
HAW!
THIS "MASCOT" MAY HAVE SAVED MY ENTIRE OPERATION, WEATHER WIZARD. HE'S KEEPING YOU ROGUES IN BUSINESS.
GOLDFACE WAS READY TO STRIKE, HUNTER ZOLOMON WAS ABOUT TO PIECE EVERY-THING TO-GETHER AND EXPOSE THE NET-WORK
I'M NOT ABOUT TO THROW FIFTEEN YEARS AWAY.
HANDS OFF, GIRDER.
VMMM
BLACKSMITH! WE HAVE TROUBLE!
WHAT'S GOING ON?
COMPUTRON UNIT EIGHT REPORTING. IT'S THE RAIDER AGAIN. STIRRING UP TROUBLE.

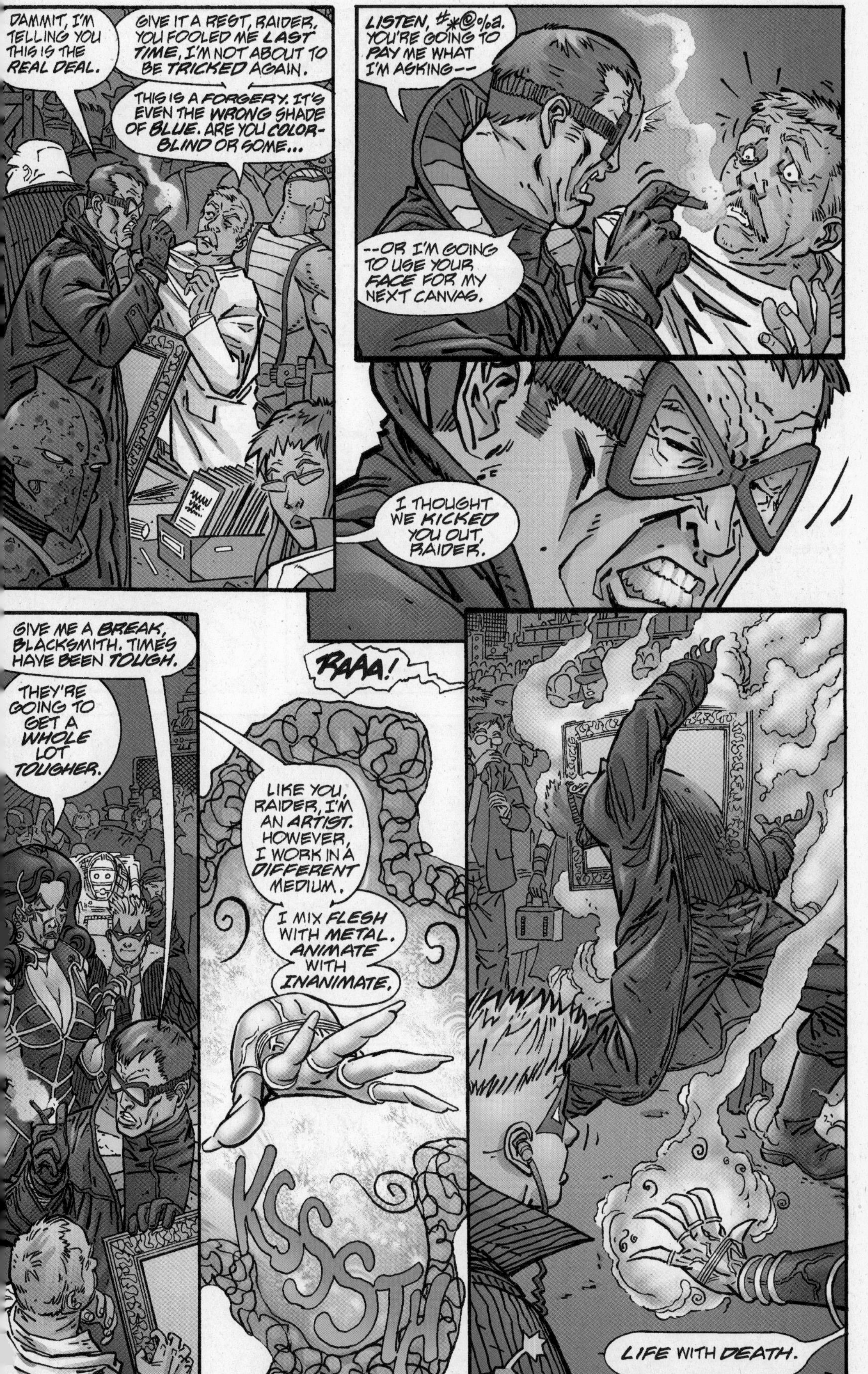

DAMMIT, I'M TELLING YOU THIS IS THE REAL DEAL.
GIVE IT A REST, RAIDER. YOU FOOLED ME LAST TIME. I'M NOT ABOUT TO BE TRICKED AGAIN.
THIS IS A FORGERY. IT'S EVEN THE WRONG SHADE OF BLUE. ARE YOU COLOR-BLIND OR SOME...
LISTEN, #*@%a. YOU'RE GOING TO PAY ME WHAT I'M ASKING--
--OR I'M GOING TO USE YOUR FACE FOR MY NEXT CANVAS.
I THOUGHT WE KICKED YOU OUT, RAIDER.
GIVE ME A BREAK, BLACKSMITH. TIMES HAVE BEEN TOUGH.
THEY'RE GOING TO GET A WHOLE LOT TOUGHER.
RAAA!
LIKE YOU, RAIDER, I'M AN ARTIST. HOWEVER, I WORK IN A DIFFERENT MEDIUM.
I MIX FLESH WITH METAL. ANIMATE WITH INANIMATE.
KSSSTH
LIFE WITH DEATH.

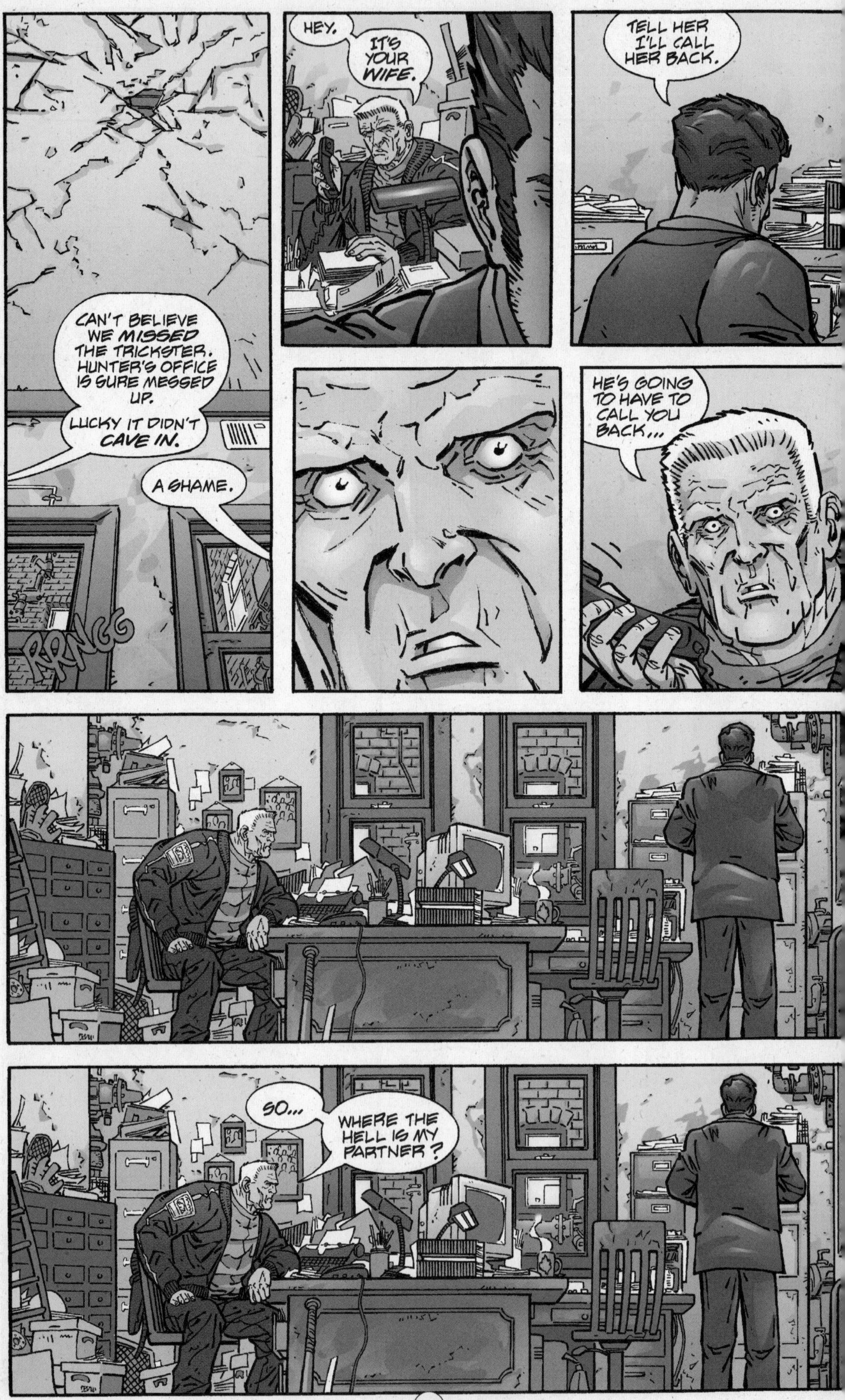

HEY.
IT'S YOUR WIFE.
TELL HER I'LL CALL HER BACK.
CAN'T BELIEVE WE MISSED THE TRICKSTER. HUNTER'S OFFICE IS SURE MESSED UP.
LUCKY IT DIDN'T CAVE IN.
A SHAME.
RRINGG
HE'S GOING TO HAVE TO CALL YOU BACK...
SO...
WHERE THE HELL IS MY PARTNER?

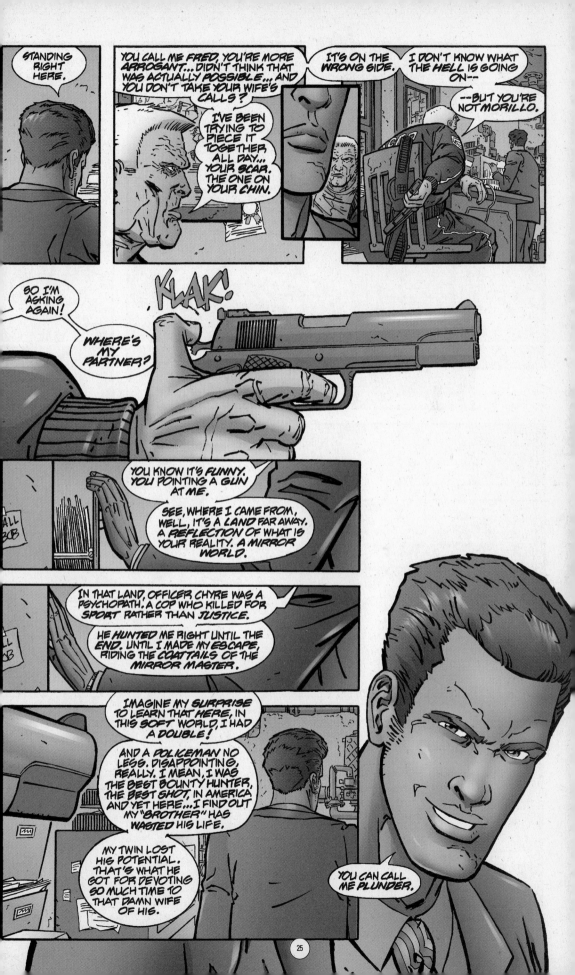

STANDING RIGHT HERE.

YOU CALL ME *FRED*, YOU'RE MORE *ARROGANT*... DIDN'T THINK THAT WAS ACTUALLY *POSSIBLE*... AND YOU DON'T TAKE YOUR *WIFE'S* CALLS?

I'VE BEEN TRYING TO *PIECE* IT TOGETHER, ALL DAY... YOUR *SCAR*. THE ONE ON YOUR *CHIN*.

IT'S ON THE *WRONG* SIDE.

I DON'T KNOW WHAT THE *HELL* IS GOING ON--

--BUT YOU'RE NOT *MORILLO*.

SO I'M ASKING *AGAIN*!

KLAK!

WHERE'S MY *PARTNER*?

ALL BOB

YOU KNOW IT'S *FUNNY*. YOU POINTING A GUN AT ME.

SEE, WHERE I CAME FROM, WELL, IT'S A *LAND* FAR AWAY. A *REFLECTION* OF WHAT IS YOUR REALITY. A *MIRROR WORLD*.

ALL BOB

IN THAT LAND, OFFICER *CHYRE* WAS A *PSYCHOPATH*. A COP WHO KILLED FOR *SPORT* RATHER THAN *JUSTICE*.

HE *HUNTED* ME RIGHT UNTIL THE *END*. UNTIL I MADE MY *ESCAPE*, RIDING THE *COATTAILS* OF THE *MIRROR MASTER*.

IMAGINE MY *SURPRISE* TO LEARN THAT *HERE*, IN THIS *SOFT* WORLD, I HAD A *DOUBLE*!

AND A *POLICEMAN* NO LESS. *DISAPPOINTING*, REALLY. I MEAN, I WAS THE *BEST* BOUNTY HUNTER, THE BEST *SHOT*, IN AMERICA AND YET *HERE*...I FIND OUT MY "*BROTHER*" HAS *WASTED* HIS LIFE.

MY TWIN LOST HIS *POTENTIAL*. THAT'S WHAT HE GOT FOR DEVOTING SO MUCH TIME TO THAT *DAMN* WIFE OF HIS.

YOU CAN CALL ME *PLUNDER*.

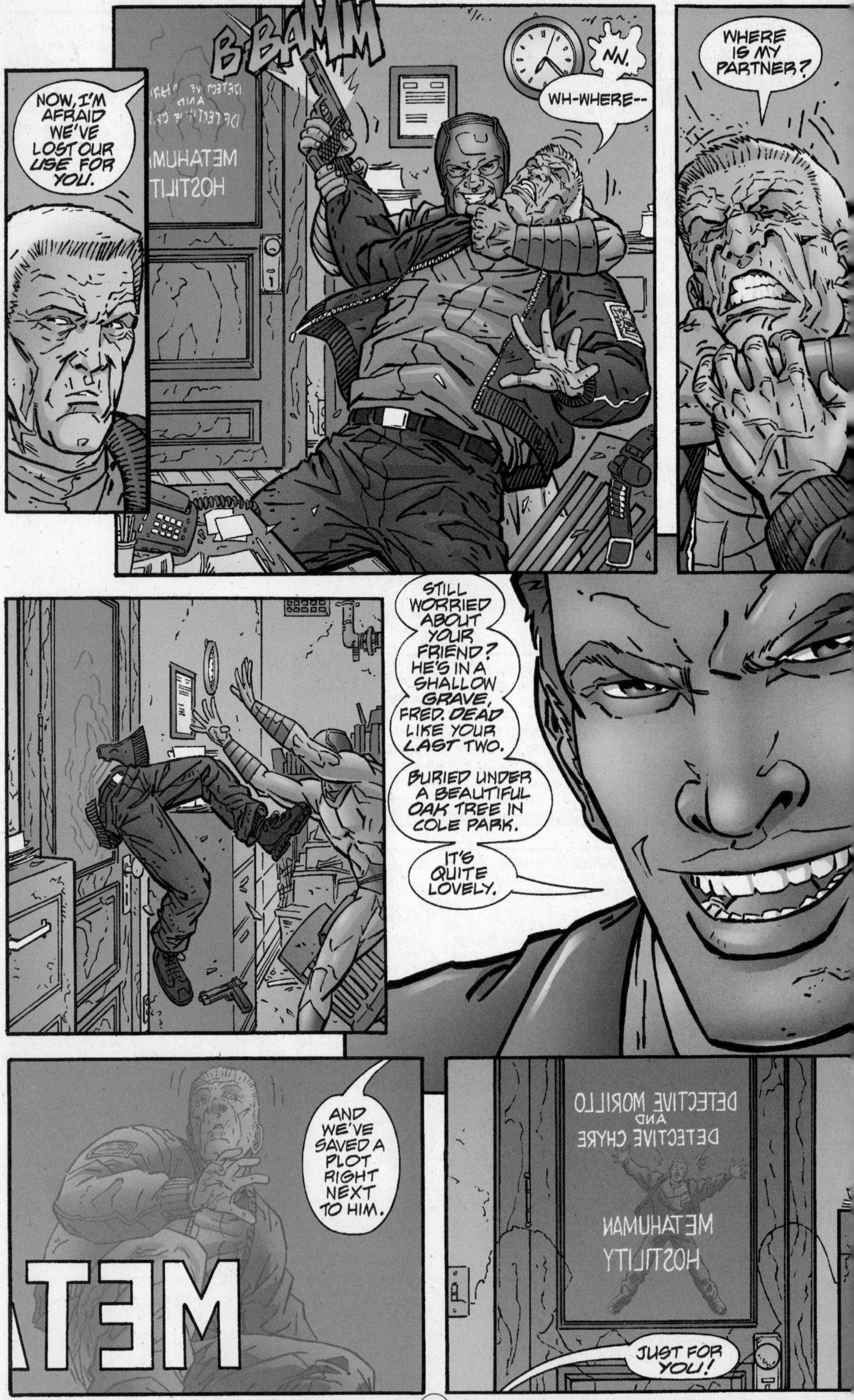
NOW, I'M AFRAID WE'VE LOST OUR USE FOR YOU.
B-BAMM
NN.
WH-WHERE--
WHERE IS MY PARTNER?
STILL WORRIED ABOUT YOUR FRIEND? HE'S IN A SHALLOW GRAVE, FRED. DEAD LIKE YOUR LAST TWO.
BURIED UNDER A BEAUTIFUL OAK TREE IN COLE PARK.
IT'S QUITE LOVELY.
AND WE'VE SAVED A PLOT RIGHT NEXT TO HIM.
DETECTIVE MORILLO AND DETECTIVE CHYRE
METAHUMAN HOSTILITY
JUST FOR YOU!

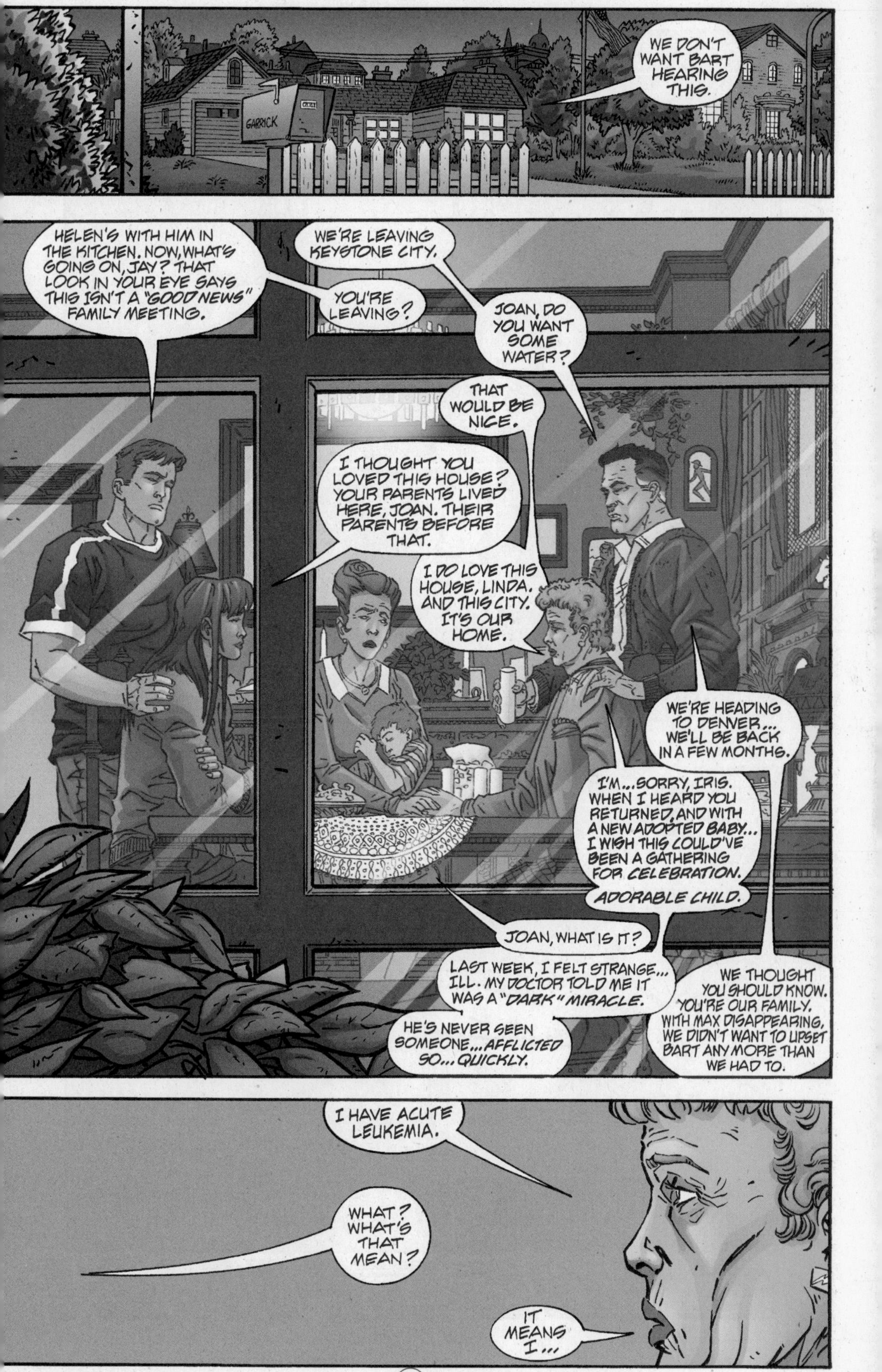
GARRICK
WE DON'T WANT BART HEARING THIS.
HELEN'S WITH HIM IN THE KITCHEN. NOW, WHAT'S GOING ON, JAY? THAT LOOK IN YOUR EYE SAYS THIS ISN'T A "GOOD NEWS" FAMILY MEETING.
WE'RE LEAVING KEYSTONE CITY.
YOU'RE LEAVING?
JOAN, DO YOU WANT SOME WATER?
THAT WOULD BE NICE.
I THOUGHT YOU LOVED THIS HOUSE? YOUR PARENTS LIVED HERE, JOAN. THEIR PARENTS BEFORE THAT.
I DO LOVE THIS HOUSE, LINDA. AND THIS CITY. IT'S OUR HOME.
WE'RE HEADING TO DENVER,... WE'LL BE BACK IN A FEW MONTHS.
I'M...SORRY, IRIS. WHEN I HEARD YOU RETURNED, AND WITH A NEW ADOPTED BABY... I WISH THIS COULD'VE BEEN A GATHERING FOR CELEBRATION.
ADORABLE CHILD.
JOAN, WHAT IS IT?
LAST WEEK, I FELT STRANGE... ILL. MY DOCTOR TOLD ME IT WAS A "DARK" MIRACLE.
HE'S NEVER SEEN SOMEONE...AFFLICTED SO...QUICKLY.
WE THOUGHT YOU SHOULD KNOW. YOU'RE OUR FAMILY. WITH MAX DISAPPEARING, WE DIDN'T WANT TO UPSET BART ANY MORE THAN WE HAD TO.
I HAVE ACUTE LEUKEMIA.
WHAT? WHAT'S THAT MEAN?
IT MEANS I...

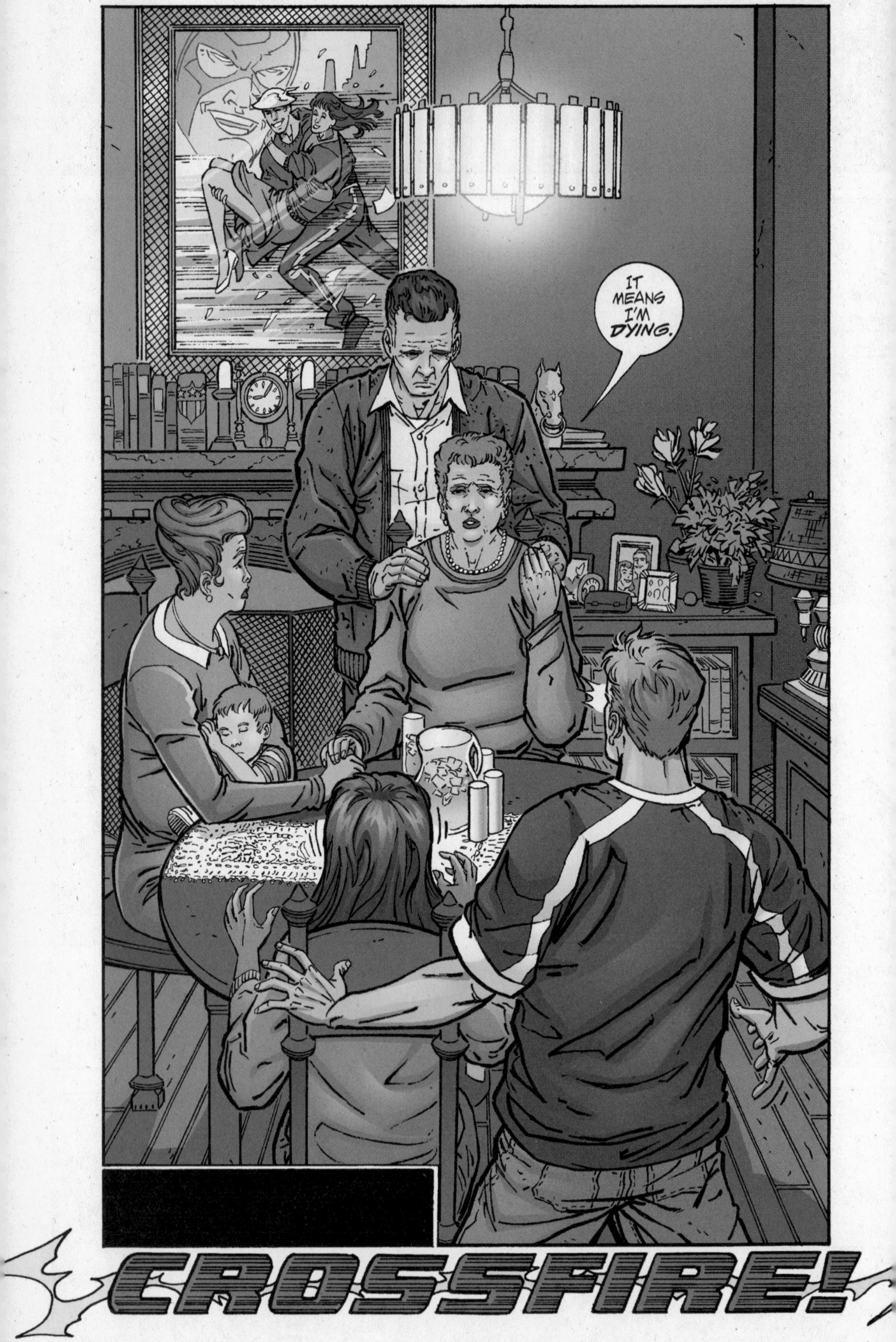
IT MEANS I'M DYING.
CROSSFIRE!

KEYSTONE CITY.

THE CITY OF INDUSTRY.

TIKA TIKA TAC TAC

BUILT IN KEYSTONE

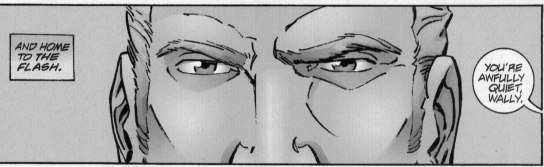

AND HOME TO THE FLASH.

YOU'RE AWFULLY QUIET, WALLY.

SO IS KEYSTONE.

I KNOW YOU'RE WORRIED ABOUT THE GARRICKS, BUT IRIS TALKED TO THEM THIS MORNING. JAY'S IMPRESSED WITH THE CANCER SPECIALIST JOAN'S SEEING.

IT'S MORE THAN THAT, LINDA.

THE GARRICKS AREN'T THE ONLY ONES TO BE HIT BY A STROKE OF *BAD* LUCK.

PIPER, CHUNK AND JESSE QUICK ARE OUT OF COMMISSION. MAX MERCURY IS STILL MISSING.

AND CYBORG... VIC HASN'T CALLED ME BACK, HAS HE?

NO. HE HASN'T.

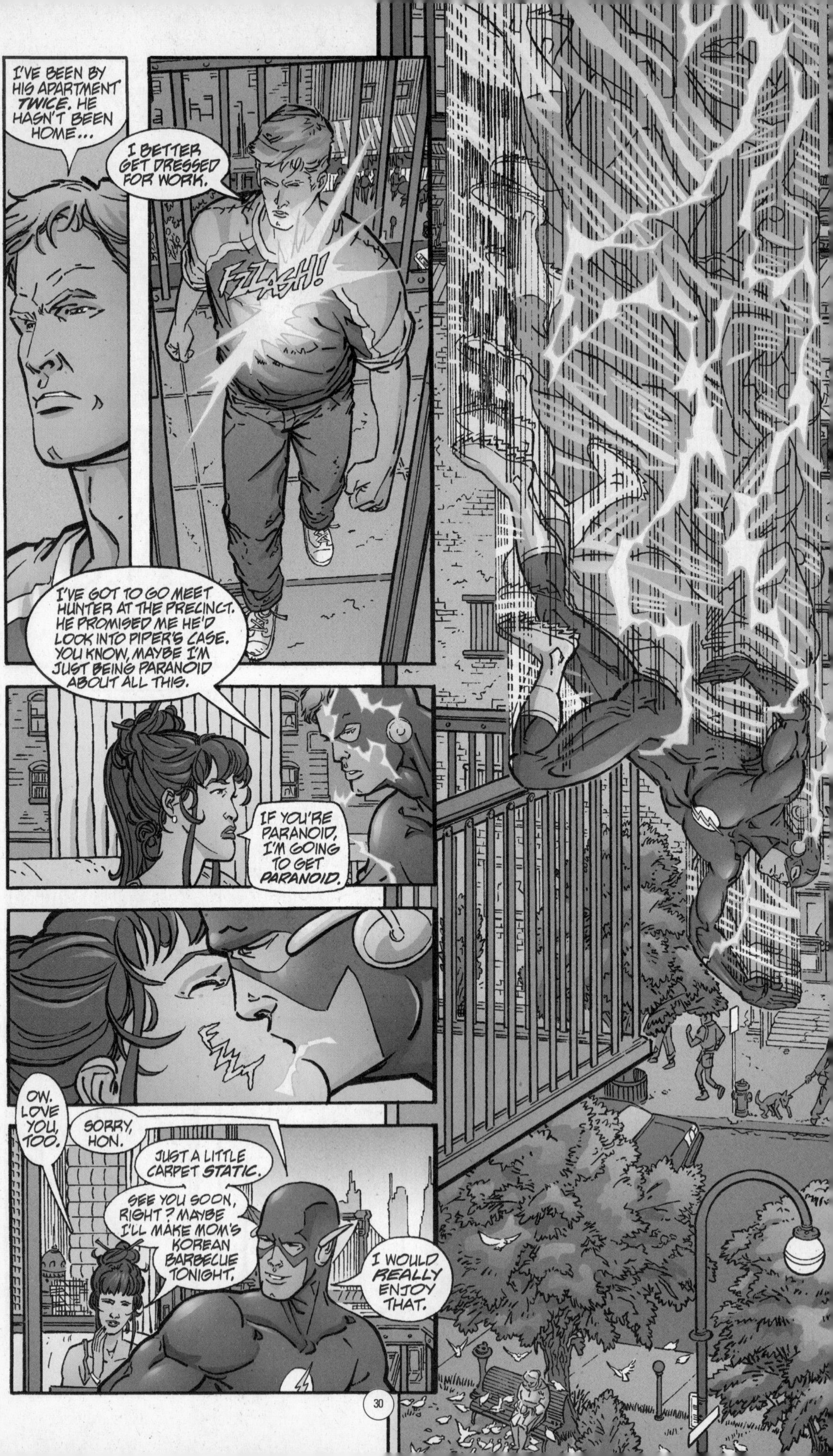
I'VE BEEN BY HIS APARTMENT TWICE. HE HASN'T BEEN HOME...
I BETTER GET DRESSED FOR WORK.
FZZASH!
I'VE GOT TO GO MEET HUNTER AT THE PRECINCT. HE PROMISED ME HE'D LOOK INTO PIPER'S CASE. YOU KNOW, MAYBE I'M JUST BEING PARANOID ABOUT ALL THIS.
IF YOU'RE PARANOID, I'M GOING TO GET PARANOID.
OW. LOVE YOU, TOO.
SORRY, HON.
JUST A LITTLE CARPET STATIC.
SEE YOU SOON, RIGHT? MAYBE I'LL MAKE MOM'S KOREAN BARBECUE TONIGHT.
I WOULD REALLY ENJOY THAT.

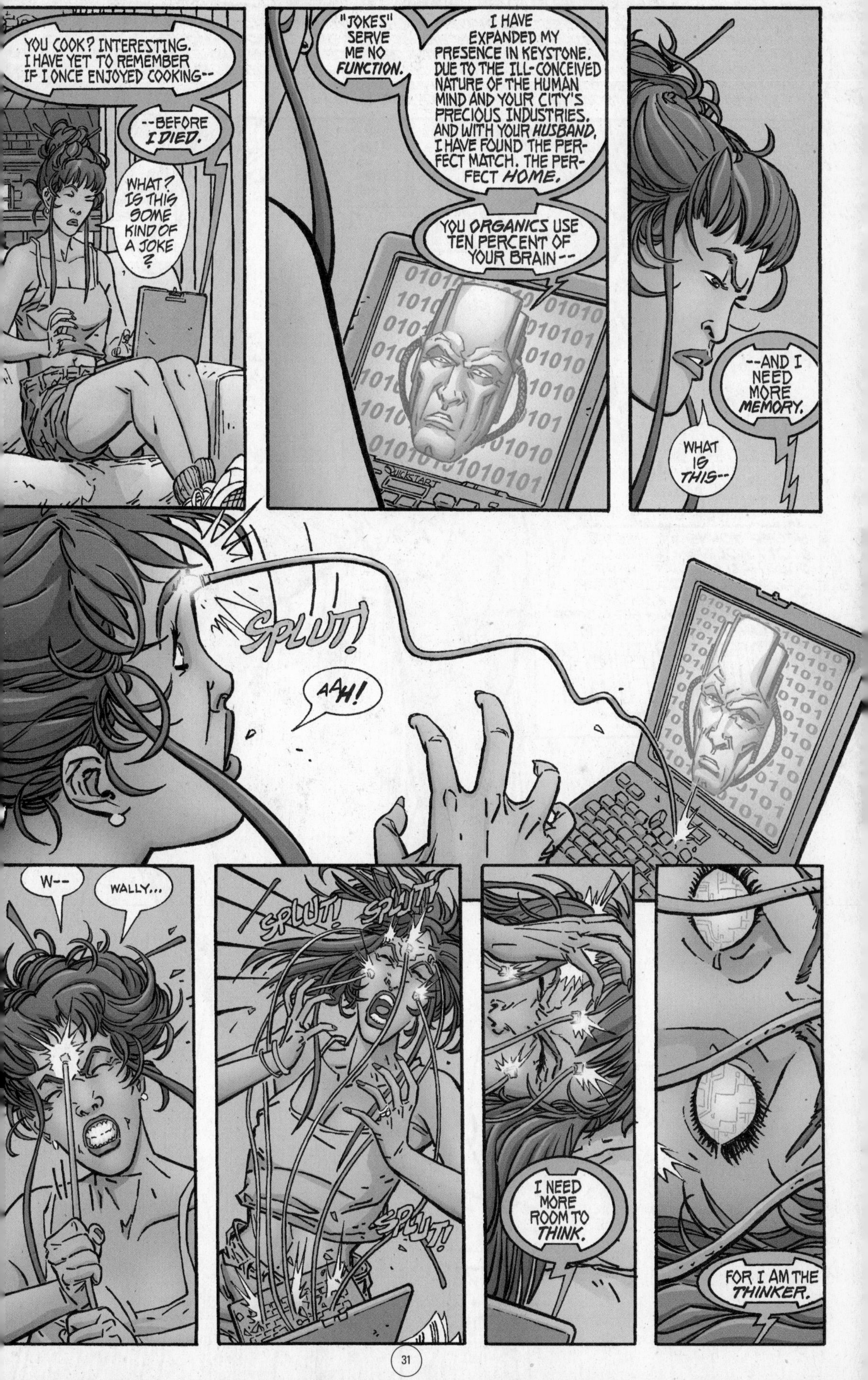
YOU COOK? INTERESTING. I HAVE YET TO REMEMBER IF I ONCE ENJOYED COOKING--
--BEFORE I DIED.
WHAT? IS THIS SOME KIND OF A JOKE?
"JOKES" SERVE ME NO FUNCTION.
I HAVE EXPANDED MY PRESENCE IN KEYSTONE. DUE TO THE ILL-CONCEIVED NATURE OF THE HUMAN MIND AND YOUR CITY'S PRECIOUS INDUSTRIES. AND WITH YOUR HUSBAND, I HAVE FOUND THE PERFECT MATCH. THE PERFECT HOME.
YOU ORGANICS USE TEN PERCENT OF YOUR BRAIN--
--AND I NEED MORE MEMORY.
WHAT IS THIS--
SPLUT!
AAH!
W--
WALLY...
SPLUT!
SPLUT!
SPLUT!
I NEED MORE ROOM TO THINK.
FOR I AM THE THINKER.

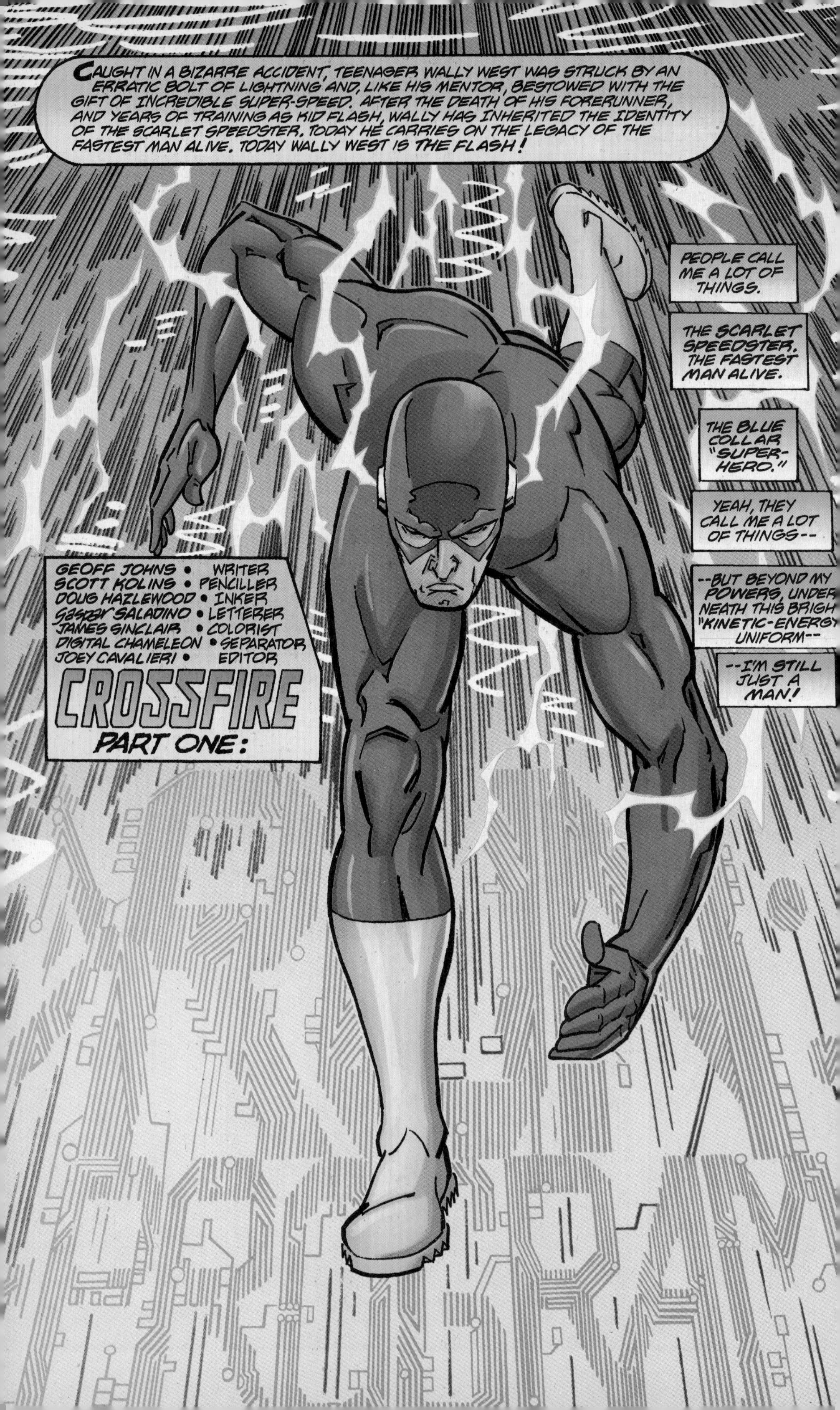
CAUGHT IN A BIZARRE ACCIDENT, TEENAGER WALLY WEST WAS STRUCK BY AN ERRATIC BOLT OF LIGHTNING AND, LIKE HIS MENTOR, BESTOWED WITH THE GIFT OF INCREDIBLE SUPER-SPEED. AFTER THE DEATH OF HIS FORERUNNER, AND YEARS OF TRAINING AS KID FLASH, WALLY HAS INHERITED THE IDENTITY OF THE SCARLET SPEEDSTER. TODAY HE CARRIES ON THE LEGACY OF THE FASTEST MAN ALIVE. TODAY WALLY WEST IS THE FLASH!
PEOPLE CALL ME A LOT OF THINGS.
THE SCARLET SPEEDSTER. THE FASTEST MAN ALIVE.
THE BLUE COLLAR "SUPER-HERO."
YEAH, THEY CALL ME A LOT OF THINGS--
--BUT BEYOND MY POWERS, UNDER NEATH THIS BRIGH "KINETIC-ENERG UNIFORM--
--I'M STILL JUST A MAN!
GEOFF JOHNS • WRITER
SCOTT KOLINS • PENCILLER
DOUG HAZLEWOOD • INKER
GASPAR SALADINO • LETTERER
JAMES SINCLAIR • COLORIST
DIGITAL CHAMELEON • SEPARATOR
JOEY CAVALIERI • EDITOR
CROSSFIRE
PART ONE:

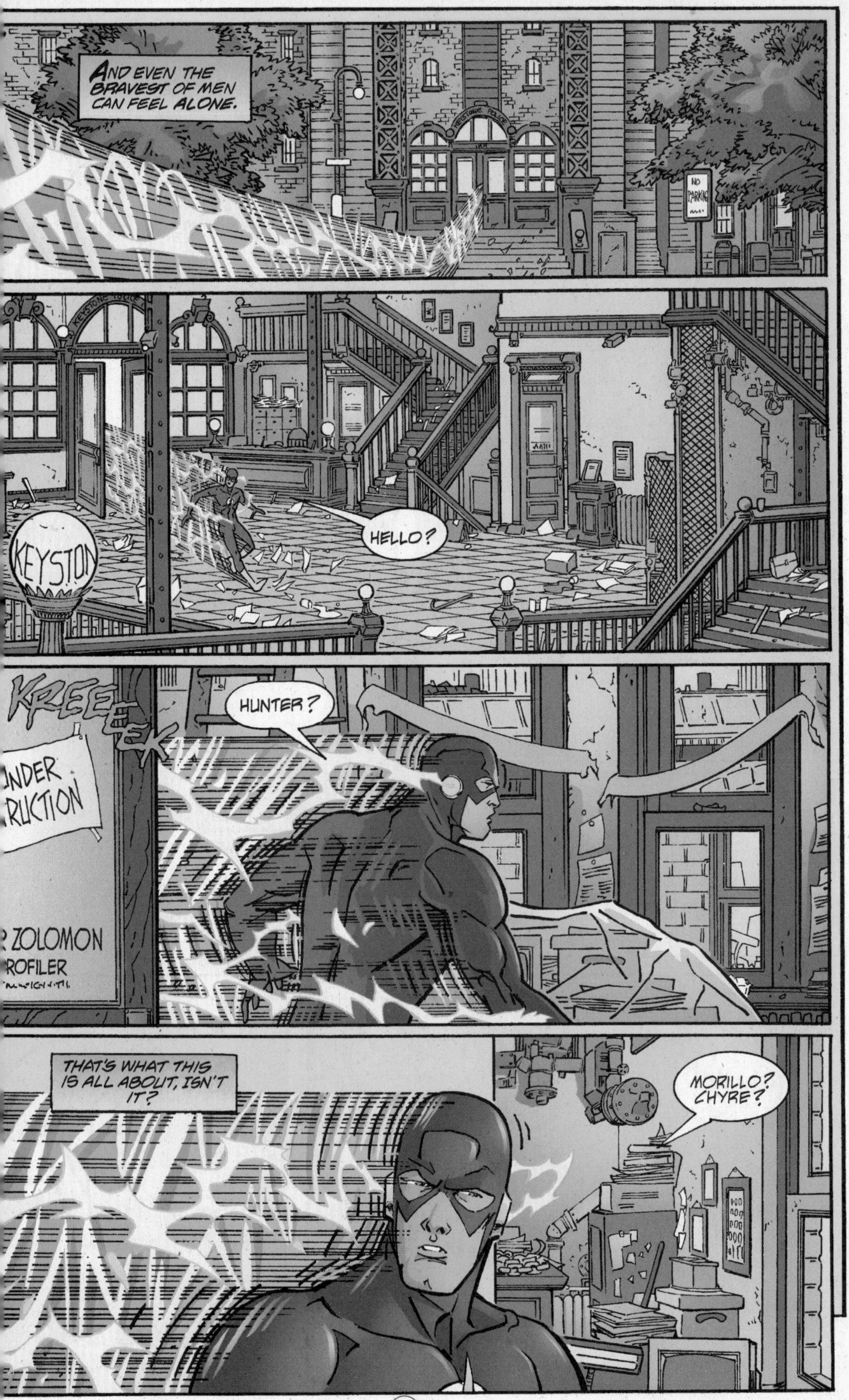
AND EVEN THE BRAVEST OF MEN CAN FEEL ALONE.
HELLO?
KEYSTON
KREEEEEK
HUNTER?
ZOLOMON
ROFILER
THAT'S WHAT THIS IS ALL ABOUT, ISN'T IT?
MORILLO? CHYRE?

I'M ALONE.

RRNGGG

RRNG

RRNG--

LOOK IN THE MIRROR, FLASHER.

MIRROR MASTER? WHAT DO YOU--

LOOK IN THE GLASS.

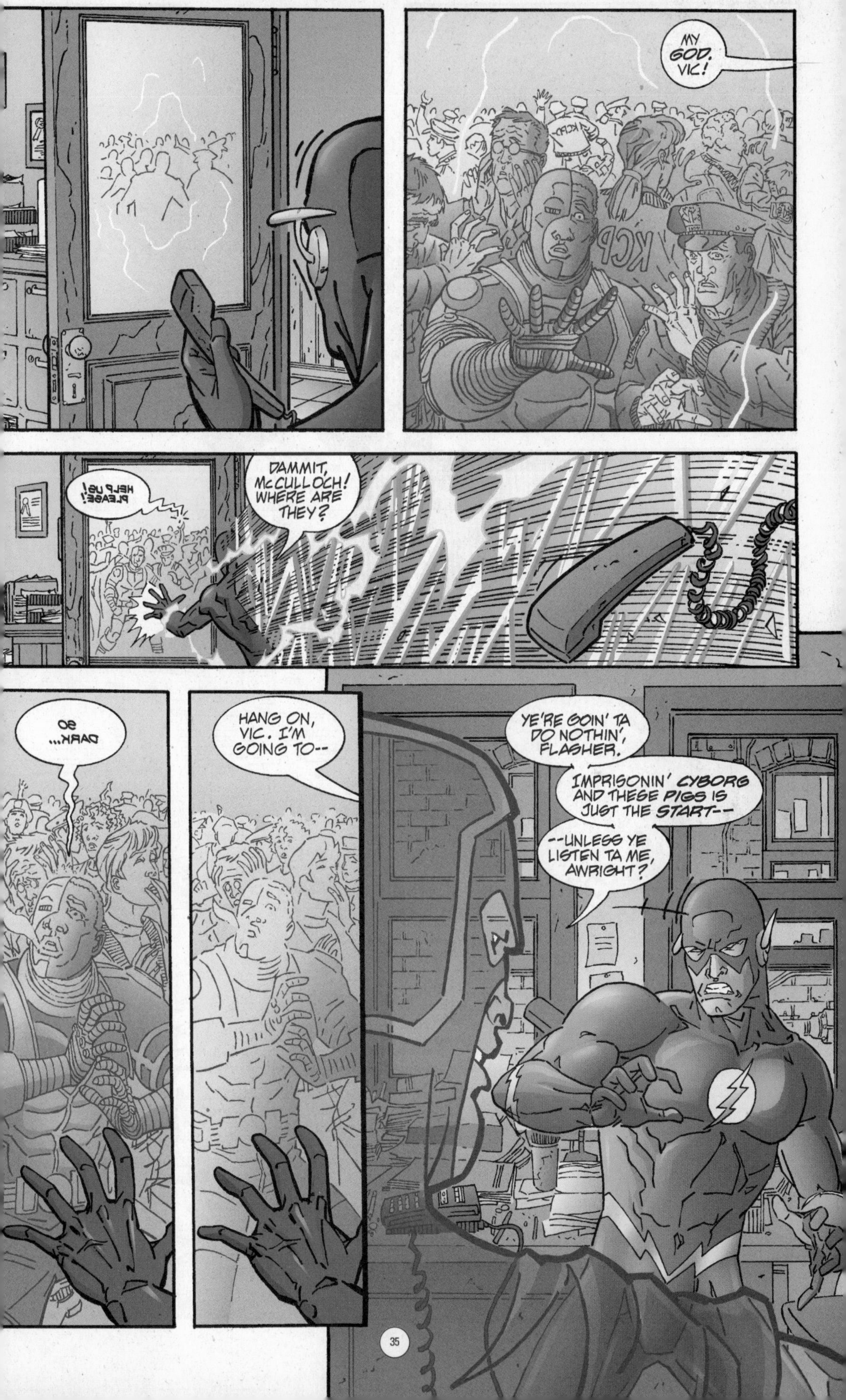
MY GOD. VIC!
HELP US! PLEASE!
DAMMIT, McCULLOCH! WHERE ARE THEY?
SO DARK...
HANG ON, VIC. I'M GOING TO--
YE'RE GOIN' TA DO NOTHIN', FLASHER.
IMPRISONIN' CYBORG AND THESE PIGS IS JUST THE START--
--UNLESS YE LISTEN TA ME, AWRIGHT?

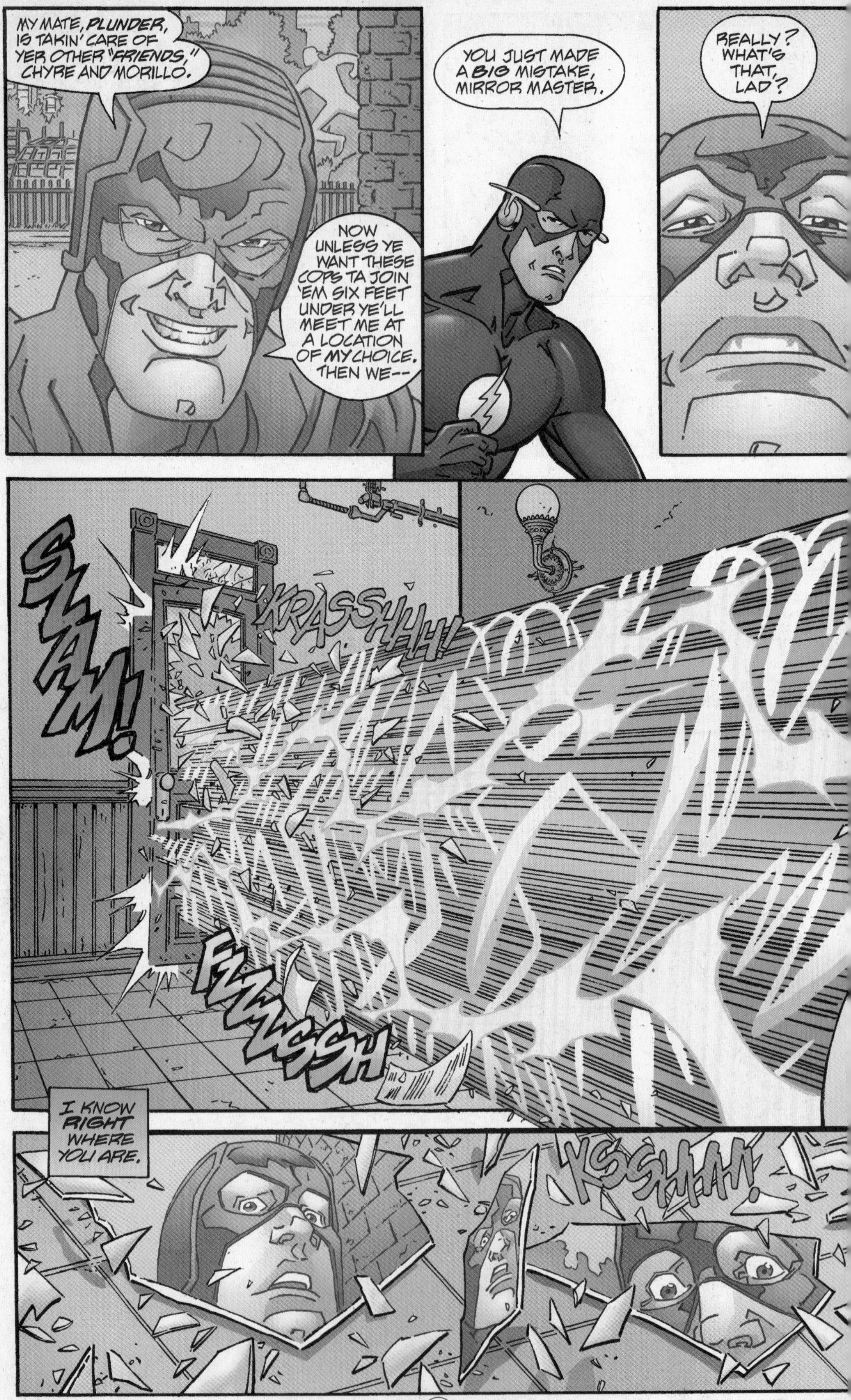
MY MATE, PLUNDER, IS TAKIN' CARE OF YER OTHER "FRIENDS," CHYRE AND MORILLO.
NOW UNLESS YE WANT THESE COPS TA JOIN 'EM SIX FEET UNDER YE'LL MEET ME AT A LOCATION OF MY CHOICE. THEN WE--
YOU JUST MADE A BIG MISTAKE, MIRROR MASTER.
REALLY? WHAT'S THAT, LAD?
SMAM!
KRASSHHH!
FZZWUSSH
I KNOW RIGHT WHERE YOU ARE.
KSSHHH!

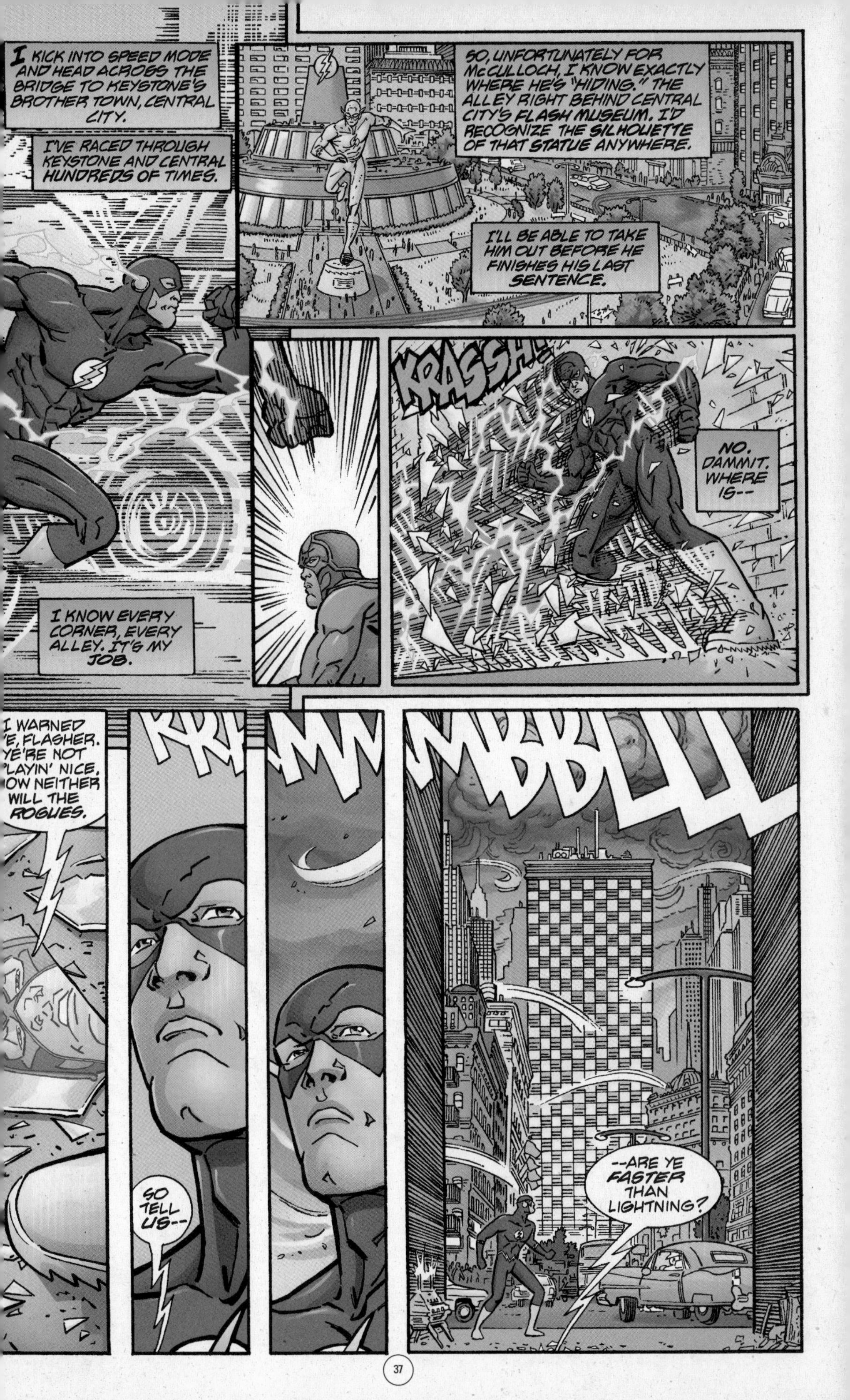

I KICK INTO SPEED MODE AND HEAD ACROSS THE BRIDGE TO KEYSTONE'S BROTHER TOWN, CENTRAL CITY.
I'VE RACED THROUGH KEYSTONE AND CENTRAL HUNDREDS OF TIMES.
SO, UNFORTUNATELY FOR McCULLOCH, I KNOW EXACTLY WHERE HE'S "HIDING." THE ALLEY RIGHT BEHIND CENTRAL CITY'S FLASH MUSEUM. I'D RECOGNIZE THE SILHOUETTE OF THAT STATUE ANYWHERE.
I'LL BE ABLE TO TAKE HIM OUT BEFORE HE FINISHES HIS LAST SENTENCE.
I KNOW EVERY CORNER, EVERY ALLEY. IT'S MY JOB.
KRASSH!
NO. DAMMIT. WHERE IS--
I WARNED 'E, FLASHER. YE'RE NOT PLAYIN' NICE, NOW NEITHER WILL THE ROGUES.
KRRAMMMBBLLL
SO TELL US--
--ARE YE FASTER THAN LIGHTNING?

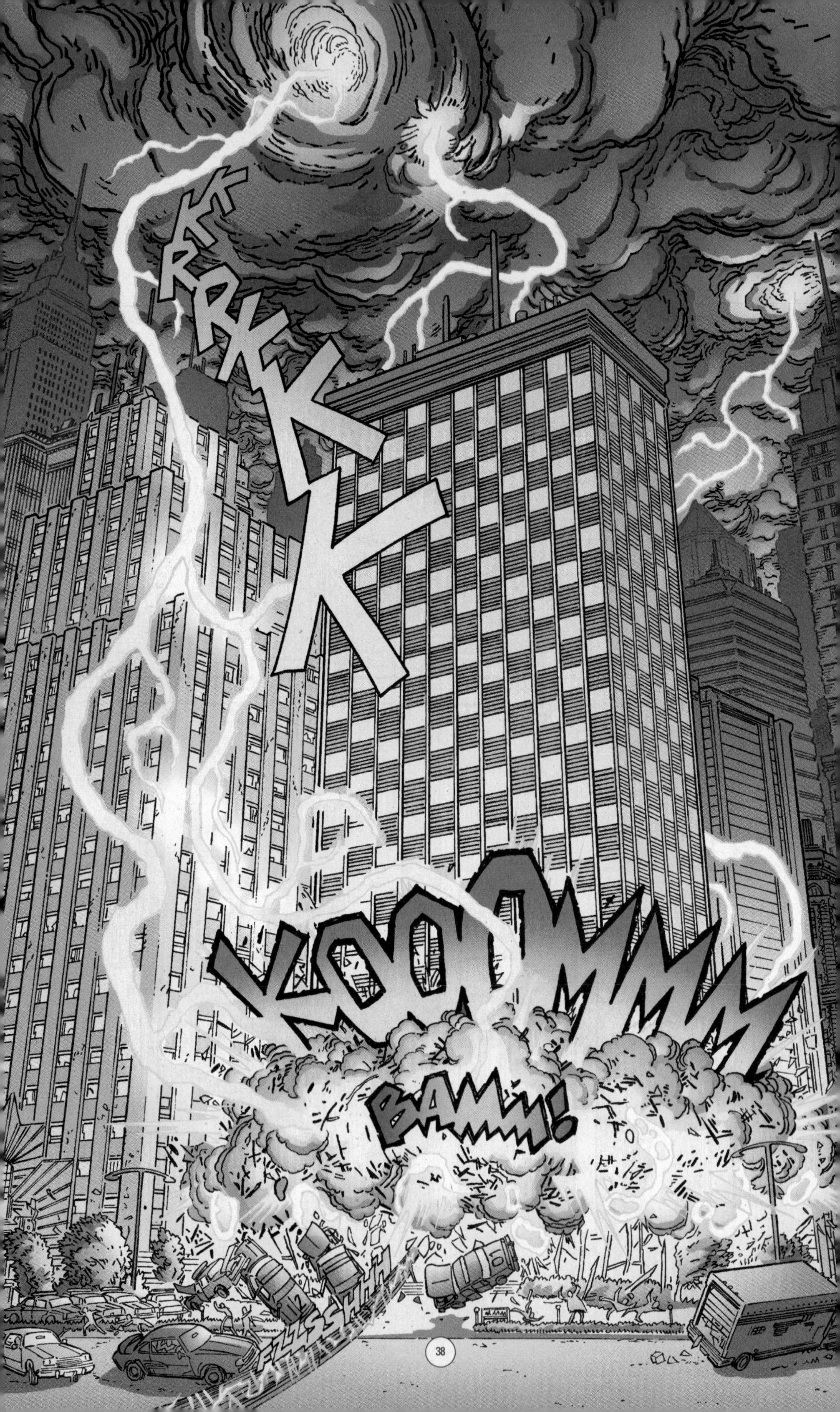
KOOMMM
BAMM!
FZZZSSHHH

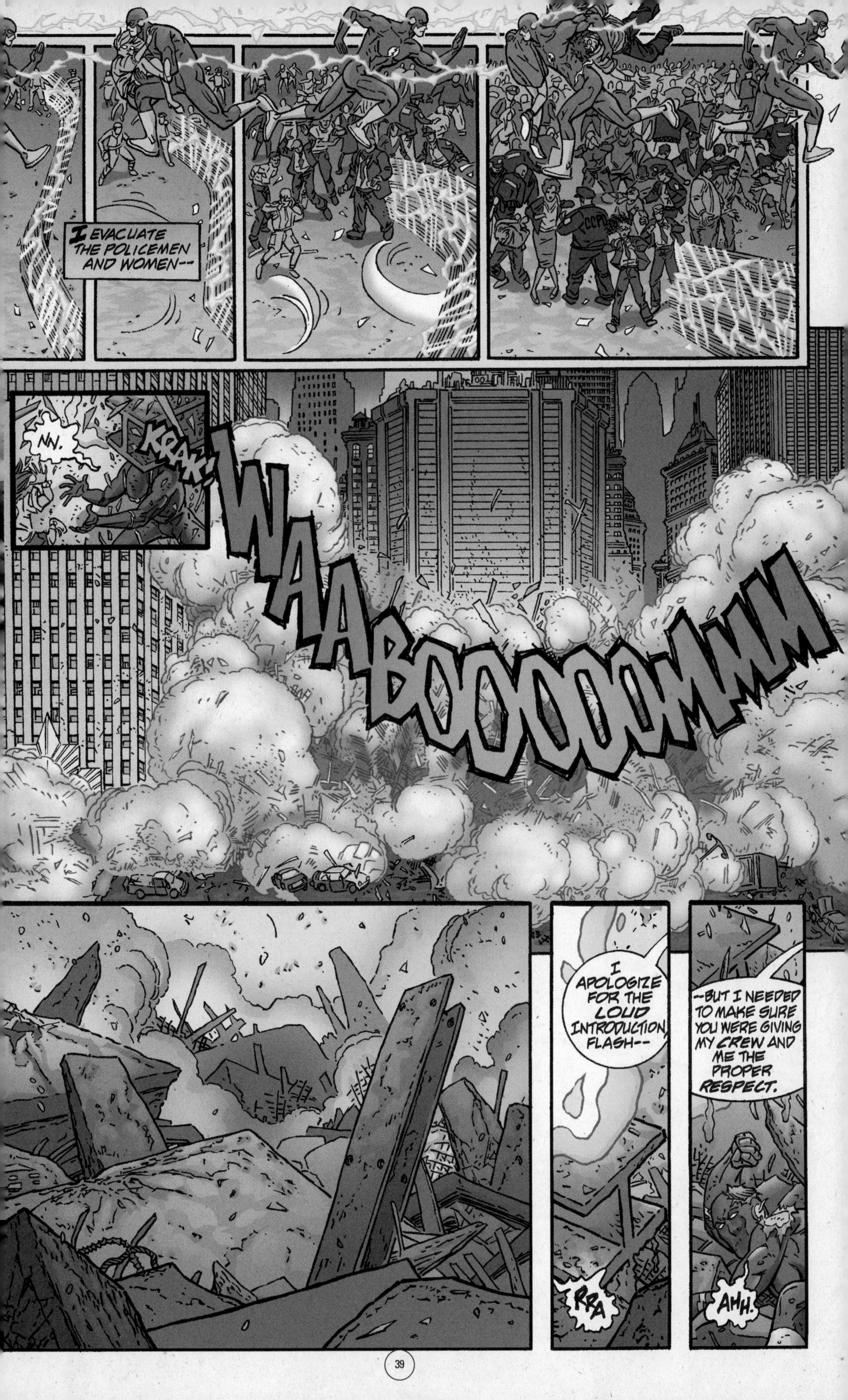

I EVACUATE THE POLICEMEN AND WOMEN--
NN.
KRAK!
WAABOOOOOMMM
I APOLOGIZE FOR THE LOUD INTRODUCTION, FLASH--
RRA
--BUT I NEEDED TO MAKE SURE YOU WERE GIVING MY CREW AND ME THE PROPER RESPECT.
AHH.

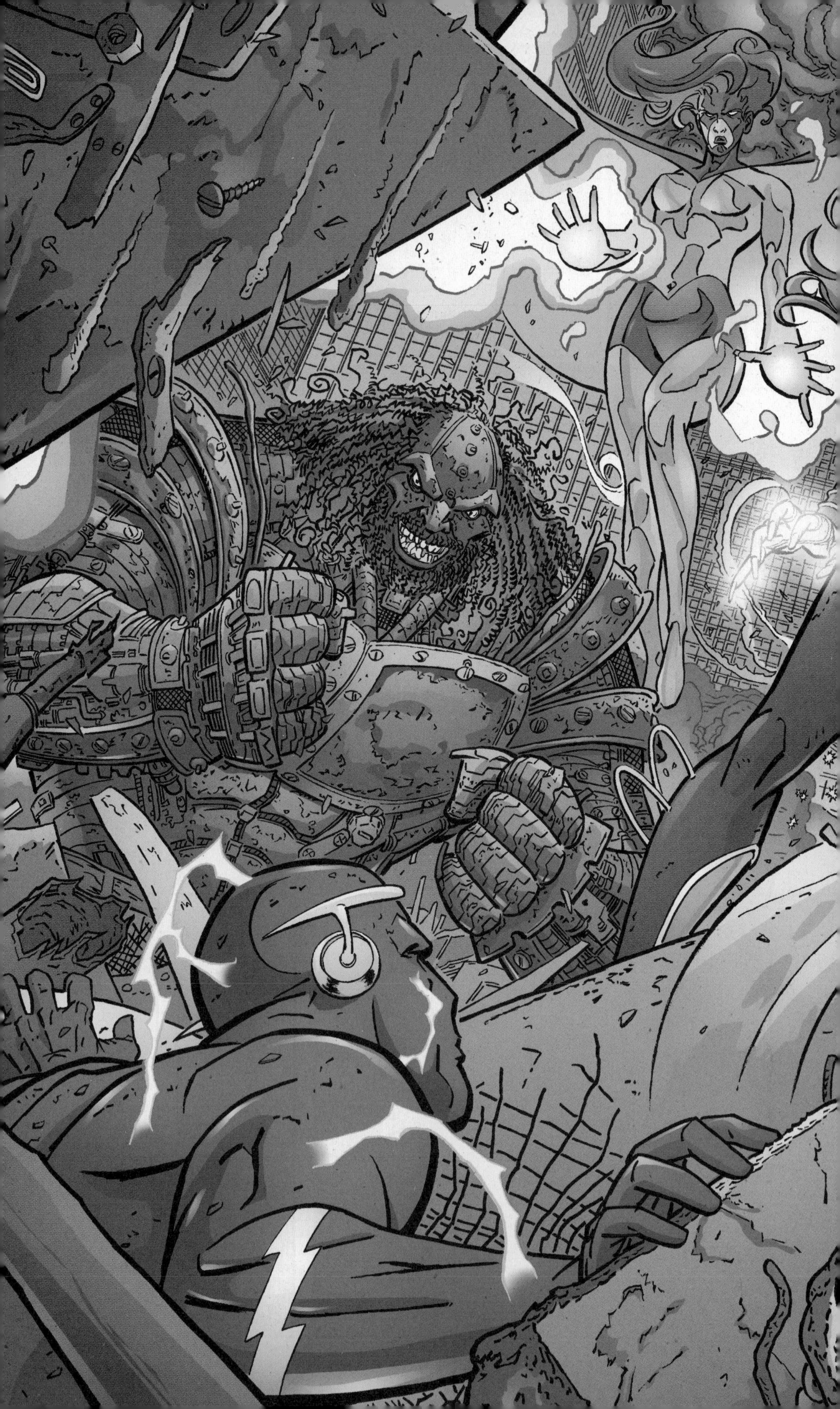

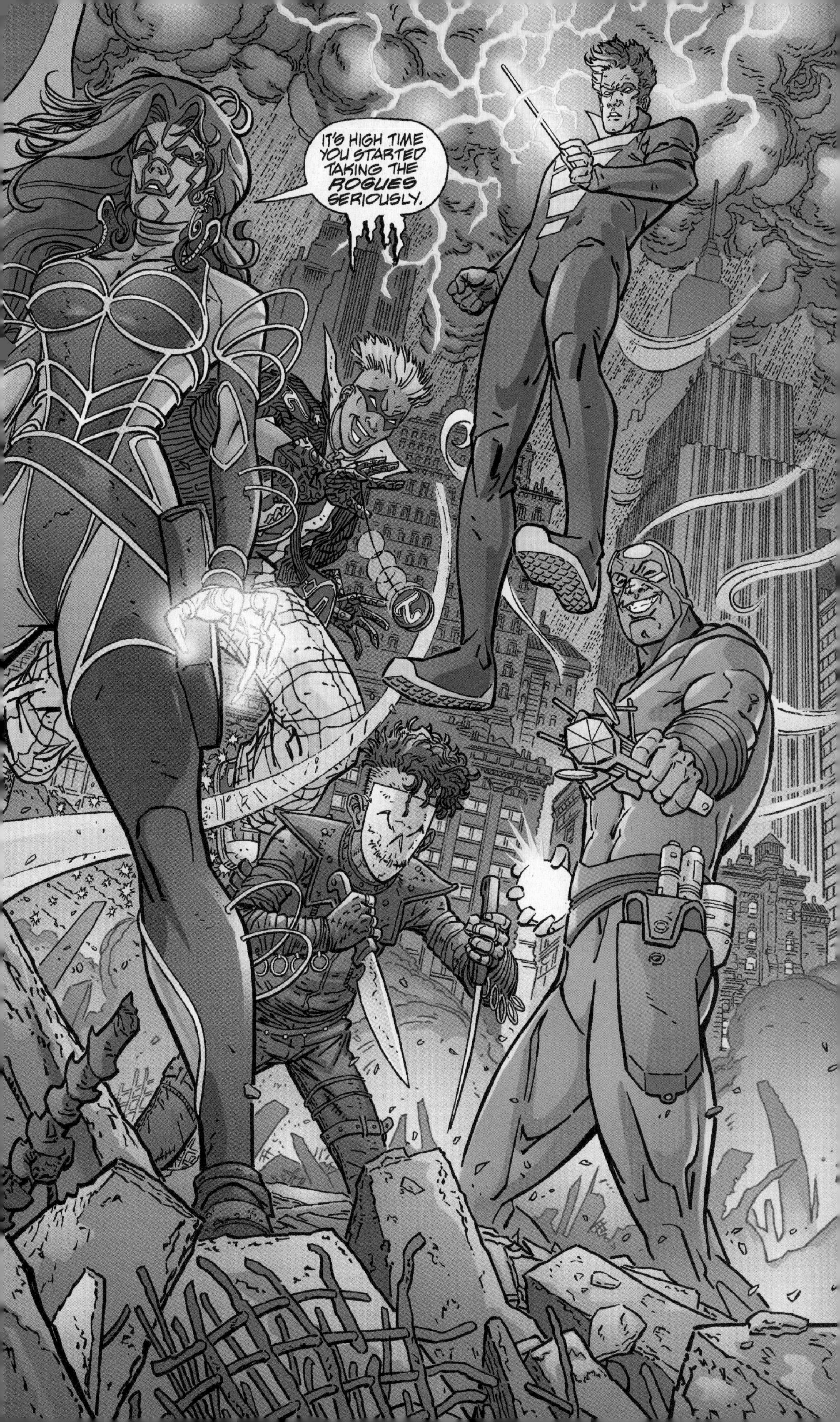
IT'S HIGH TIME YOU STARTED TAKING THE *ROGUES* SERIOUSLY.

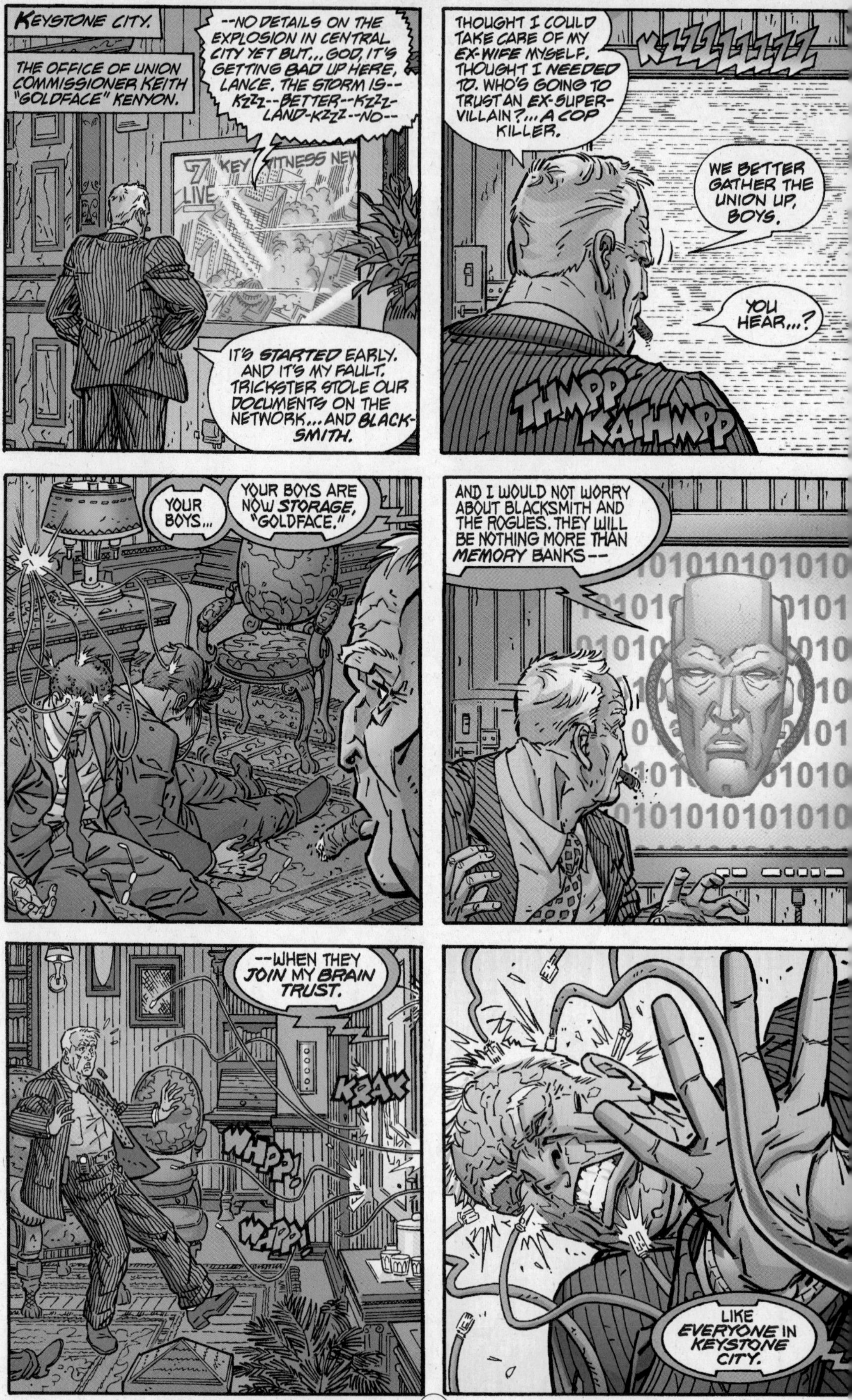
KEYSTONE CITY.
THE OFFICE OF UNION COMMISSIONER KEITH "GOLDFACE" KENYON.
--NO DETAILS ON THE EXPLOSION IN CENTRAL CITY YET BUT... GOD, IT'S GETTING BAD UP HERE, LANCE. THE STORM IS--KZZZ--BETTER--KZZZ-LAND-KZZZ--NO--
7 LIVE
KEY
ITNESS NEW
IT'S STARTED EARLY. AND IT'S MY FAULT. TRICKSTER STOLE OUR DOCUMENTS ON THE NETWORK... AND BLACK-SMITH.
THOUGHT I COULD TAKE CARE OF MY EX-WIFE MYSELF. THOUGHT I NEEDED TO. WHO'S GOING TO TRUST AN EX-SUPER-VILLAIN?... A COP KILLER.
KZZZZZZZ
WE BETTER GATHER THE UNION UP, BOYS.
YOU HEAR...?
THMPP
KATHMPP
YOUR BOYS...
YOUR BOYS ARE NOW STORAGE, "GOLDFACE."
AND I WOULD NOT WORRY ABOUT BLACKSMITH AND THE ROGUES. THEY WILL BE NOTHING MORE THAN MEMORY BANKS--
--WHEN THEY JOIN MY BRAIN TRUST.
KRAK
WHPP
WAPP
LIKE EVERYONE IN KEYSTONE CITY.

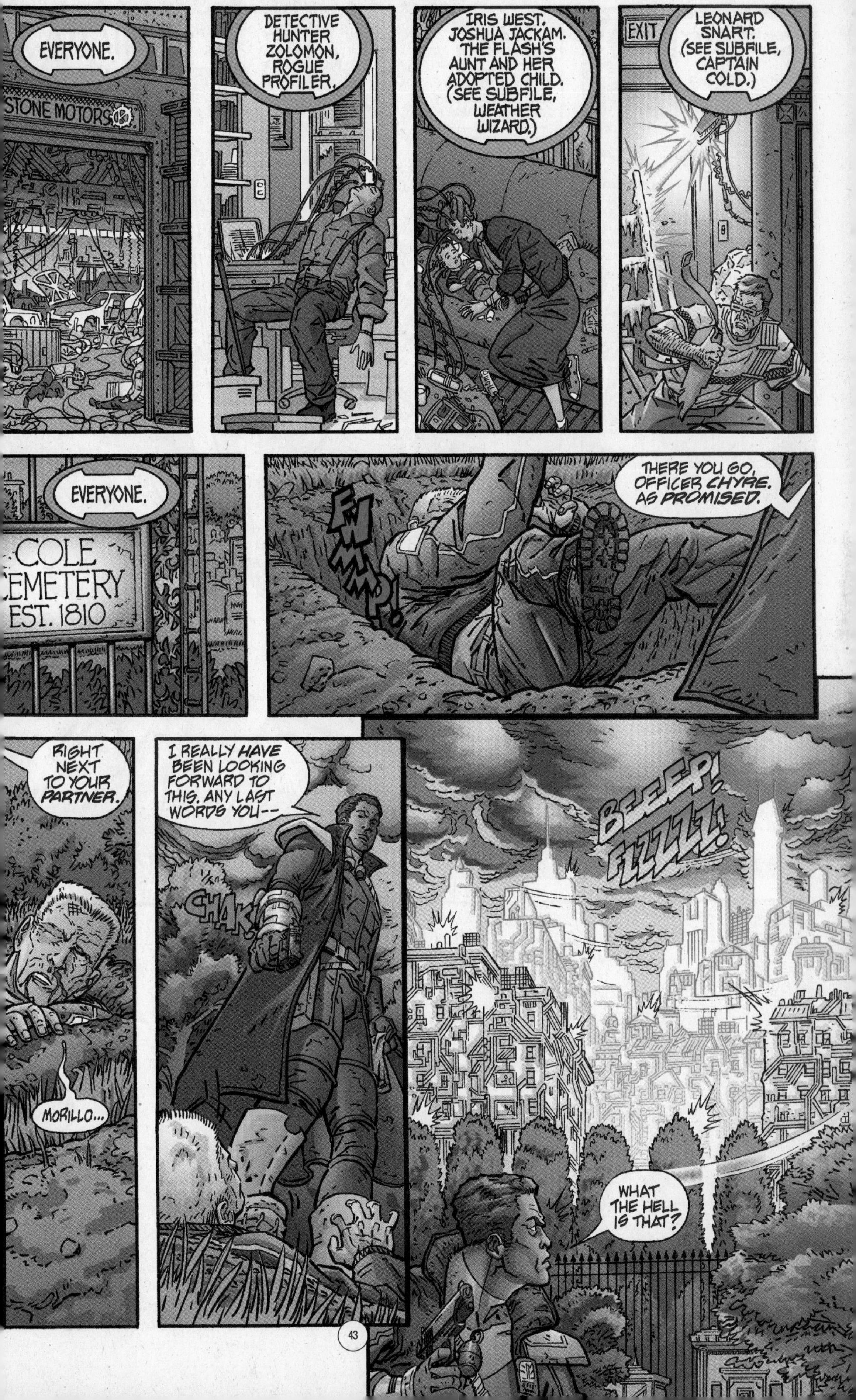
EVERYONE.
STONE MOTORS
DETECTIVE HUNTER ZOLOMON, ROGUE PROFILER.
IRIS WEST. JOSHUA JACKAM. THE FLASH'S AUNT AND HER ADOPTED CHILD. (SEE SUBFILE, WEATHER WIZARD.)
EXIT
LEONARD SNART. (SEE SUBFILE, CAPTAIN COLD.)
EVERYONE.
COLE CEMETERY EST. 1810
FWUMP!
THERE YOU GO, OFFICER CHYRE. AS PROMISED.
RIGHT NEXT TO YOUR PARTNER.
I REALLY HAVE BEEN LOOKING FORWARD TO THIS. ANY LAST WORDS YOU--
CHAK
MORILLO...
BEEEP! FZZZZ!
WHAT THE HELL IS THAT?

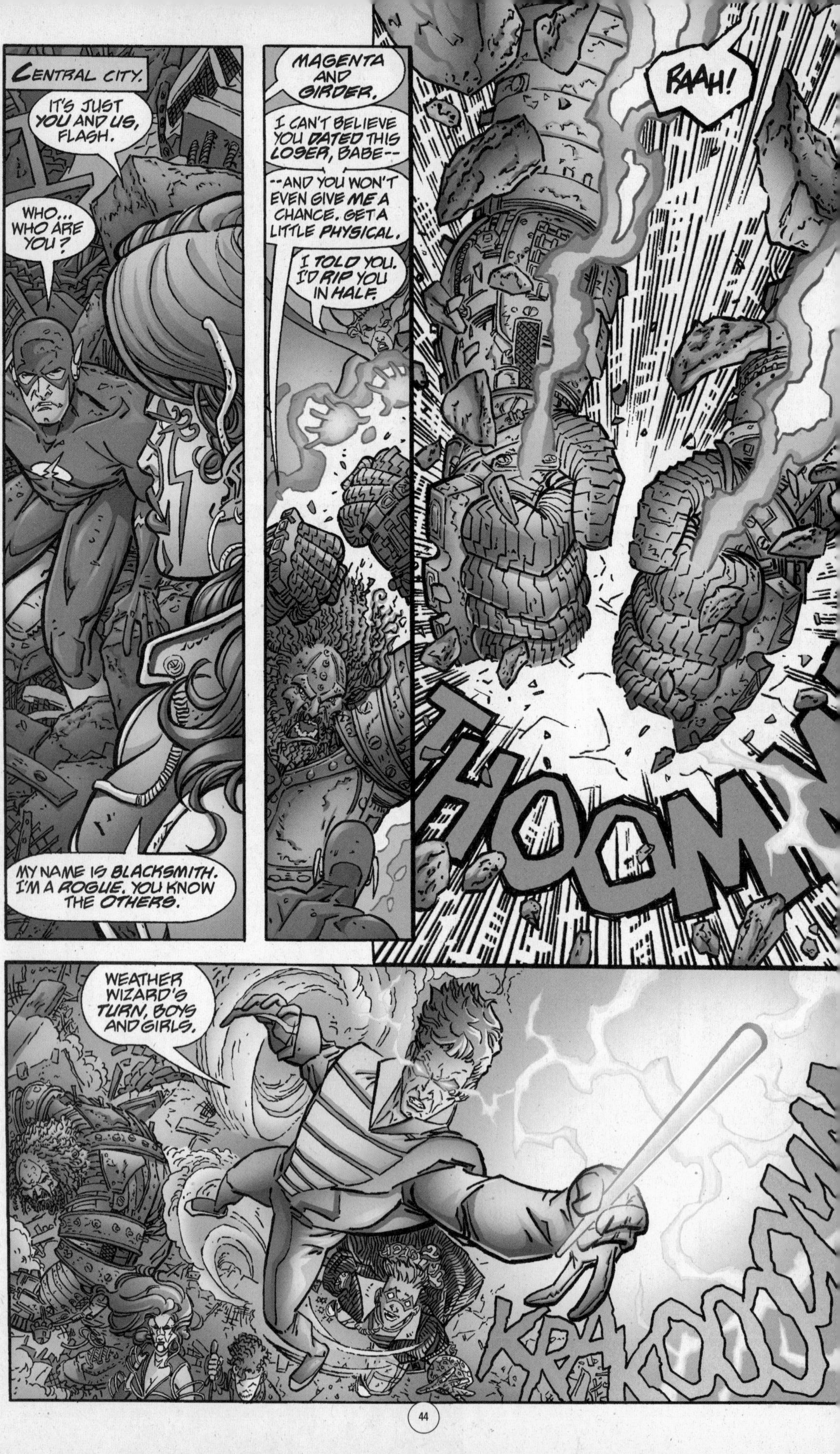
CENTRAL CITY.
IT'S JUST YOU AND US, FLASH.
WHO... WHO ARE YOU?
MY NAME IS BLACKSMITH. I'M A ROGUE. YOU KNOW THE OTHERS.
MAGENTA AND GIRDER.
I CAN'T BELIEVE YOU DATED THIS LOSER, BABE--
--AND YOU WON'T EVEN GIVE ME A CHANCE. GET A LITTLE PHYSICAL.
I TOLD YOU. I'D RIP YOU IN HALF.
RAAH!
THOOM
WEATHER WIZARD'S TURN, BOYS AND GIRLS.
KRAKOOOM

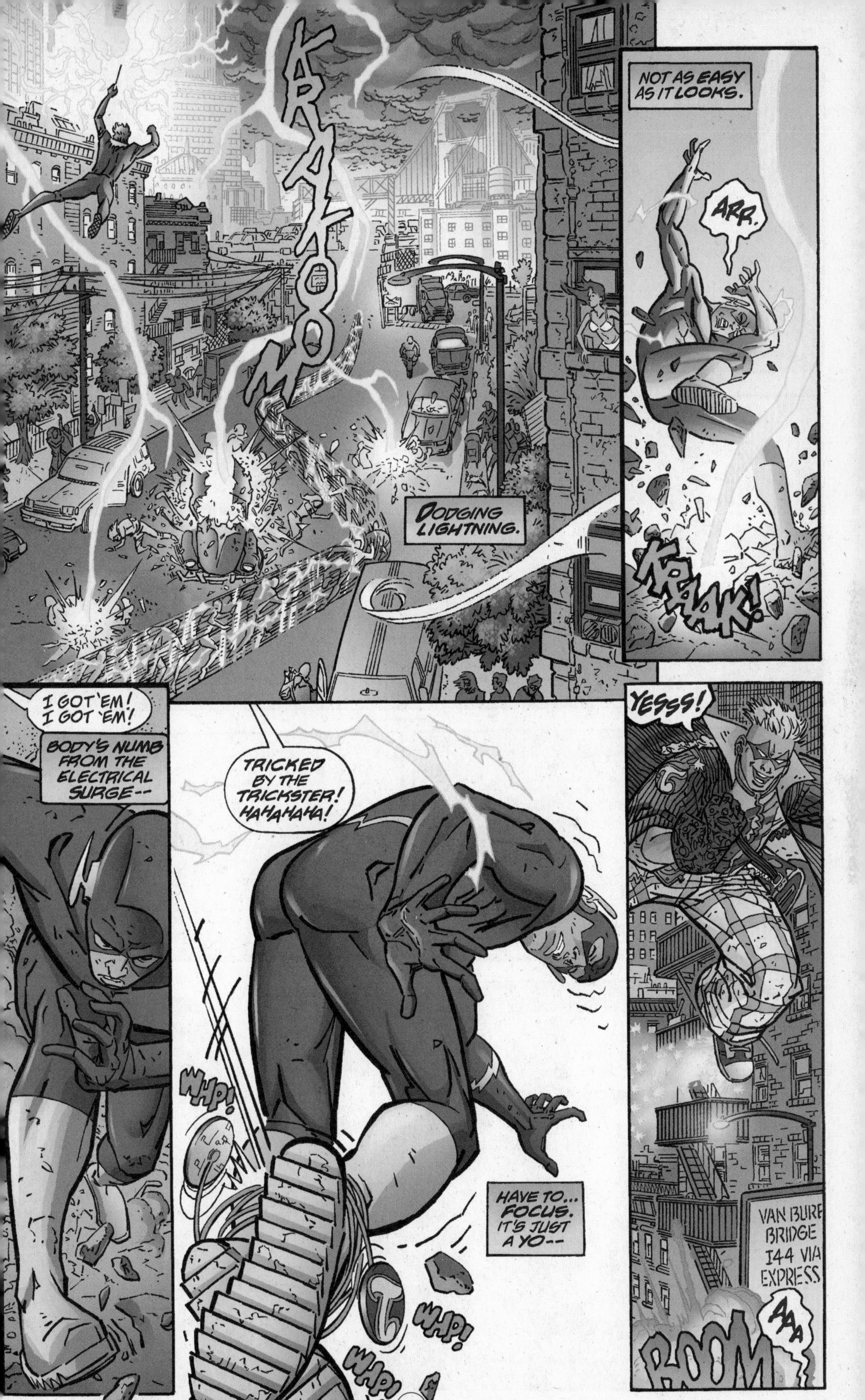

KRAKOOM
DODGING LIGHTNING.
NOT AS EASY AS IT LOOKS.
ARR.
KRAAK!
I GOT 'EM! I GOT 'EM!
BODY'S NUMB FROM THE ELECTRICAL SURGE--
TRICKED BY THE TRICKSTER! HAHAHAHA!
WHP!
HAVE TO... FOCUS. IT'S JUST A YO--
WHP!
WHP!
YESSS!
VAN BURE
BRIDGE
I44 VIA
EXPRESS
AAA
BOOM

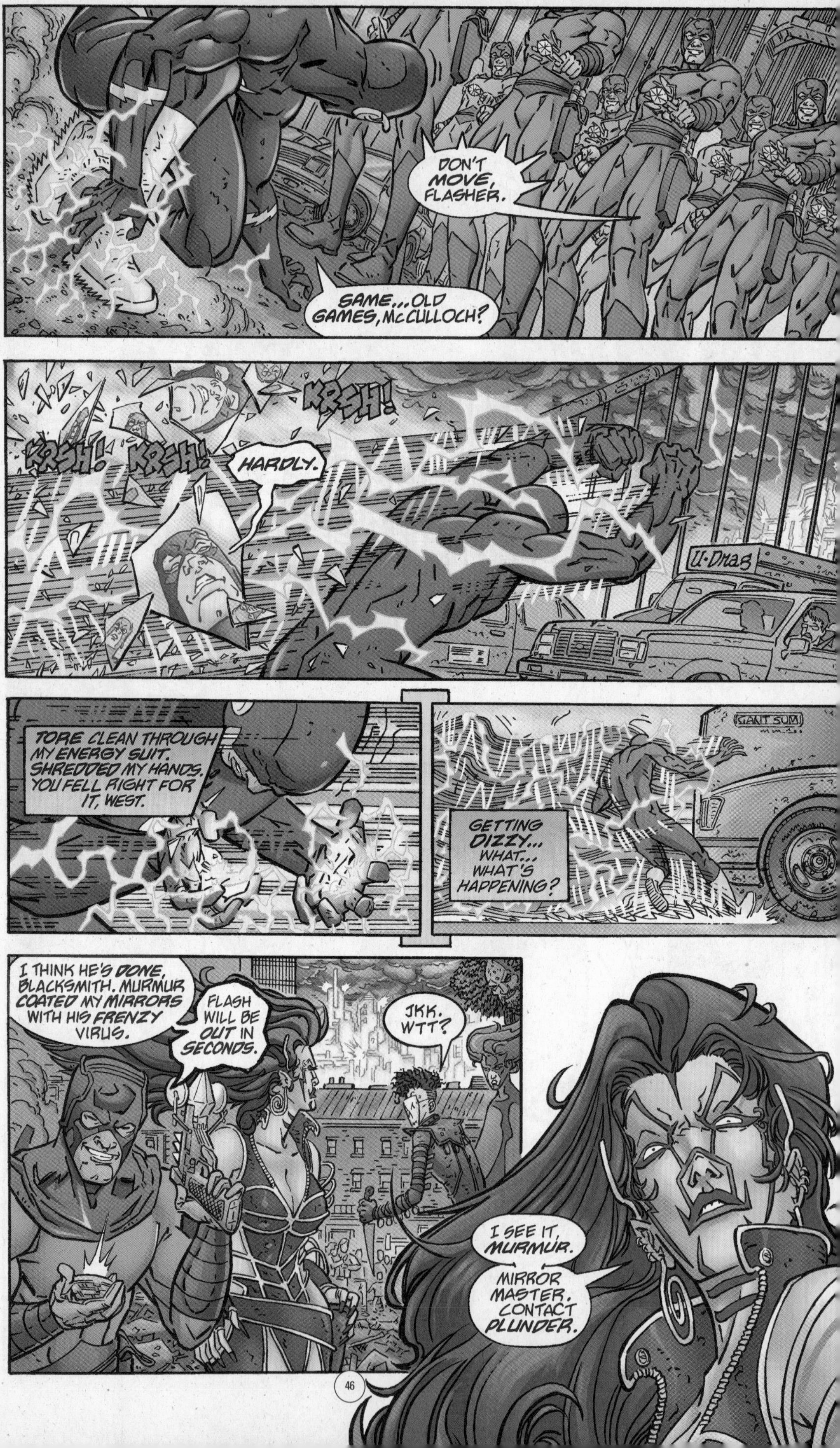

DON'T MOVE, FLASHER.
SAME...OLD GAMES, McCULLOCH?
KRSH! KRSH!
KRSH!
HARDLY.
U-Drag
TORE CLEAN THROUGH MY ENERGY SUIT. SHREDDED MY HANDS. YOU FELL RIGHT FOR IT, WEST.
GETTING DIZZY... WHAT... WHAT'S HAPPENING?
I THINK HE'S DONE, BLACKSMITH. MURMUR COATED MY MIRRORS WITH HIS FRENZY VIRUS.
FLASH WILL BE OUT IN SECONDS.
JKK. WTT?
I SEE IT, MURMUR.
MIRROR MASTER. CONTACT PLUNDER.

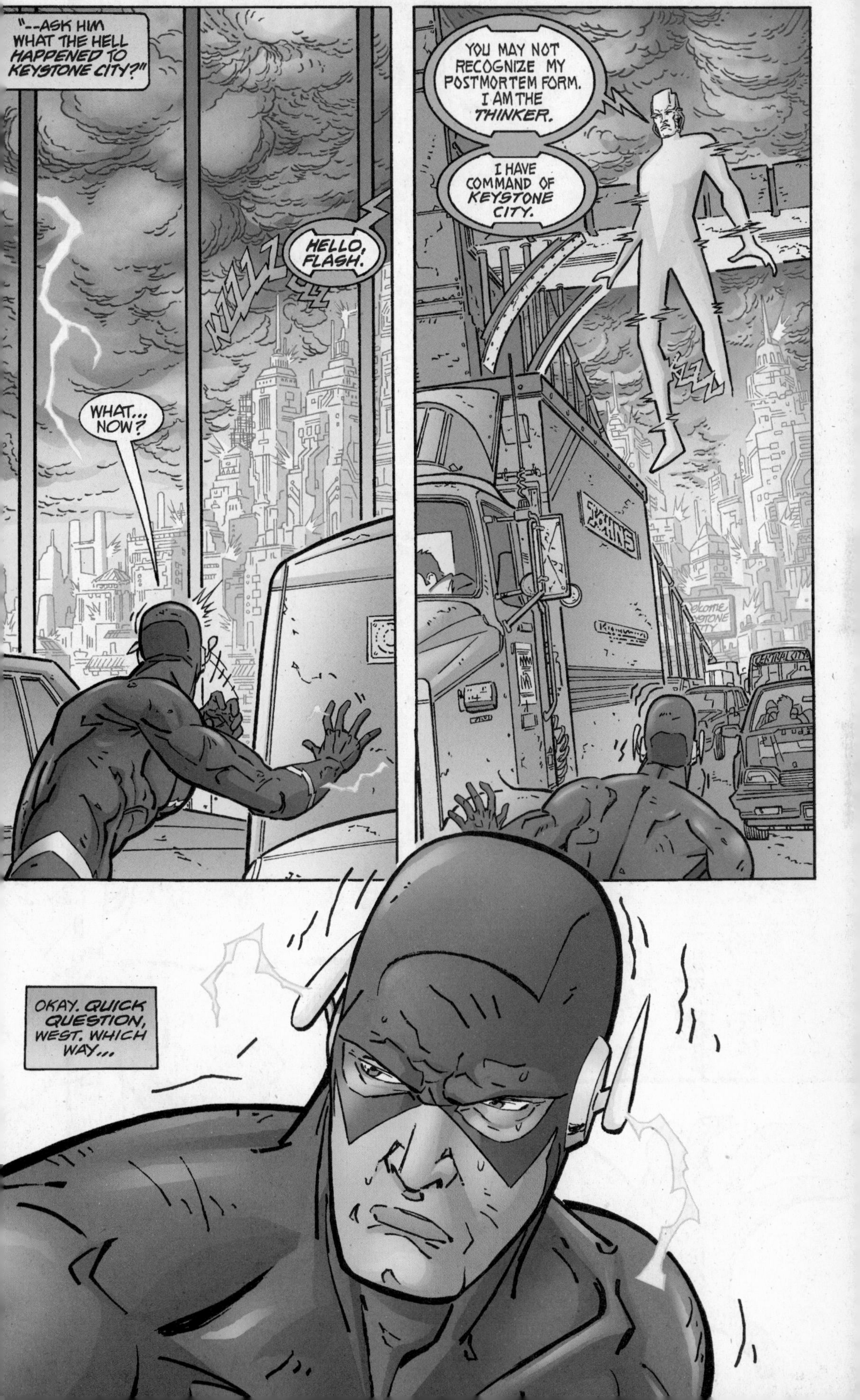
"--ASK HIM WHAT THE HELL HAPPENED TO KEYSTONE CITY?"
KZZZZZ
HELLO, FLASH.
WHAT... NOW?
YOU MAY NOT RECOGNIZE MY POSTMORTEM FORM. I AM THE THINKER.
I HAVE COMMAND OF KEYSTONE CITY.
OKAY. QUICK QUESTION, WEST. WHICH WAY...

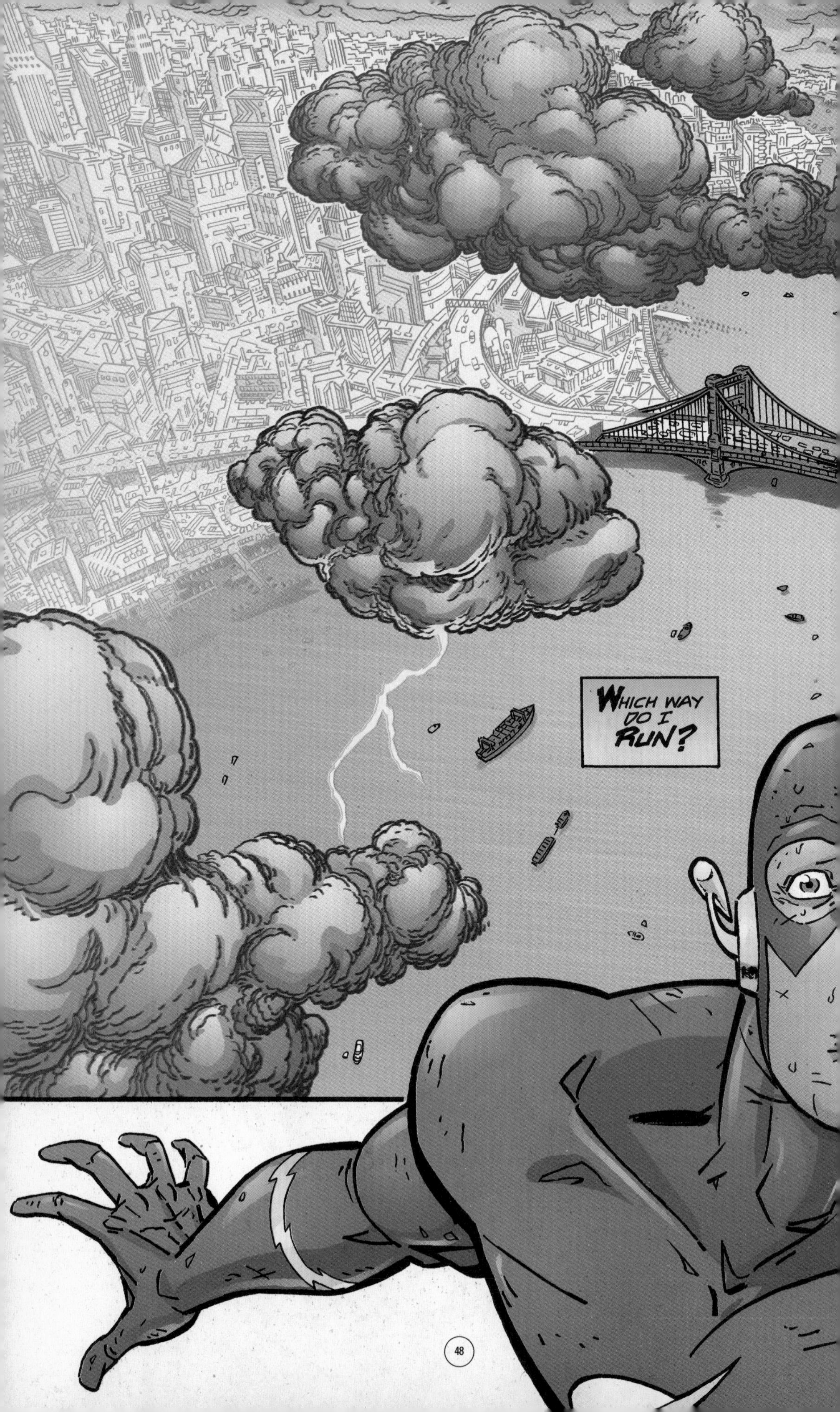
WHICH WAY DO I RUN?

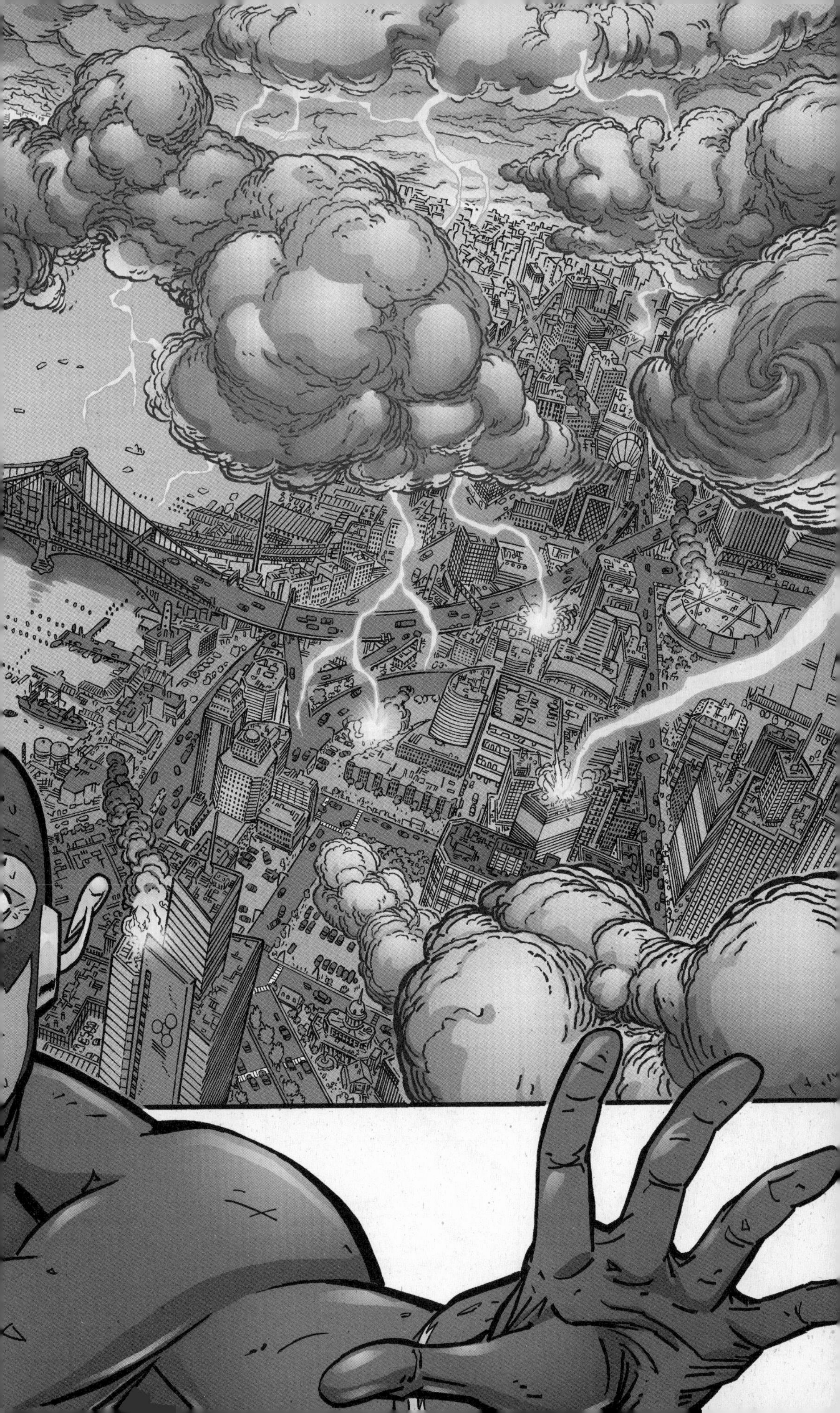

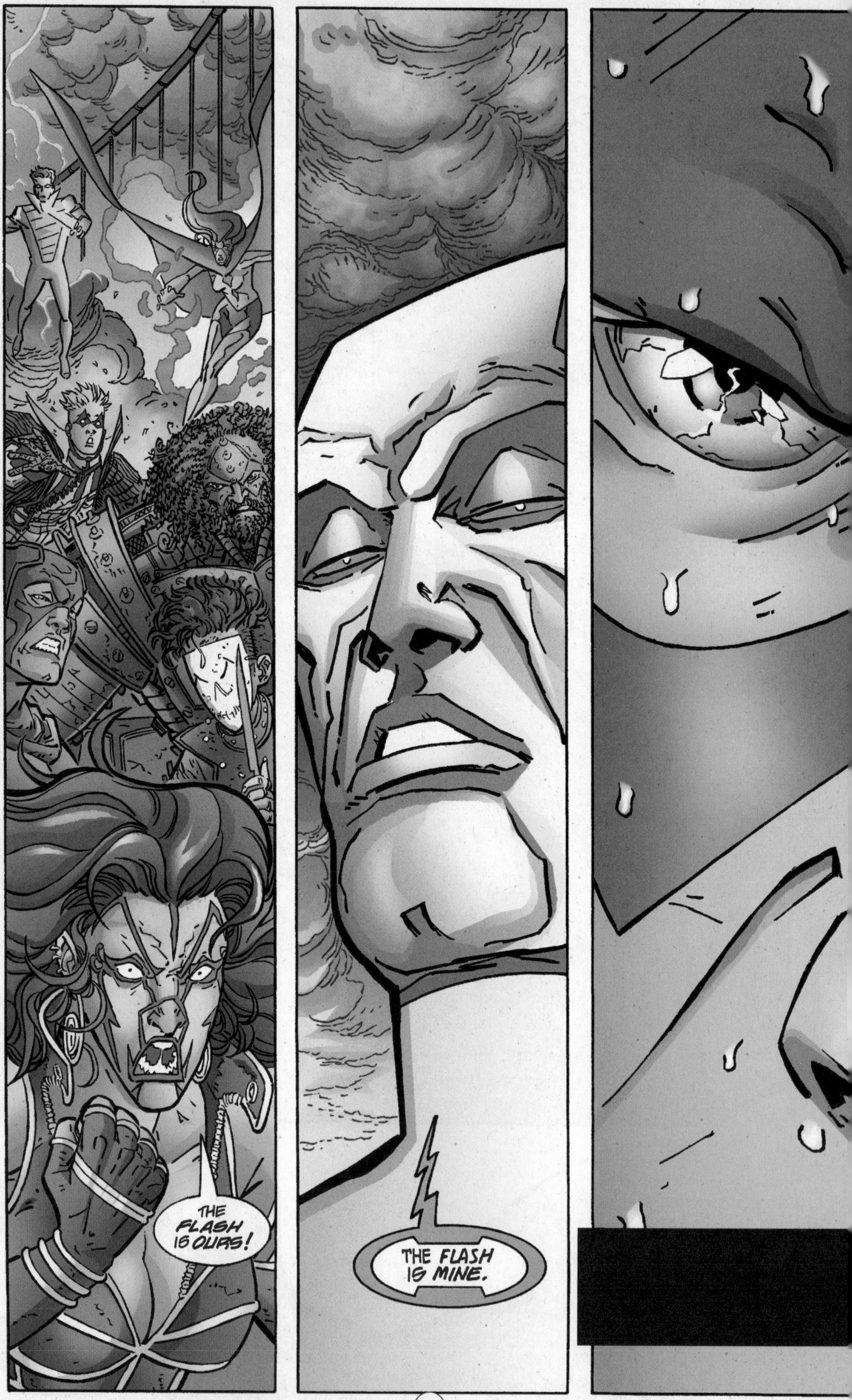
THE FLASH IS OURS!
THE FLASH IS MINE.
[redacted]

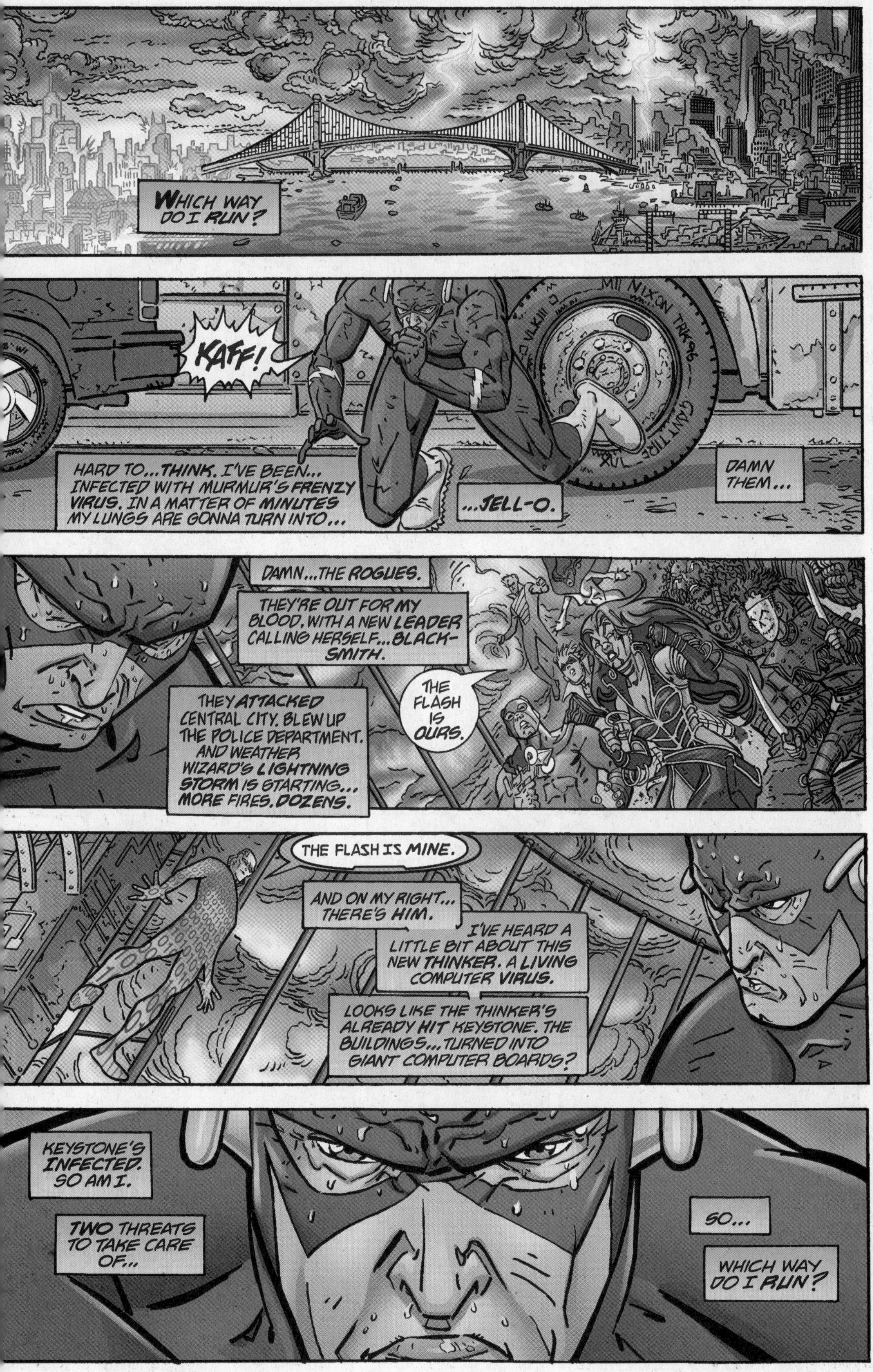
WHICH WAY DO I RUN?
KAFF!
MII NIXON TRK 96
HARD TO...THINK. I'VE BEEN... INFECTED WITH MURMUR'S FRENZY VIRUS. IN A MATTER OF MINUTES MY LUNGS ARE GONNA TURN INTO...
...JELL-O.
DAMN THEM...
DAMN...THE ROGUES.
THEY'RE OUT FOR MY BLOOD, WITH A NEW LEADER CALLING HERSELF...BLACKSMITH.
THE FLASH IS OURS.
THEY ATTACKED CENTRAL CITY. BLEW UP THE POLICE DEPARTMENT. AND WEATHER WIZARD'S LIGHTNING STORM IS STARTING... MORE FIRES. DOZENS.
THE FLASH IS MINE.
AND ON MY RIGHT... THERE'S HIM.
I'VE HEARD A LITTLE BIT ABOUT THIS NEW THINKER. A LIVING COMPUTER VIRUS.
LOOKS LIKE THE THINKER'S ALREADY HIT KEYSTONE. THE BUILDINGS...TURNED INTO GIANT COMPUTER BOARDS?
KEYSTONE'S INFECTED. SO AM I.
TWO THREATS TO TAKE CARE OF...
SO...
WHICH WAY DO I RUN?

RIGHT NOW I DON'T HAVE MUCH CHOICE.

I HEAD WEST.

I'M.... DYING.

AND IF I WANT TO STOP...THESE MONSTERS...

I'VE GOT TO... STAY ALIVE.

I SEE THE DAMAGE THE THINKER HAS DONE. EVERY LIVING THING HAS BEEN ENSNARED IN A WEB OF WIRES.

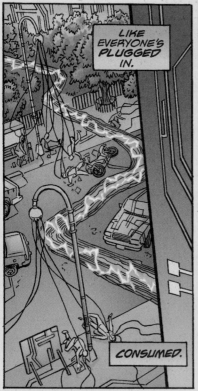

LIKE EVERYONE'S PLUGGED IN.

CONSUMED.

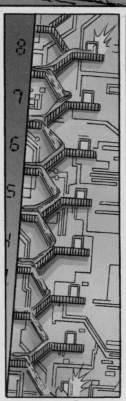

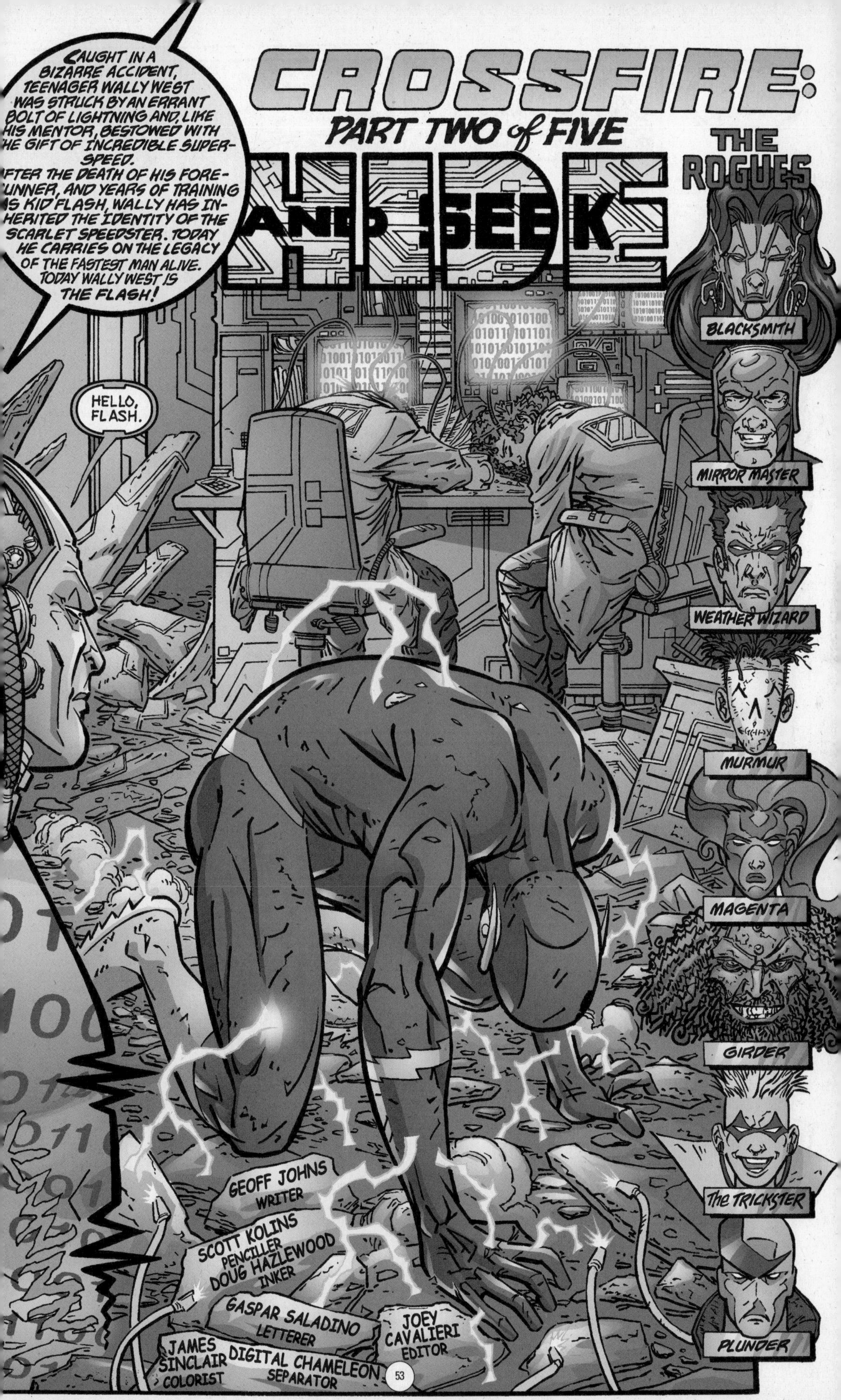
CAUGHT IN A BIZARRE ACCIDENT, TEENAGER WALLY WEST WAS STRUCK BY AN ERRANT BOLT OF LIGHTNING AND, LIKE HIS MENTOR, BESTOWED WITH THE GIFT OF INCREDIBLE SUPER-SPEED. AFTER THE DEATH OF HIS FORE-RUNNER, AND YEARS OF TRAINING AS KID FLASH, WALLY HAS IN-HERITED THE IDENTITY OF THE SCARLET SPEEDSTER. TODAY HE CARRIES ON THE LEGACY OF THE FASTEST MAN ALIVE. TODAY WALLY WEST IS THE FLASH!
CROSSFIRE:
PART TWO of FIVE
HIDE AND SEEK
THE ROGUES
BLACKSMITH
MIRROR MASTER
WEATHER WIZARD
MURMUR
MAGENTA
GIRDER
The TRICKSTER
PLUNDER
HELLO, FLASH.
GEOFF JOHNS WRITER
SCOTT KOLINS PENCILLER
DOUG HAZLEWOOD INKER
GASPAR SALADINO LETTERER
JOEY CAVALIERI EDITOR
JAMES SINCLAIR COLORIST
DIGITAL CHAMELEON SEPARATOR

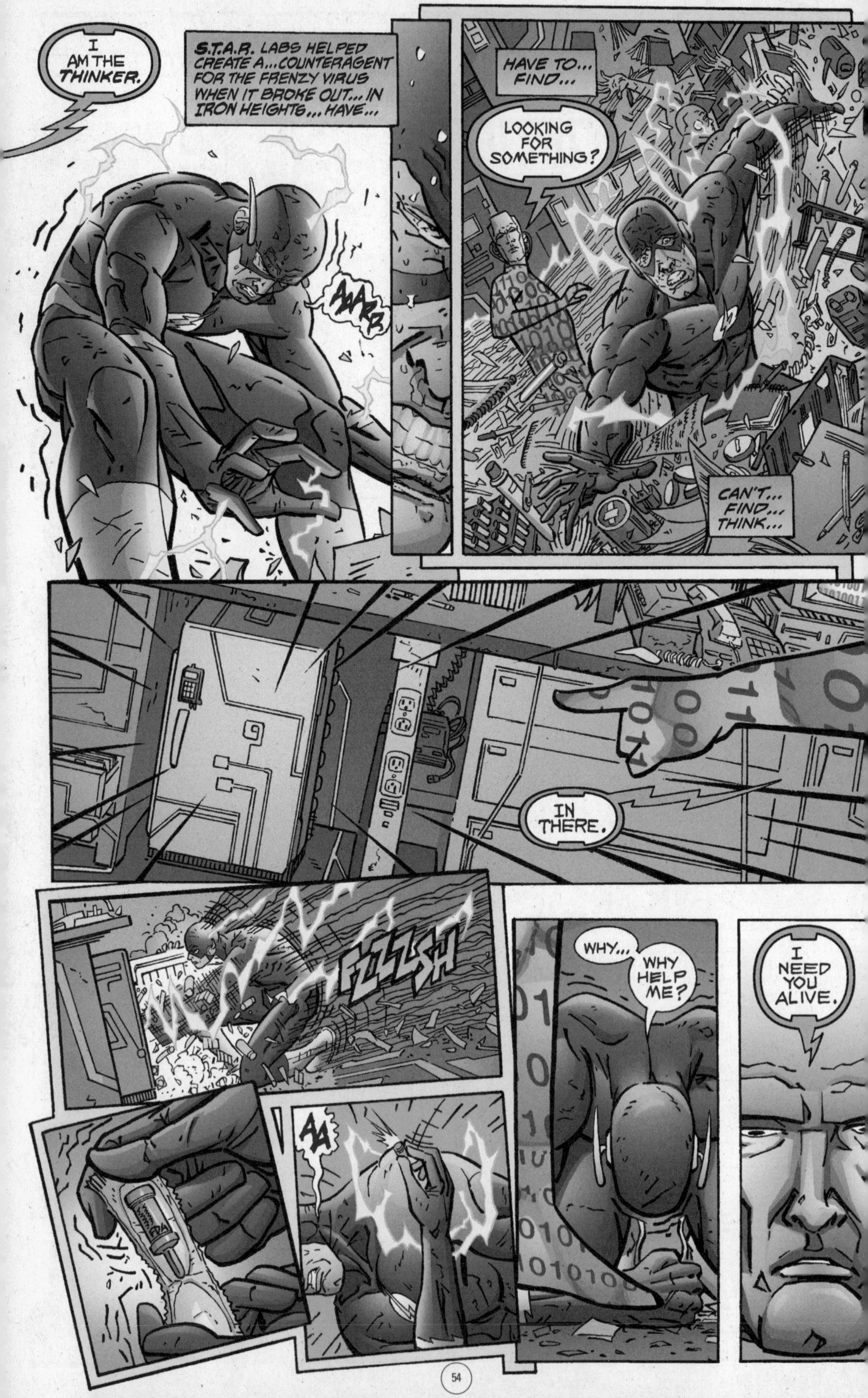

I AM THE THINKER.
S.T.A.R. LABS HELPED CREATE A...COUNTERAGENT FOR THE FRENZY VIRUS WHEN IT BROKE OUT... IN IRON HEIGHTS... HAVE...
AAARR
HAVE TO... FIND...
LOOKING FOR SOMETHING?
CAN'T... FIND... THINK...
IN THERE.
FZZZSH
AA
WHY... WHY HELP ME?
I NEED YOU ALIVE.

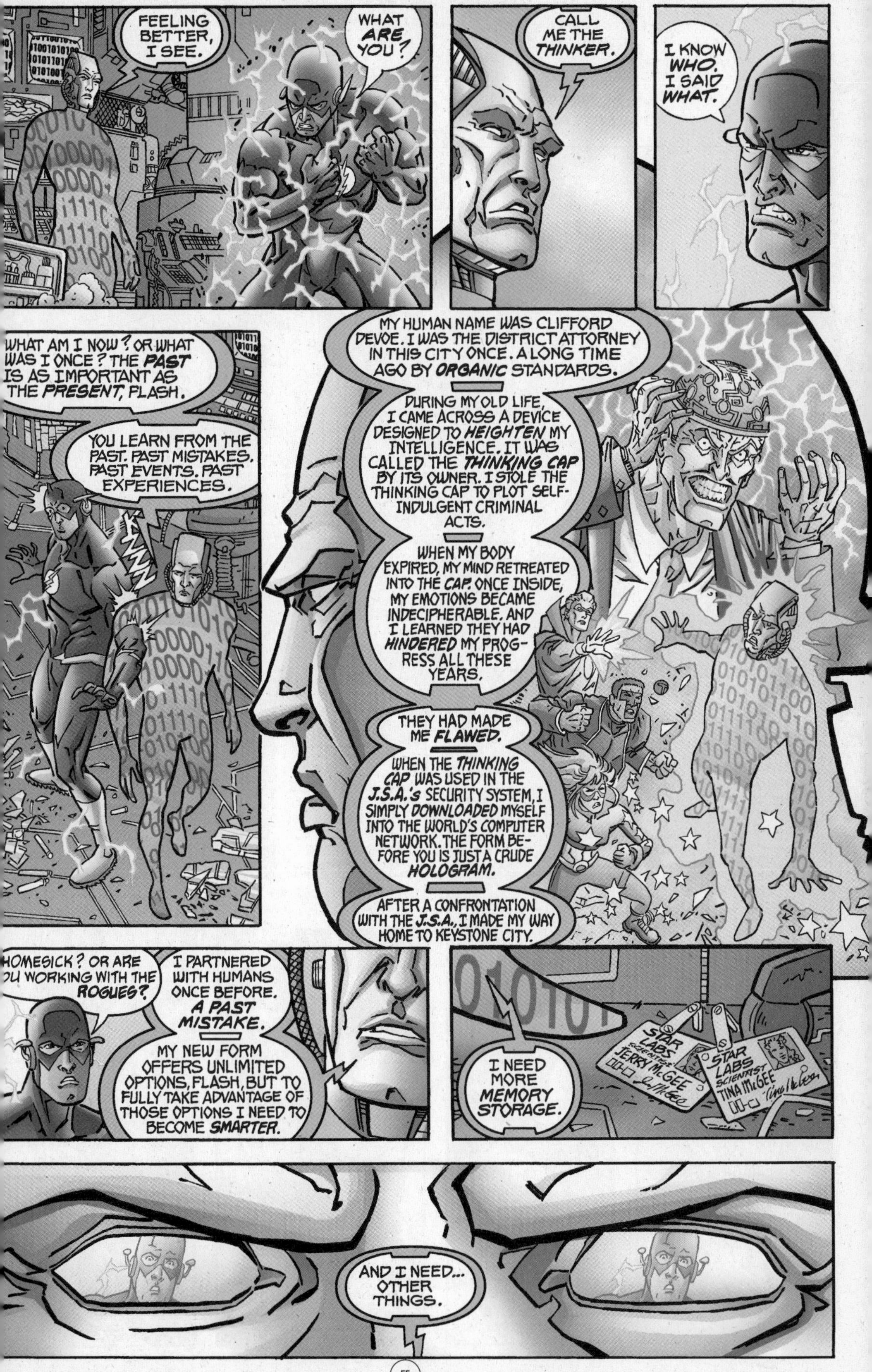
FEELING BETTER, I SEE.
WHAT ARE YOU?
CALL ME THE THINKER.
I KNOW WHO. I SAID WHAT.
WHAT AM I NOW? OR WHAT WAS I ONCE? THE PAST IS AS IMPORTANT AS THE PRESENT, FLASH.
YOU LEARN FROM THE PAST. PAST MISTAKES. PAST EVENTS. PAST EXPERIENCES.
MY HUMAN NAME WAS CLIFFORD DEVOE. I WAS THE DISTRICT ATTORNEY IN THIS CITY ONCE. A LONG TIME AGO BY ORGANIC STANDARDS.
DURING MY OLD LIFE, I CAME ACROSS A DEVICE DESIGNED TO HEIGHTEN MY INTELLIGENCE. IT WAS CALLED THE THINKING CAP BY ITS OWNER. I STOLE THE THINKING CAP TO PLOT SELF-INDULGENT CRIMINAL ACTS.
WHEN MY BODY EXPIRED, MY MIND RETREATED INTO THE CAP. ONCE INSIDE, MY EMOTIONS BECAME INDECIPHERABLE. AND I LEARNED THEY HAD HINDERED MY PROGRESS ALL THESE YEARS.
THEY HAD MADE ME FLAWED.
WHEN THE THINKING CAP WAS USED IN THE J.S.A.'s SECURITY SYSTEM, I SIMPLY DOWNLOADED MYSELF INTO THE WORLD'S COMPUTER NETWORK. THE FORM BEFORE YOU IS JUST A CRUDE HOLOGRAM.
AFTER A CONFRONTATION WITH THE J.S.A., I MADE MY WAY HOME TO KEYSTONE CITY.
HOMESICK? OR ARE OU WORKING WITH THE ROGUES?
I PARTNERED WITH HUMANS ONCE BEFORE. A PAST MISTAKE.
MY NEW FORM OFFERS UNLIMITED OPTIONS, FLASH, BUT TO FULLY TAKE ADVANTAGE OF THOSE OPTIONS I NEED TO BECOME SMARTER.
I NEED MORE MEMORY STORAGE.
STAR LABS SCIENTIST JERRY McGEE
STAR LABS SCIENTIST TINA McGEE
AND I NEED... OTHER THINGS.

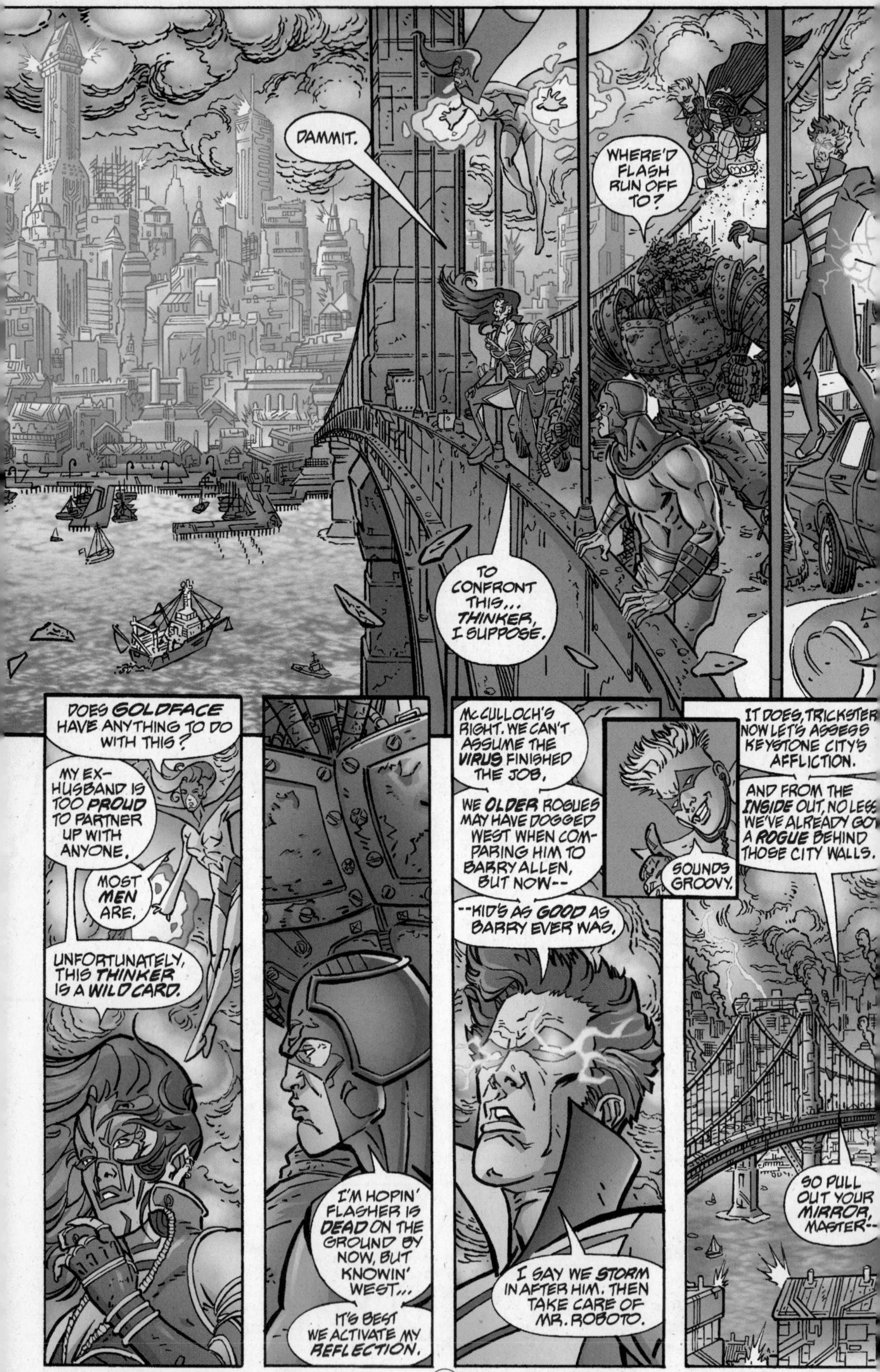
DAMMIT.
WHERE'D FLASH RUN OFF TO?
TO CONFRONT THIS... THINKER, I SUPPOSE.
DOES GOLDFACE HAVE ANYTHING TO DO WITH THIS?
MY EX-HUSBAND IS TOO PROUD TO PARTNER UP WITH ANYONE.
MOST MEN ARE.
UNFORTUNATELY, THIS THINKER IS A WILD CARD.
I'M HOPIN' FLASHER IS DEAD ON THE GROUND BY NOW, BUT KNOWIN' WEST...
IT'S BEST WE ACTIVATE MY REFLECTION.
McCULLOCH'S RIGHT. WE CAN'T ASSUME THE VIRUS FINISHED THE JOB.
WE OLDER ROGUES MAY HAVE DOGGED WEST WHEN COMPARING HIM TO BARRY ALLEN, BUT NOW--
--KID'S AS GOOD AS BARRY EVER WAS.
I SAY WE STORM IN AFTER HIM. THEN TAKE CARE OF MR. ROBOTO.
SOUNDS GROOVY.
IT DOES, TRICKSTER. NOW LET'S ASSESS KEYSTONE CITY'S AFFLICTION.
AND FROM THE INSIDE OUT, NO LESS. WE'VE ALREADY GOT A ROGUE BEHIND THOSE CITY WALLS.
SO PULL OUT YOUR MIRROR, MASTER--

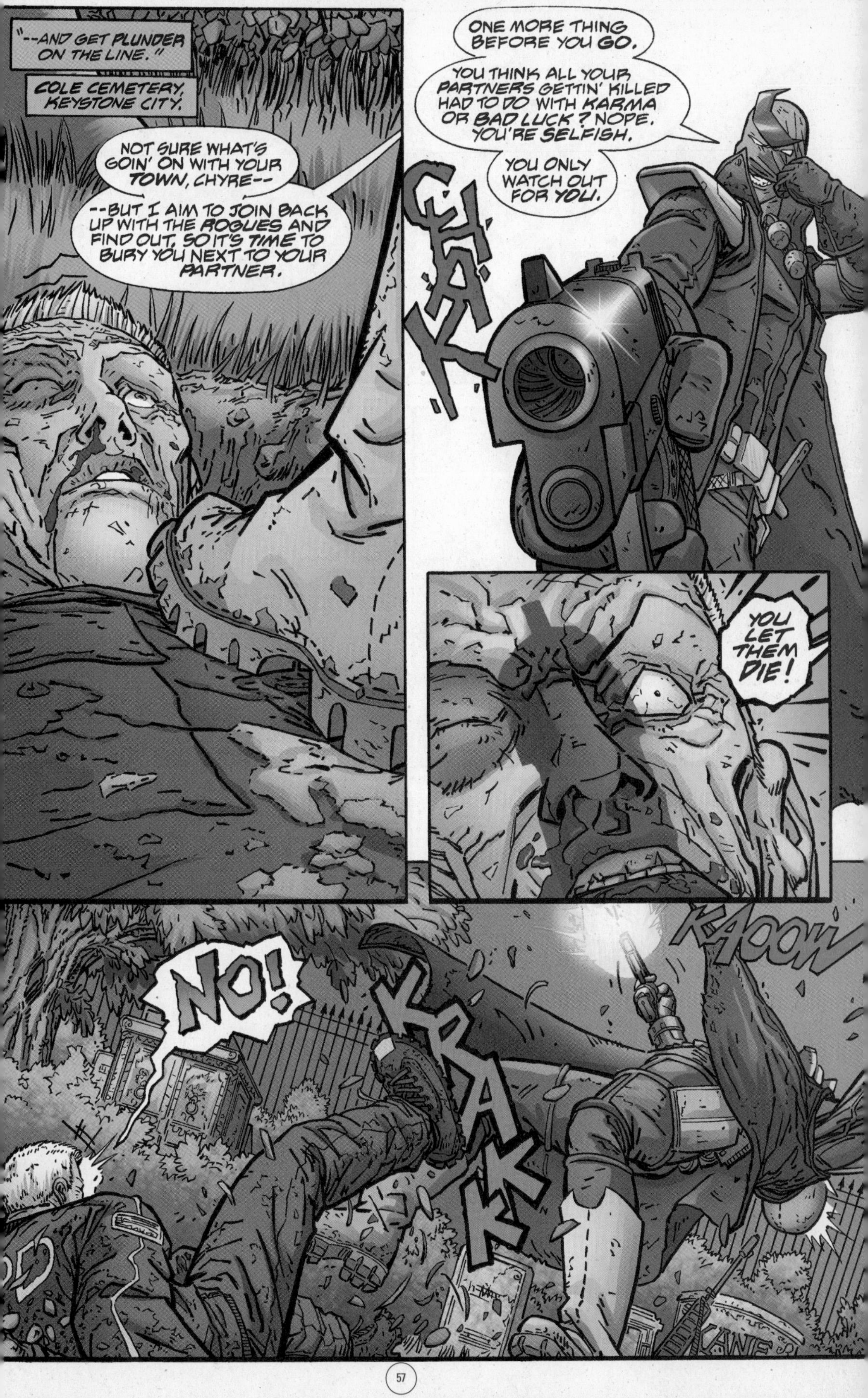
"--AND GET PLUNDER ON THE LINE."
COLE CEMETERY, KEYSTONE CITY.
NOT SURE WHAT'S GOIN' ON WITH YOUR TOWN, CHYRE--
--BUT I AIM TO JOIN BACK UP WITH THE ROGUES AND FIND OUT, SO IT'S TIME TO BURY YOU NEXT TO YOUR PARTNER.
ONE MORE THING BEFORE YOU GO.
YOU THINK ALL YOUR PARTNERS GETTIN' KILLED HAD TO DO WITH KARMA OR BAD LUCK? NOPE. YOU'RE SELFISH.
YOU ONLY WATCH OUT FOR YOU.
CHAK
YOU LET THEM DIE!
KAOOW
NO!
KRAKK

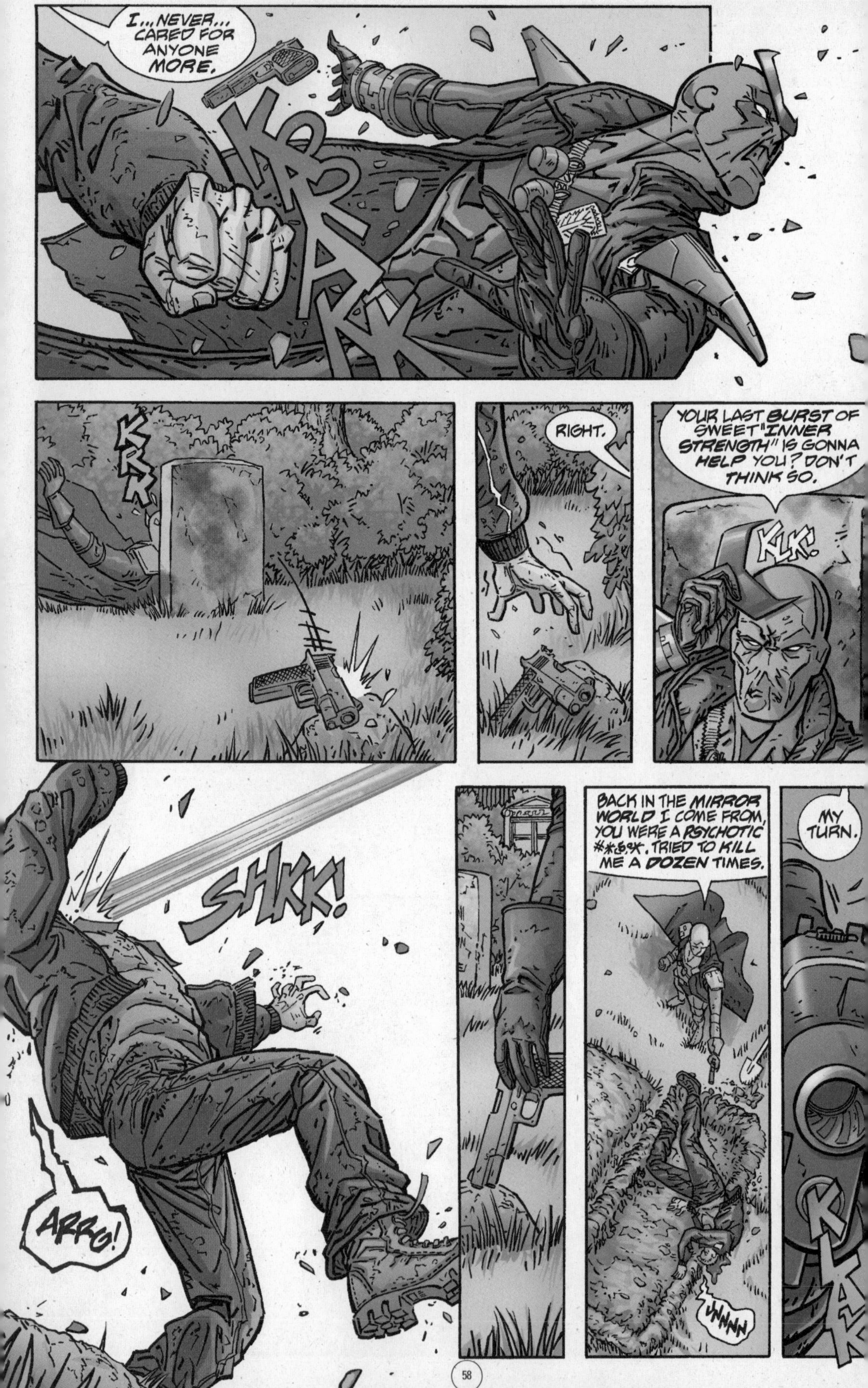

I... NEVER... CARED FOR ANYONE MORE.
KRRAKK
KRRR
RIGHT.
YOUR LAST BURST OF SWEET "INNER STRENGTH" IS GONNA HELP YOU? DON'T THINK SO.
KLIK!
SHKK!
ARRG!
BACK IN THE MIRROR WORLD I COME FROM, YOU WERE A PSYCHOTIC #*&%. TRIED TO KILL ME A DOZEN TIMES.
UNNNN
MY TURN.
KLAK

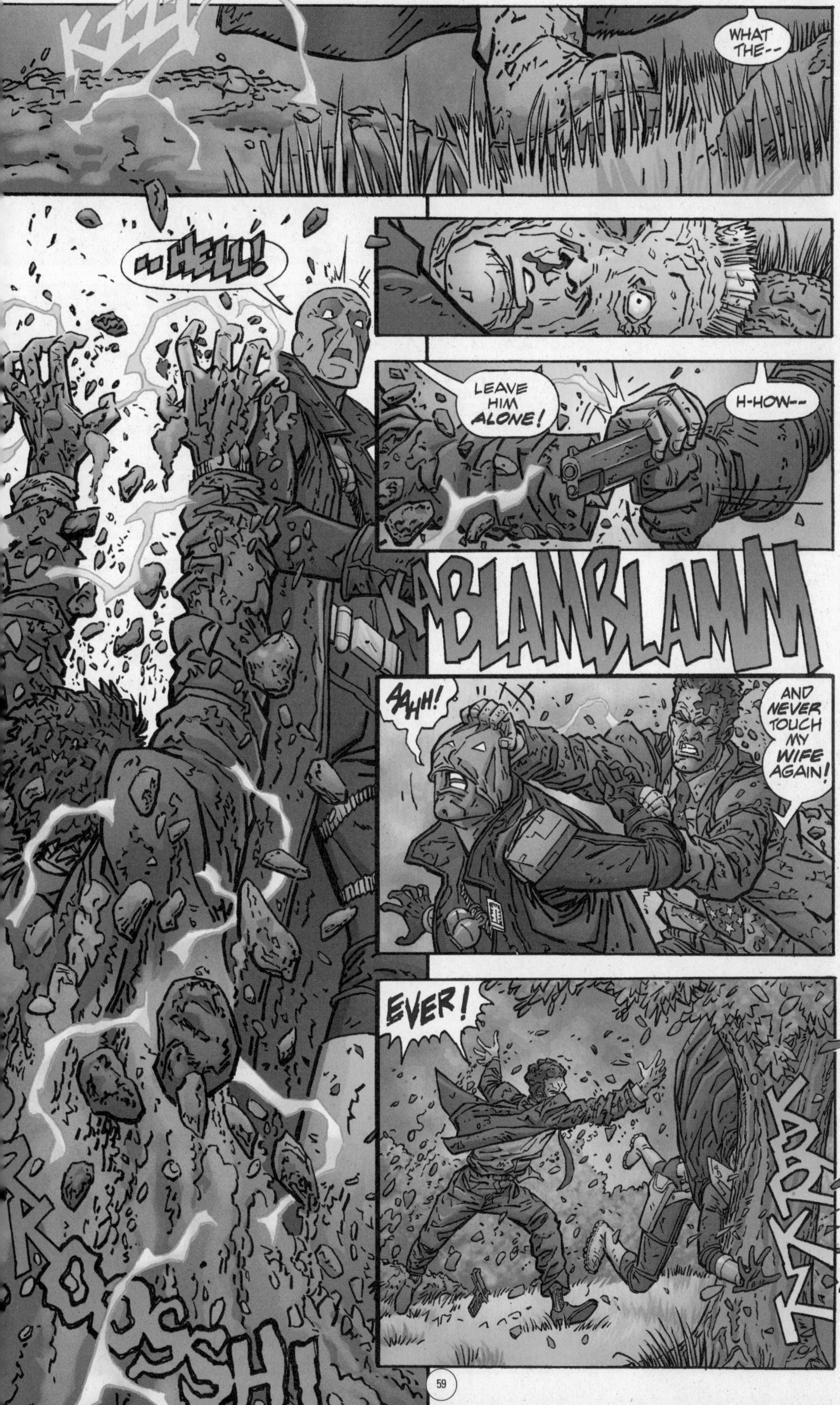
KZZT
WHAT THE--
--HELL!
LEAVE HIM ALONE!
H-HOW--
KABLAMBLAMM
AAHH!
AND NEVER TOUCH MY WIFE AGAIN!
EVER!

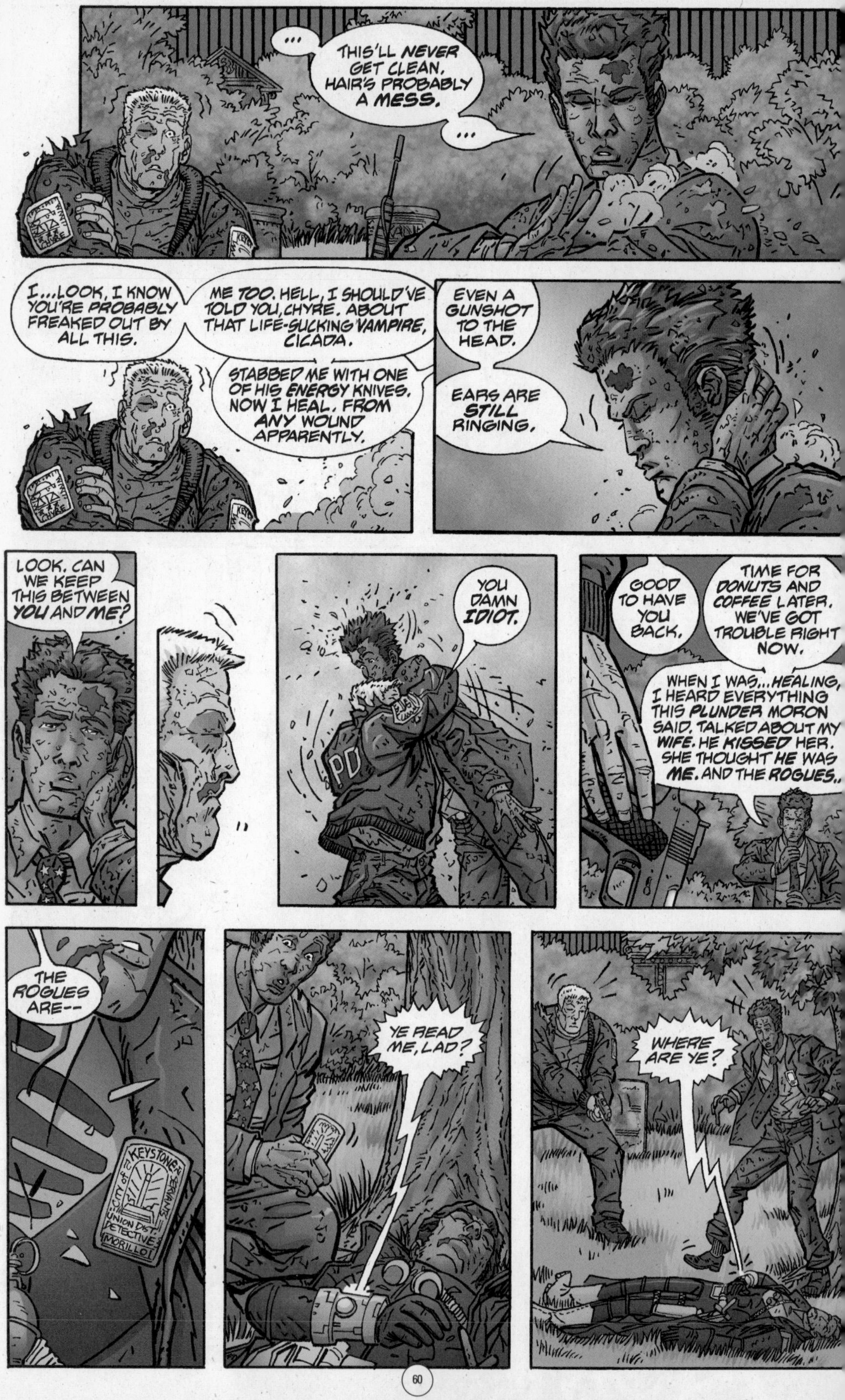
...
THIS'LL NEVER GET CLEAN. HAIR'S PROBABLY A MESS.
...
I...LOOK, I KNOW YOU'RE PROBABLY FREAKED OUT BY ALL THIS.
ME TOO. HELL, I SHOULD'VE TOLD YOU, CHYRE. ABOUT THAT LIFE-SUCKING VAMPIRE, CICADA.
STABBED ME WITH ONE OF HIS ENERGY KNIVES. NOW I HEAL. FROM ANY WOUND APPARENTLY.
EVEN A GUNSHOT TO THE HEAD.
EARS ARE STILL RINGING.
LOOK. CAN WE KEEP THIS BETWEEN YOU AND ME?
YOU DAMN IDIOT.
GOOD TO HAVE YOU BACK.
TIME FOR DONUTS AND COFFEE LATER. WE'VE GOT TROUBLE RIGHT NOW.
WHEN I WAS...HEALING, I HEARD EVERYTHING THIS PLUNDER MORON SAID. TALKED ABOUT MY WIFE. HE KISSED HER. SHE THOUGHT HE WAS ME. AND THE ROGUES...
THE ROGUES ARE--
CITY OF KEYSTONE SERVANTS UNION DIST. DETECTIVE MORILLO
YE READ ME, LAD?
WHERE ARE YE?

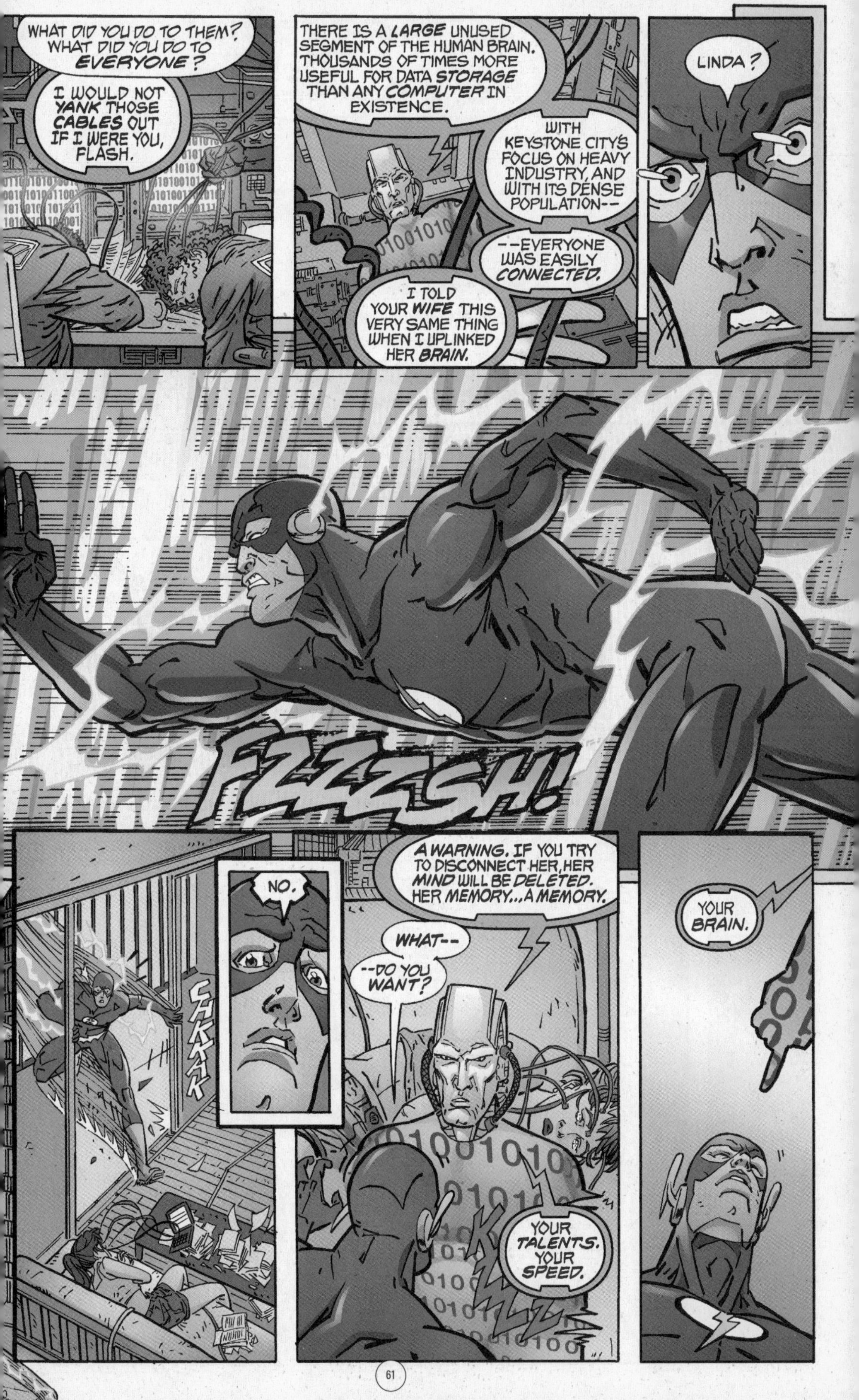
WHAT DID YOU DO TO THEM? WHAT DID YOU DO TO EVERYONE?
I WOULD NOT YANK THOSE CABLES OUT IF I WERE YOU, FLASH.
THERE IS A LARGE UNUSED SEGMENT OF THE HUMAN BRAIN. THOUSANDS OF TIMES MORE USEFUL FOR DATA STORAGE THAN ANY COMPUTER IN EXISTENCE.
WITH KEYSTONE CITY'S FOCUS ON HEAVY INDUSTRY, AND WITH ITS DENSE POPULATION--
--EVERYONE WAS EASILY CONNECTED.
I TOLD YOUR WIFE THIS VERY SAME THING WHEN I UPLINKED HER BRAIN.
LINDA?
FZZZSH!
CHKKAK
NO.
A WARNING. IF YOU TRY TO DISCONNECT HER, HER MIND WILL BE DELETED. HER MEMORY... A MEMORY.
WHAT--
--DO YOU WANT?
YOUR TALENTS. YOUR SPEED.
YOUR BRAIN.

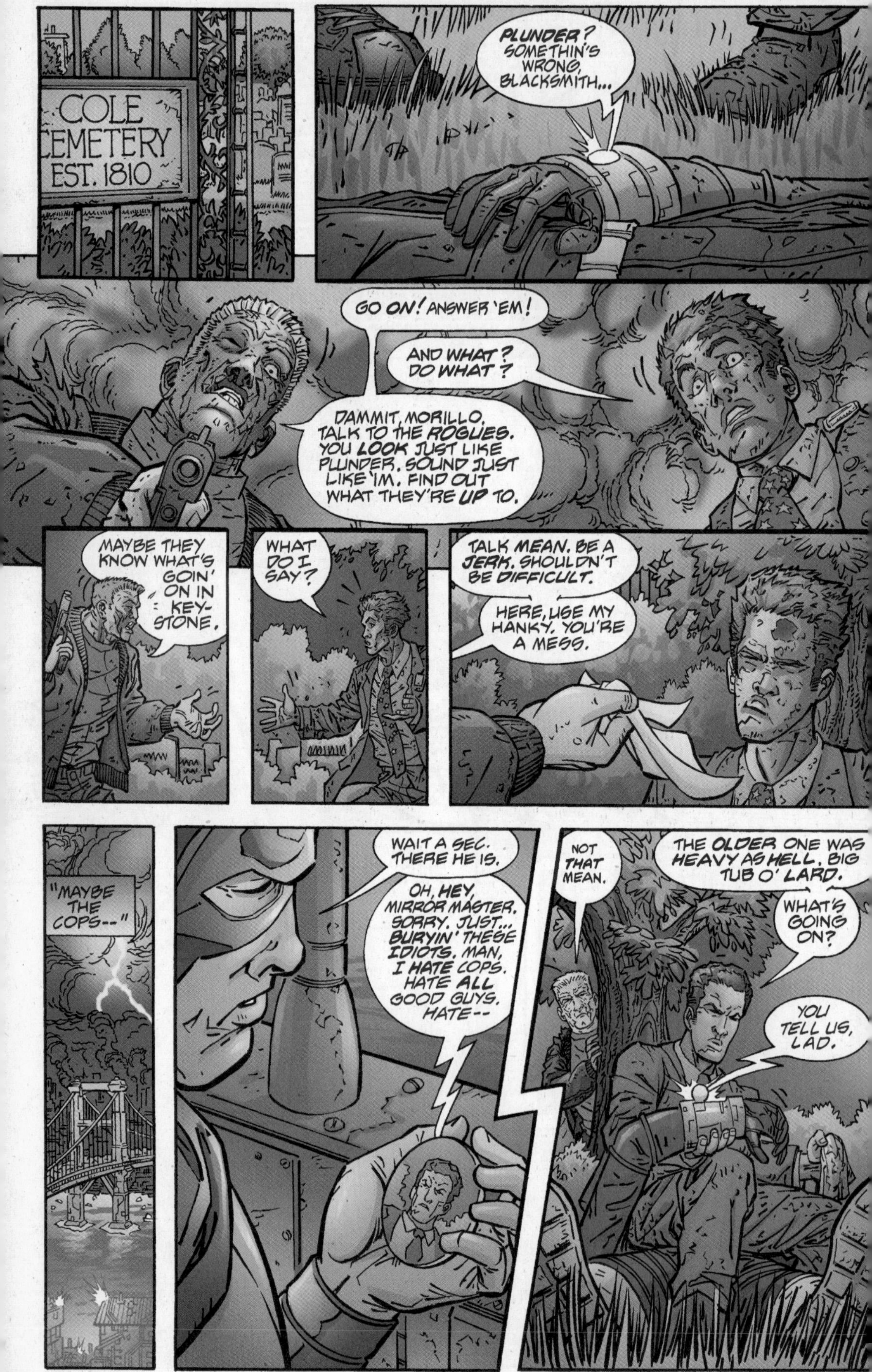
COLE CEMETERY EST. 1810
PLUNDER? SOMETHIN'S WRONG, BLACKSMITH...
GO ON! ANSWER 'EM!
AND WHAT? DO WHAT?
DAMMIT, MORILLO, TALK TO THE ROGUES. YOU LOOK JUST LIKE PLUNDER. SOUND JUST LIKE 'IM. FIND OUT WHAT THEY'RE UP TO.
MAYBE THEY KNOW WHAT'S GOIN' ON IN KEYSTONE.
WHAT DO I SAY?
TALK MEAN. BE A JERK. SHOULDN'T BE DIFFICULT.
HERE, USE MY HANKY. YOU'RE A MESS.
"MAYBE THE COPS--"
WAIT A SEC. THERE HE IS.
OH, HEY, MIRROR MASTER. SORRY. JUST... BURYIN' THESE IDIOTS. MAN, I HATE COPS. HATE ALL GOOD GUYS. HATE--
NOT THAT MEAN.
THE OLDER ONE WAS HEAVY AS HELL. BIG TUB O' LARD.
WHAT'S GOING ON?
YOU TELL US, LAD.

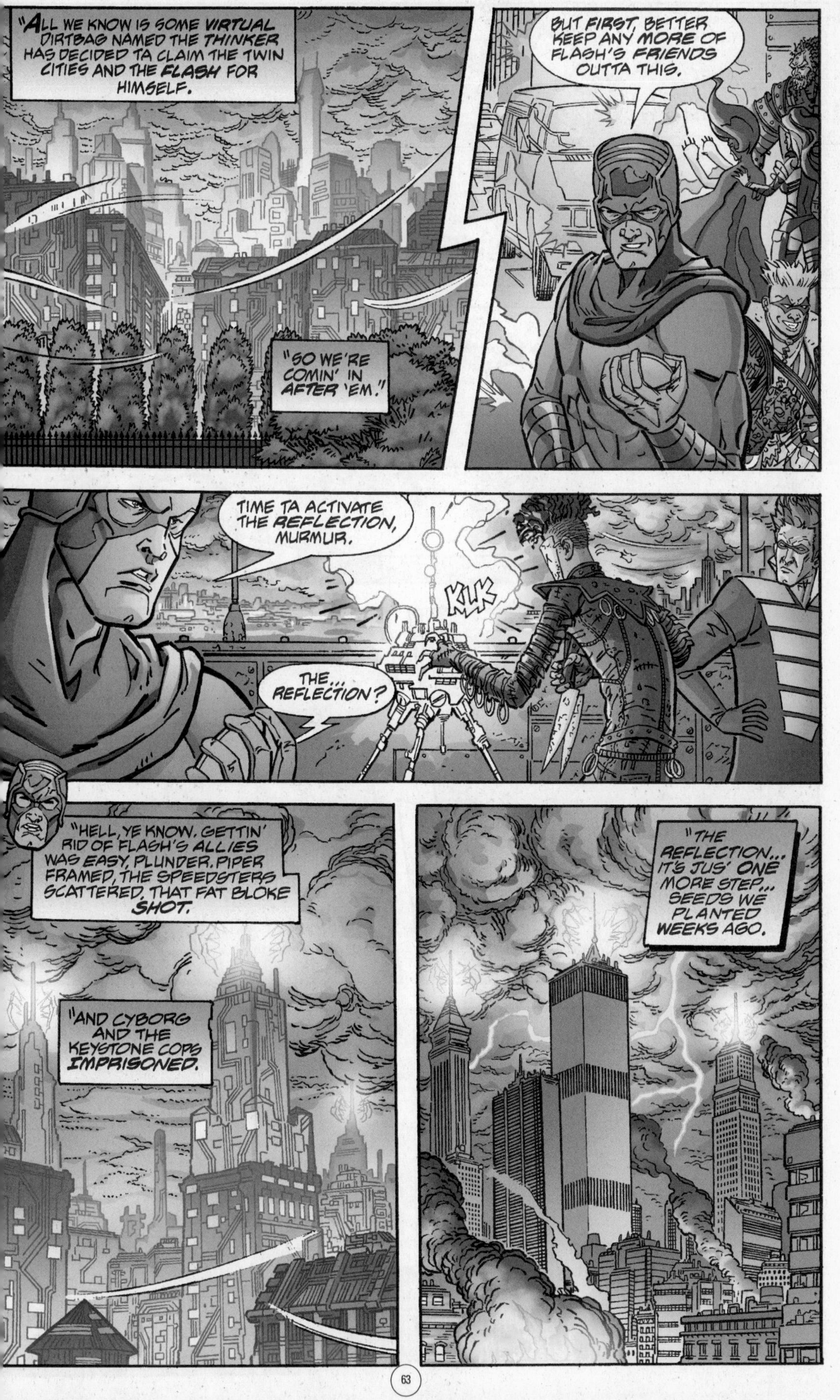
"ALL WE KNOW IS SOME VIRTUAL DIRTBAG NAMED THE THINKER HAS DECIDED TA CLAIM THE TWIN CITIES AND THE FLASH FOR HIMSELF.
"SO WE'RE COMIN' IN AFTER 'EM."
BUT FIRST, BETTER KEEP ANY MORE OF FLASH'S FRIENDS OUTTA THIS.
TIME TA ACTIVATE THE REFLECTION, MURMUR.
KLIK
THE... REFLECTION?
"HELL, YE KNOW. GETTIN' RID OF FLASH'S ALLIES WAS EASY, PLUNDER. PIPER FRAMED, THE SPEEDSTERS SCATTERED, THAT FAT BLOKE SHOT.
"AND CYBORG AND THE KEYSTONE COPS IMPRISONED.
"THE REFLECTION... IT'S JUS' ONE MORE STEP... SEEDS WE PLANTED WEEKS AGO.

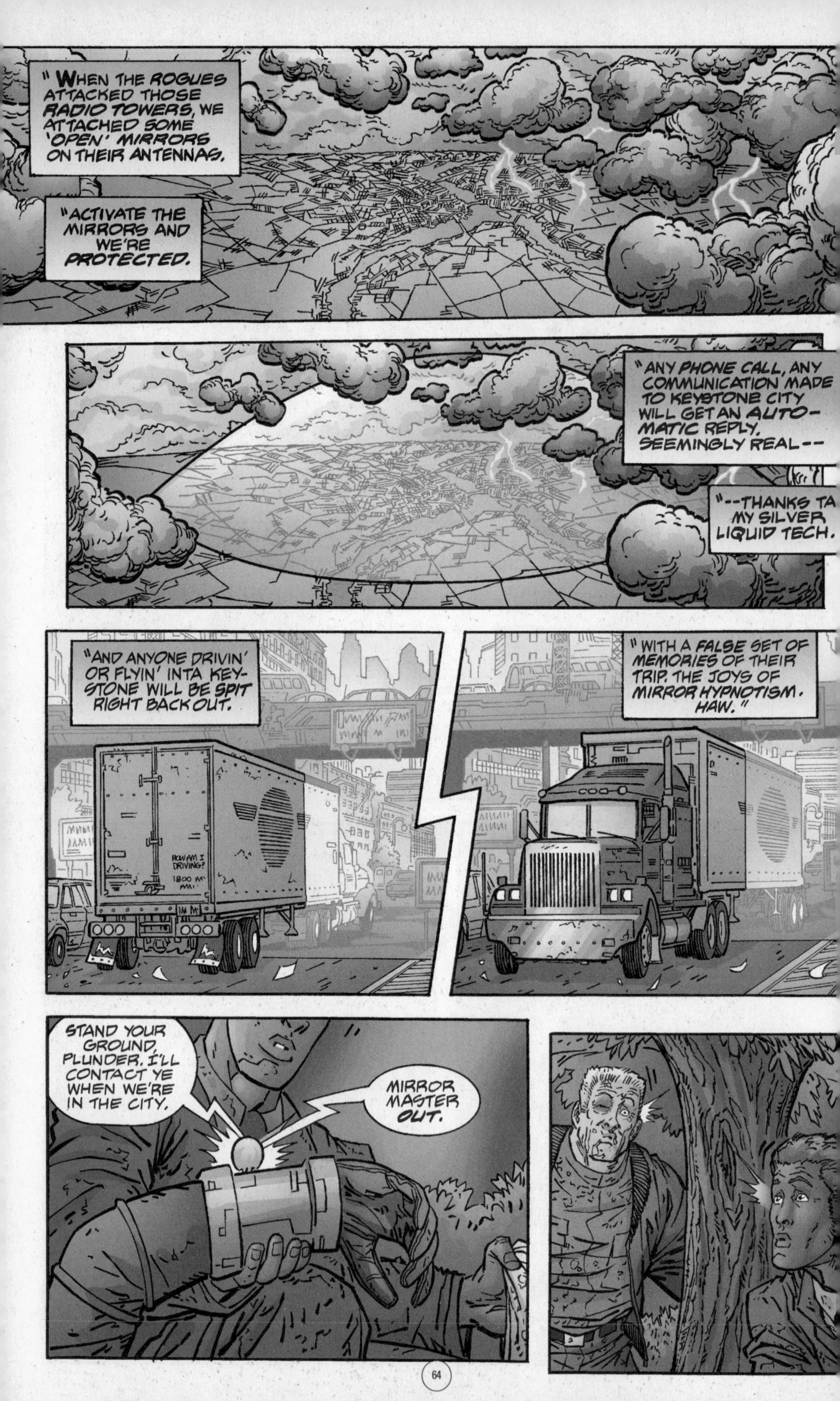
"WHEN THE ROGUES ATTACHED THOSE RADIO TOWERS, WE ATTACHED SOME 'OPEN' MIRRORS ON THEIR ANTENNAS.
"ACTIVATE THE MIRRORS AND WE'RE PROTECTED.
"ANY PHONE CALL, ANY COMMUNICATION MADE TO KEYSTONE CITY WILL GET AN AUTO-MATIC REPLY. SEEMINGLY REAL--
"--THANKS TA MY SILVER LIQUID TECH.
"AND ANYONE DRIVIN' OR FLYIN' INTA KEY-STONE WILL BE SPIT RIGHT BACK OUT.
HOW AM I DRIVING?
"WITH A FALSE SET OF MEMORIES OF THEIR TRIP. THE JOYS OF MIRROR HYPNOTISM. HAW."
STAND YOUR GROUND, PLUNDER. I'LL CONTACT YE WHEN WE'RE IN THE CITY.
MIRROR MASTER OUT.

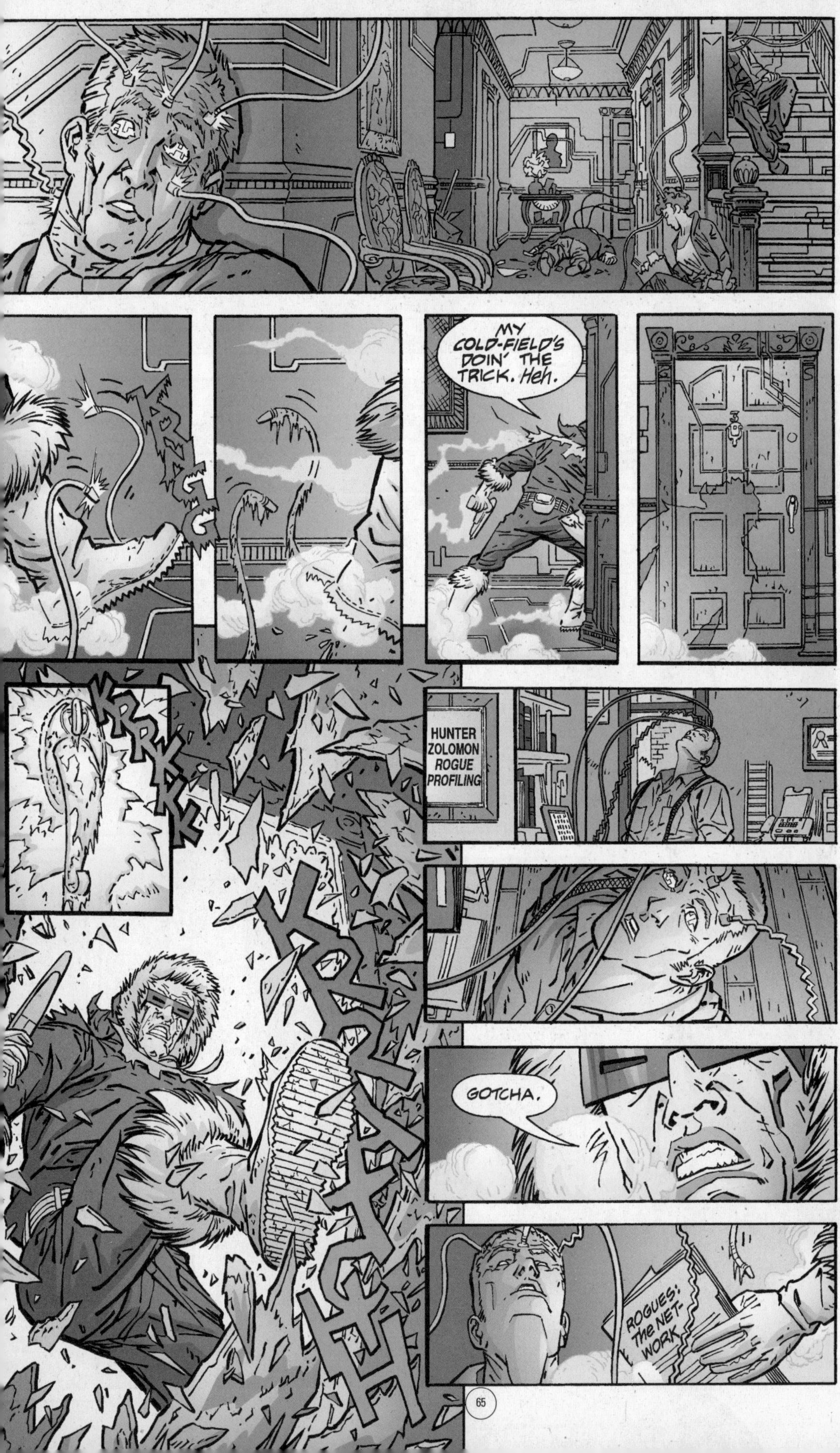
KRAGG
MY COLD-FIELD'S DOIN' THE TRICK. Heh.
KRRKKK
HUNTER ZOLOMON ROGUE PROFILING
KRRRKKSSHH
GOTCHA.
ROGUES: The NET-WORK

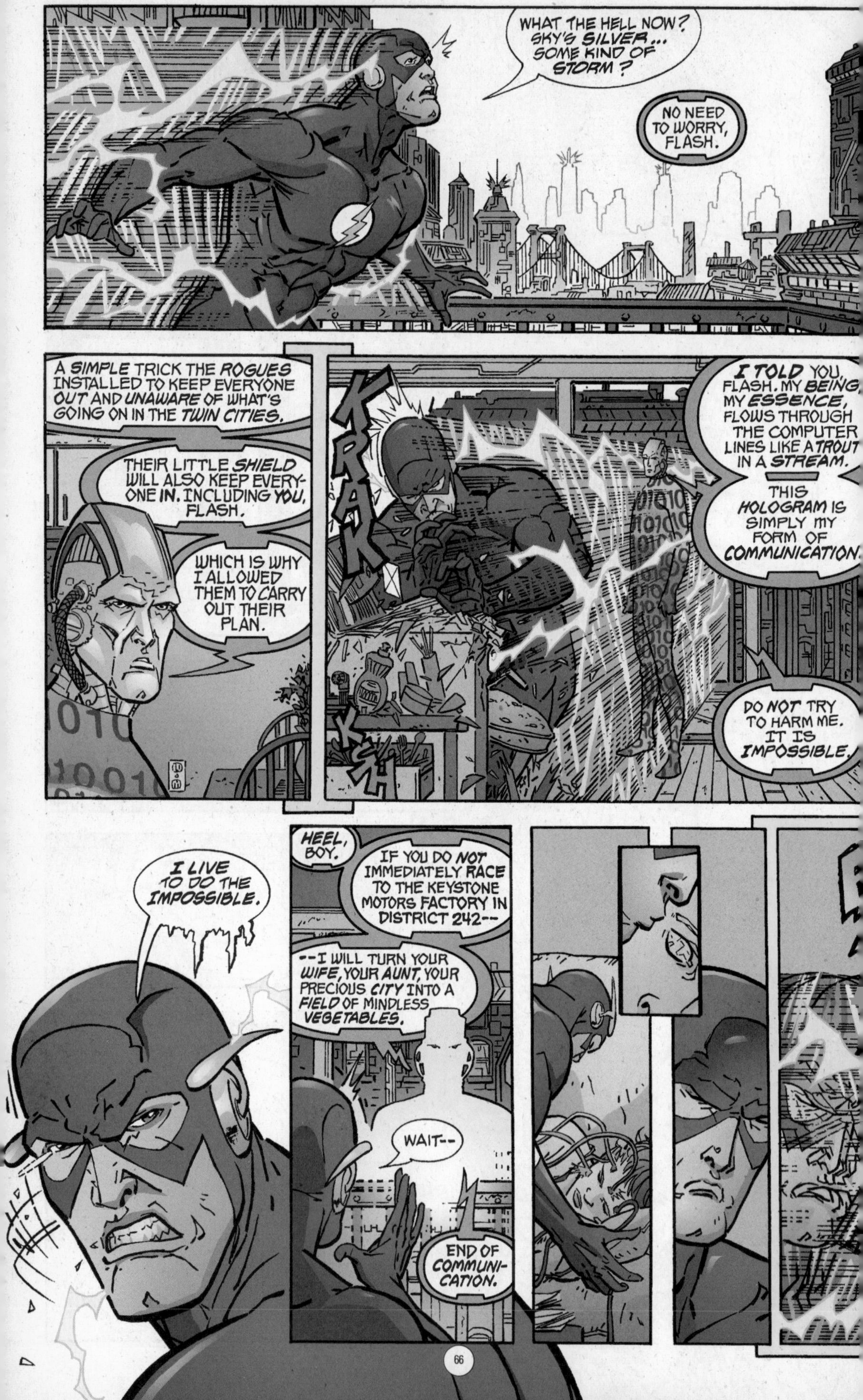
WHAT THE HELL NOW? SKY'S SILVER... SOME KIND OF STORM?
NO NEED TO WORRY, FLASH.
A SIMPLE TRICK THE ROGUES INSTALLED TO KEEP EVERYONE OUT AND UNAWARE OF WHAT'S GOING ON IN THE TWIN CITIES.
THEIR LITTLE SHIELD WILL ALSO KEEP EVERYONE IN. INCLUDING YOU, FLASH.
WHICH IS WHY I ALLOWED THEM TO CARRY OUT THEIR PLAN.
KRAK
I TOLD YOU, FLASH. MY BEING, MY ESSENCE, FLOWS THROUGH THE COMPUTER LINES LIKE A TROUT IN A STREAM.
THIS HOLOGRAM IS SIMPLY MY FORM OF COMMUNICATION.
DO NOT TRY TO HARM ME. IT IS IMPOSSIBLE.
I LIVE TO DO THE IMPOSSIBLE.
HEEL, BOY.
IF YOU DO NOT IMMEDIATELY RACE TO THE KEYSTONE MOTORS FACTORY IN DISTRICT 242--
--I WILL TURN YOUR WIFE, YOUR AUNT, YOUR PRECIOUS CITY INTO A FIELD OF MINDLESS VEGETABLES.
WAIT--
END OF COMMUNICATION.

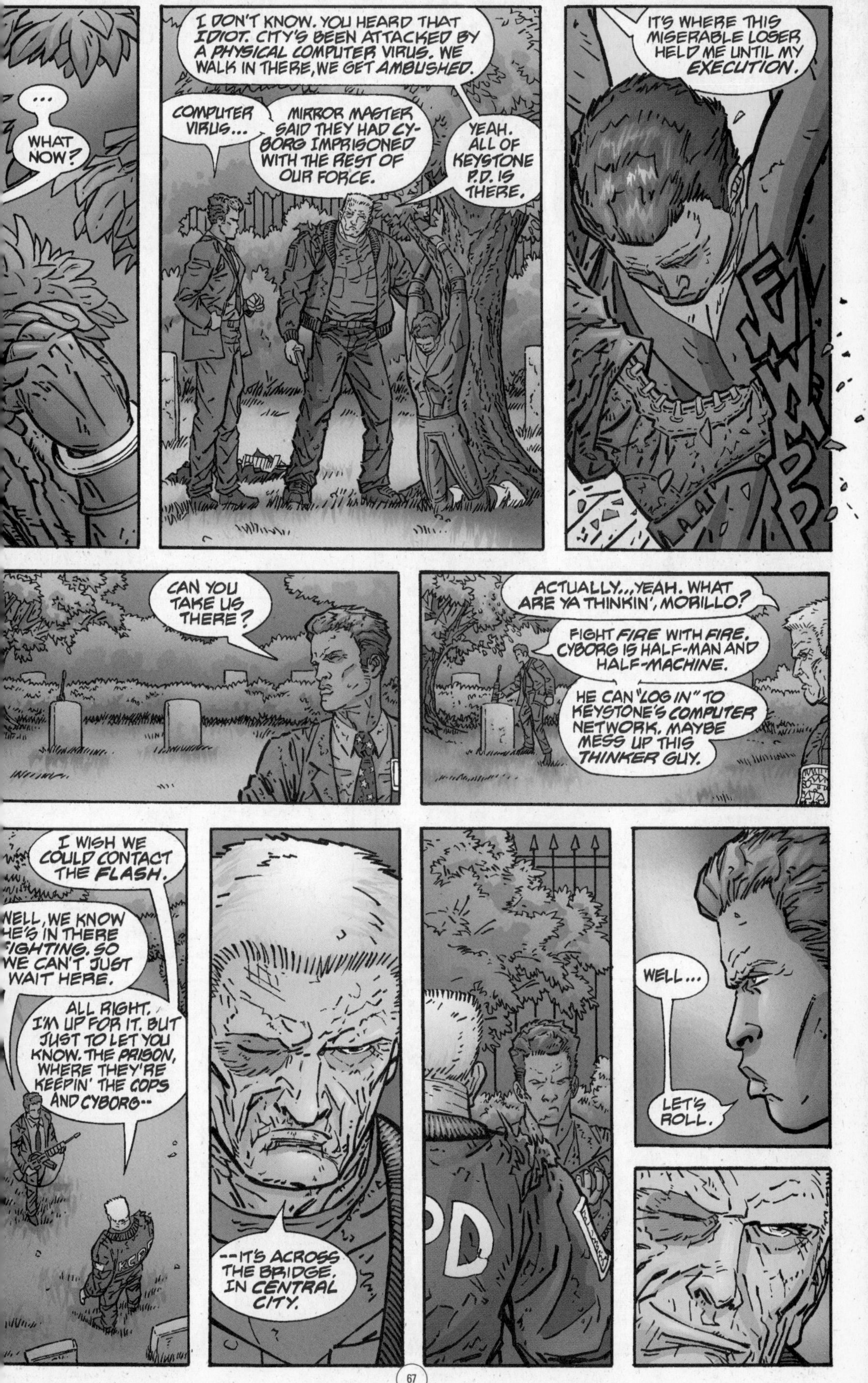
...
WHAT NOW?
I DON'T KNOW. YOU HEARD THAT IDIOT. CITY'S BEEN ATTACKED BY A PHYSICAL COMPUTER VIRUS. WE WALK IN THERE, WE GET AMBUSHED.
COMPUTER VIRUS...
MIRROR MASTER SAID THEY HAD CYBORG IMPRISONED WITH THE REST OF OUR FORCE.
YEAH. ALL OF KEYSTONE P.D. IS THERE.
IT'S WHERE THIS MISERABLE LOSER HELD ME UNTIL MY EXECUTION.
FWAMP
CAN YOU TAKE US THERE?
ACTUALLY... YEAH. WHAT ARE YA THINKIN', MORILLO?
FIGHT FIRE WITH FIRE. CYBORG IS HALF-MAN AND HALF-MACHINE.
HE CAN "LOG IN" TO KEYSTONE'S COMPUTER NETWORK. MAYBE MESS UP THIS THINKER GUY.
I WISH WE COULD CONTACT THE FLASH.
WELL, WE KNOW HE'S IN THERE FIGHTING. SO WE CAN'T JUST WAIT HERE.
ALL RIGHT. I'M UP FOR IT. BUT JUST TO LET YOU KNOW. THE PRISON, WHERE THEY'RE KEEPIN' THE COPS AND CYBORG--
--IT'S ACROSS THE BRIDGE. IN CENTRAL CITY.
WELL...
LET'S ROLL.

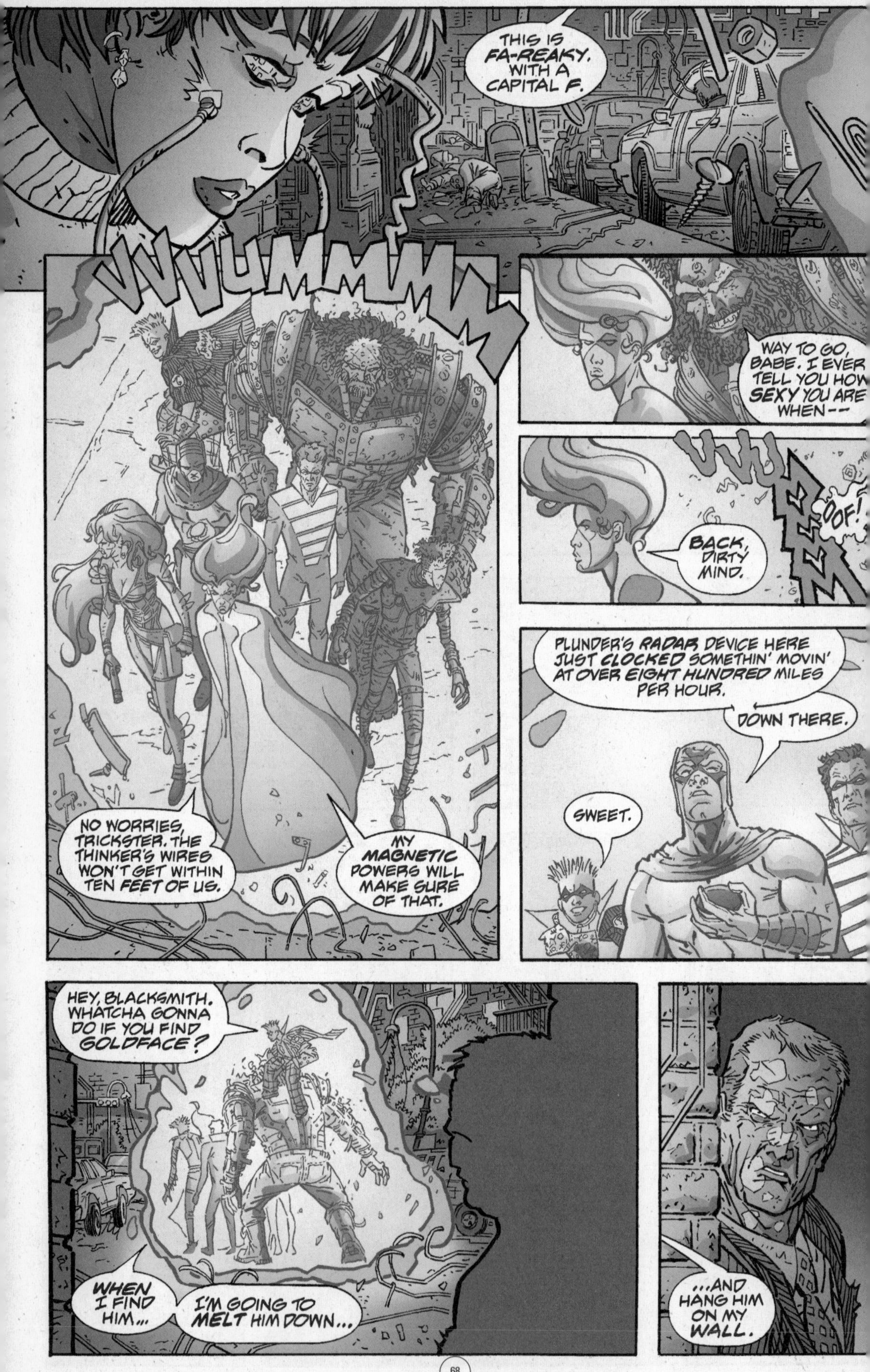
THIS IS FA-REAKY. WITH A CAPITAL F.
VVVUMMMMM
WAY TO GO, BABE. I EVER TELL YOU HOW SEXY YOU ARE WHEN--
VVVUMM
OOF!
BACK, DIRTY MIND.
NO WORRIES, TRICKSTER. THE THINKER'S WIRES WON'T GET WITHIN TEN FEET OF US.
MY MAGNETIC POWERS WILL MAKE SURE OF THAT.
PLUNDER'S RADAR DEVICE HERE JUST CLOCKED SOMETHIN' MOVIN' AT OVER EIGHT HUNDRED MILES PER HOUR.
DOWN THERE.
SWEET.
HEY, BLACKSMITH. WHATCHA GONNA DO IF YOU FIND GOLDFACE?
WHEN I FIND HIM...
I'M GOING TO MELT HIM DOWN...
...AND HANG HIM ON MY WALL.

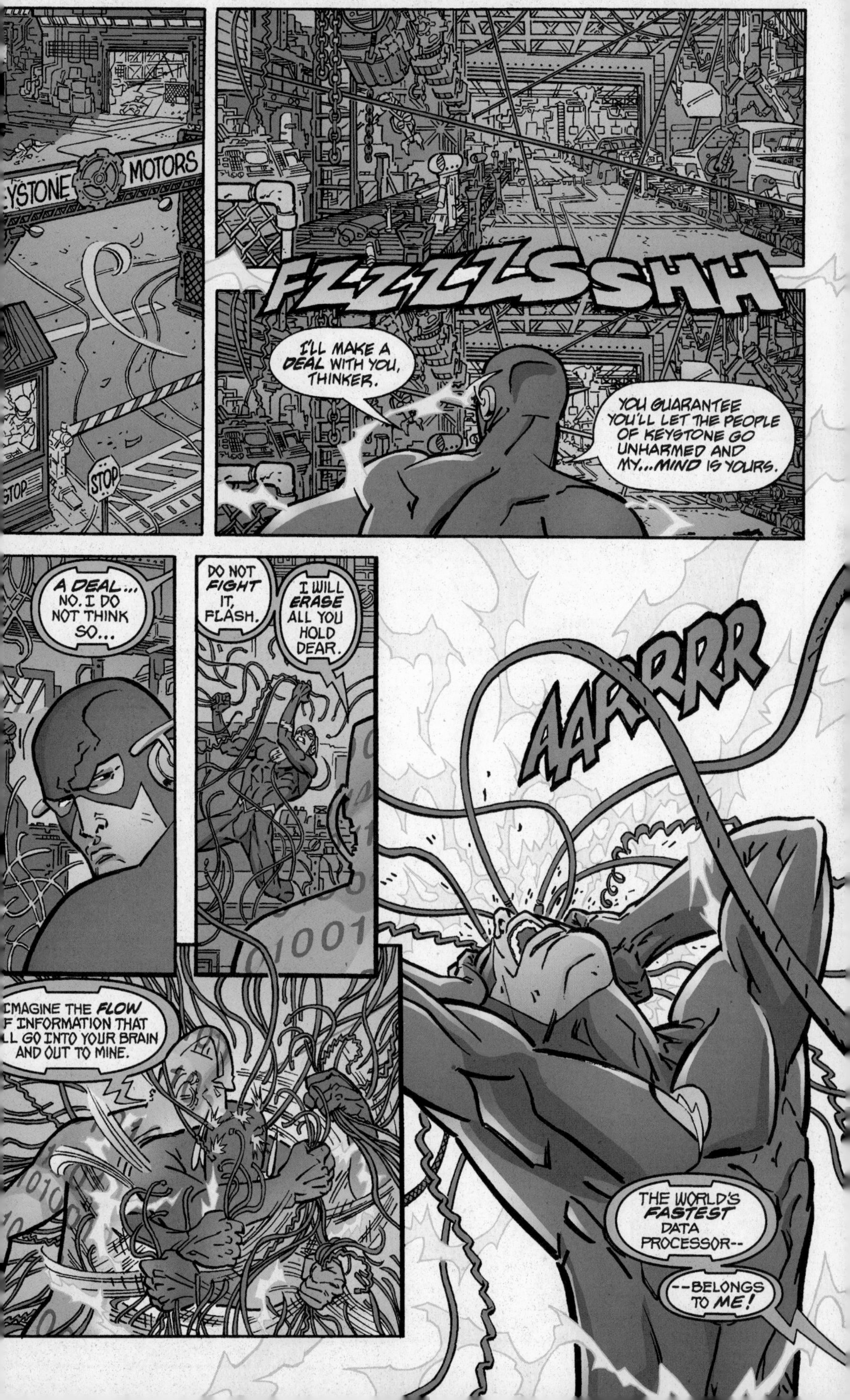

KEYSTONE MOTORS
STOP
STOP
FZZZZSSHH
I'LL MAKE A DEAL WITH YOU, THINKER.
YOU GUARANTEE YOU'LL LET THE PEOPLE OF KEYSTONE GO UNHARMED AND MY... MIND IS YOURS.
A DEAL... NO. I DO NOT THINK SO...
DO NOT FIGHT IT, FLASH.
I WILL ERASE ALL YOU HOLD DEAR.
AARRRR
IMAGINE THE FLOW OF INFORMATION THAT WILL GO INTO YOUR BRAIN AND OUT TO MINE.
THE WORLD'S FASTEST DATA PROCESSOR--
--BELONGS TO ME!

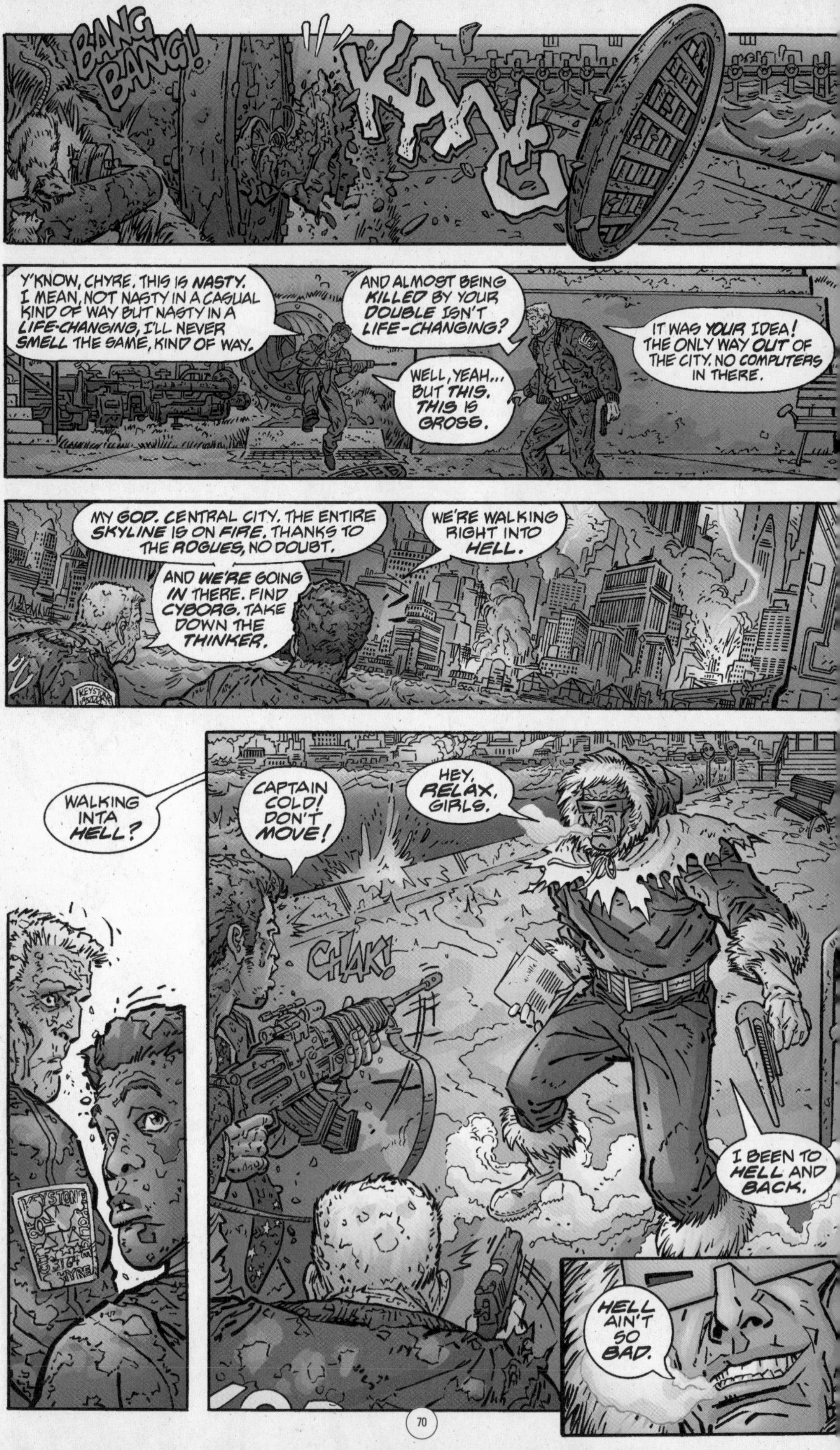
BANG BANG!
KAK
Y'KNOW, CHYRE, THIS IS NASTY. I MEAN, NOT NASTY IN A CASUAL KIND OF WAY BUT NASTY IN A LIFE-CHANGING, I'LL NEVER SMELL THE SAME, KIND OF WAY.
AND ALMOST BEING KILLED BY YOUR DOUBLE ISN'T LIFE-CHANGING?
WELL, YEAH... BUT THIS. THIS IS GROSS.
IT WAS YOUR IDEA! THE ONLY WAY OUT OF THE CITY. NO COMPUTERS IN THERE.
MY GOD. CENTRAL CITY. THE ENTIRE SKYLINE IS ON FIRE. THANKS TO THE ROGUES, NO DOUBT.
AND WE'RE GOING IN THERE. FIND CYBORG. TAKE DOWN THE THINKER.
WE'RE WALKING RIGHT INTO HELL.
WALKING INTA HELL?
CAPTAIN COLD! DON'T MOVE!
HEY, RELAX, GIRLS.
CHAK!
I BEEN TO HELL AND BACK.
HELL AIN'T SO BAD.

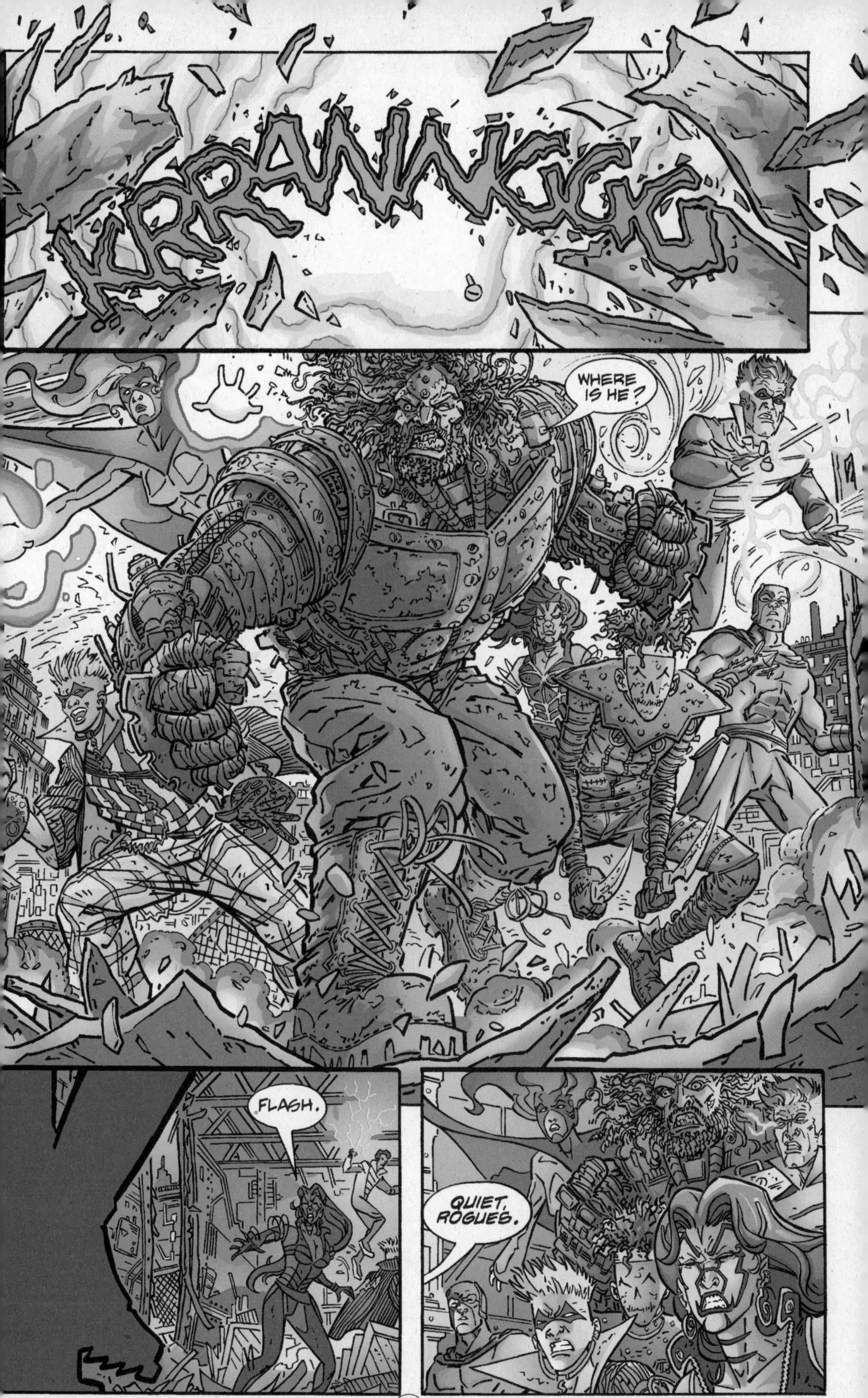
KRRAWWGGG
WHERE IS HE?
FLASH.
QUIET, ROGUES.

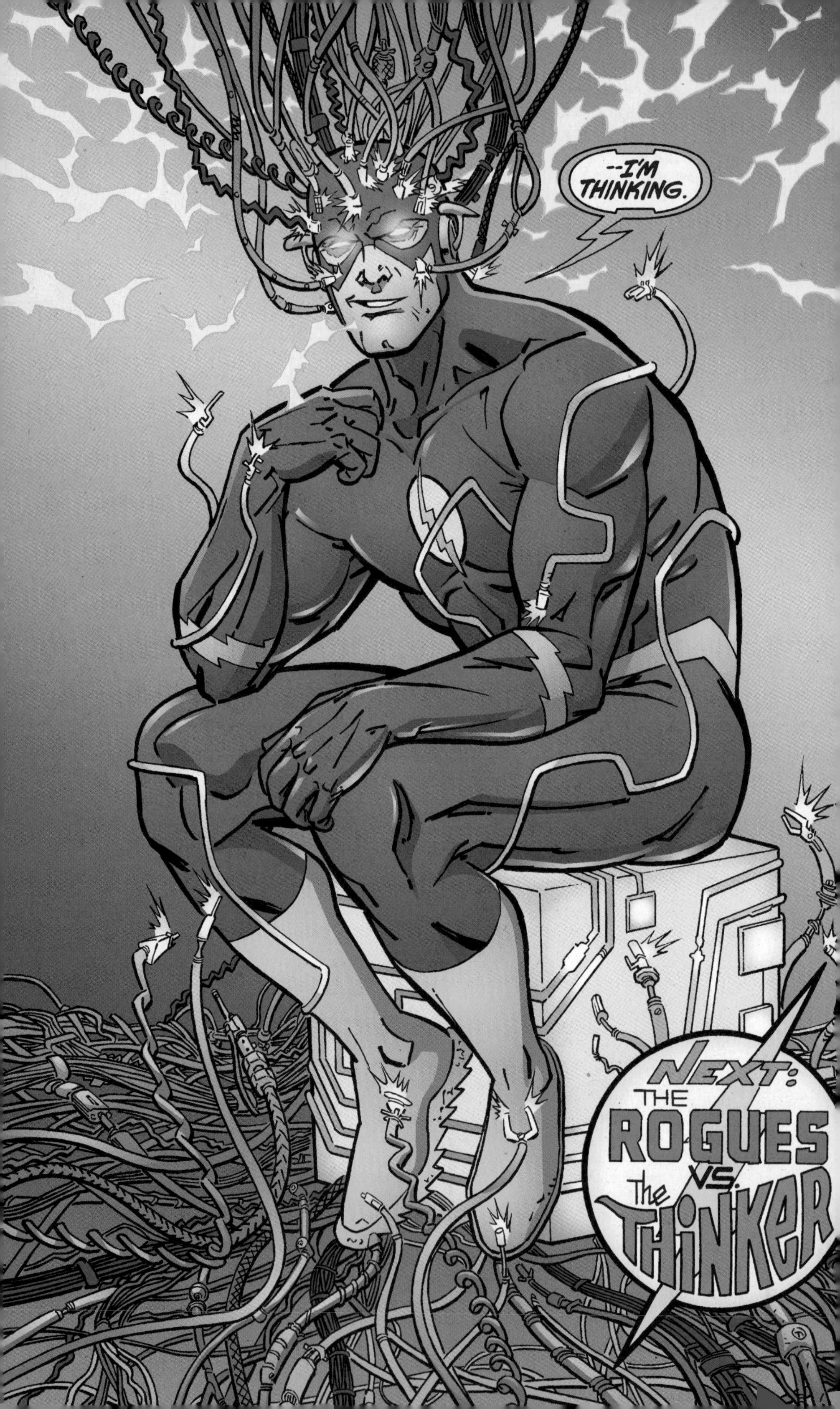
--I'M THINKING.
NEXT: THE ROGUES VS. THE THINKER

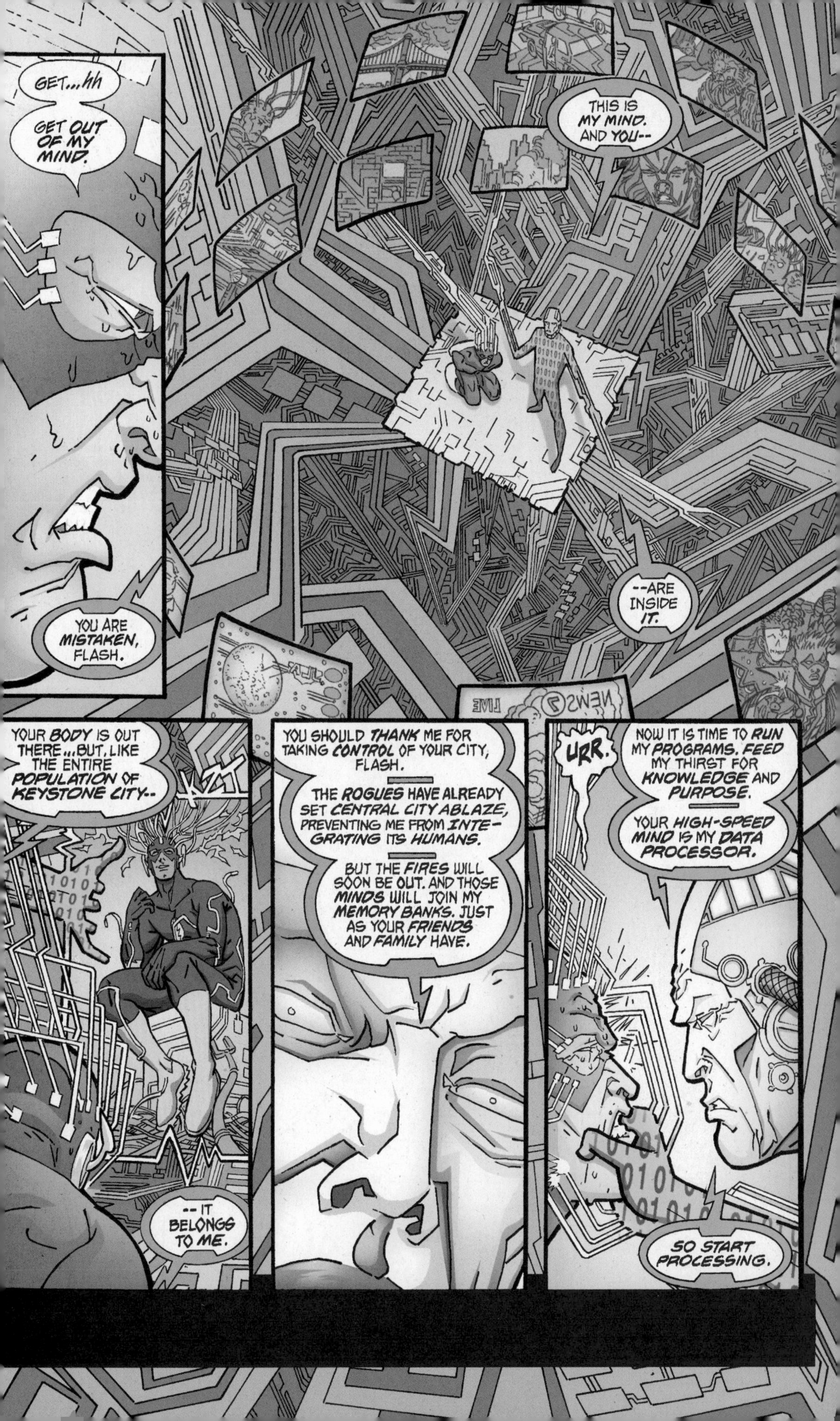
GET...hh
GET OUT OF MY MIND.
THIS IS MY MIND. AND YOU--
--ARE INSIDE IT.
YOU ARE MISTAKEN, FLASH.
YOUR BODY IS OUT THERE...BUT, LIKE THE ENTIRE POPULATION OF KEYSTONE CITY--
-- IT BELONGS TO ME.
YOU SHOULD THANK ME FOR TAKING CONTROL OF YOUR CITY, FLASH.
THE ROGUES HAVE ALREADY SET CENTRAL CITY ABLAZE, PREVENTING ME FROM INTEGRATING ITS HUMANS.
BUT THE FIRES WILL SOON BE OUT. AND THOSE MINDS WILL JOIN MY MEMORY BANKS. JUST AS YOUR FRIENDS AND FAMILY HAVE.
URR.
NOW IT IS TIME TO RUN MY PROGRAMS. FEED MY THIRST FOR KNOWLEDGE AND PURPOSE.
YOUR HIGH-SPEED MIND IS MY DATA PROCESSOR.
SO START PROCESSING.

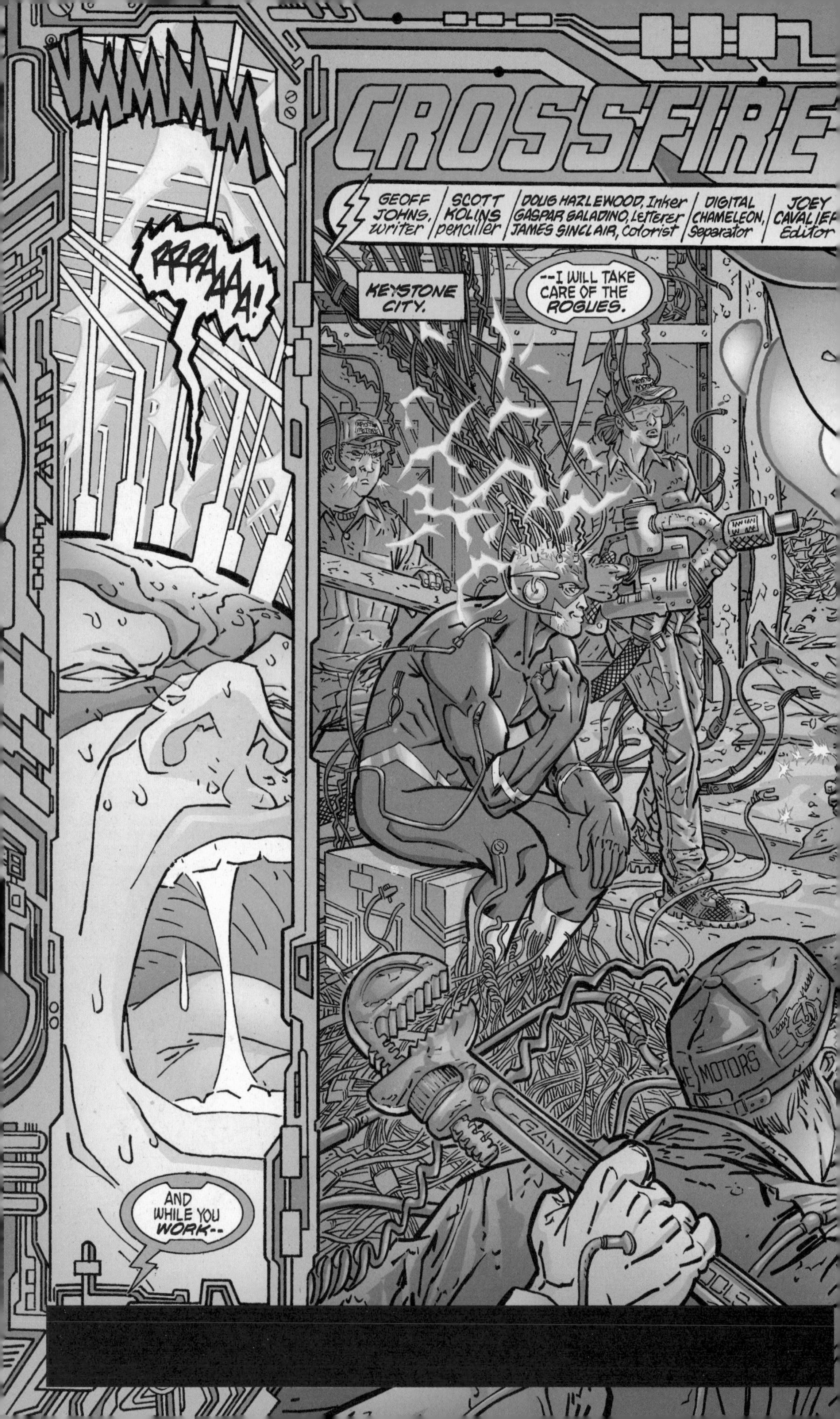
VMMMMM
RRRAAAA!
AND WHILE YOU WORK--
CROSSFIRE
GEOFF JOHNS, writer
SCOTT KOLINS penciller
DOUG HAZLEWOOD, Inker
GASPAR SALADINO, Letterer
JAMES SINCLAIR, Colorist
DIGITAL CHAMELEON, Separator
JOEY CAVALIE Editor
KEYSTONE CITY.
--I WILL TAKE CARE OF THE ROGUES.
MOTORS
GANT

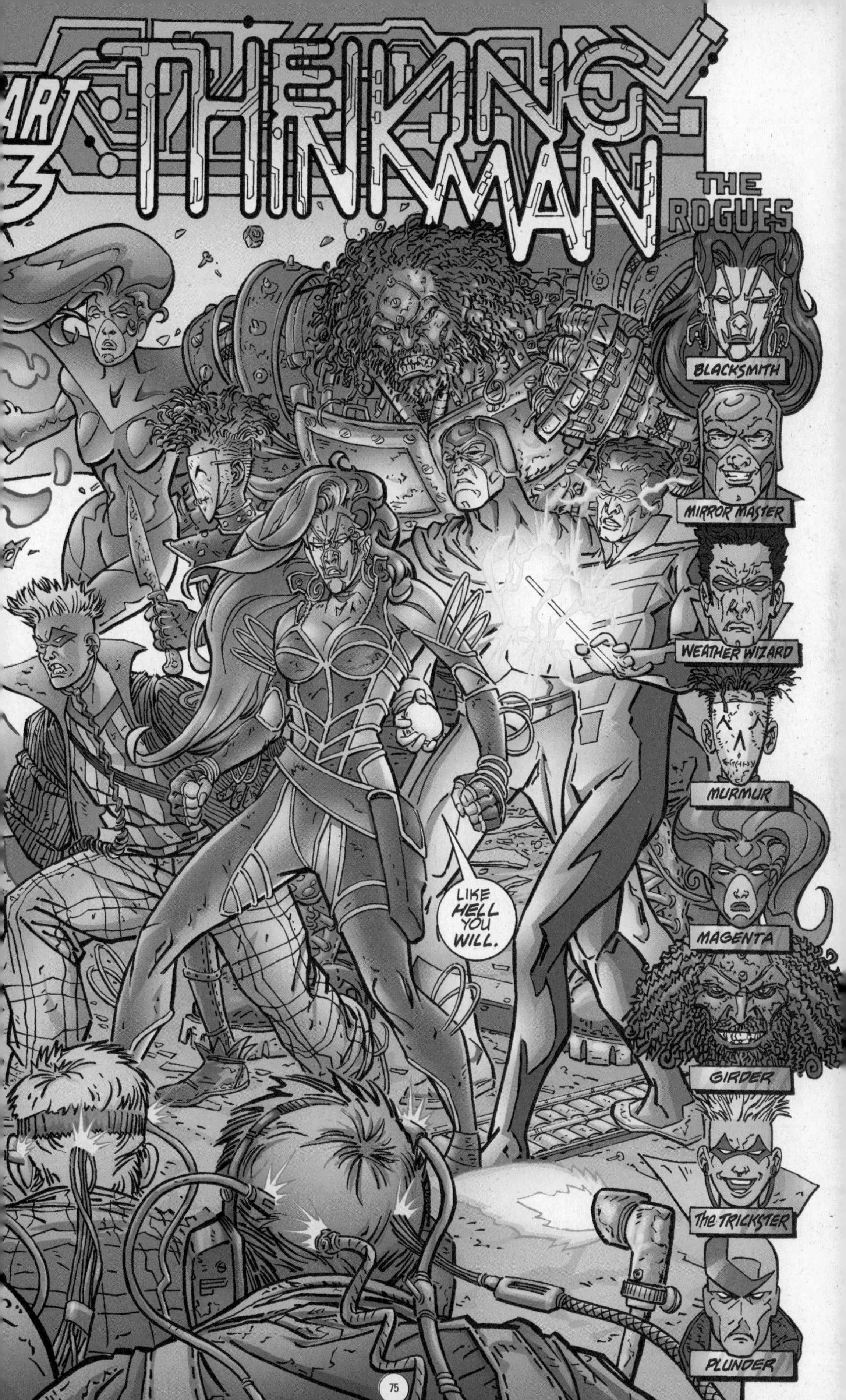
ART 3
THINKMAN
THE ROGUES
BLACKSMITH
MIRROR MASTER
WEATHER WIZARD
MURMUR
MAGENTA
GIRDER
The TRICKSTER
PLUNDER
LIKE HELL YOU WILL.

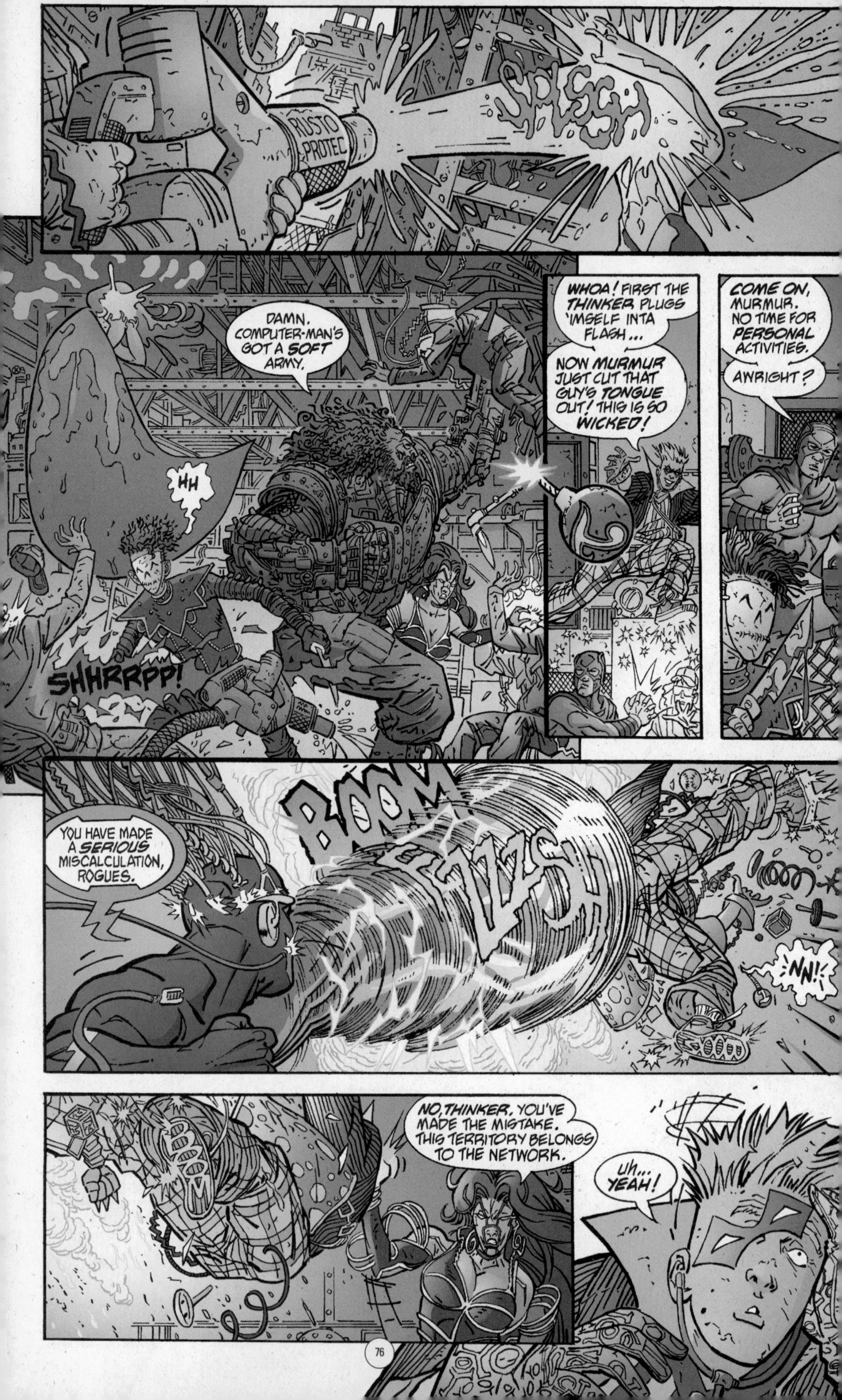
RUSTO PROTEC
SPLSSH
DAMN. COMPUTER-MAN'S GOT A SOFT ARMY.
HH
SHHRRPP!
WHOA! FIRST THE THINKER PLUGS 'IMSELF INTA FLASH...
NOW MURMUR JUST CUT THAT GUY'S TONGUE OUT! THIS IS SO WICKED!
COME ON, MURMUR. NO TIME FOR PERSONAL ACTIVITIES.
AWRIGHT?
YOU HAVE MADE A SERIOUS MISCALCULATION, ROGUES.
BOOM
ZZZS
NN!
NO, THINKER. YOU'VE MADE THE MISTAKE. THIS TERRITORY BELONGS TO THE NETWORK.
UH... YEAH!

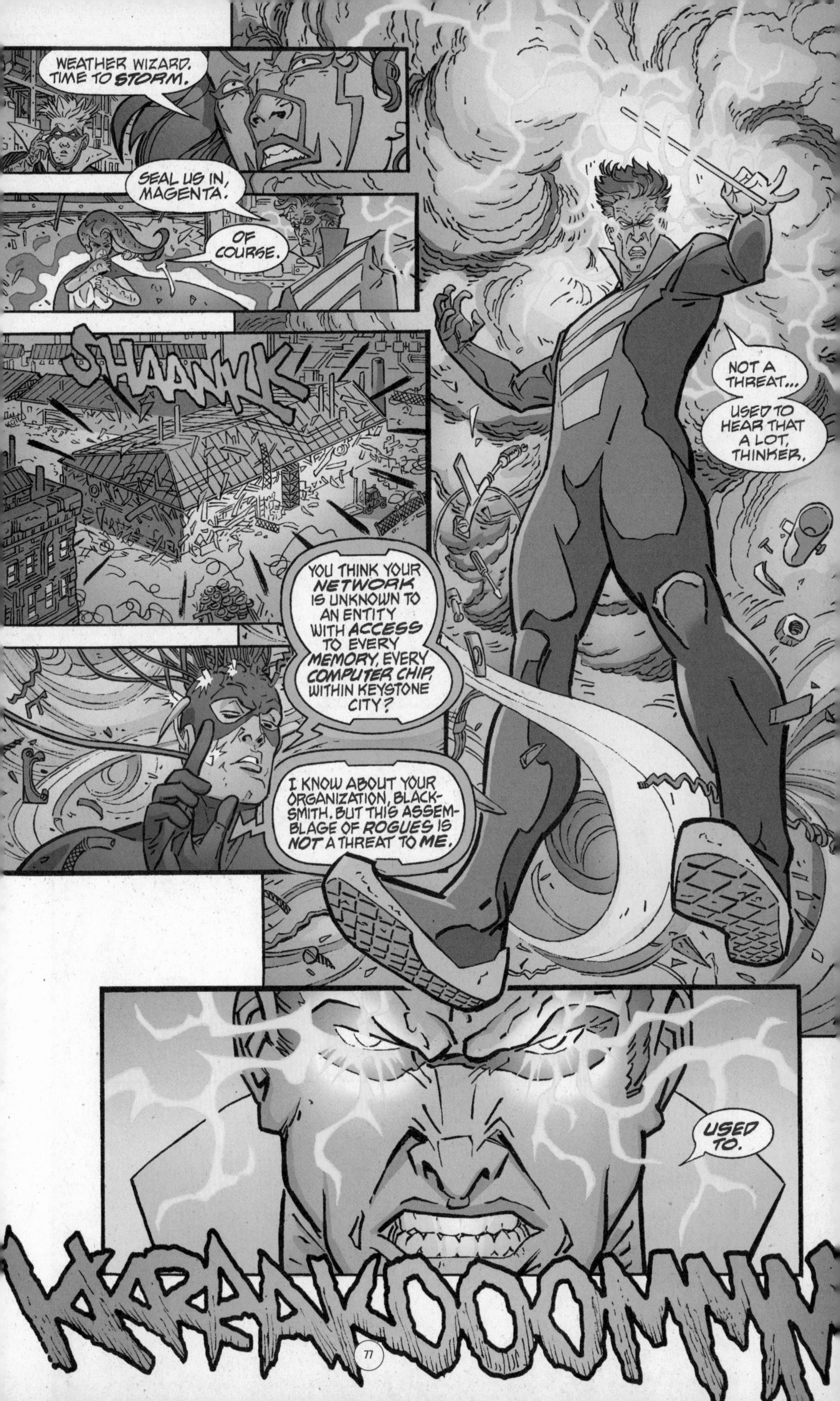

WEATHER WIZARD. TIME TO STORM.
SEAL US IN, MAGENTA.
OF COURSE.
SHAANK!
YOU THINK YOUR NETWORK IS UNKNOWN TO AN ENTITY WITH ACCESS TO EVERY MEMORY, EVERY COMPUTER CHIP, WITHIN KEYSTONE CITY?
I KNOW ABOUT YOUR ORGANIZATION, BLACKSMITH. BUT THIS ASSEMBLAGE OF ROGUES IS NOT A THREAT TO ME.
NOT A THREAT...
USED TO HEAR THAT A LOT, THINKER.
USED TO.
KRAAKOOOMM

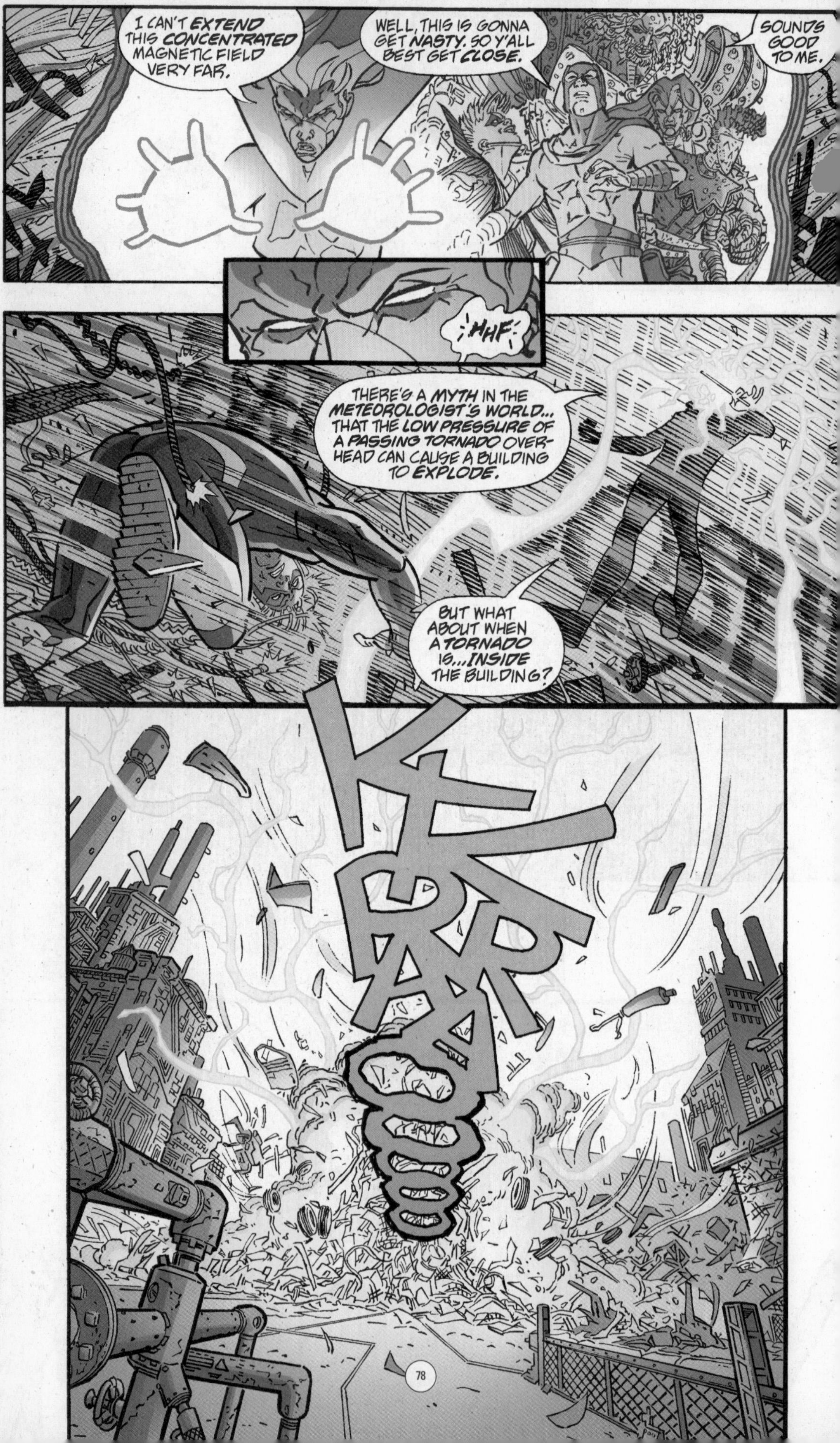
I CAN'T EXTEND THIS CONCENTRATED MAGNETIC FIELD VERY FAR.
WELL, THIS IS GONNA GET NASTY. SO Y'ALL BEST GET CLOSE.
SOUNDS GOOD TO ME.
HHF
THERE'S A MYTH IN THE METEOROLOGIST'S WORLD... THAT THE LOW PRESSURE OF A PASSING TORNADO OVER-HEAD CAN CAUSE A BUILDING TO EXPLODE.
BUT WHAT ABOUT WHEN A TORNADO IS... INSIDE THE BUILDING?
KRRBRRAAOOOOO

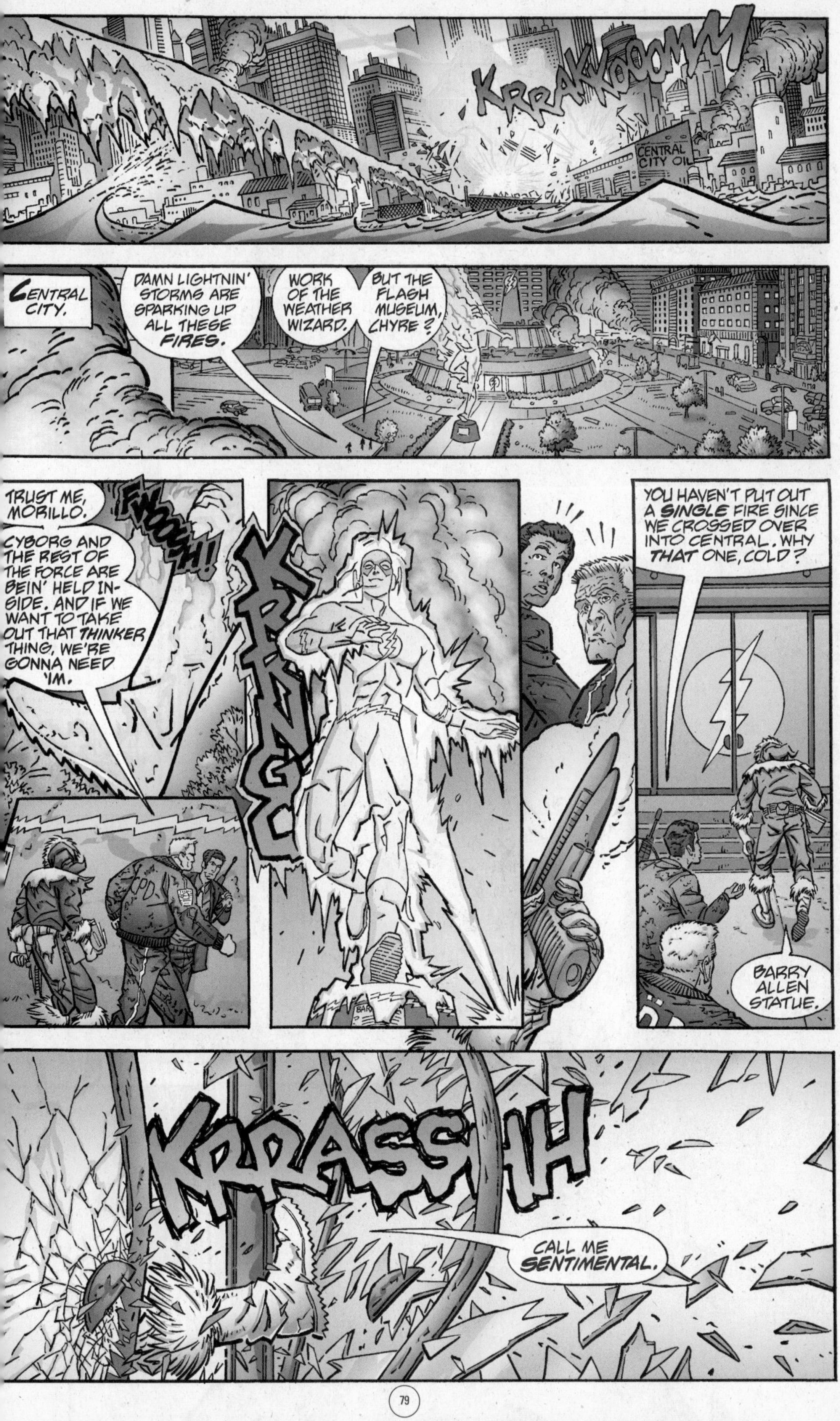

KRRAKOOOMM
CENTRAL CITY OIL
CENTRAL CITY.
DAMN LIGHTNIN' STORMS ARE SPARKING UP ALL THESE FIRES.
WORK OF THE WEATHER WIZARD.
BUT THE FLASH MUSEUM, CHYRE?
TRUST ME, MORILLO.
CYBORG AND THE REST OF THE FORCE ARE BEIN' HELD INSIDE. AND IF WE WANT TO TAKE OUT THAT THINKER THING, WE'RE GONNA NEED 'IM.
FWOOSH!
KRINGG
YOU HAVEN'T PUT OUT A SINGLE FIRE SINCE WE CROSSED OVER INTO CENTRAL. WHY THAT ONE, COLD?
BARRY ALLEN STATUE.
KRRASSHH
CALL ME SENTIMENTAL.

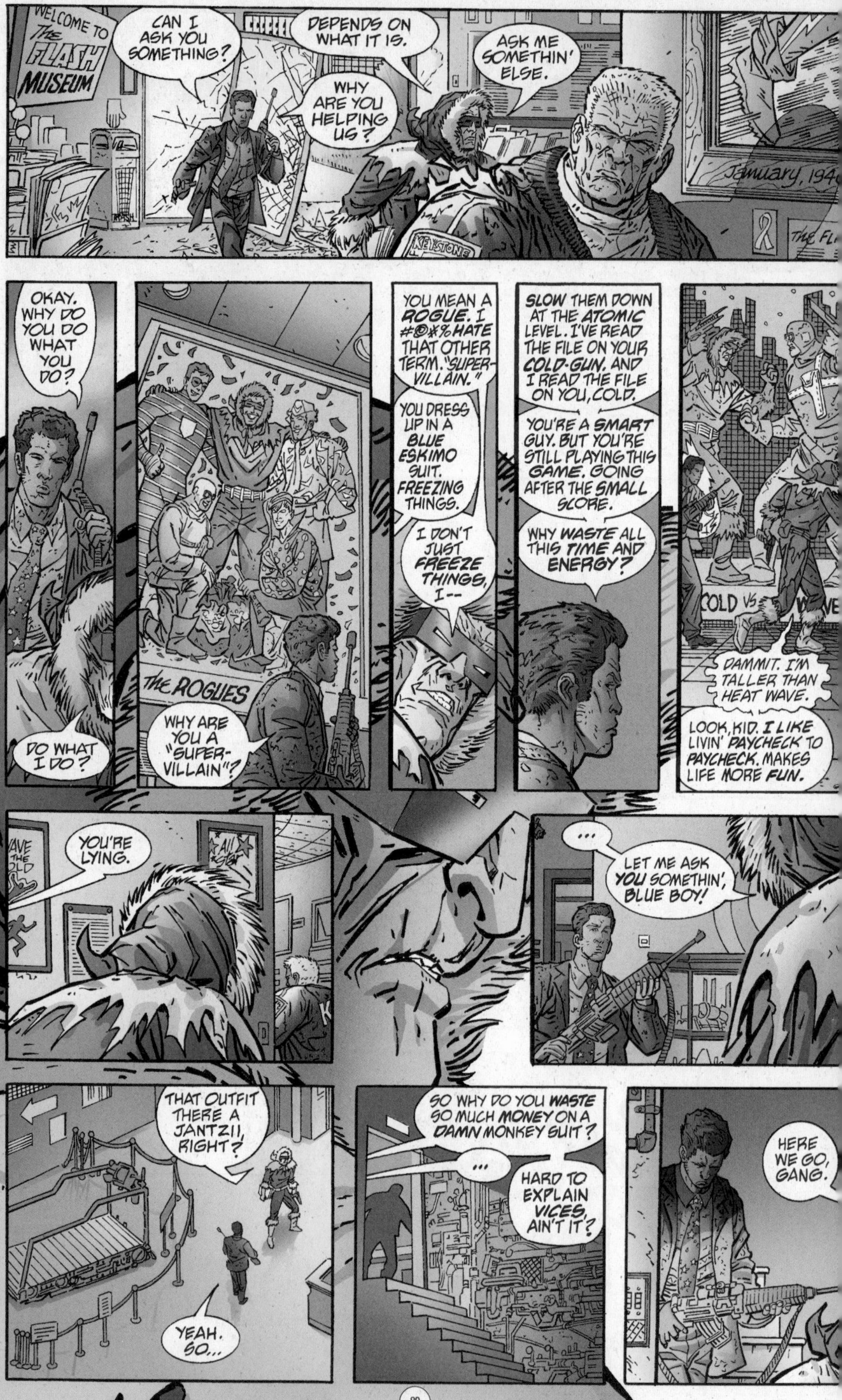
WELCOME TO The FLASH MUSEUM
CAN I ASK YOU SOMETHING?
DEPENDS ON WHAT IT IS.
WHY ARE YOU HELPING US?
ASK ME SOMETHIN' ELSE.
January, 194
KEYSTONE
OKAY. WHY DO YOU DO WHAT YOU DO?
DO WHAT I DO?
THE ROGUES
WHY ARE YOU A "SUPER-VILLAIN"?
YOU MEAN A ROGUE. I #@*% HATE THAT OTHER TERM. "SUPER-VILLAIN."
YOU DRESS UP IN A BLUE ESKIMO SUIT. FREEZING THINGS.
I DON'T JUST FREEZE THINGS, I--
SLOW THEM DOWN AT THE ATOMIC LEVEL. I'VE READ THE FILE ON YOUR COLD-GUN. AND I READ THE FILE ON YOU, COLD.
YOU'RE A SMART GUY. BUT YOU'RE STILL PLAYING THIS GAME. GOING AFTER THE SMALL SCORE.
WHY WASTE ALL THIS TIME AND ENERGY?
COLD VS
DAMMIT. I'M TALLER THAN HEAT WAVE.
LOOK, KID. I LIKE LIVIN' PAYCHECK TO PAYCHECK. MAKES LIFE MORE FUN.
YOU'RE LYING.
...
LET ME ASK YOU SOMETHIN', BLUE BOY!
THAT OUTFIT THERE A JANTZII, RIGHT?
YEAH. SO...
SO WHY DO YOU WASTE SO MUCH MONEY ON A DAMN MONKEY SUIT?
...
HARD TO EXPLAIN VICES, AIN'T IT?
HERE WE GO, GANG.

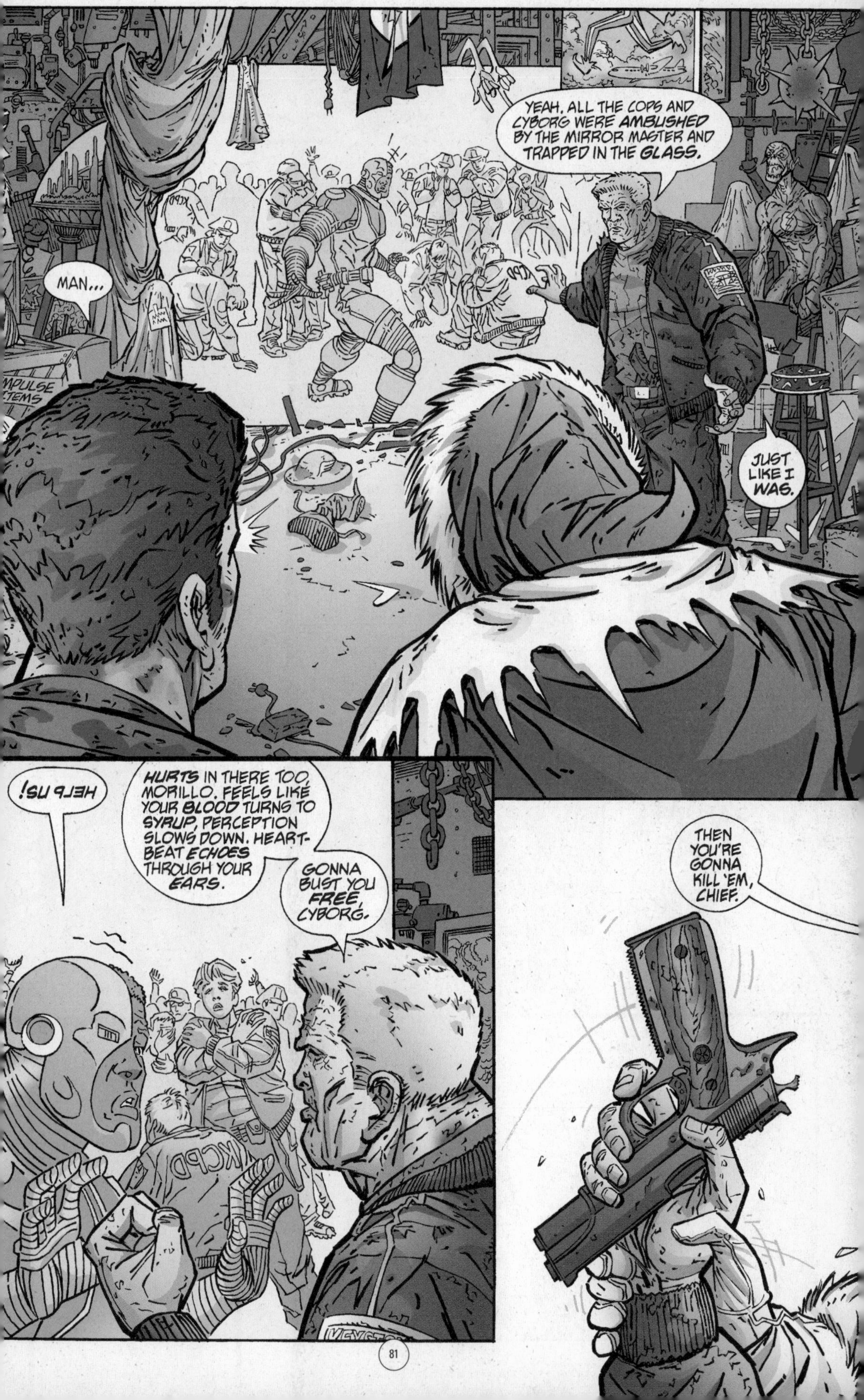
YEAH, ALL THE COPS AND CYBORG WERE AMBUSHED BY THE MIRROR MASTER AND TRAPPED IN THE GLASS.
MAN...
JUST LIKE I WAS.
HELP US!
HURTS IN THERE TOO, MORILLO. FEELS LIKE YOUR BLOOD TURNS TO SYRUP, PERCEPTION SLOWS DOWN. HEART-BEAT ECHOES THROUGH YOUR EARS.
GONNA BUST YOU FREE, CYBORG.
THEN YOU'RE GONNA KILL 'EM, CHIEF.

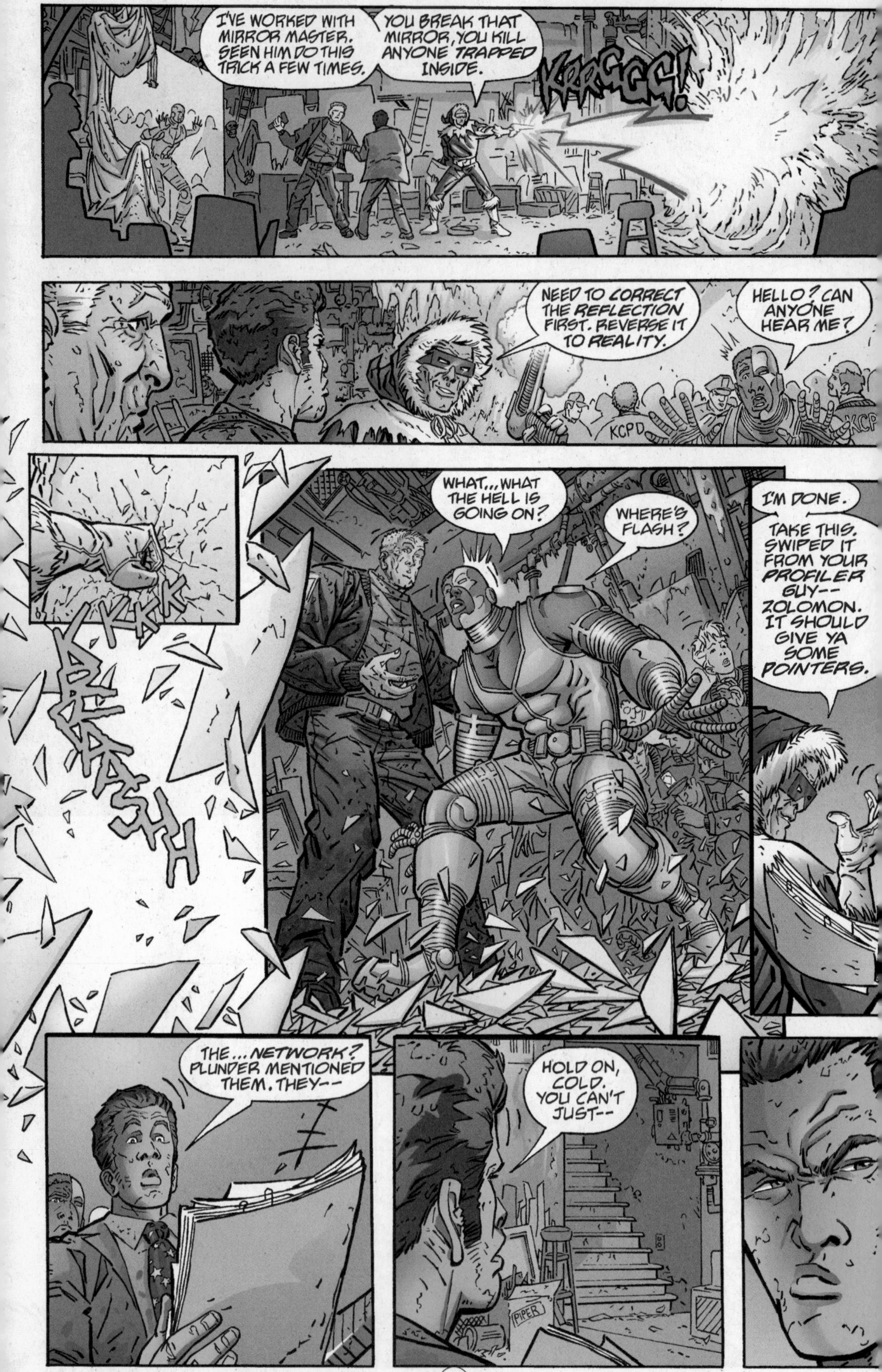

I'VE WORKED WITH MIRROR MASTER. SEEN HIM DO THIS TRICK A FEW TIMES.
YOU BREAK THAT MIRROR, YOU KILL ANYONE TRAPPED INSIDE.
KRRGGG!
NEED TO CORRECT THE REFLECTION FIRST. REVERSE IT TO REALITY.
HELLO? CAN ANYONE HEAR ME?
KCPD
KCP
KKKK
BRASHH
WHAT... WHAT THE HELL IS GOING ON?
WHERE'S FLASH?
I'M DONE.
TAKE THIS. SWIPED IT FROM YOUR PROFILER GUY-- ZOLOMON. IT SHOULD GIVE YA SOME POINTERS.
THE... NETWORK? PLUNDER MENTIONED THEM. THEY--
HOLD ON, COLD. YOU CAN'T JUST--
PIPER

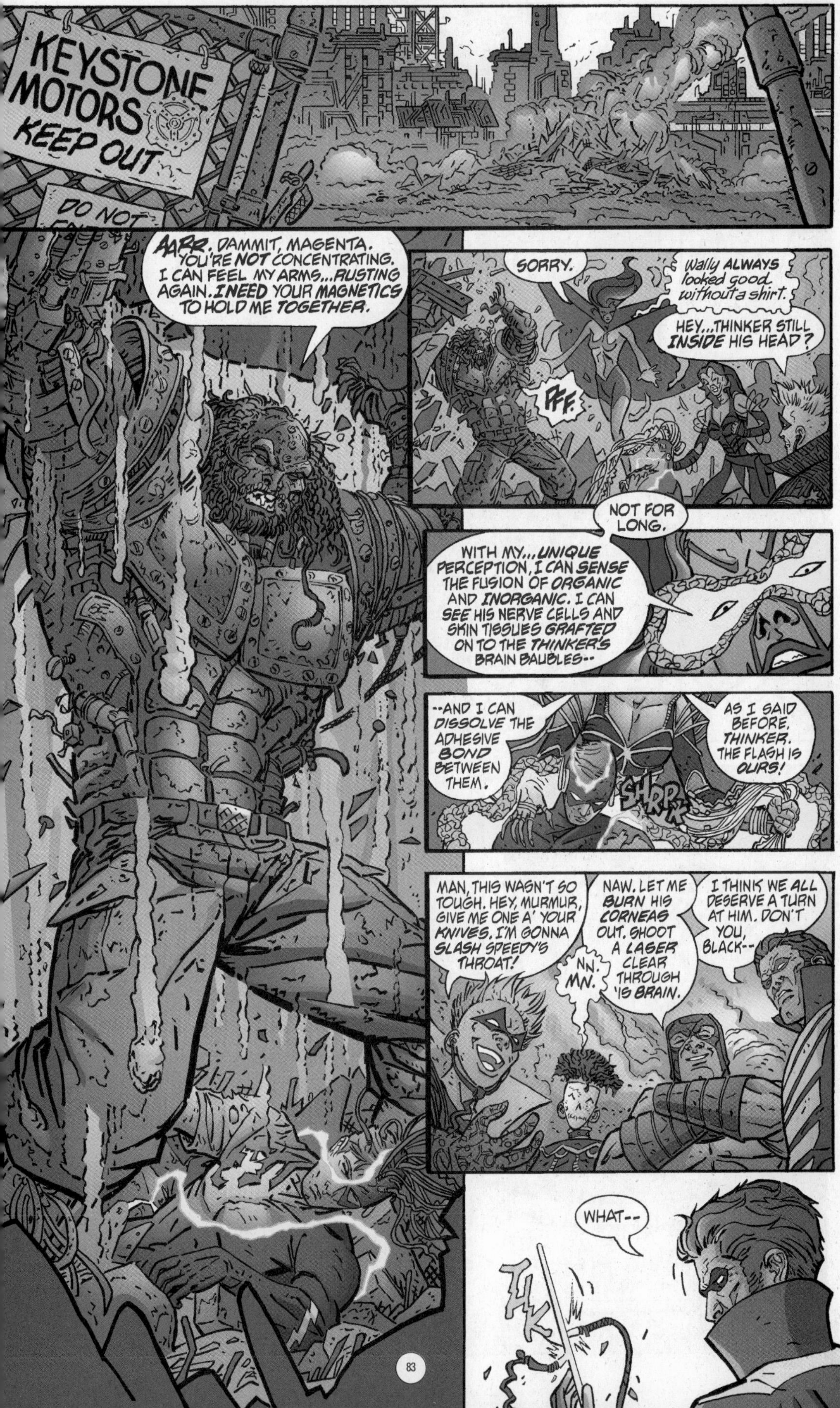

KEYSTONE MOTORS KEEP OUT
DO NOT
AARR. DAMMIT, MAGENTA. YOU'RE NOT CONCENTRATING. I CAN FEEL MY ARMS...RUSTING AGAIN. I NEED YOUR MAGNETICS TO HOLD ME TOGETHER.
SORRY.
Wally ALWAYS looked good without a shirt.
HEY...THINKER STILL INSIDE HIS HEAD?
PFF.
NOT FOR LONG.
WITH MY...UNIQUE PERCEPTION, I CAN SENSE THE FUSION OF ORGANIC AND INORGANIC. I CAN SEE HIS NERVE CELLS AND SKIN TISSUES GRAFTED ON TO THE THINKER'S BRAIN BAUBLES--
--AND I CAN DISSOLVE THE ADHESIVE BOND BETWEEN THEM.
AS I SAID BEFORE, THINKER. THE FLASH IS OURS!
SHRRK
MAN, THIS WASN'T SO TOUGH. HEY, MURMUR, GIVE ME ONE A' YOUR KNIVES. I'M GONNA SLASH SPEEDY'S THROAT!
NN. MN.
NAW. LET ME BURN HIS CORNEAS OUT. SHOOT A LASER CLEAR THROUGH 'IS BRAIN.
I THINK WE ALL DESERVE A TURN AT HIM. DON'T YOU, BLACK--
WHAT--
THK

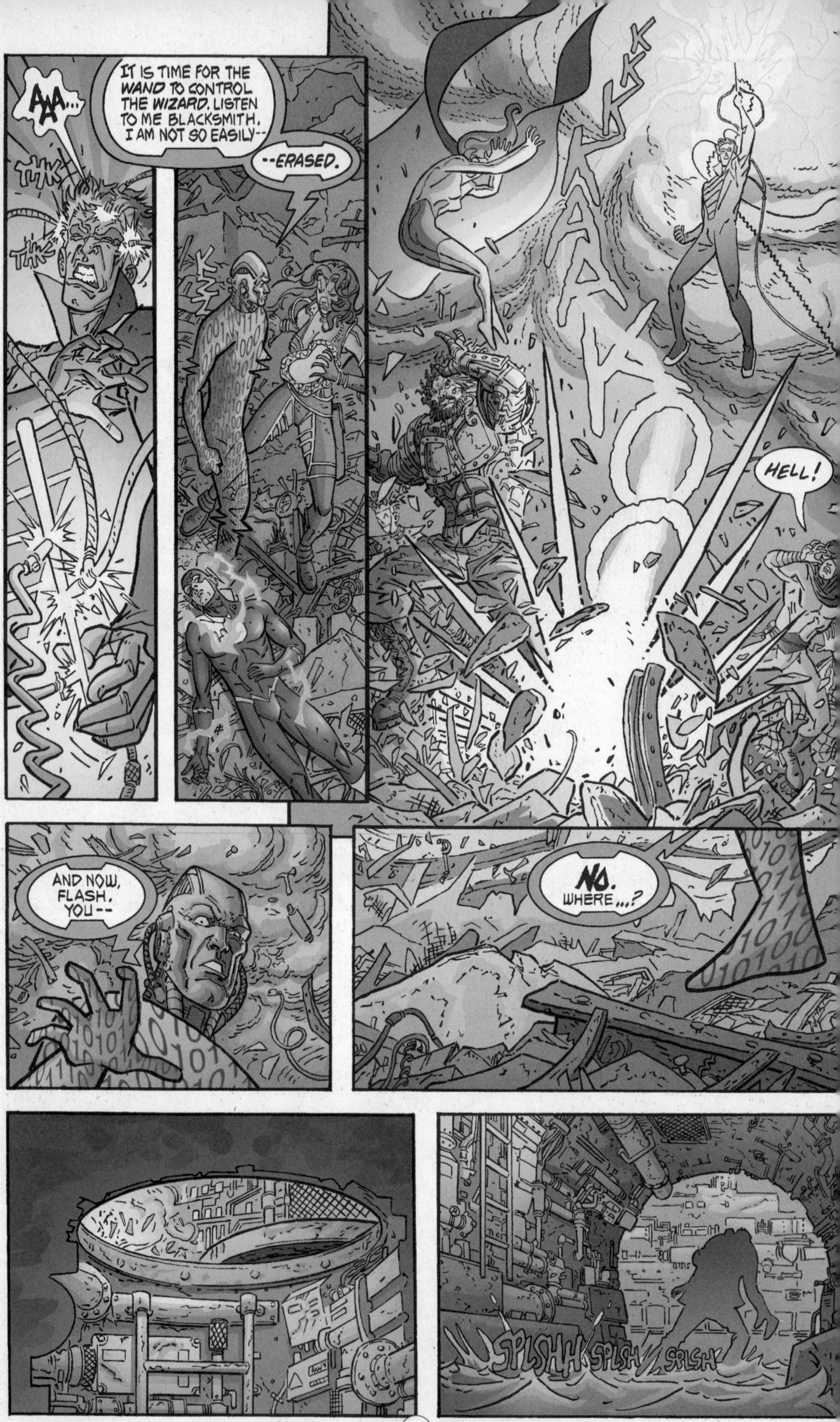
AAA...
THK
THK
IT IS TIME FOR THE WAND TO CONTROL THE WIZARD. LISTEN TO ME BLACKSMITH. I AM NOT SO EASILY--
--ERASED.
KKKK
KAAKOOM
HELL!
AND NOW, FLASH, YOU--
NO. WHERE...?
SPLSHH SPLSH SPLSH

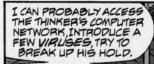

THE REST OF OUR *FORCE* IS STAYING BEHIND IN *CENTRAL*, TRYING TO HELP SAVE LIVES.

LEAVING IT UP TO *US* TO FIND *FLASH*.

I CAN PROBABLY ACCESS THE THINKER'S COMPUTER NETWORK, INTRODUCE A FEW *VIRUSES*, TRY TO BREAK UP HIS HOLD.

FROM THERE... WE COULD DISCONNECT HIS POWER,... ATTACK HIM WITH SOMETHING LESS CONCRETE...

LESS TECHNOLOGICAL...?

I KNOW THERE AREN'T ANY GUARANTEES, CYBORG.

WELL, I'M GOING TO *TRY*, *DIE TRYING* IF I'VE GOT TO.

THE *FLASH* IS IN *TROUBLE*.

I HAVEN'T STUDIED *A.I.* SPECIFICALLY. WAS ALWAYS MORE INTO *SPORTS* THAN *VIDEO GAMES*, THOUGH I'M NO *SLOUCH* IN THE COMPUTER DEPARTMENT.

KID SPEAKS REALLY HIGHLY OF YOU. WHEN'D YOU MEET HIM?

RIGHT AFTER MY *ACCIDENT*, AFTER HALF MY BODY WAS REPLACED WITH MACHINERY.

WE WERE IN THE *TEEN TITANS* BACK THEN...

IT'S *FUNNY*. I DIDN'T THINK TOO MUCH OF WEST AT FIRST. HE WAS KIND OF *EVASIVE*, HAD A *TEMPER*, FELL IN *LOVE* TOO EASY...

BUT REALLY, I WAS WRONG. HE WAS DOING WHAT I FORGOT TO DO. WHAT I THOUGHT I LOST.

HE WAS SHOWING HIS *EMOTIONS*.

IT'S *AMAZING* TO ME SOMETIMES. TO THINK BACK, WHAT WALLY *WAS* ONCE LIKE. WHAT HE IS *TODAY*.

SO MANY HEROES DON'T *LEARN* OR *EVOLVE*. THEY DON'T *GROW UP*.

I MEAN THE GUY'S *STILL* SMILING.

THAT'S *INSPIRING*.

AND *THIS* IS AMAZING.

WHAT?

THE *NETWORK*. THE *ROGUES*...

WALLY HAS. MORE THAN ALMOST ANY OF THE OTHER TITANS. HE'S GOTTEN THROUGH A LOT OF *HARD TIMES*, AND HE'S STILL NOT *JADED*.

THIS *WHOLE MESS* TIES INTO *ONE PERSON*...

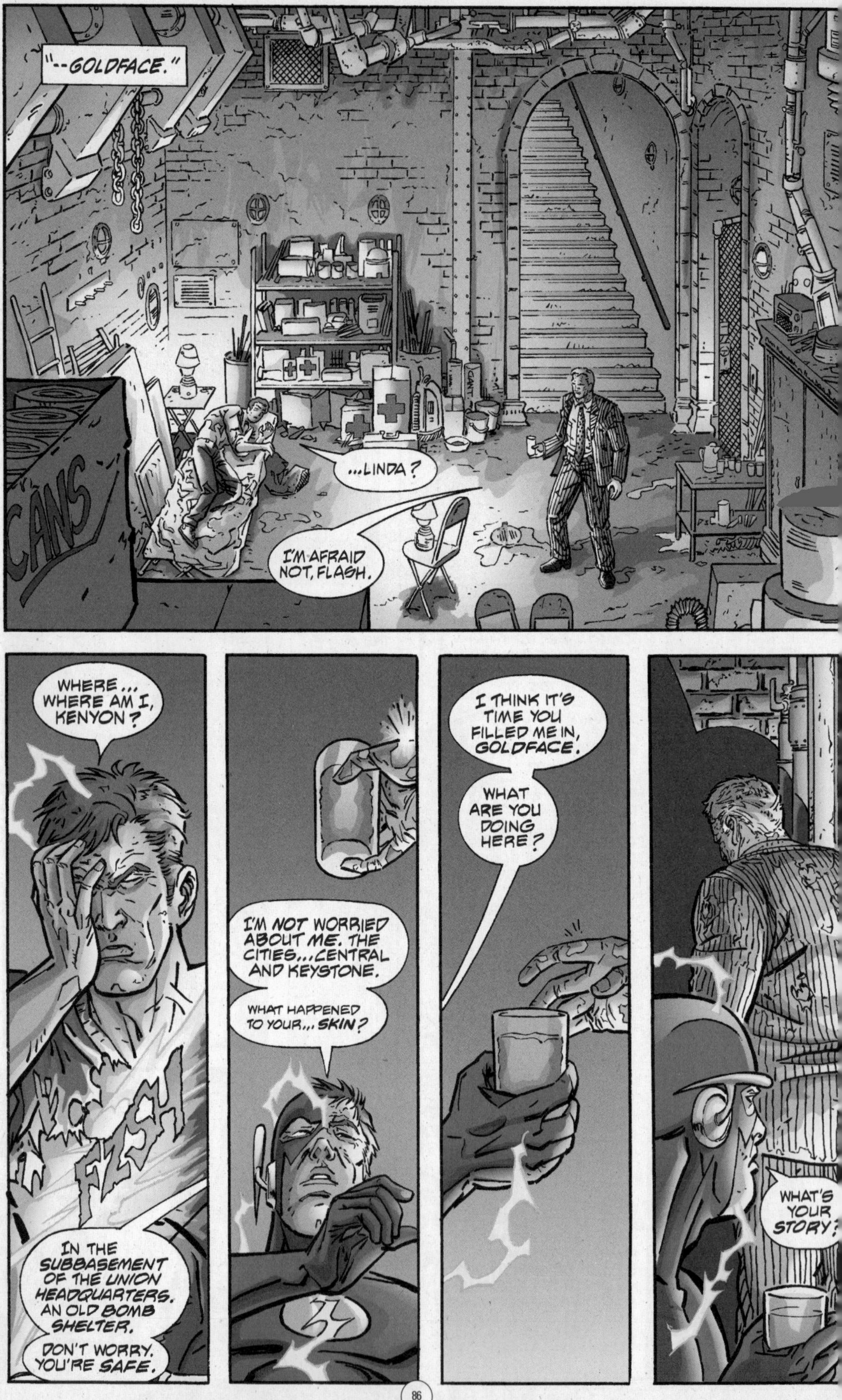
"--GOLDFACE."
...LINDA?
I'M AFRAID NOT, FLASH.
WHERE... WHERE AM I, KENYON?
IN THE SUBBASEMENT OF THE UNION HEADQUARTERS. AN OLD BOMB SHELTER.
DON'T WORRY. YOU'RE SAFE.
FZSH
I'M NOT WORRIED ABOUT ME. THE CITIES... CENTRAL AND KEYSTONE.
WHAT HAPPENED TO YOUR... SKIN?
I THINK IT'S TIME YOU FILLED ME IN, GOLDFACE.
WHAT ARE YOU DOING HERE?
WHAT'S YOUR STORY?

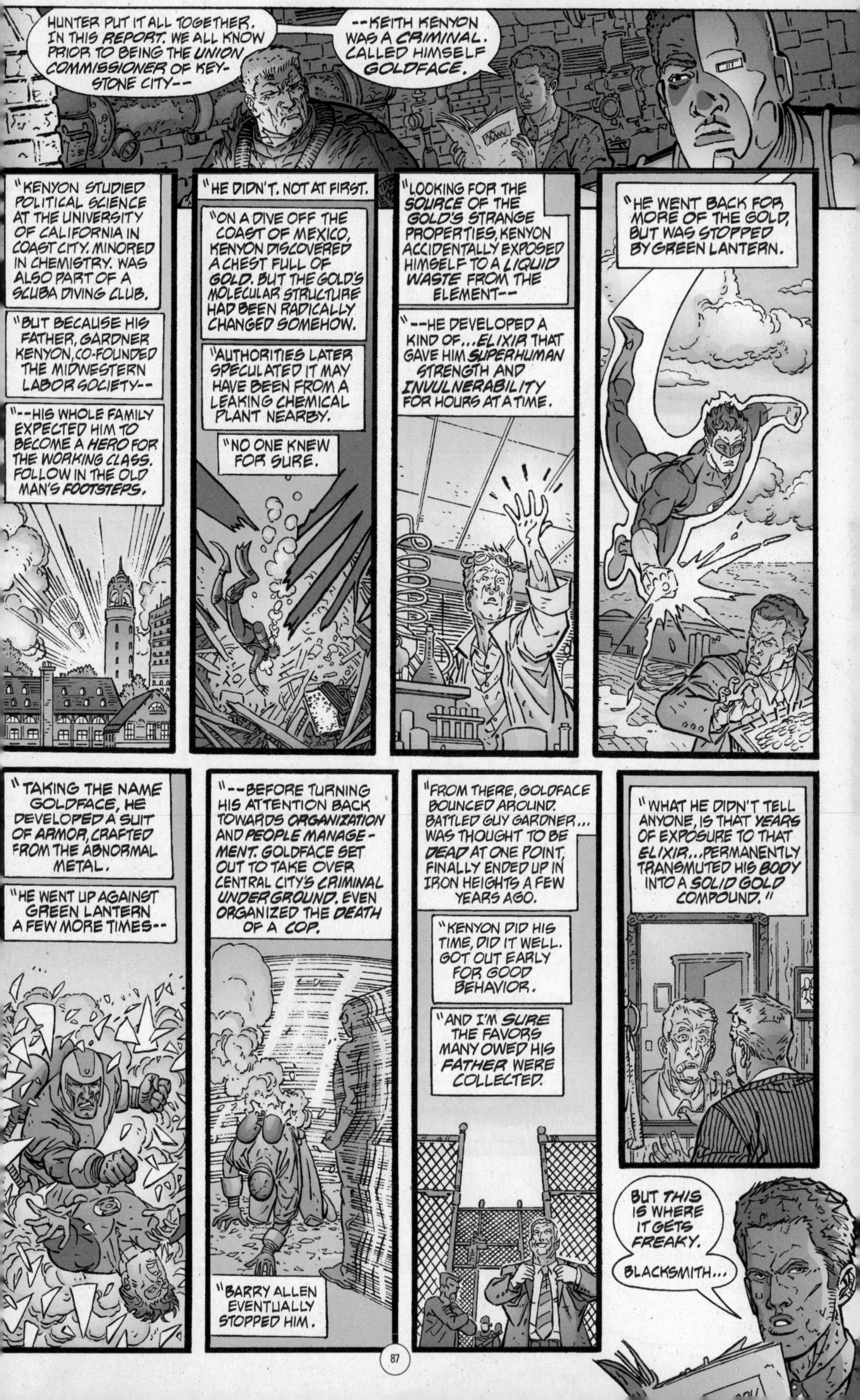
HUNTER PUT IT ALL TOGETHER. IN THIS REPORT. WE ALL KNOW PRIOR TO BEING THE UNION COMMISSIONER OF KEY-STONE CITY--
--KEITH KENYON WAS A CRIMINAL. CALLED HIMSELF GOLDFACE.
"KENYON STUDIED POLITICAL SCIENCE AT THE UNIVERSITY OF CALIFORNIA IN COAST CITY. MINORED IN CHEMISTRY. WAS ALSO PART OF A SCUBA DIVING CLUB.
"BUT BECAUSE HIS FATHER, GARDNER KENYON, CO-FOUNDED THE MIDWESTERN LABOR SOCIETY--
"--HIS WHOLE FAMILY EXPECTED HIM TO BECOME A HERO FOR THE WORKING CLASS. FOLLOW IN THE OLD MAN'S FOOTSTEPS.
"HE DIDN'T. NOT AT FIRST.
"ON A DIVE OFF THE COAST OF MEXICO, KENYON DISCOVERED A CHEST FULL OF GOLD. BUT THE GOLD'S MOLECULAR STRUCTURE HAD BEEN RADICALLY CHANGED SOMEHOW.
"AUTHORITIES LATER SPECULATED IT MAY HAVE BEEN FROM A LEAKING CHEMICAL PLANT NEARBY.
"NO ONE KNEW FOR SURE.
"LOOKING FOR THE SOURCE OF THE GOLD'S STRANGE PROPERTIES, KENYON ACCIDENTALLY EXPOSED HIMSELF TO A LIQUID WASTE FROM THE ELEMENT--
"--HE DEVELOPED A KIND OF...ELIXIR THAT GAVE HIM SUPERHUMAN STRENGTH AND INVULNERABILITY FOR HOURS AT A TIME.
"HE WENT BACK FOR MORE OF THE GOLD, BUT WAS STOPPED BY GREEN LANTERN.
"TAKING THE NAME GOLDFACE, HE DEVELOPED A SUIT OF ARMOR, CRAFTED FROM THE ABNORMAL METAL.
"HE WENT UP AGAINST GREEN LANTERN A FEW MORE TIMES--
"--BEFORE TURNING HIS ATTENTION BACK TOWARDS ORGANIZATION AND PEOPLE MANAGE-MENT. GOLDFACE SET OUT TO TAKE OVER CENTRAL CITY'S CRIMINAL UNDERGROUND. EVEN ORGANIZED THE DEATH OF A COP.
"BARRY ALLEN EVENTUALLY STOPPED HIM.
"FROM THERE, GOLDFACE BOUNCED AROUND. BATTLED GUY GARDNER... WAS THOUGHT TO BE DEAD AT ONE POINT. FINALLY ENDED UP IN IRON HEIGHTS A FEW YEARS AGO.
"KENYON DID HIS TIME, DID IT WELL. GOT OUT EARLY FOR GOOD BEHAVIOR.
"AND I'M SURE THE FAVORS MANY OWED HIS FATHER WERE COLLECTED.
"WHAT HE DIDN'T TELL ANYONE, IS THAT YEARS OF EXPOSURE TO THAT ELIXIR...PERMANENTLY TRANSMUTED HIS BODY INTO A SOLID GOLD COMPOUND."
BUT THIS IS WHERE IT GETS FREAKY.
BLACKSMITH...

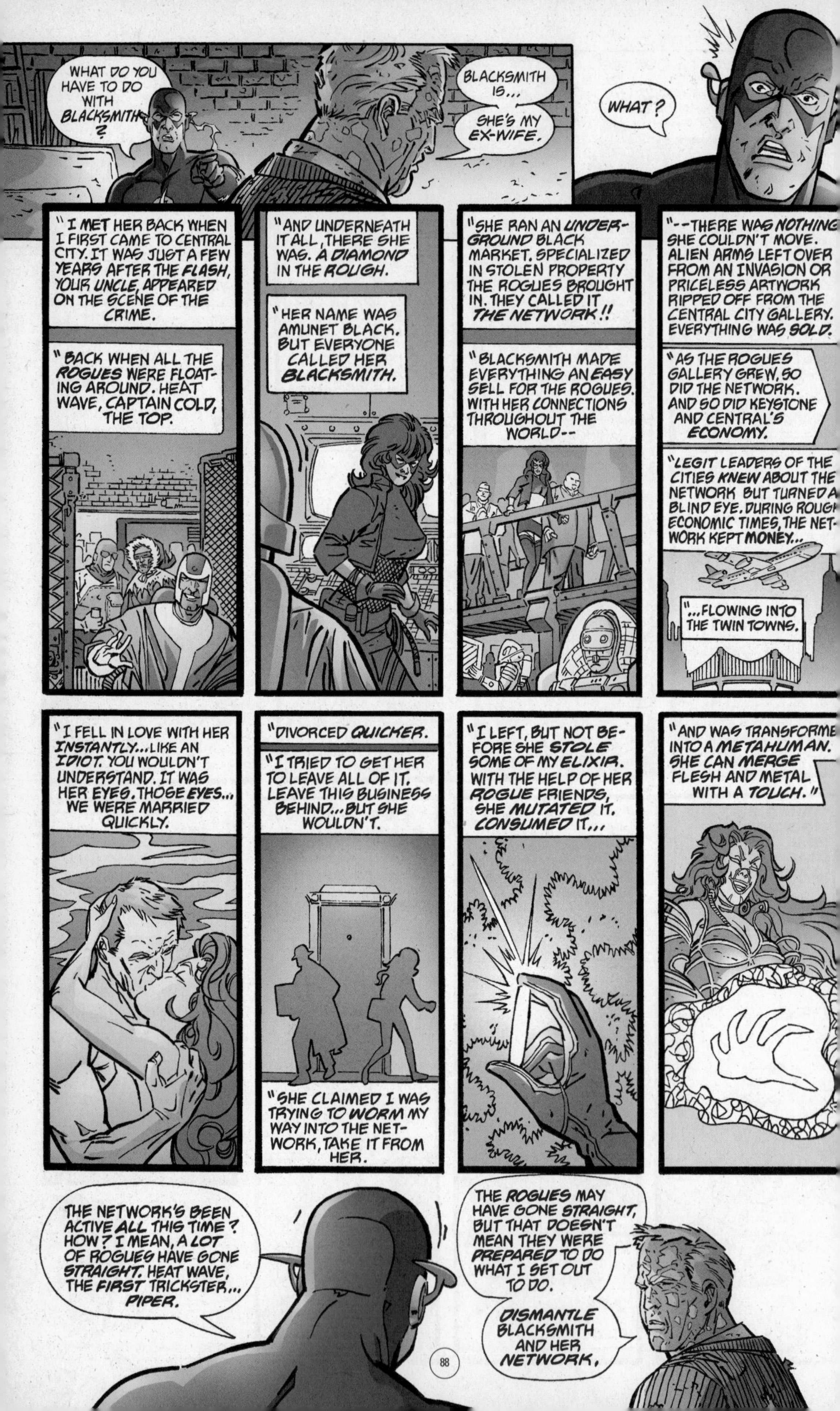
WHAT DO YOU HAVE TO DO WITH BLACKSMITH?
BLACKSMITH IS...
SHE'S MY EX-WIFE.
WHAT?
"I MET HER BACK WHEN I FIRST CAME TO CENTRAL CITY. IT WAS JUST A FEW YEARS AFTER THE FLASH, YOUR UNCLE, APPEARED ON THE SCENE OF THE CRIME.
"BACK WHEN ALL THE ROGUES WERE FLOATING AROUND. HEAT WAVE, CAPTAIN COLD, THE TOP.
"AND UNDERNEATH IT ALL, THERE SHE WAS. A DIAMOND IN THE ROUGH.
"HER NAME WAS AMUNET BLACK. BUT EVERYONE CALLED HER BLACKSMITH.
"SHE RAN AN UNDERGROUND BLACK MARKET. SPECIALIZED IN STOLEN PROPERTY THE ROGUES BROUGHT IN. THEY CALLED IT THE NETWORK!!
"BLACKSMITH MADE EVERYTHING AN EASY SELL FOR THE ROGUES. WITH HER CONNECTIONS THROUGHOUT THE WORLD--
"--THERE WAS NOTHING SHE COULDN'T MOVE. ALIEN ARMS LEFT OVER FROM AN INVASION OR PRICELESS ARTWORK RIPPED OFF FROM THE CENTRAL CITY GALLERY. EVERYTHING WAS SOLD.
"AS THE ROGUES GALLERY GREW, SO DID THE NETWORK. AND SO DID KEYSTONE AND CENTRAL'S ECONOMY.
"LEGIT LEADERS OF THE CITIES KNEW ABOUT THE NETWORK BUT TURNED A BLIND EYE. DURING ROUGH ECONOMIC TIMES, THE NETWORK KEPT MONEY...
"...FLOWING INTO THE TWIN TOWNS.
"I FELL IN LOVE WITH HER INSTANTLY... LIKE AN IDIOT. YOU WOULDN'T UNDERSTAND. IT WAS HER EYES. THOSE EYES... WE WERE MARRIED QUICKLY.
"DIVORCED QUICKER.
"I TRIED TO GET HER TO LEAVE ALL OF IT. LEAVE THIS BUSINESS BEHIND... BUT SHE WOULDN'T.
"SHE CLAIMED I WAS TRYING TO WORM MY WAY INTO THE NETWORK, TAKE IT FROM HER.
"I LEFT, BUT NOT BEFORE SHE STOLE SOME OF MY ELIXIR. WITH THE HELP OF HER ROGUE FRIENDS, SHE MUTATED IT. CONSUMED IT...
"AND WAS TRANSFORMED INTO A METAHUMAN. SHE CAN MERGE FLESH AND METAL WITH A TOUCH."
THE NETWORK'S BEEN ACTIVE ALL THIS TIME? HOW? I MEAN, A LOT OF ROGUES HAVE GONE STRAIGHT. HEAT WAVE, THE FIRST TRICKSTER... PIPER.
THE ROGUES MAY HAVE GONE STRAIGHT, BUT THAT DOESN'T MEAN THEY WERE PREPARED TO DO WHAT I SET OUT TO DO.
DISMANTLE BLACKSMITH AND HER NETWORK.

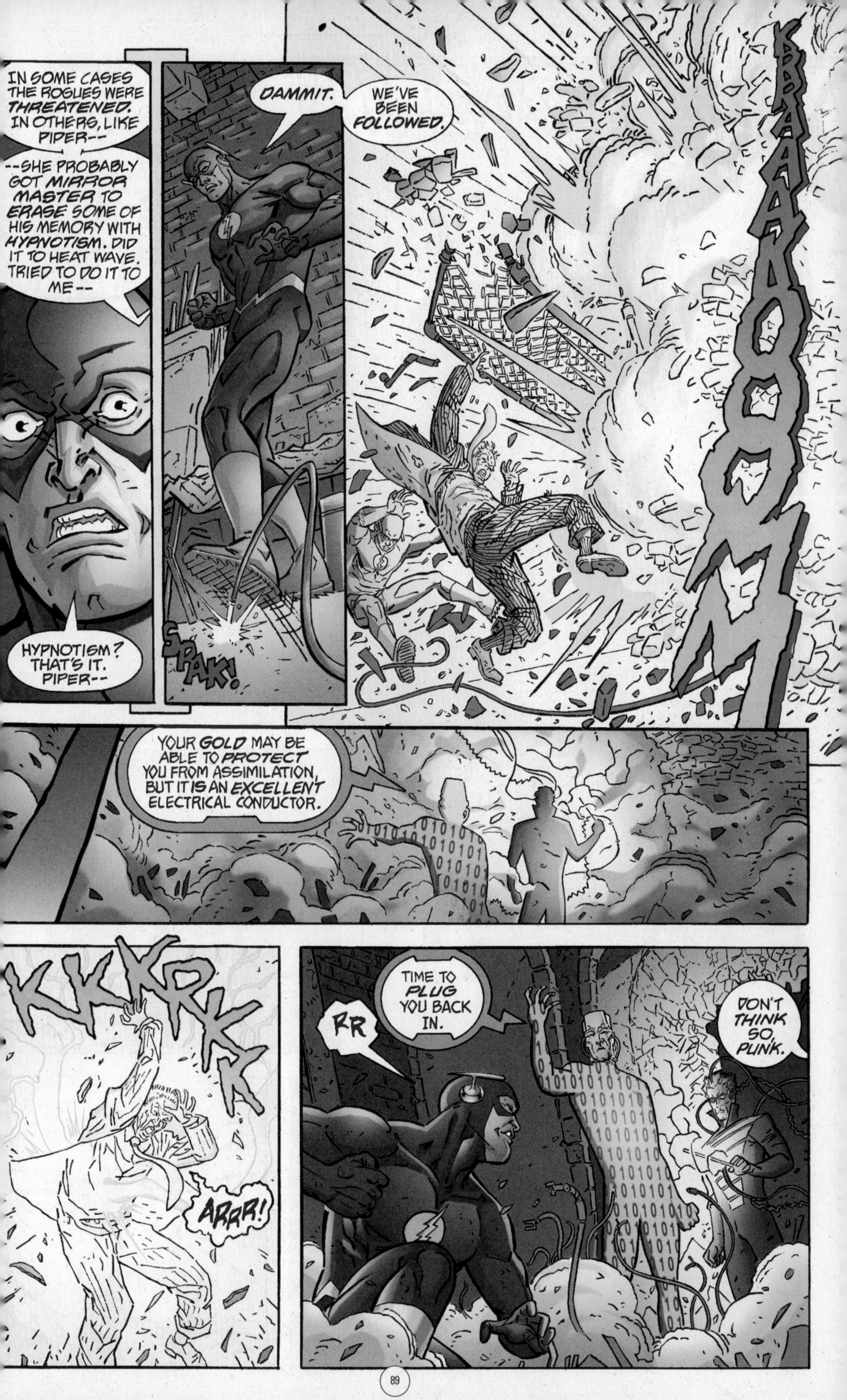
IN SOME CASES THE ROGUES WERE THREATENED. IN OTHERS, LIKE PIPER--
--SHE PROBABLY GOT MIRROR MASTER TO ERASE SOME OF HIS MEMORY WITH HYPNOTISM. DID IT TO HEAT WAVE. TRIED TO DO IT TO ME--
HYPNOTISM? THAT'S IT. PIPER--
DAMMIT.
WE'VE BEEN FOLLOWED.
SPAK!
KBRAAAAAOOOM
YOUR GOLD MAY BE ABLE TO PROTECT YOU FROM ASSIMILATION, BUT IT IS AN EXCELLENT ELECTRICAL CONDUCTOR.
KKKRKK
ARRR!
RR
TIME TO PLUG YOU BACK IN.
DON'T THINK SO, PUNK.

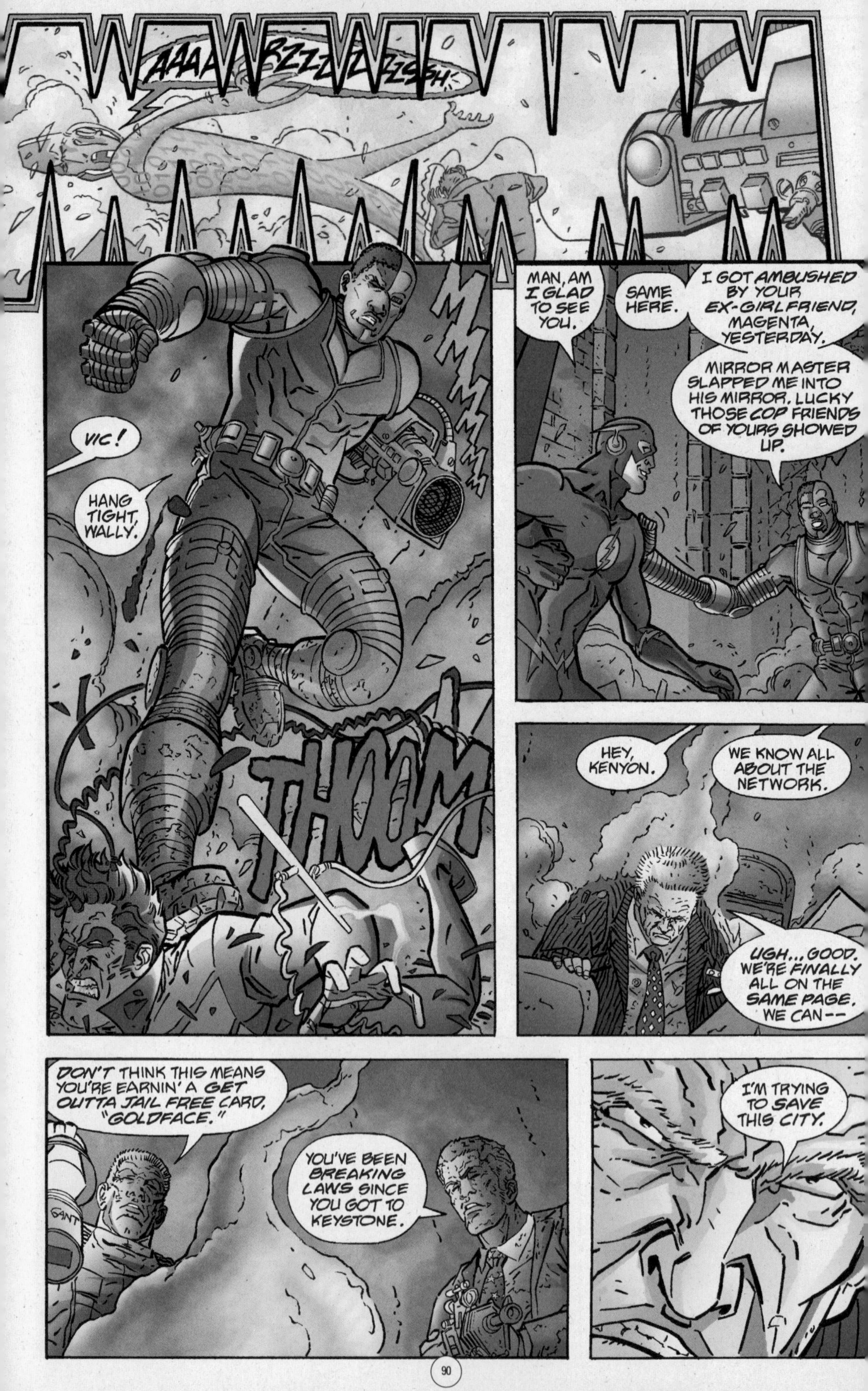
AAAARZZZZZZZSSH!
VIC!
HANG TIGHT, WALLY.
MMMMMMM
THOOM
MAN, AM I GLAD TO SEE YOU.
SAME HERE.
I GOT AMBUSHED BY YOUR EX-GIRLFRIEND, MAGENTA, YESTERDAY.
MIRROR MASTER SLAPPED ME INTO HIS MIRROR. LUCKY THOSE COP FRIENDS OF YOURS SHOWED UP.
HEY, KENYON.
WE KNOW ALL ABOUT THE NETWORK.
UGH... GOOD. WE'RE FINALLY ALL ON THE SAME PAGE. WE CAN--
DON'T THINK THIS MEANS YOU'RE EARNIN' A GET OUTTA JAIL FREE CARD, "GOLDFACE."
GANT
YOU'VE BEEN BREAKING LAWS SINCE YOU GOT TO KEYSTONE.
I'M TRYING TO SAVE THIS CITY.

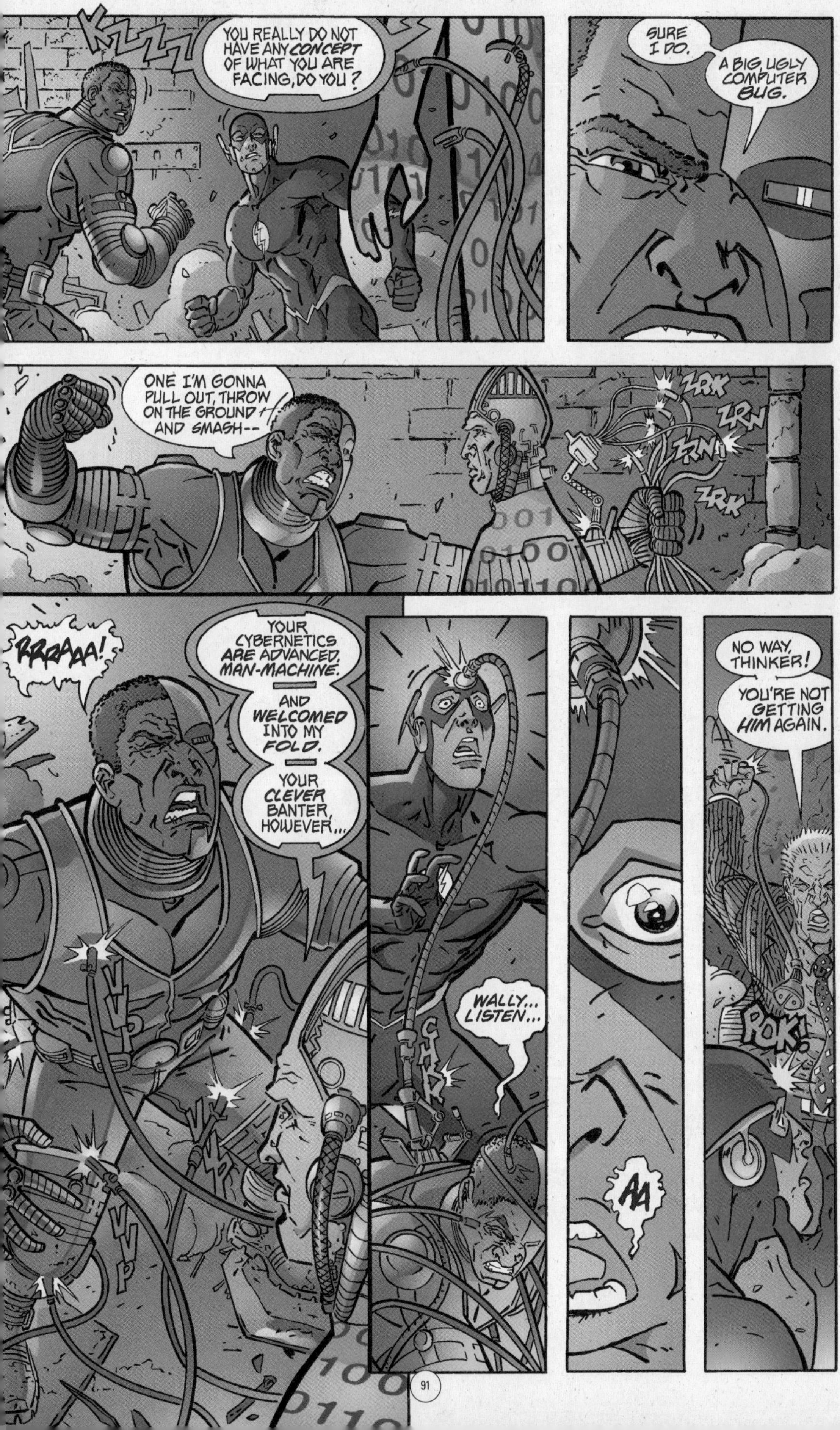
KZZZT
YOU REALLY DO NOT HAVE ANY CONCEPT OF WHAT YOU ARE FACING, DO YOU?
SURE I DO.
A BIG, UGLY COMPUTER BUG.
ONE I'M GONNA PULL OUT, THROW ON THE GROUND AND SMASH--
ZRK
ZRN
ZRN
ZRK
RRRAAAA!
YOUR CYBERNETICS ARE ADVANCED, MAN-MACHINE.
AND WELCOMED INTO MY FOLD.
YOUR CLEVER BANTER, HOWEVER...
WALLY... LISTEN...
AA
NO WAY, THINKER!
YOU'RE NOT GETTING HIM AGAIN.
POK!

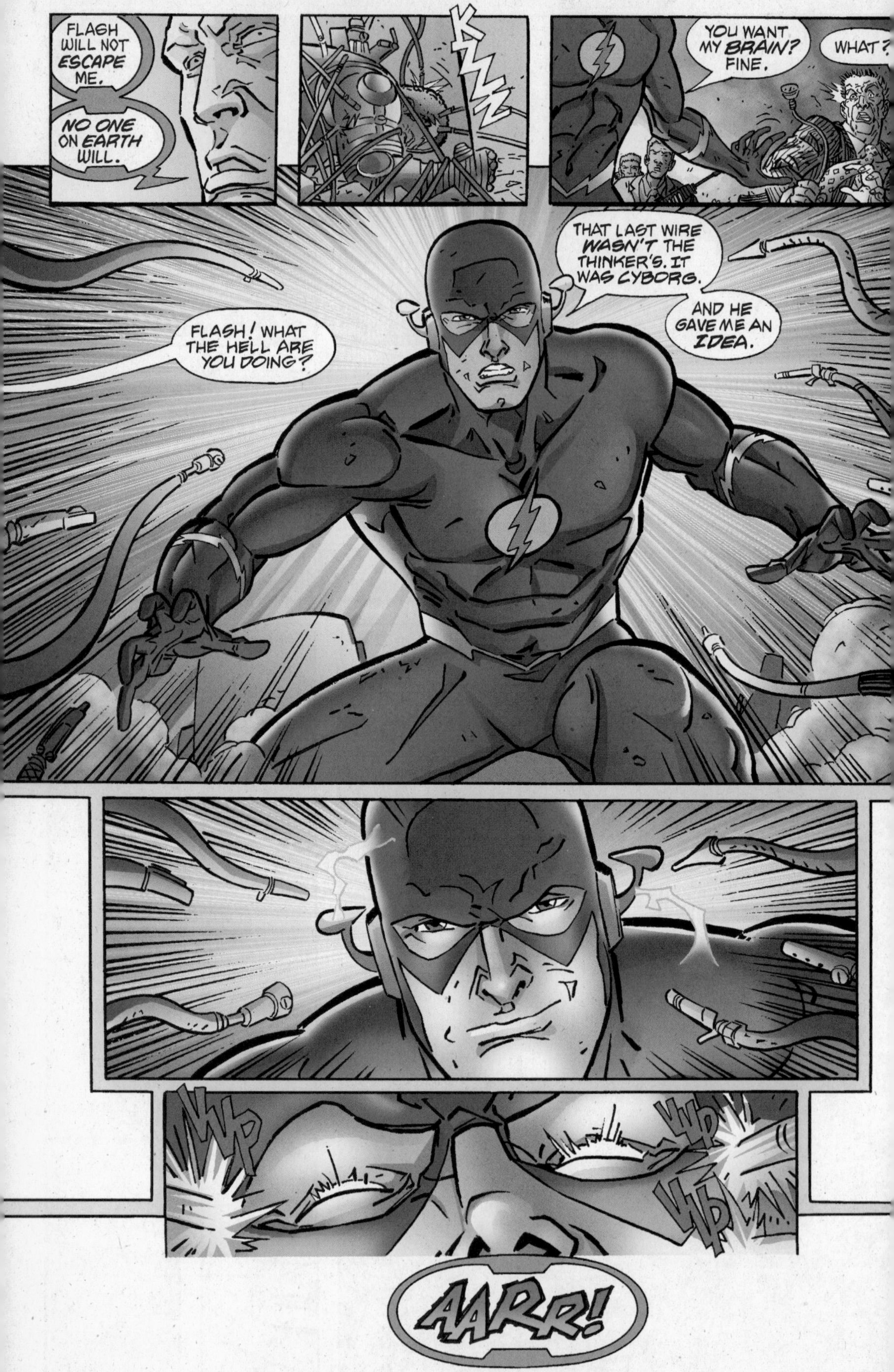
FLASH WILL NOT ESCAPE ME.
NO ONE ON EARTH WILL.
K-ZZZZ
YOU WANT MY BRAIN? FINE.
WHAT?
THAT LAST WIRE WASN'T THE THINKER'S. IT WAS CYBORG.
AND HE GAVE ME AN IDEA.
FLASH! WHAT THE HELL ARE YOU DOING?
VWP
VWP
VWP
AARR!

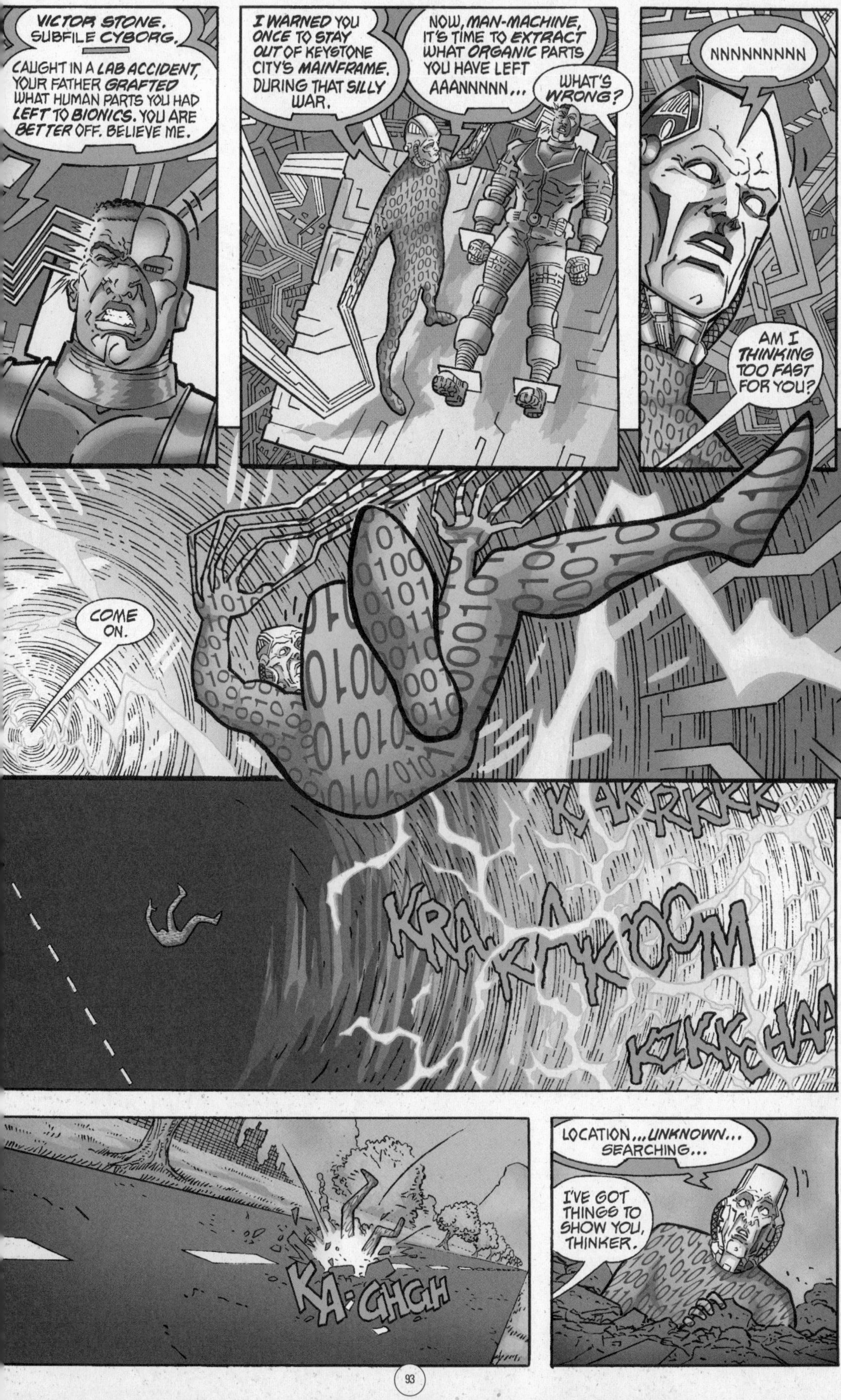
VICTOR STONE. SUBFILE CYBORG.
CAUGHT IN A LAB ACCIDENT, YOUR FATHER GRAFTED WHAT HUMAN PARTS YOU HAD LEFT TO BIONICS. YOU ARE BETTER OFF. BELIEVE ME.
I WARNED YOU ONCE TO STAY OUT OF KEYSTONE CITY'S MAINFRAME. DURING THAT SILLY WAR.
NOW, MAN-MACHINE, IT'S TIME TO EXTRACT WHAT ORGANIC PARTS YOU HAVE LEFT AAANNNNN...
WHAT'S WRONG?
NNNNNNNNN
AM I THINKING TOO FAST FOR YOU?
COME ON.
KAKRKKK
KRAAKTKOOM
KZKKCHAA
KA-GHGH
LOCATION... UNKNOWN... SEARCHING...
I'VE GOT THINGS TO SHOW YOU, THINKER.

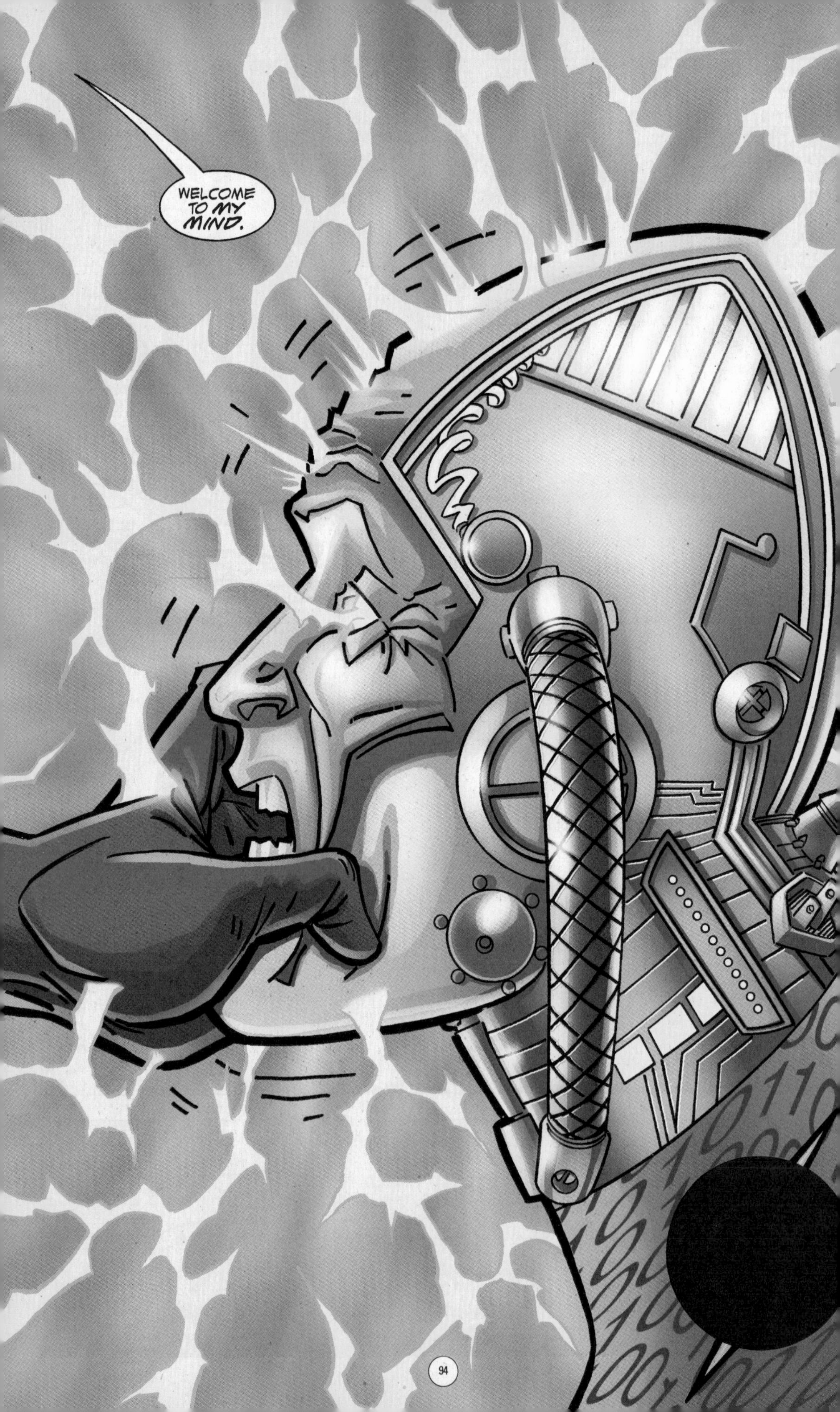
WELCOME TO MY MIND.

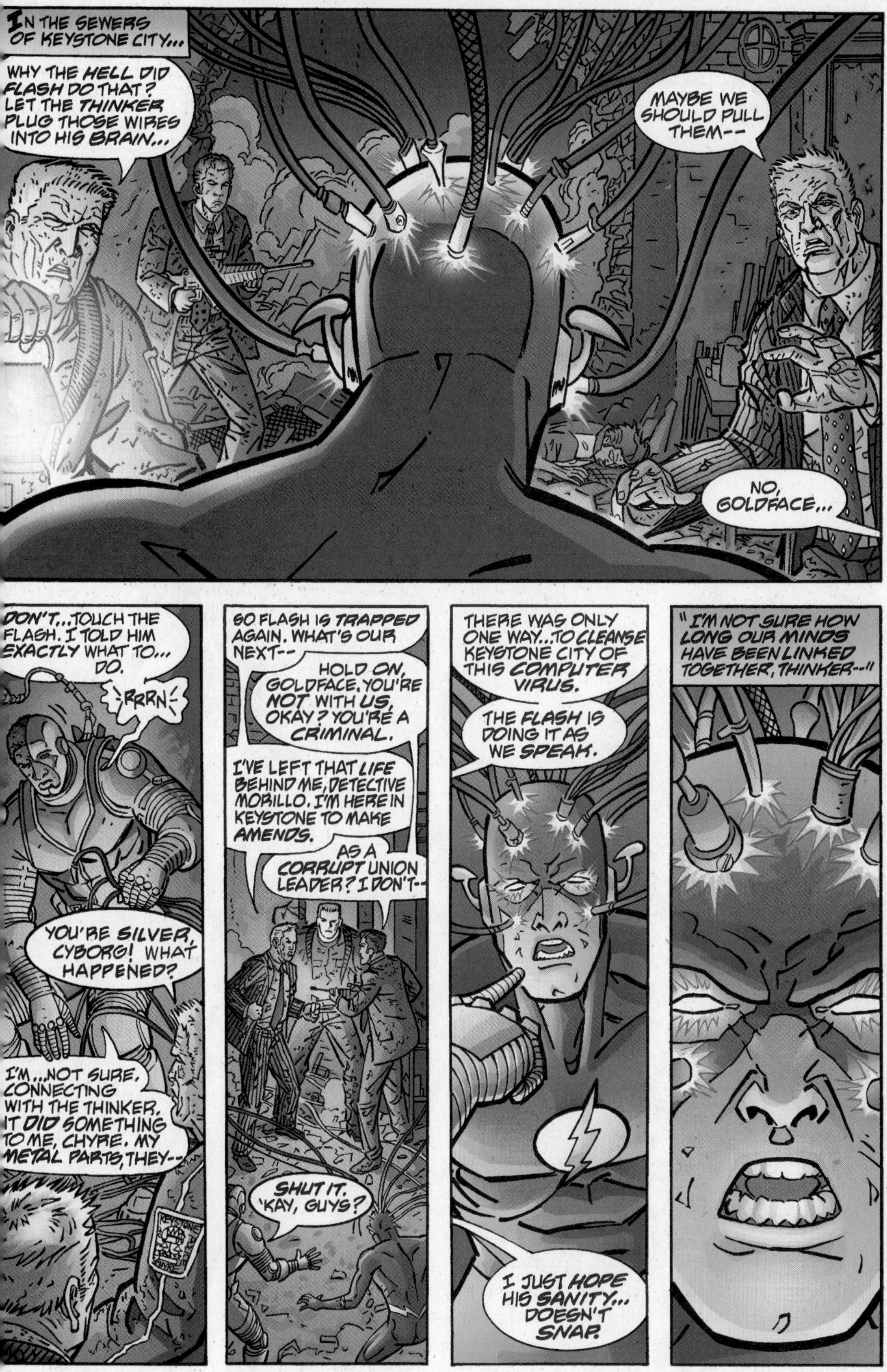
IN THE SEWERS OF KEYSTONE CITY...
WHY THE HELL DID FLASH DO THAT? LET THE THINKER PLUG THOSE WIRES INTO HIS BRAIN...
MAYBE WE SHOULD PULL THEM--
NO, GOLDFACE...
DON'T...TOUCH THE FLASH. I TOLD HIM EXACTLY WHAT TO... DO.
RRRN
YOU'RE SILVER, CYBORG! WHAT HAPPENED?
I'M...NOT SURE. CONNECTING WITH THE THINKER. IT DID SOMETHING TO ME, CHYRE. MY METAL PARTS, THEY--
SO FLASH IS TRAPPED AGAIN. WHAT'S OUR NEXT--
HOLD ON, GOLDFACE. YOU'RE NOT WITH US, OKAY? YOU'RE A CRIMINAL.
I'VE LEFT THAT LIFE BEHIND ME, DETECTIVE MORILLO. I'M HERE IN KEYSTONE TO MAKE AMENDS.
AS A CORRUPT UNION LEADER? I DON'T--
SHUT IT. 'KAY, GUYS?
THERE WAS ONLY ONE WAY...TO CLEANSE KEYSTONE CITY OF THIS COMPUTER VIRUS.
THE FLASH IS DOING IT AS WE SPEAK.
I JUST HOPE HIS SANITY... DOESN'T SNAP.
"I'M NOT SURE HOW LONG OUR MINDS HAVE BEEN LINKED TOGETHER, THINKER--"

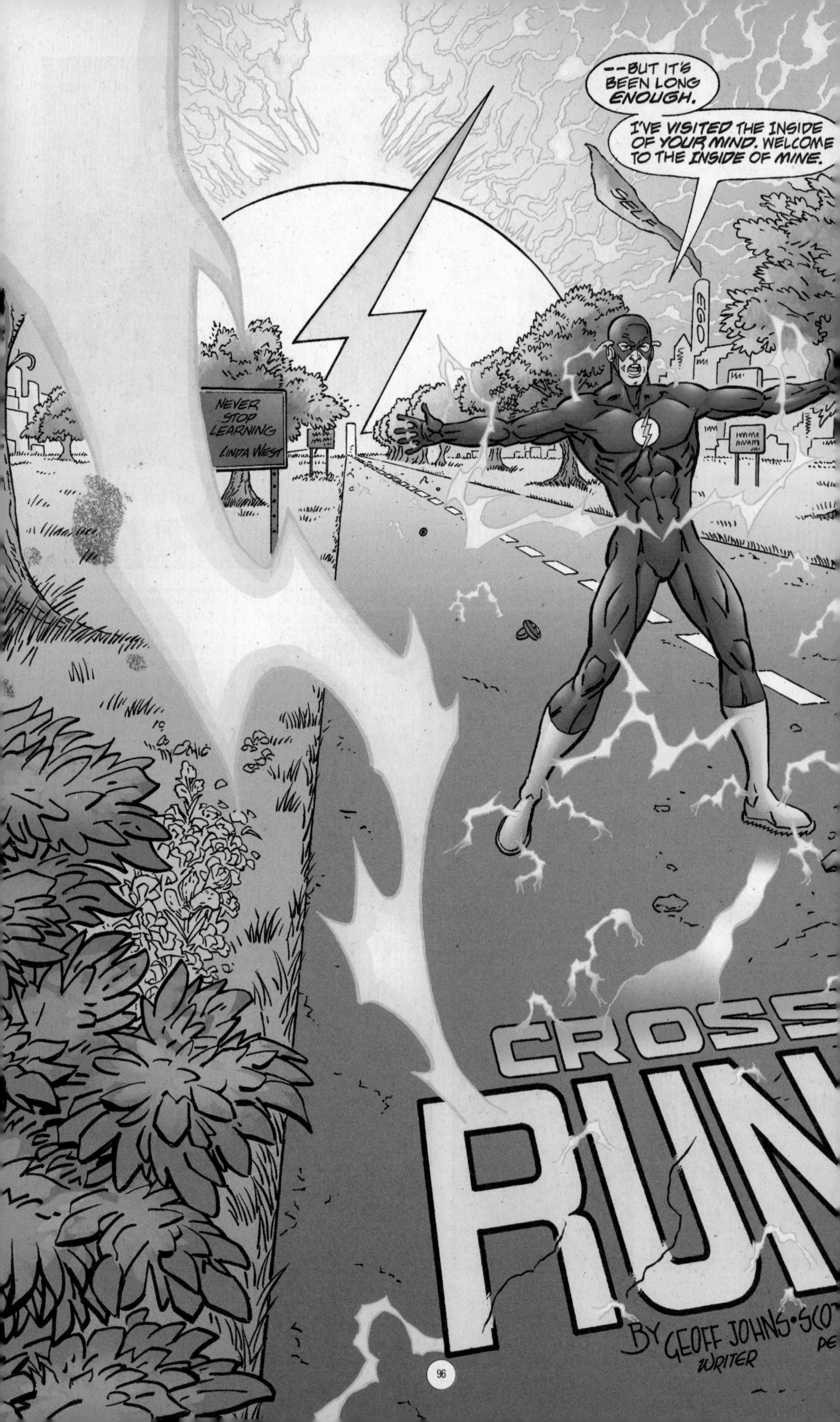

--BUT IT'S BEEN LONG ENOUGH.
I'VE VISITED THE INSIDE OF YOUR MIND. WELCOME TO THE INSIDE OF MINE.
SELF
EGO
NEVER STOP LEARNING LINDA WEST
CROSS
RUN
BY GEOFF JOHNS WRITER

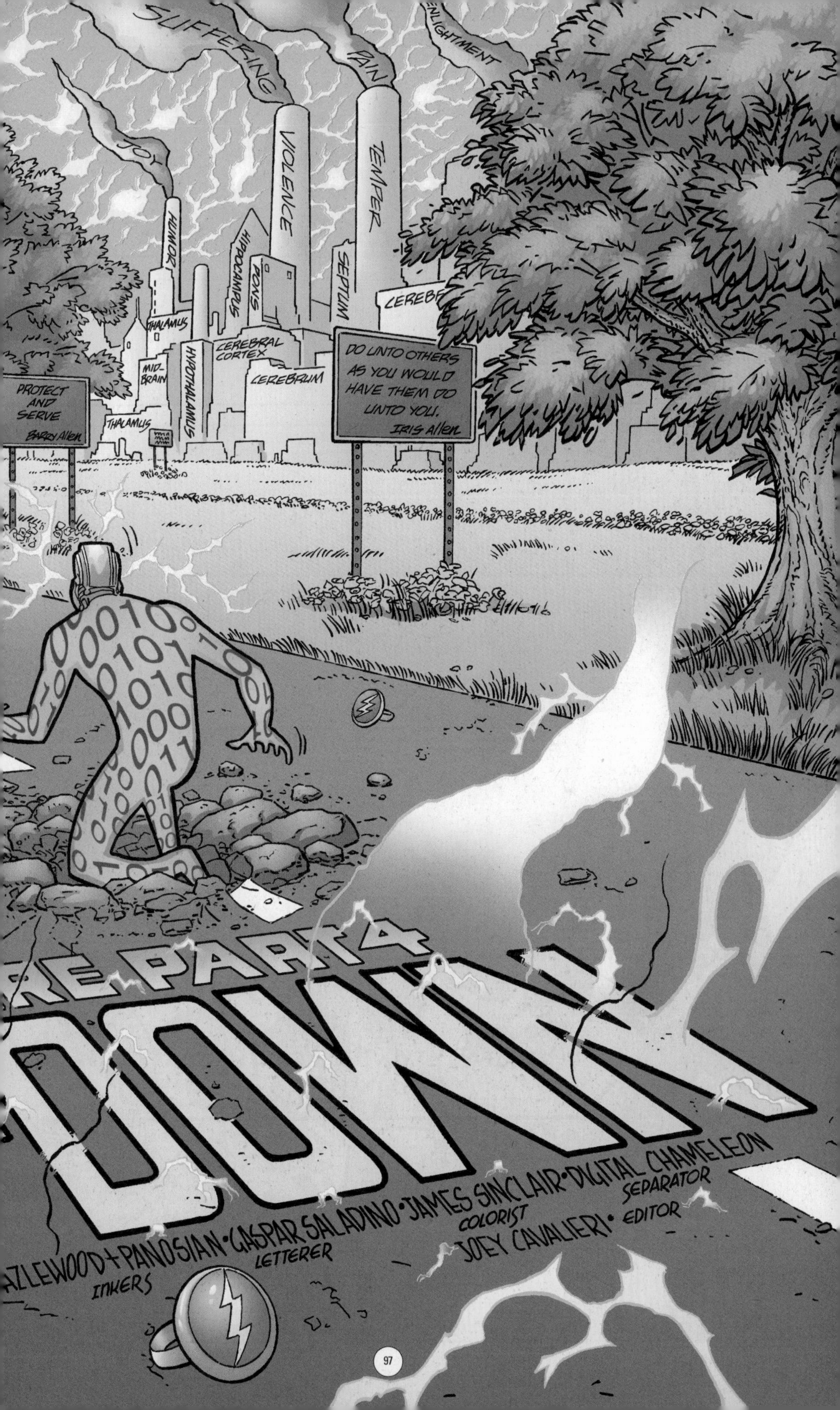

SUFFERING
PAIN
ENLIGHTMENT
JOY
VIOLENCE
TEMPER
HUMOR
HIPPOCAMPUS
PONS
SEPTUM
CEREBR
THALAMUS
CEREBRAL CORTEX
MID-BRAIN
HYPOTHALAMUS
CEREBRUM
THALAMUS
PROTECT AND SERVE
BARRY ALLEN
DO UNTO OTHERS AS YOU WOULD HAVE THEM DO UNTO YOU.
IRIS ALLEN
RE PART 4
DOWN
AZLEWOOD + PANOSIAN · INKERS
GASPAR SALADINO · LETTERER
JAMES SINCLAIR · COLORIST
DIGITAL CHAMELEON · SEPARATOR
JOEY CAVALIERI · EDITOR

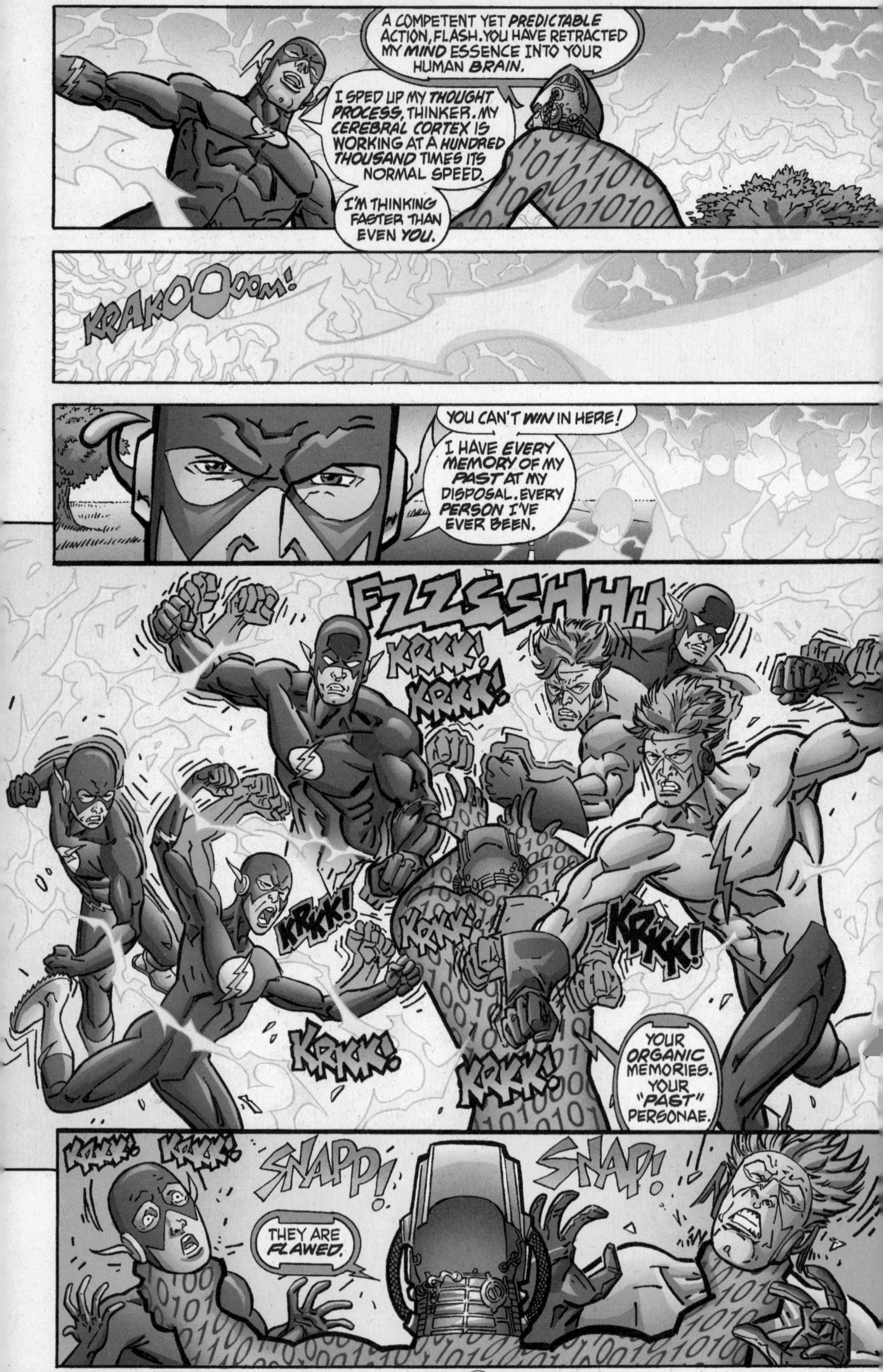
A COMPETENT YET PREDICTABLE ACTION, FLASH. YOU HAVE RETRACTED MY MIND ESSENCE INTO YOUR HUMAN BRAIN.
I SPED UP MY THOUGHT PROCESS, THINKER. MY CEREBRAL CORTEX IS WORKING AT A HUNDRED THOUSAND TIMES ITS NORMAL SPEED.
I'M THINKING FASTER THAN EVEN YOU.
KRAKOOOoom!
YOU CAN'T WIN IN HERE!
I HAVE EVERY MEMORY OF MY PAST AT MY DISPOSAL. EVERY PERSON I'VE EVER BEEN.
FZZSSHHH
KRKK! KRKK!
KRKK!
KRKK!
KRKK!
KRKK!
KRKK!
YOUR ORGANIC MEMORIES. YOUR "PAST" PERSONAE.
KRKK! KRKK!
SNAPP!
SNAP!
THEY ARE FLAWED.

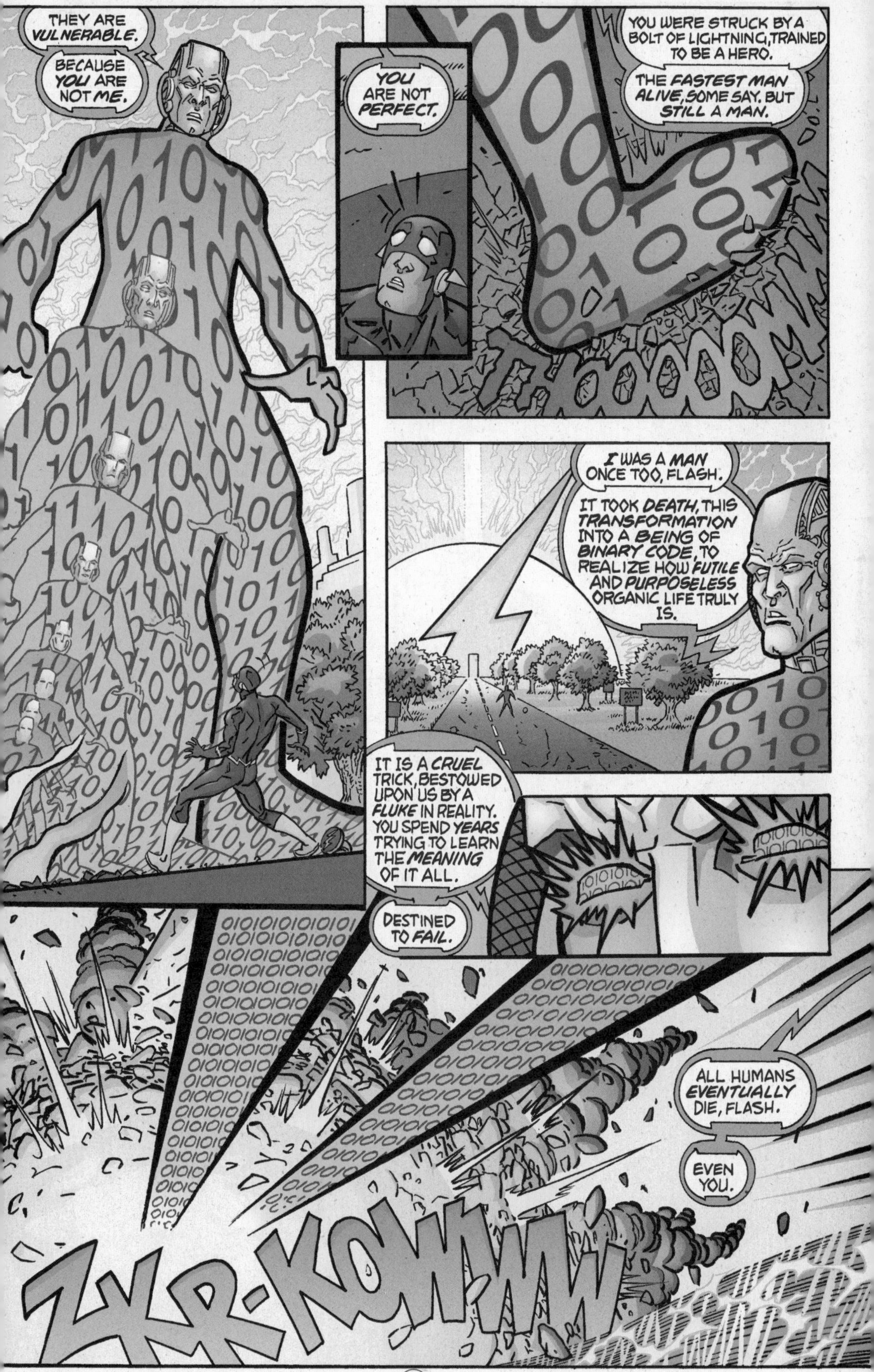
THEY ARE VULNERABLE.
BECAUSE YOU ARE NOT ME.
YOU ARE NOT PERFECT.
YOU WERE STRUCK BY A BOLT OF LIGHTNING, TRAINED TO BE A HERO.
THE FASTEST MAN ALIVE, SOME SAY. BUT STILL A MAN.
I WAS A MAN ONCE TOO, FLASH.
IT TOOK DEATH, THIS TRANSFORMATION INTO A BEING OF BINARY CODE, TO REALIZE HOW FUTILE AND PURPOSELESS ORGANIC LIFE TRULY IS.
IT IS A CRUEL TRICK, BESTOWED UPON US BY A FLUKE IN REALITY. YOU SPEND YEARS TRYING TO LEARN THE MEANING OF IT ALL.
DESTINED TO FAIL.
ALL HUMANS EVENTUALLY DIE, FLASH.
EVEN YOU.
ZZR-KOWWW

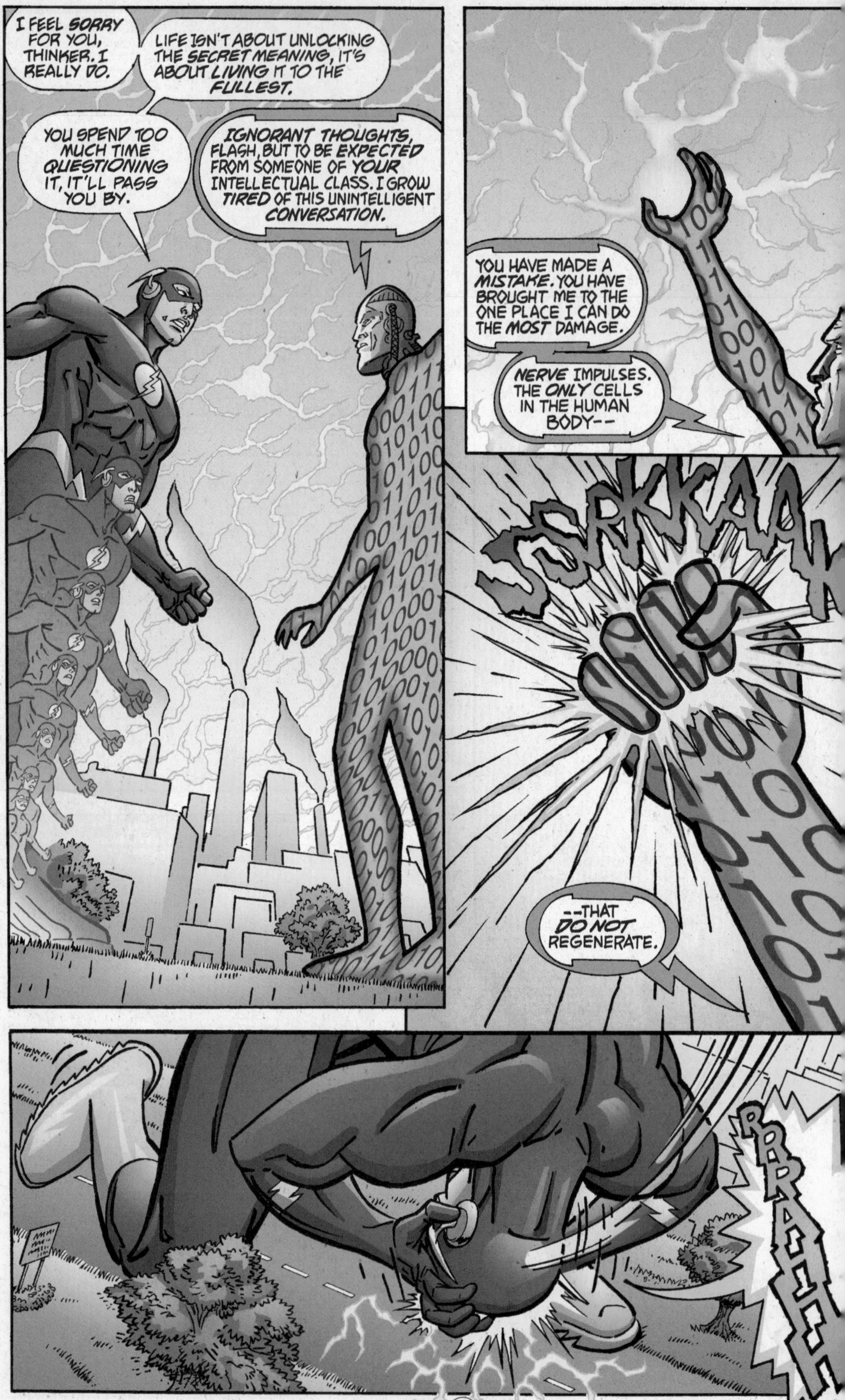
I FEEL SORRY FOR YOU, THINKER. I REALLY DO.
LIFE ISN'T ABOUT UNLOCKING THE SECRET MEANING, IT'S ABOUT LIVING IT TO THE FULLEST.
YOU SPEND TOO MUCH TIME QUESTIONING IT, IT'LL PASS YOU BY.
IGNORANT THOUGHTS, FLASH, BUT TO BE EXPECTED FROM SOMEONE OF YOUR INTELLECTUAL CLASS. I GROW TIRED OF THIS UNINTELLIGENT CONVERSATION.
YOU HAVE MADE A MISTAKE. YOU HAVE BROUGHT ME TO THE ONE PLACE I CAN DO THE MOST DAMAGE.
NERVE IMPULSES. THE ONLY CELLS IN THE HUMAN BODY--
SSRKKAAAK
--THAT DO NOT REGENERATE.

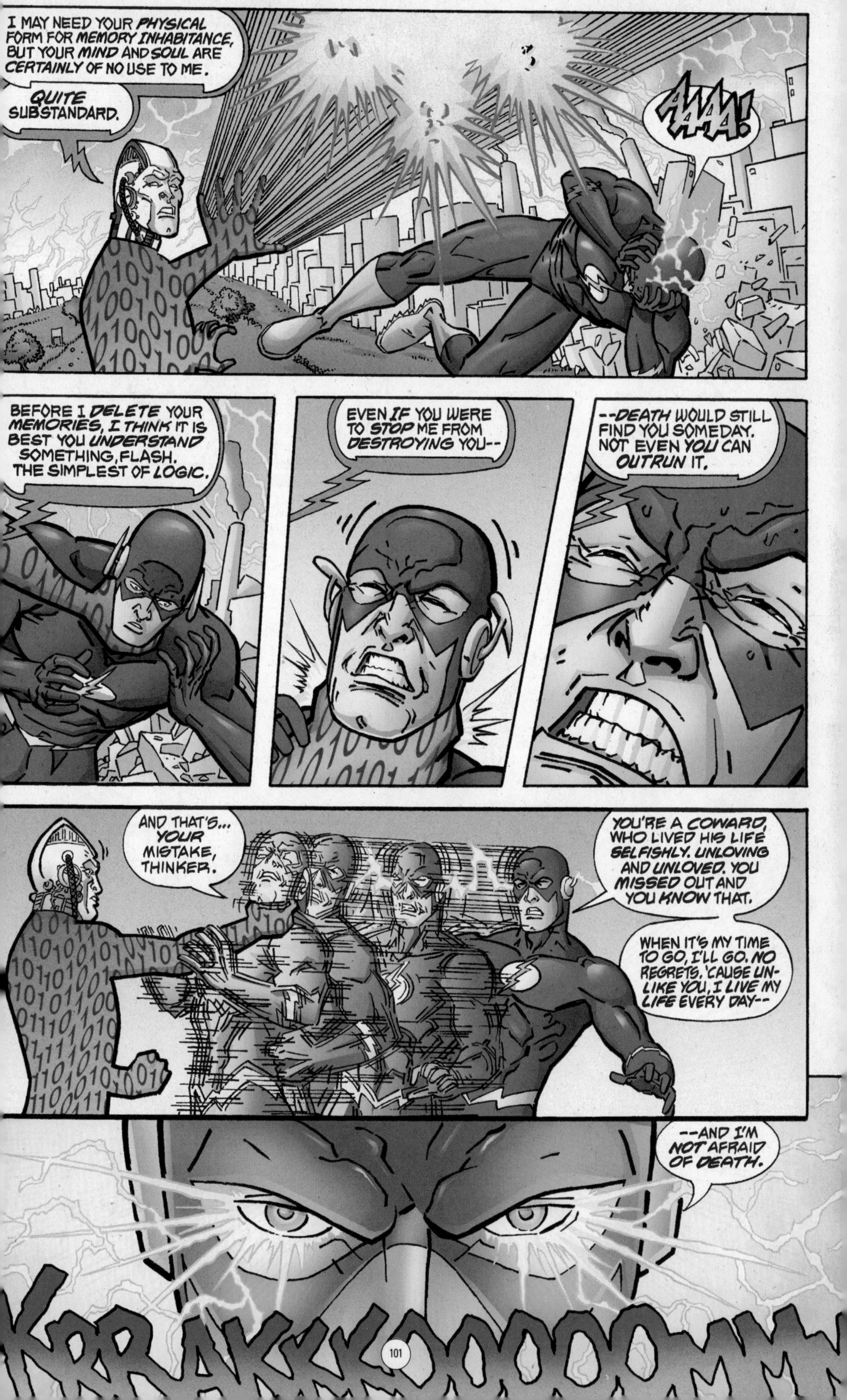

I MAY NEED YOUR PHYSICAL FORM FOR MEMORY INHABITANCE, BUT YOUR MIND AND SOUL ARE CERTAINLY OF NO USE TO ME.
QUITE SUBSTANDARD.
AAAA!
BEFORE I DELETE YOUR MEMORIES, I THINK IT IS BEST YOU UNDERSTAND SOMETHING, FLASH. THE SIMPLEST OF LOGIC.
EVEN IF YOU WERE TO STOP ME FROM DESTROYING YOU--
--DEATH WOULD STILL FIND YOU SOMEDAY. NOT EVEN YOU CAN OUTRUN IT.
AND THAT'S... YOUR MISTAKE, THINKER.
YOU'RE A COWARD, WHO LIVED HIS LIFE SELFISHLY. UNLOVING AND UNLOVED. YOU MISSED OUT AND YOU KNOW THAT.
WHEN IT'S MY TIME TO GO, I'LL GO. NO REGRETS. 'CAUSE UN-LIKE YOU, I LIVE MY LIFE EVERY DAY--
--AND I'M NOT AFRAID OF DEATH.
KRRAKKOOOOOMM

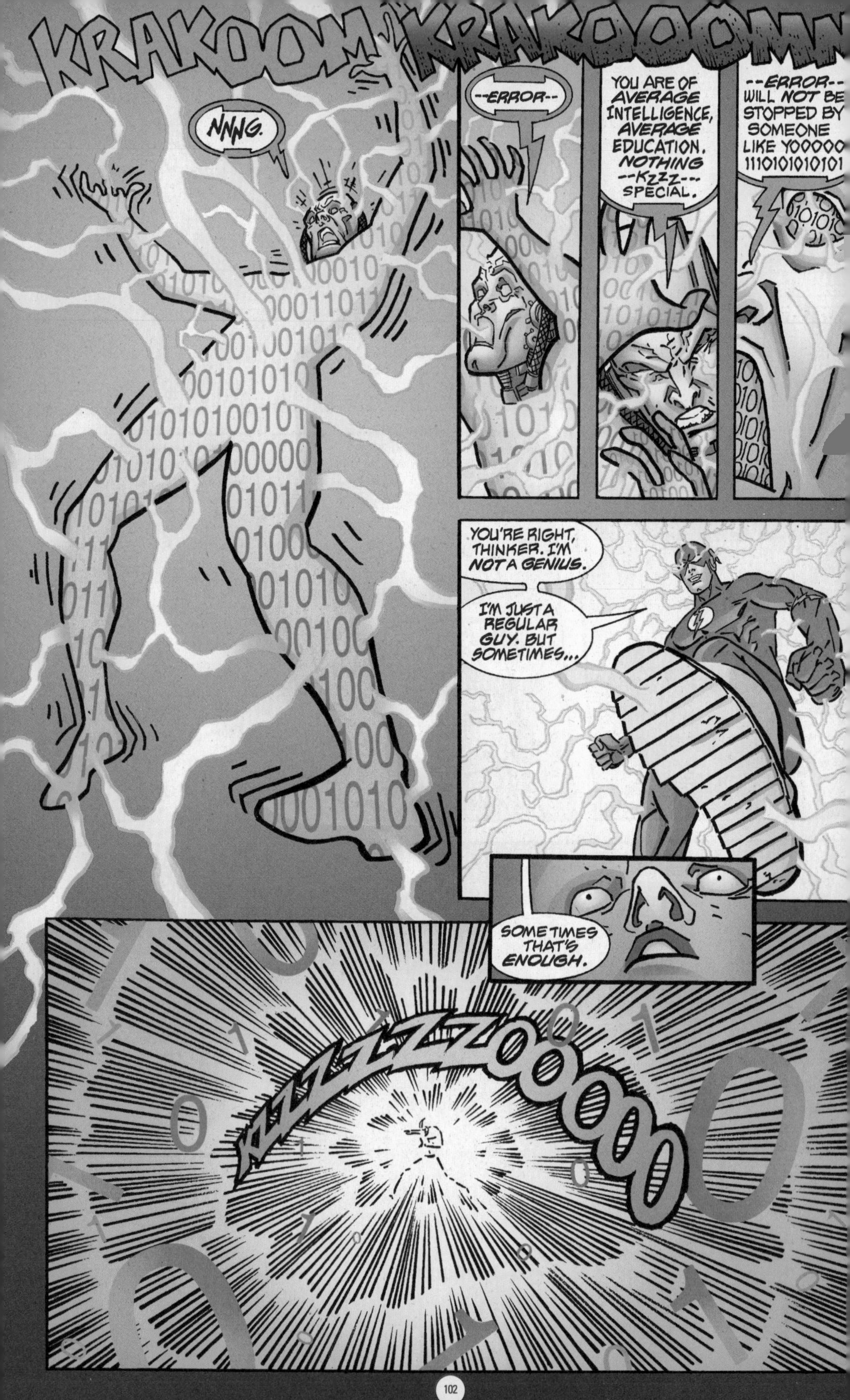
KRAKOOM KRAKOOOM
NNNG.
--ERROR--
YOU ARE OF AVERAGE INTELLIGENCE, AVERAGE EDUCATION. NOTHING --KZZZ--- SPECIAL.
--ERROR-- WILL NOT BE STOPPED BY SOMEONE LIKE YOOOOO 1110101010101
YOU'RE RIGHT, THINKER. I'M NOT A GENIUS.
I'M JUST A REGULAR GUY. BUT SOMETIMES...
SOMETIMES THAT'S ENOUGH.
KZZZZZOOOOOO

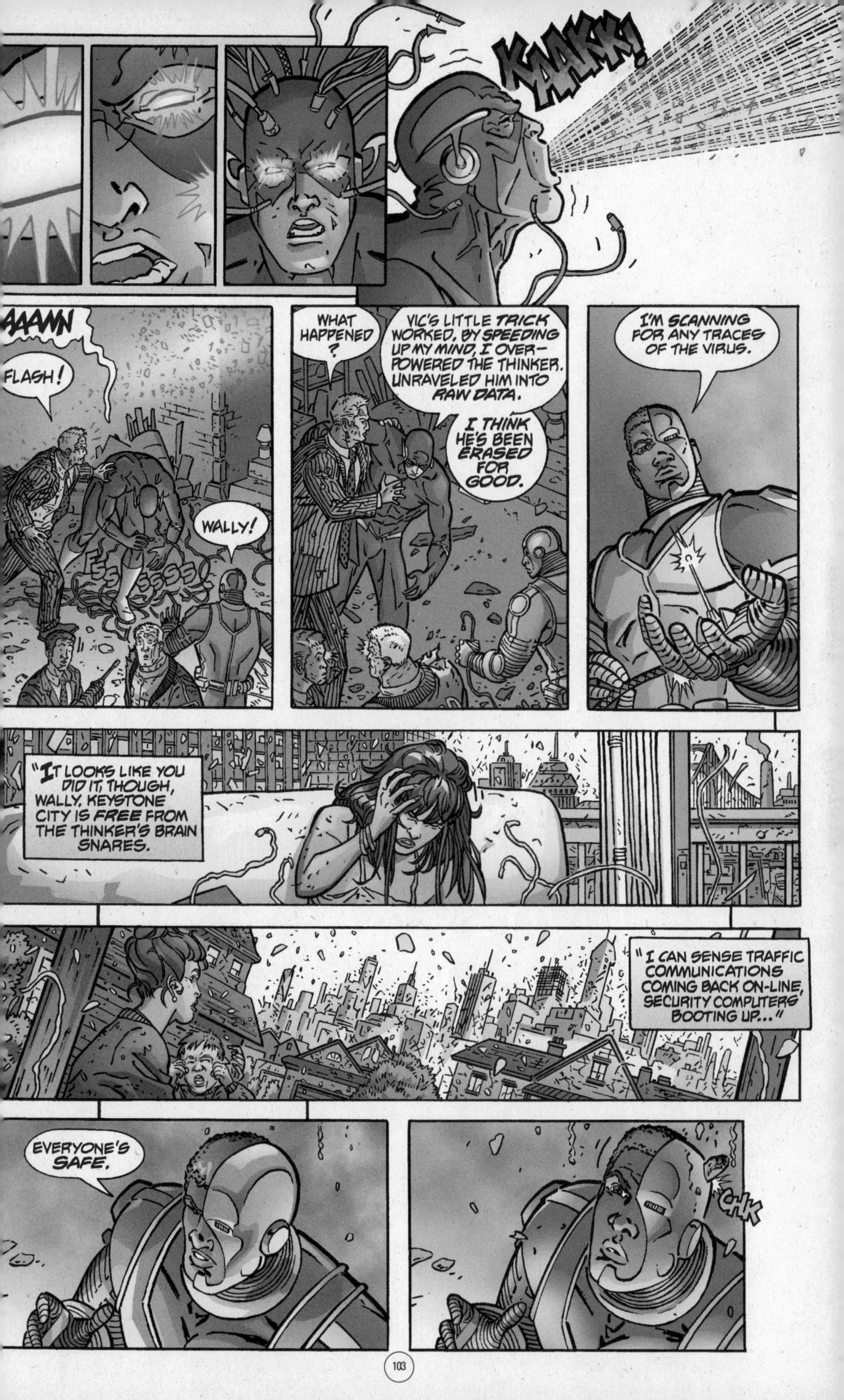
KAAKK!
AAAWN
FLASH!
WALLY!
FSSSSSSSS
WHAT HAPPENED?
VIC'S LITTLE TRICK WORKED. BY SPEEDING UP MY MIND, I OVER-POWERED THE THINKER. UNRAVELED HIM INTO RAW DATA.
I THINK HE'S BEEN ERASED FOR GOOD.
I'M SCANNING FOR ANY TRACES OF THE VIRUS.
"IT LOOKS LIKE YOU DID IT, THOUGH, WALLY. KEYSTONE CITY IS FREE FROM THE THINKER'S BRAIN SNARES.
"I CAN SENSE TRAFFIC COMMUNICATIONS COMING BACK ON-LINE, SECURITY COMPUTERS BOOTING UP..."
EVERYONE'S SAFE.
CHK

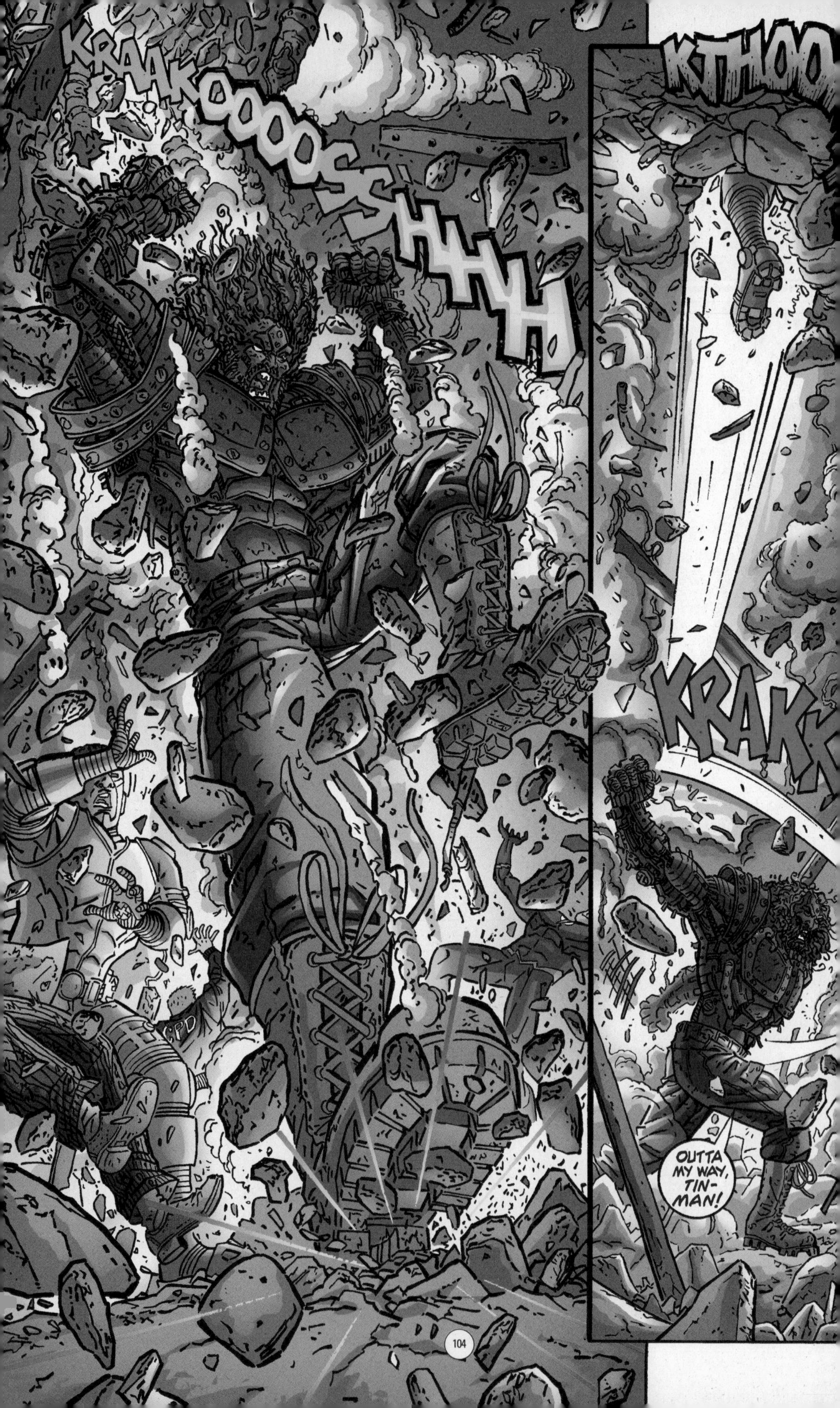

KRAAKOOOOSSHHHH
KTHOO
KRAKK
OUTTA MY WAY, TIN-MAN!

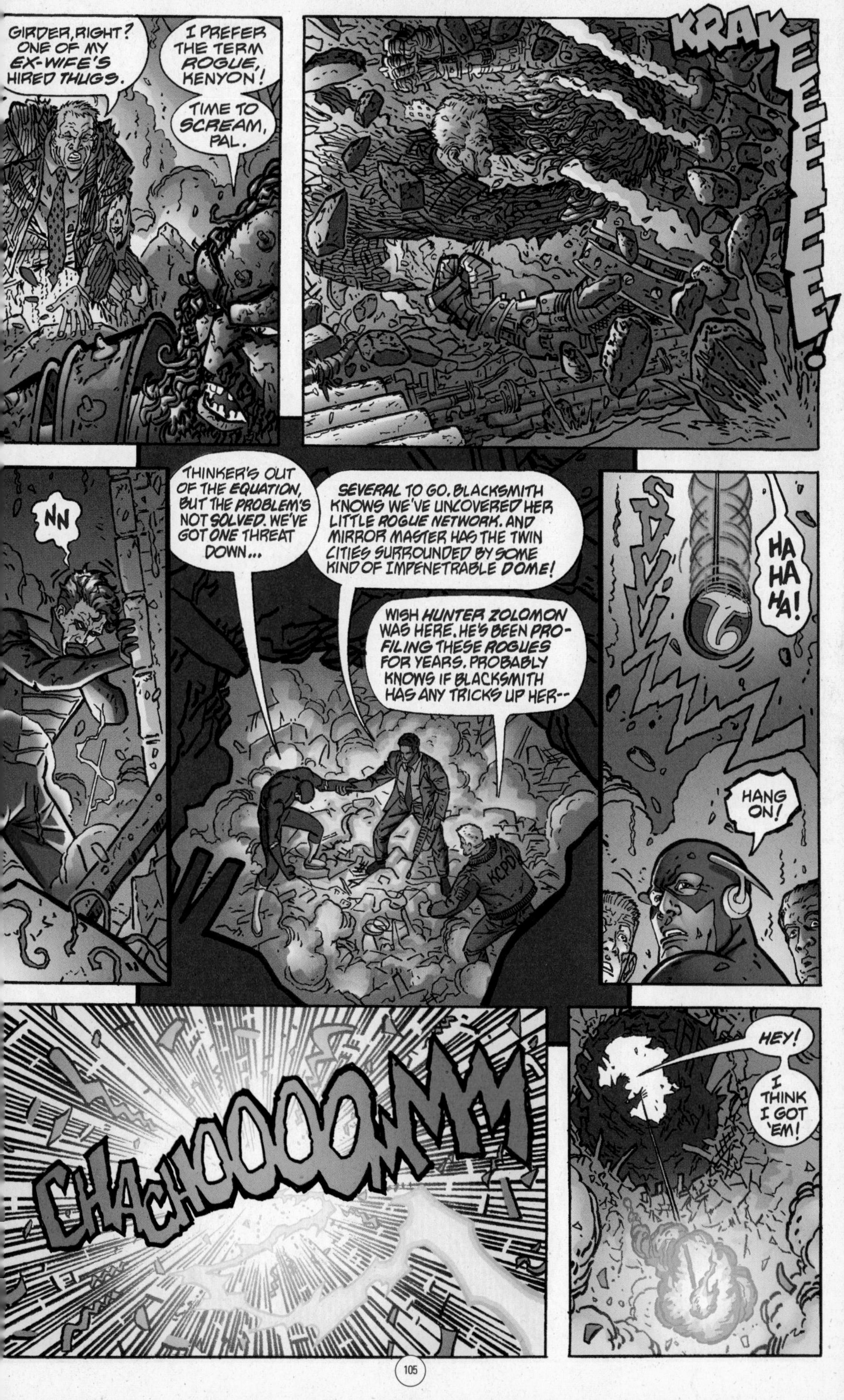
GIRDER, RIGHT? ONE OF MY EX-WIFE'S HIRED THUGS.
I PREFER THE TERM ROGUE, KENYON!
TIME TO SCREAM, PAL.
KRAKEEEEEE!
NN
THINKER'S OUT OF THE EQUATION, BUT THE PROBLEM'S NOT SOLVED. WE'VE GOT ONE THREAT DOWN...
SEVERAL TO GO. BLACKSMITH KNOWS WE'VE UNCOVERED HER LITTLE ROGUE NETWORK. AND MIRROR MASTER HAS THE TWIN CITIES SURROUNDED BY SOME KIND OF IMPENETRABLE DOME!
WISH HUNTER ZOLOMON WAS HERE. HE'S BEEN PROFILING THESE ROGUES FOR YEARS. PROBABLY KNOWS IF BLACKSMITH HAS ANY TRICKS UP HER--
KCPD
HA HA HA!
HANG ON!
CHACHOOOOMMM
HEY!
I THINK I GOT 'EM!

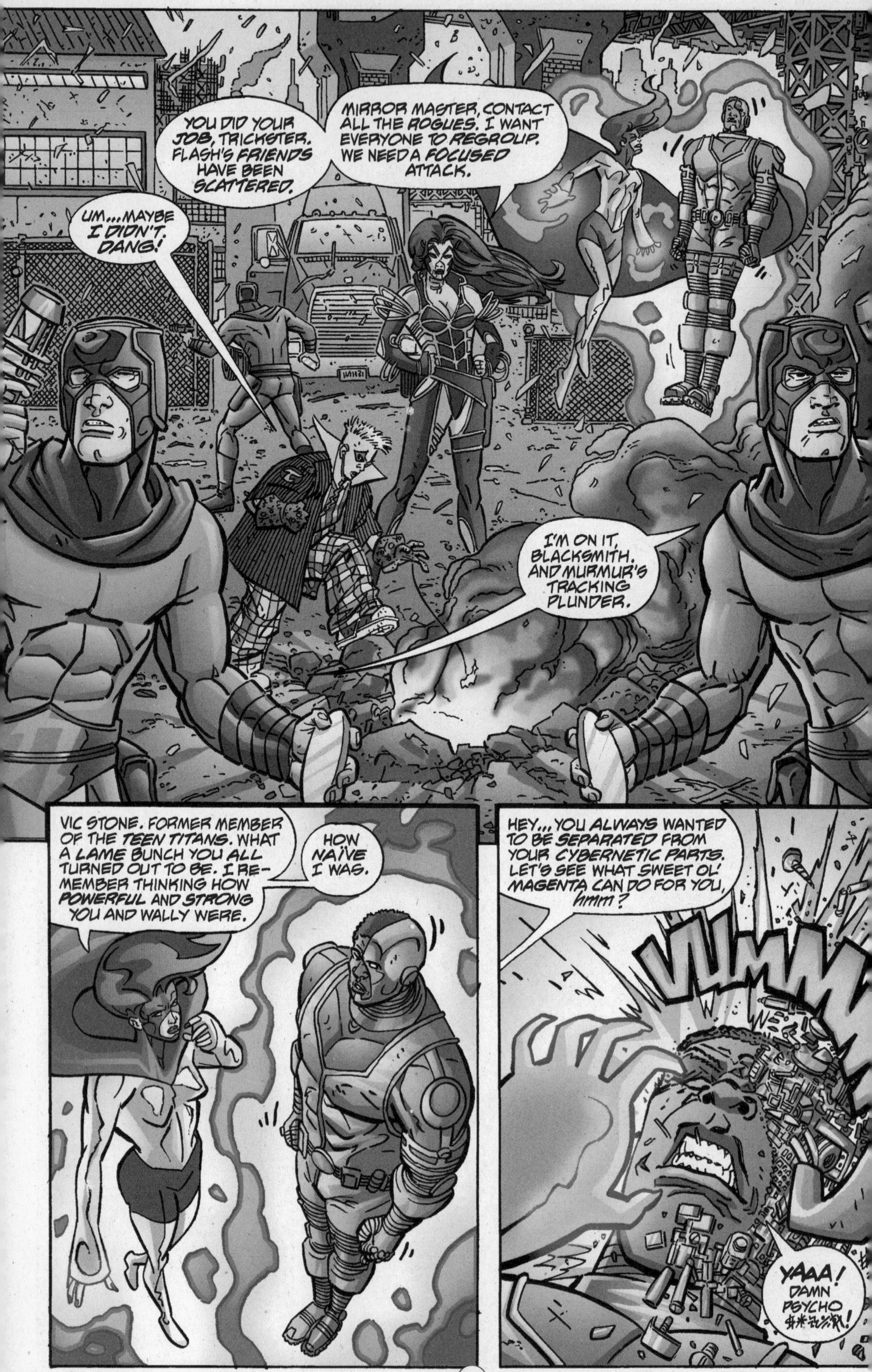
YOU DID YOUR JOB, TRICKSTER. FLASH'S FRIENDS HAVE BEEN SCATTERED.
MIRROR MASTER, CONTACT ALL THE ROGUES. I WANT EVERYONE TO REGROUP. WE NEED A FOCUSED ATTACK.
UM...MAYBE I DIDN'T. DANG!
I'M ON IT, BLACKSMITH. AND MURMUR'S TRACKING PLUNDER.
VIC STONE. FORMER MEMBER OF THE TEEN TITANS. WHAT A LAME BUNCH YOU ALL TURNED OUT TO BE. I REMEMBER THINKING HOW POWERFUL AND STRONG YOU AND WALLY WERE.
HOW NAÏVE I WAS.
HEY... YOU ALWAYS WANTED TO BE SEPARATED FROM YOUR CYBERNETIC PARTS. LET'S SEE WHAT SWEET OL' MAGENTA CAN DO FOR YOU, hmm?
VUMMM
YAAA! DAMN PSYCHO $*%#!

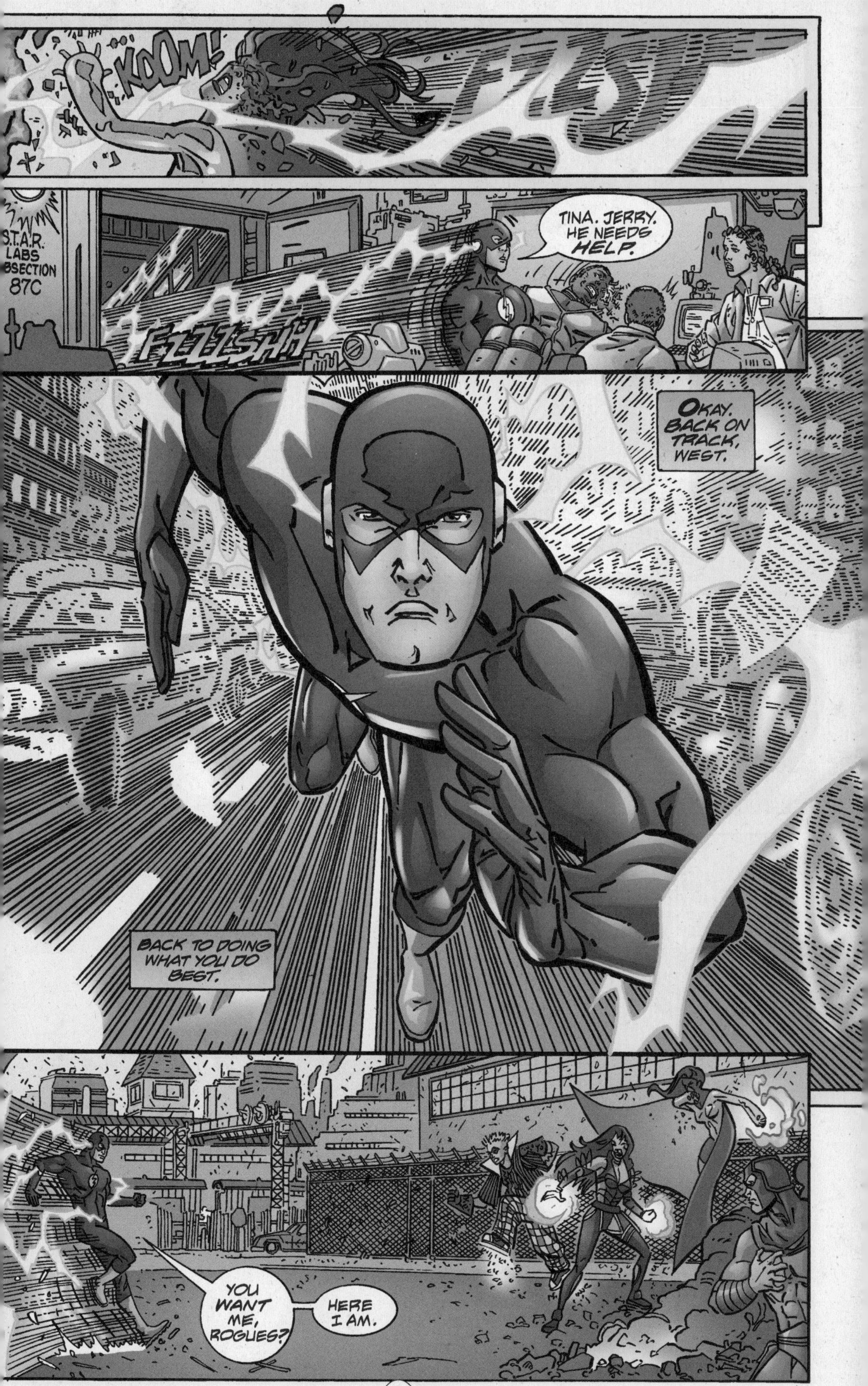
KOOM!
FZZST
S.T.A.R. LABS SUBSECTION 87C
TINA. JERRY. HE NEEDS HELP.
FZZSHH
OKAY. BACK ON TRACK, WEST.
BACK TO DOING WHAT YOU DO BEST.
YOU WANT ME, ROGUES?
HERE I AM.

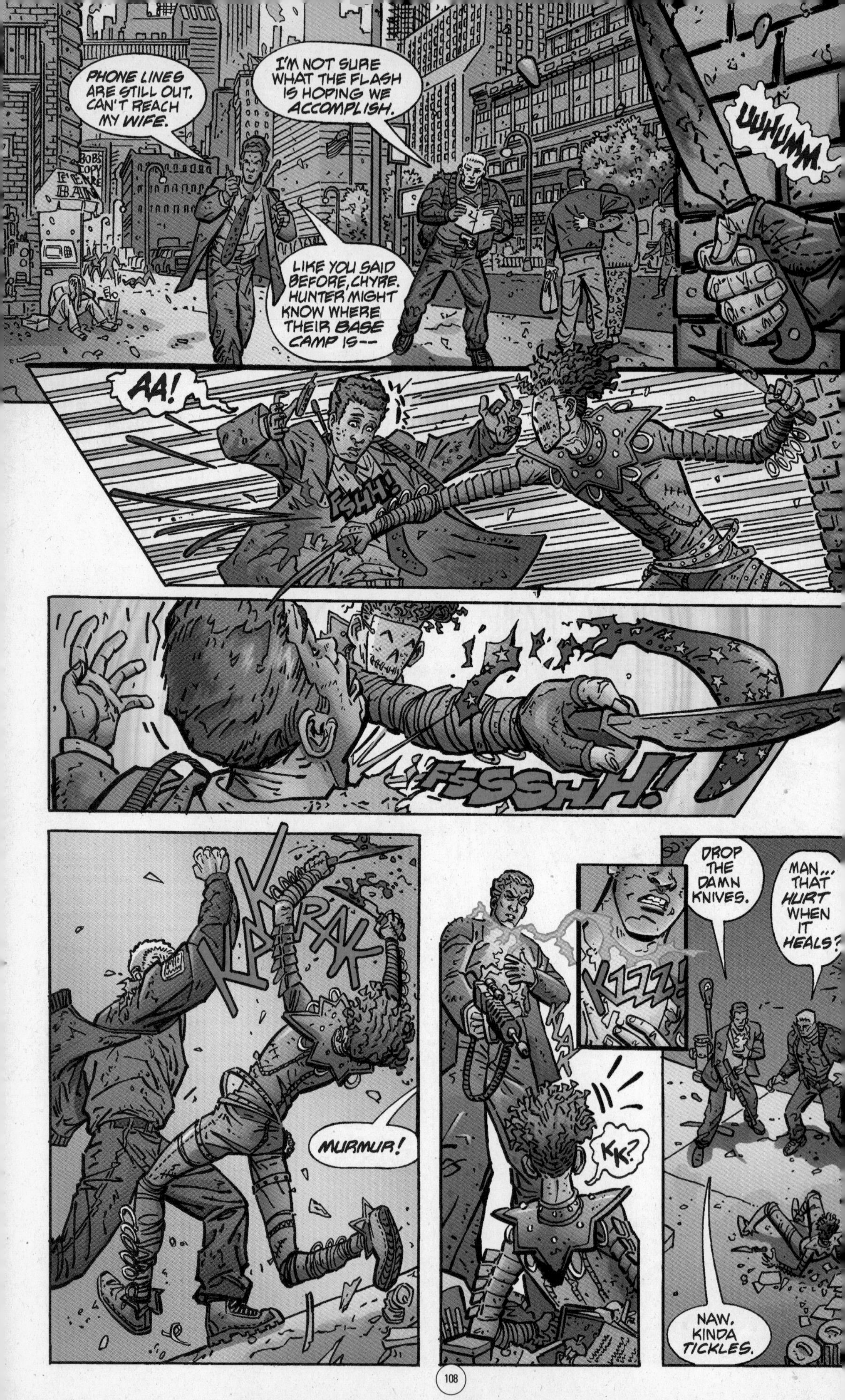
PHONE LINES ARE STILL OUT. CAN'T REACH MY WIFE.
I'M NOT SURE WHAT THE FLASH IS HOPING WE ACCOMPLISH.
LIKE YOU SAID BEFORE, CHYRE. HUNTER MIGHT KNOW WHERE THEIR BASE CAMP IS--
UUHUMM.
AA!
FSHH!
FSSSHH!
KRAK
MURMUR!
KIZZ!
DROP THE DAMN KNIVES.
KK?
MAN... THAT HURT WHEN IT HEALS?
NAW. KINDA TICKLES.

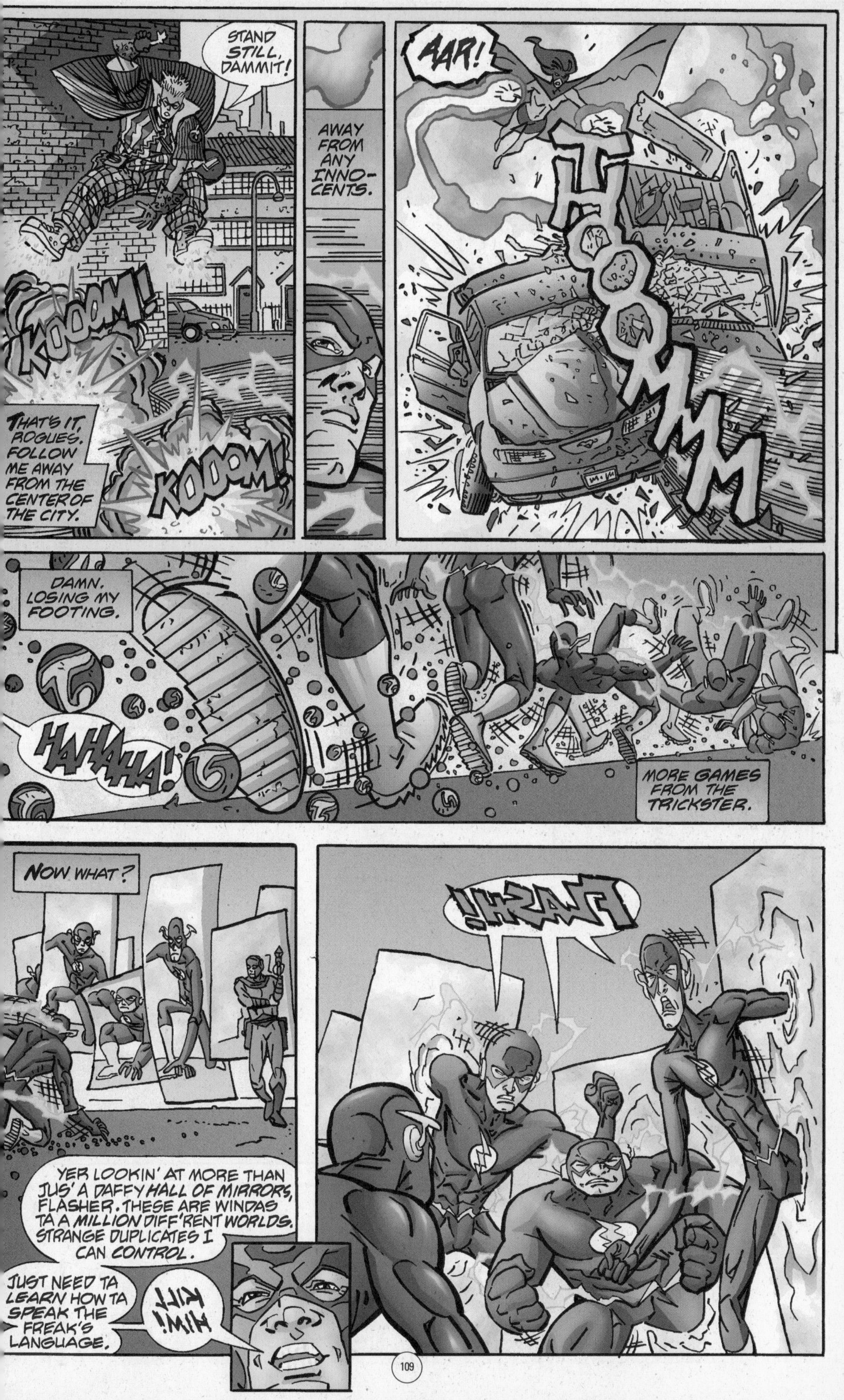

STAND STILL, DAMMIT!
KOOOM!
THAT'S IT, ROGUES. FOLLOW ME AWAY FROM THE CENTER OF THE CITY.
KOOOM!
AWAY FROM ANY INNOCENTS.
AAR!
THOOMMM
DAMN. LOSING MY FOOTING.
HAHAHA!
MORE GAMES FROM THE TRICKSTER.
NOW WHAT?
YER LOOKIN' AT MORE THAN JUS' A DAFFY HALL OF MIRRORS, FLASHER. THESE ARE WINDAS TA A MILLION DIFF'RENT WORLDS. STRANGE DUPLICATES I CAN CONTROL.
JUST NEED TA LEARN HOW TA SPEAK THE FREAK'S LANGUAGE.
KILL HIM!
FLASH!

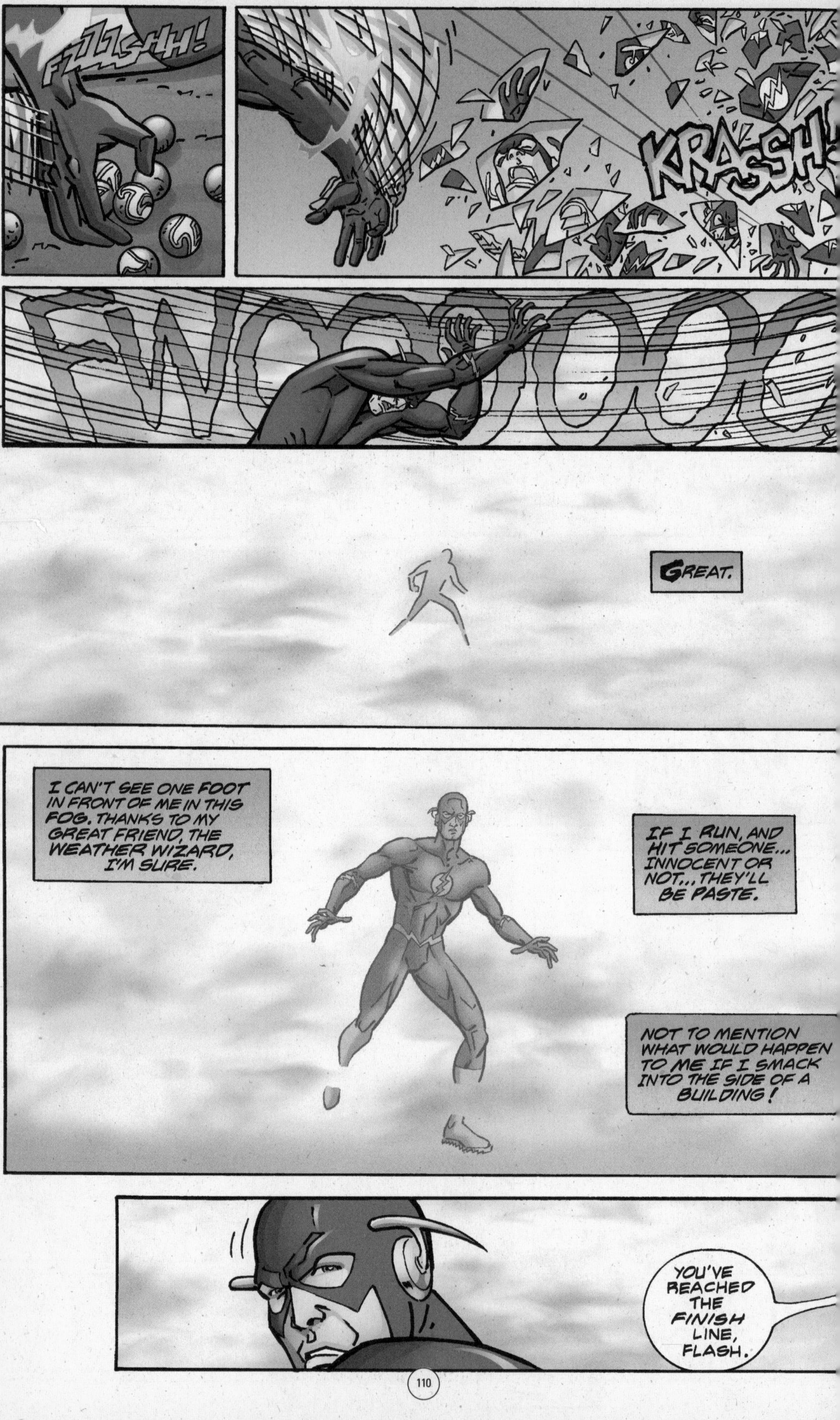

FZZZSHH!
KRASSH!
FWOOOOOOOOM
GREAT.
I CAN'T SEE ONE FOOT IN FRONT OF ME IN THIS FOG. THANKS TO MY GREAT FRIEND, THE WEATHER WIZARD, I'M SURE.
IF I RUN, AND HIT SOMEONE... INNOCENT OR NOT... THEY'LL BE PASTE.
NOT TO MENTION WHAT WOULD HAPPEN TO ME IF I SMACK INTO THE SIDE OF A BUILDING!
YOU'VE REACHED THE FINISH LINE, FLASH.

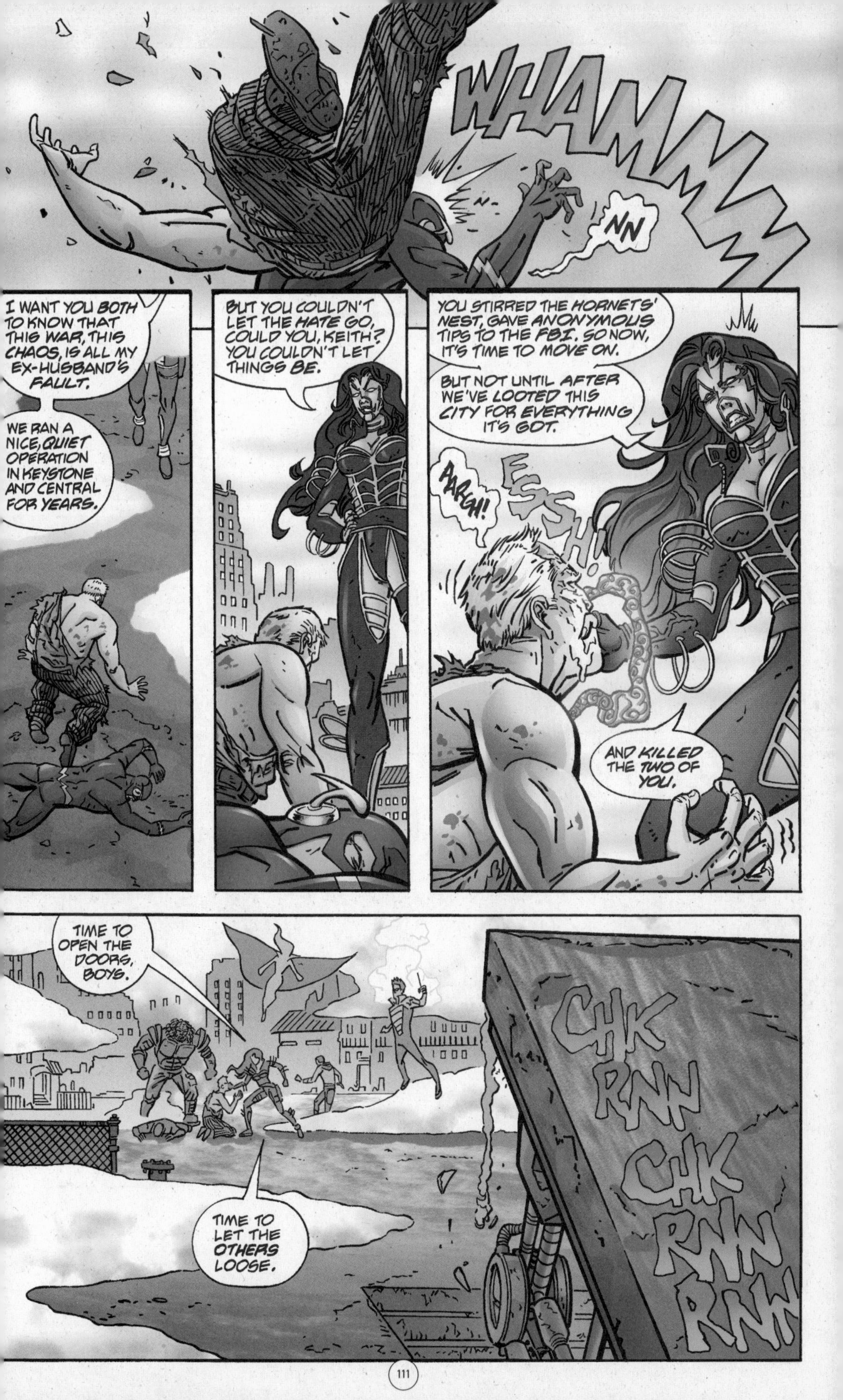
WHAMMMM
NN
I WANT YOU BOTH TO KNOW THAT THIS WAR, THIS CHAOS, IS ALL MY EX-HUSBAND'S FAULT.
WE RAN A NICE, QUIET OPERATION IN KEYSTONE AND CENTRAL FOR YEARS.
BUT YOU COULDN'T LET THE HATE GO, COULD YOU, KEITH? YOU COULDN'T LET THINGS BE.
YOU STIRRED THE HORNETS' NEST, GAVE ANONYMOUS TIPS TO THE FBI. SO NOW, IT'S TIME TO MOVE ON.
BUT NOT UNTIL AFTER WE'VE LOOTED THIS CITY FOR EVERYTHING IT'S GOT.
AARGH!
ESSSH!
AND KILLED THE TWO OF YOU.
TIME TO OPEN THE DOORS, BOYS.
TIME TO LET THE OTHERS LOOSE.
CHK RNN
CHK RNN RNN

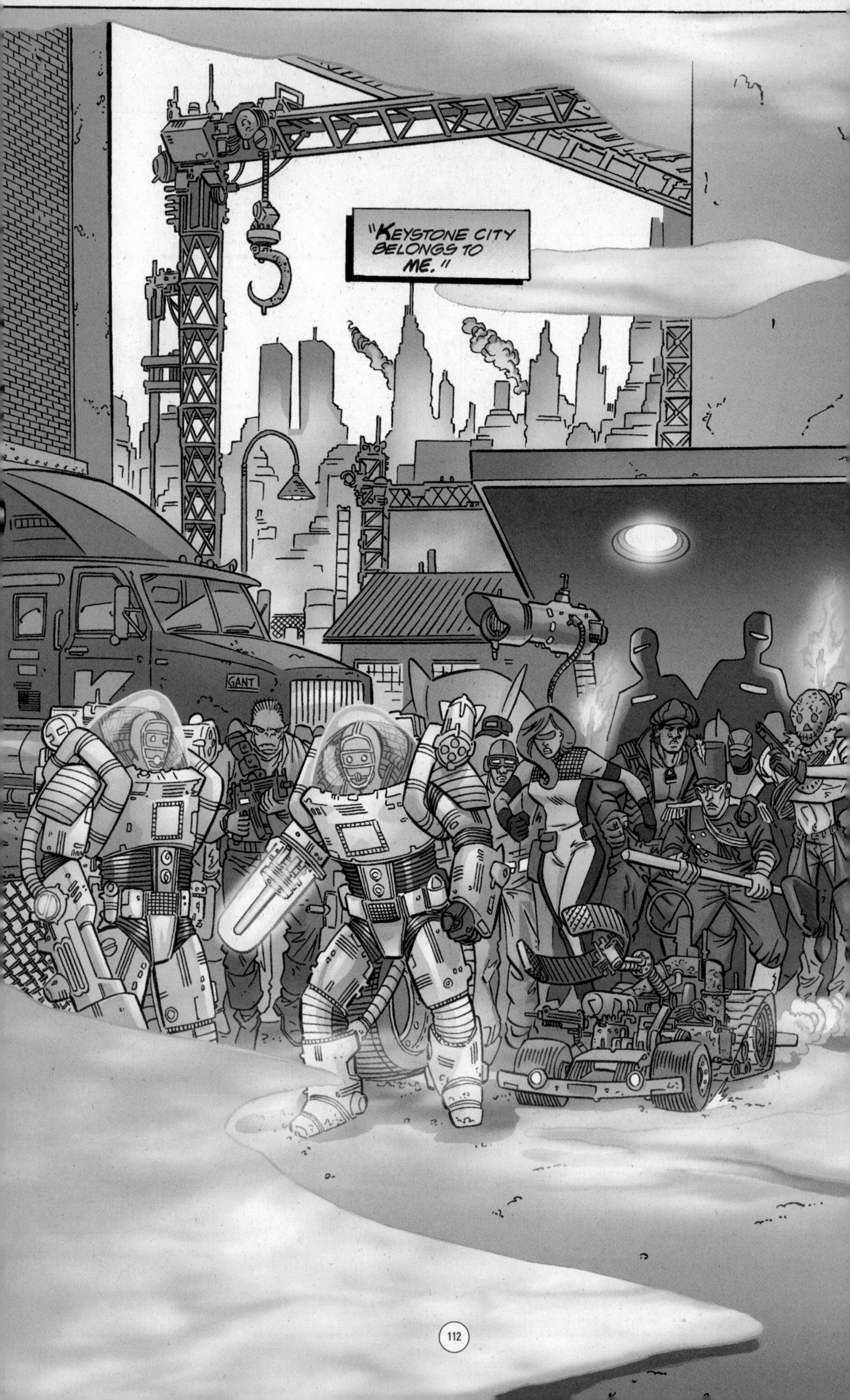
"KEYSTONE CITY BELONGS TO ME."
GANT

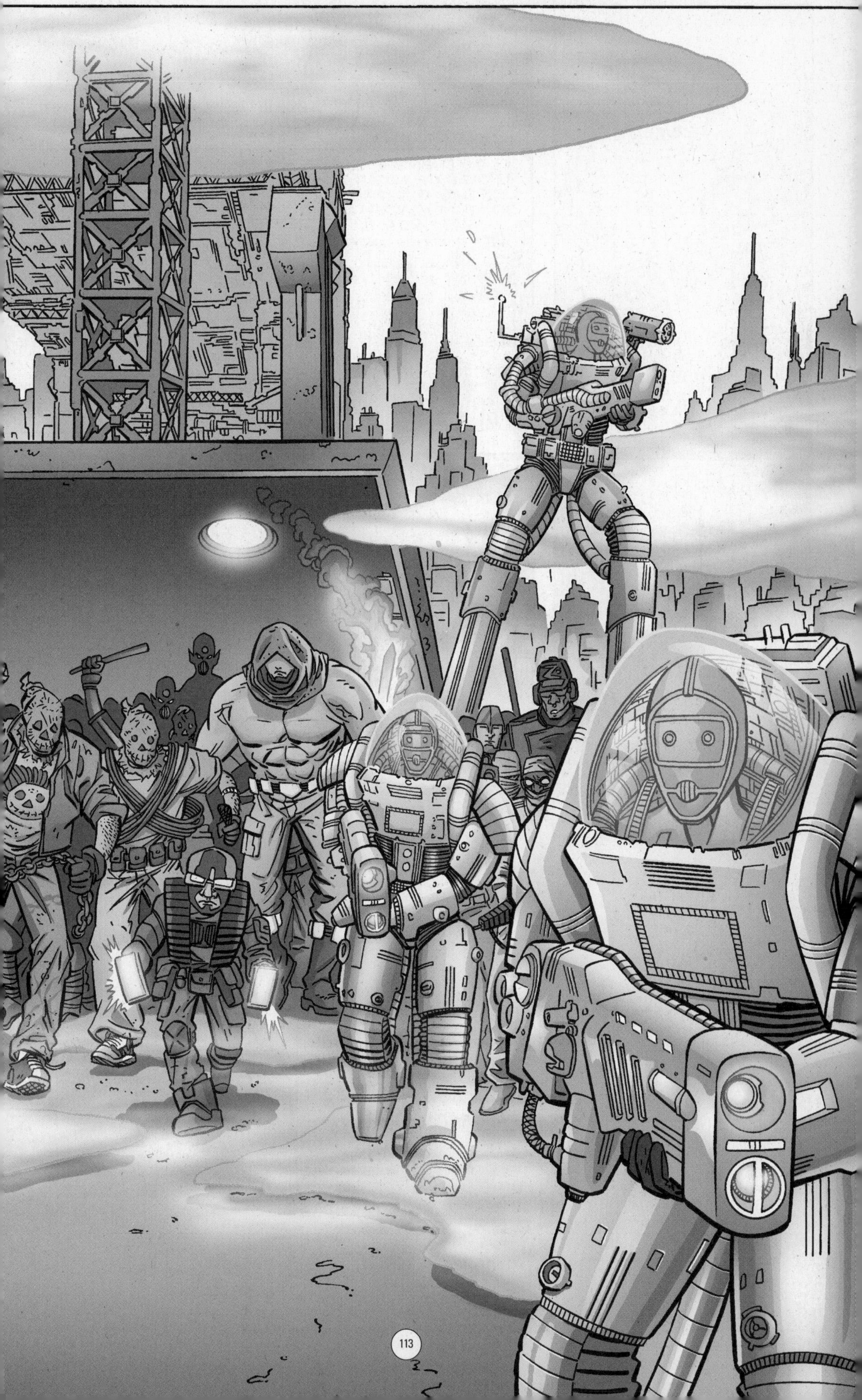

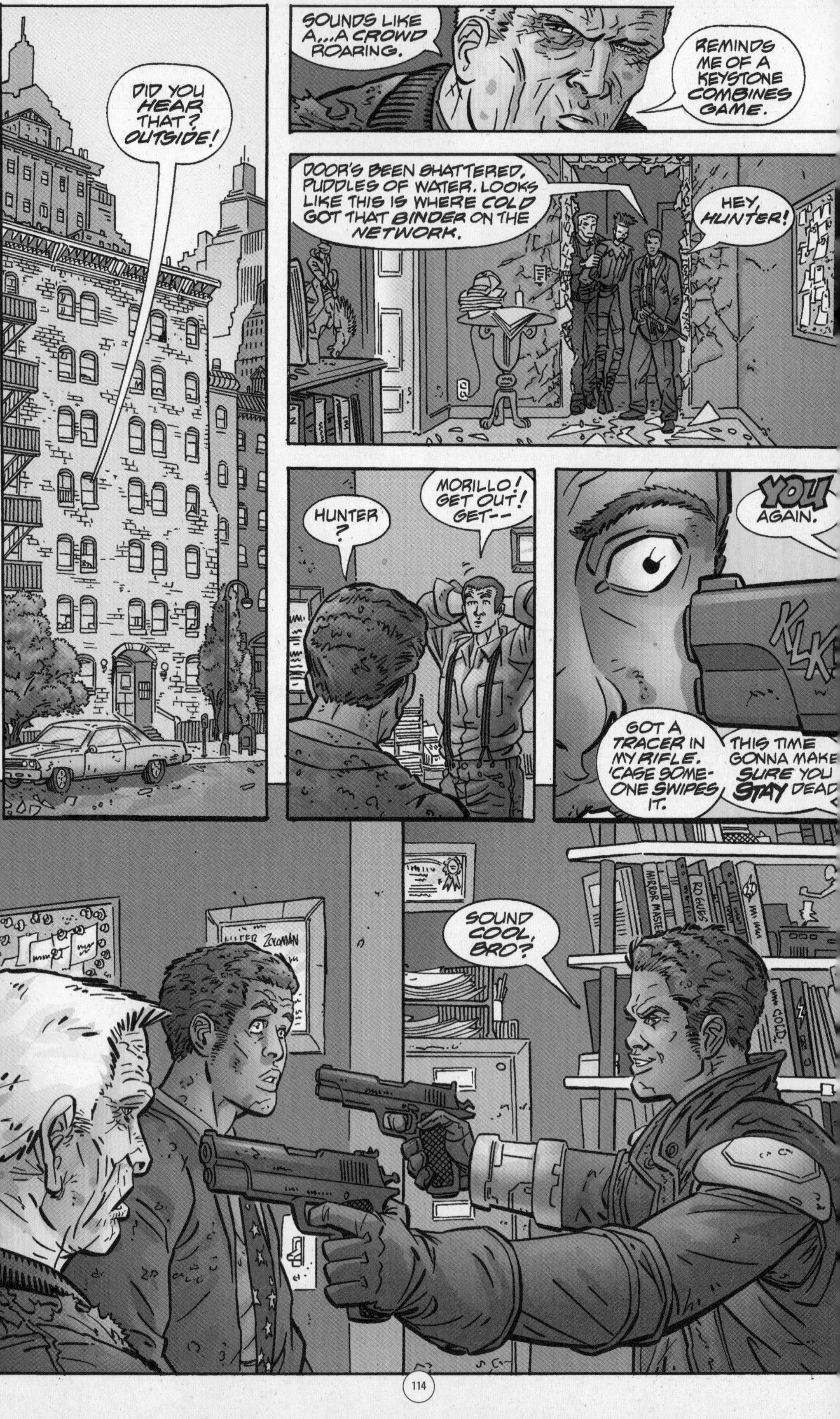
DID YOU HEAR THAT? OUTSIDE!
SOUNDS LIKE A...A CROWD ROARING.
REMINDS ME OF A KEYSTONE COMBINES GAME.
DOOR'S BEEN SHATTERED, PUDDLES OF WATER. LOOKS LIKE THIS IS WHERE COLD GOT THAT BINDER ON THE NETWORK.
HEY, HUNTER!
HUNTER?
MORILLO! GET OUT! GET--
YOU AGAIN.
KLK
GOT A TRACER IN MY RIFLE. 'CASE SOME-ONE SWIPES IT.
THIS TIME GONNA MAKE SURE YOU STAY DEAD
SOUND COOL, BRO?
MIRROR MASTER
RD GUSS
COLD

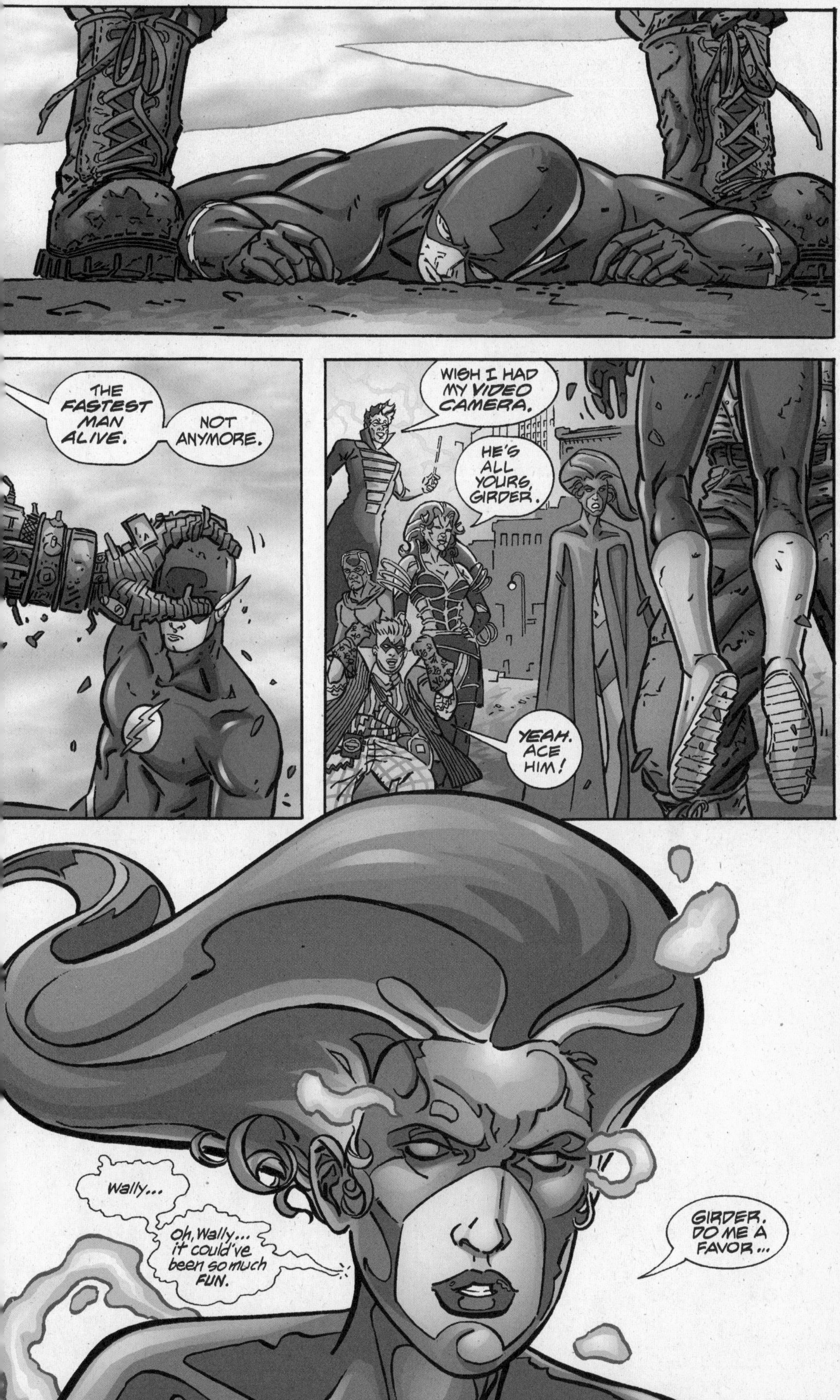
THE FASTEST MAN ALIVE.
NOT ANYMORE.
WISH I HAD MY VIDEO CAMERA.
HE'S ALL YOURS, GIRDER.
YEAH. ACE HIM!
Wally...
Oh, Wally... it could've been so much FUN.
GIRDER. DO ME A FAVOR...

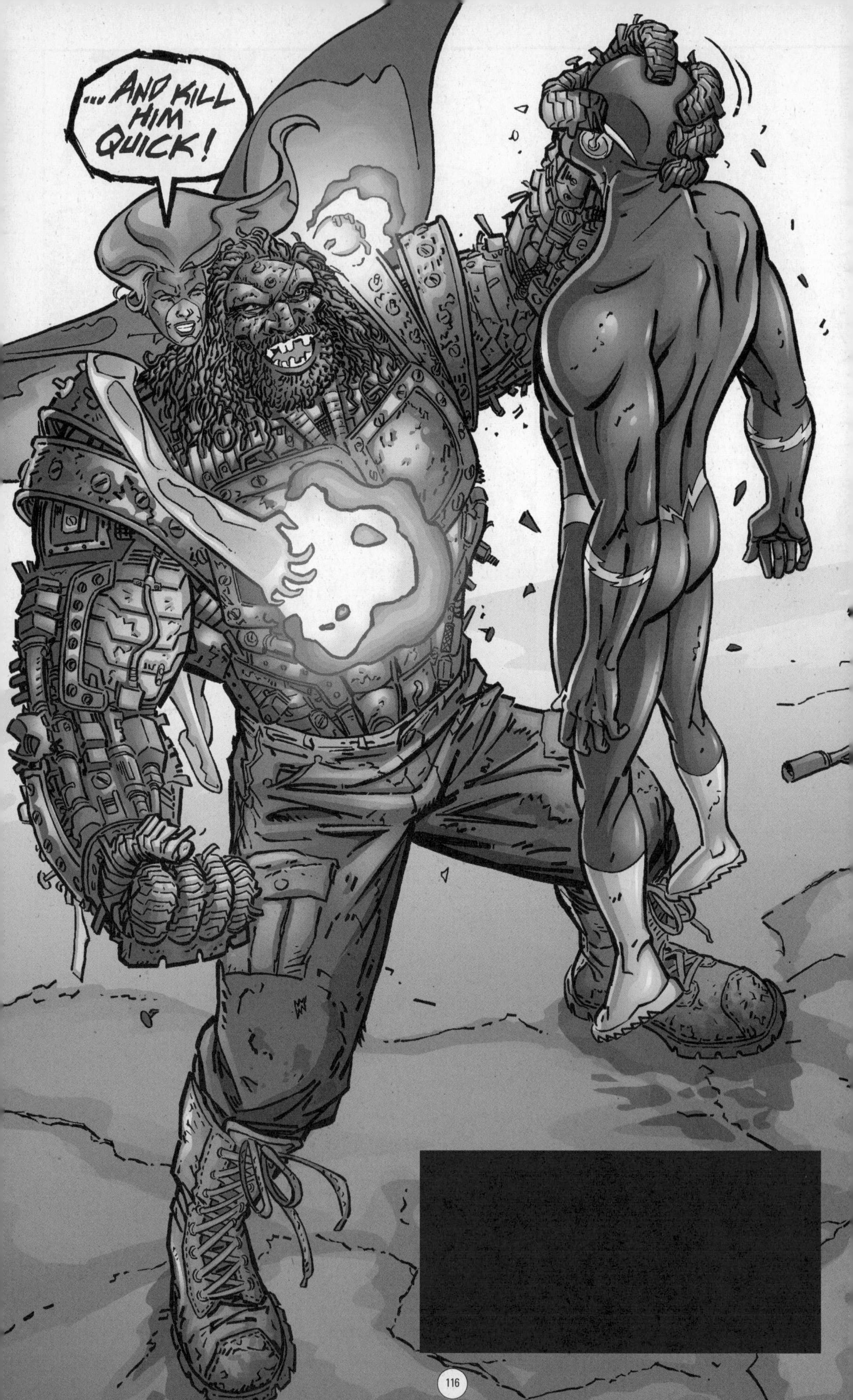
...AND KILL HIM QUICK!
[redacted]

KEYSTONE CITY.

MY DEAR *EX-HUSBAND.* YOU'VE MADE ME SO *ECSTATIC.*

I COULD *KISS* THAT BEAUTIFUL *GOLDEN FACE* OF YOURS.

FSSSSSSSSSSSSSSS

HMMMMN!

NIGHT, SPEEDY.

KRRK!

KILL HIM, GIRDER! KILL WALLY WEST.

WHHMP. UHHH!

TNK. TNK. TNK.

I HATE... I....

NO.

GOT AN IDEA, MAGENTA. I POP HIS HEAD LIKE A *GRAPE*--

--THEN YOU AND ME'LL FIND A NICE, QUIET ROOM IN KEYSTONE.

I TOLD YOU *BEFORE*--

VUMMMMMM

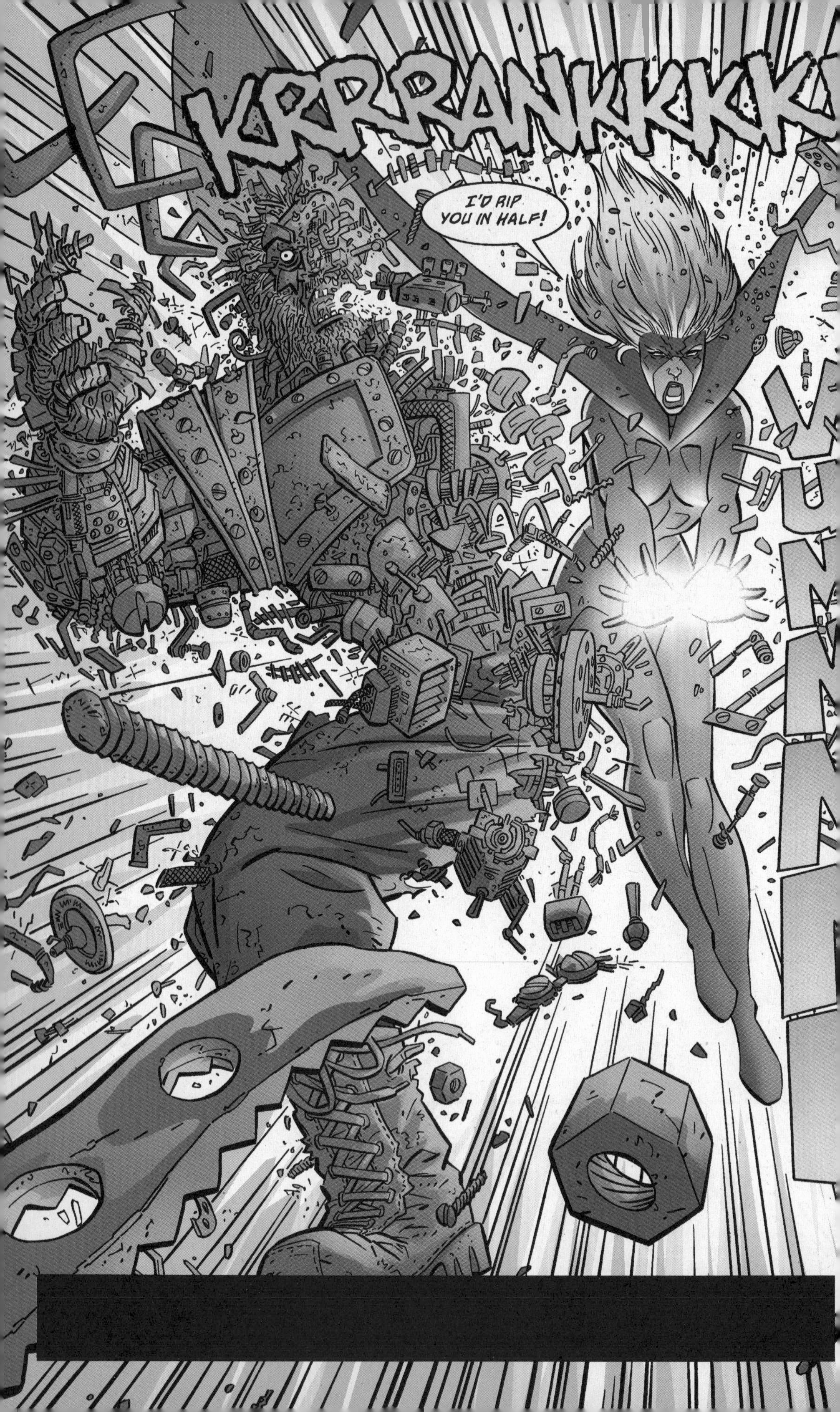
KRRANKKKKK
I'D RIP YOU IN HALF!
[redacted]

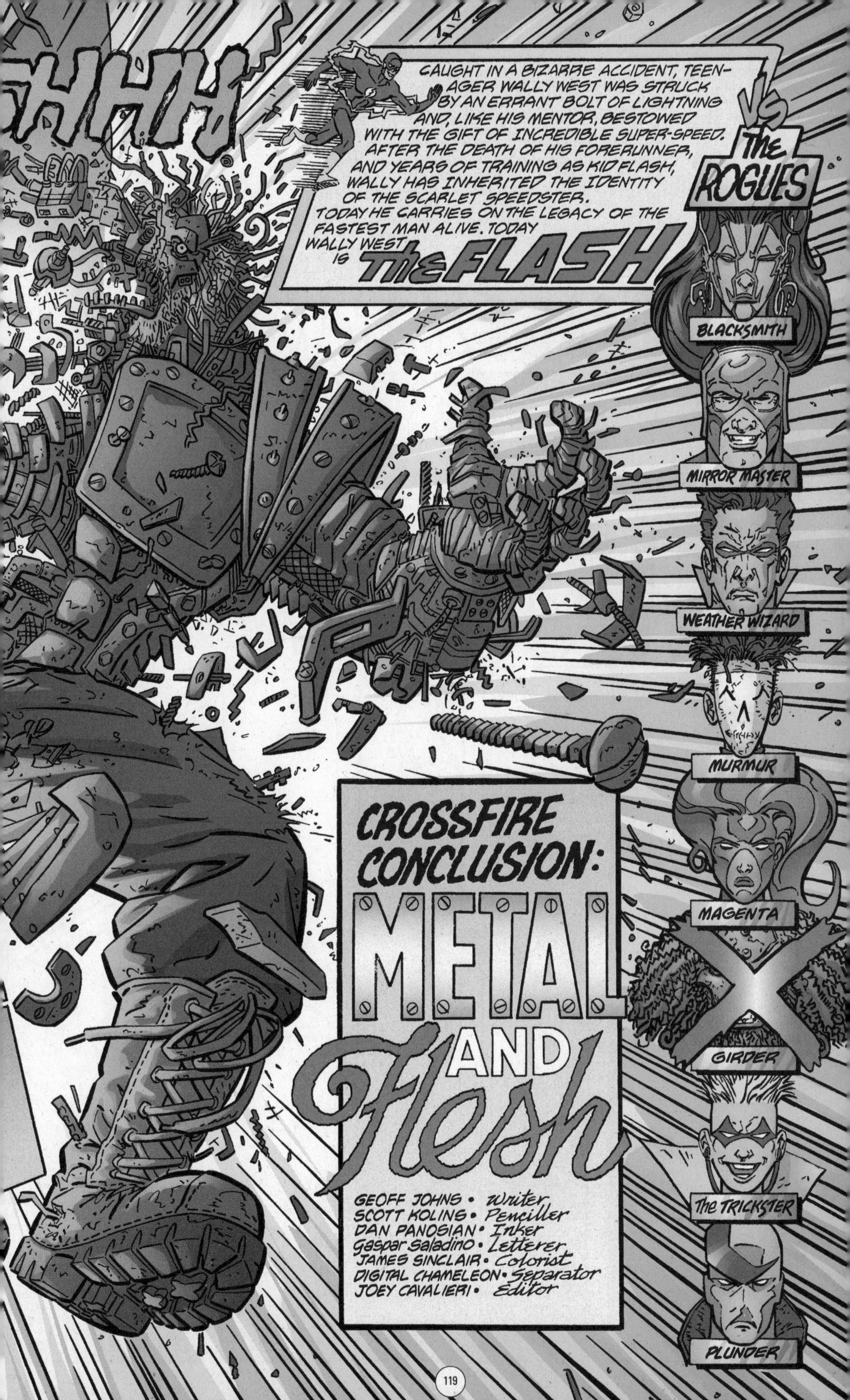

SHHHH
CAUGHT IN A BIZARRE ACCIDENT, TEEN-AGER WALLY WEST WAS STRUCK BY AN ERRANT BOLT OF LIGHTNING AND, LIKE HIS MENTOR, BESTOWED WITH THE GIFT OF INCREDIBLE SUPER-SPEED. AFTER THE DEATH OF HIS FORERUNNER, AND YEARS OF TRAINING AS KID FLASH, WALLY HAS INHERITED THE IDENTITY OF THE SCARLET SPEEDSTER. TODAY HE CARRIES ON THE LEGACY OF THE FASTEST MAN ALIVE. TODAY WALLY WEST IS THE FLASH
VS THE ROGUES
BLACKSMITH
MIRROR MASTER
WEATHER WIZARD
MURMUR
MAGENTA
GIRDER
The TRICKSTER
PLUNDER
CROSSFIRE CONCLUSION:
METAL AND Flesh
GEOFF JOHNS • Writer
SCOTT KOLINS • Penciller
DAN PANOSIAN • Inker
Gaspar Saladino • Letterer
JAMES SINCLAIR • Colorist
DIGITAL CHAMELEON • Separator
JOEY CAVALIERI • Editor

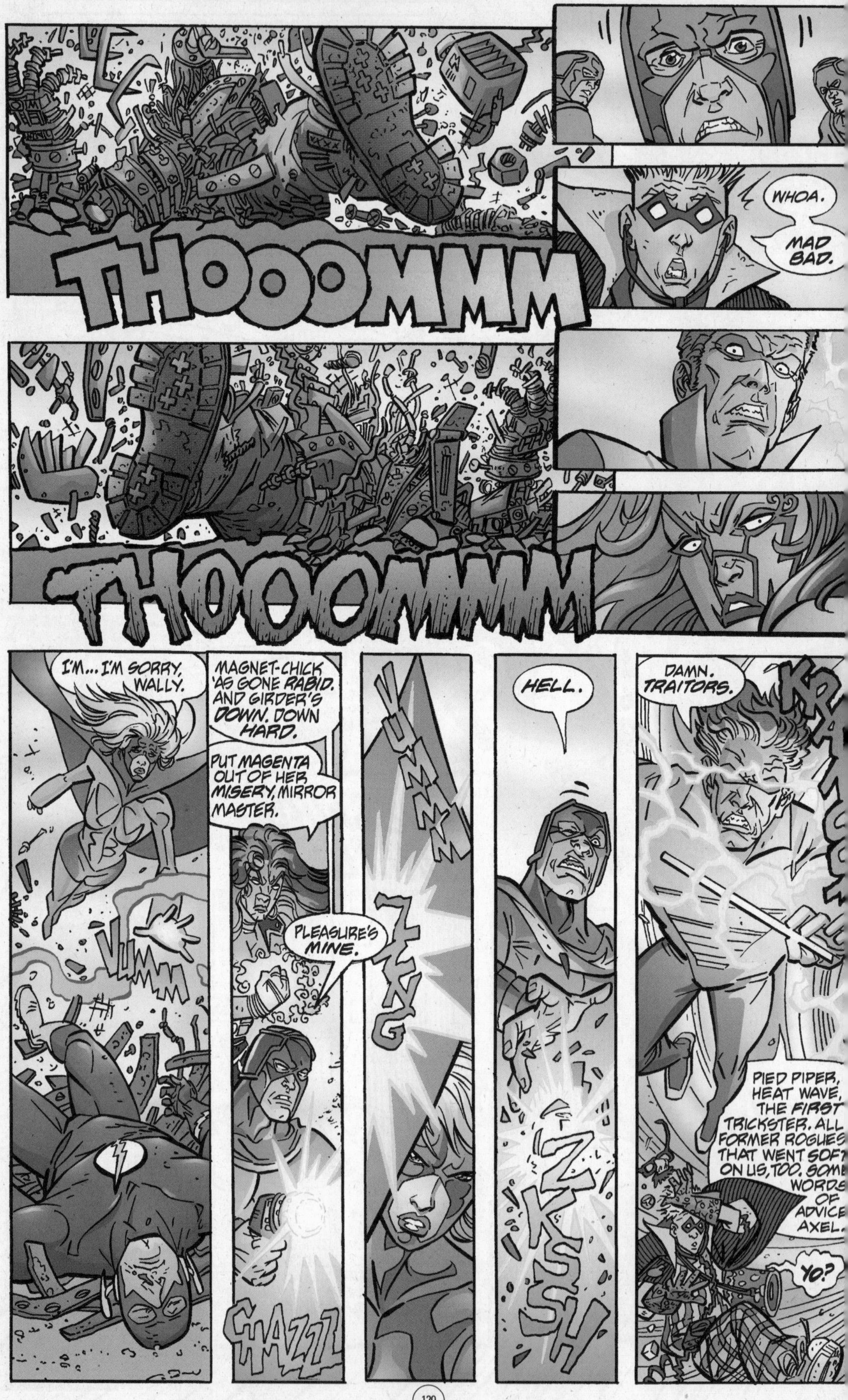
THOOOMMMM
WHOA.
MAD BAD.
THOOOMMMM
I'M... I'M SORRY, WALLY.
VUMMM
MAGNET-CHICK 'AS GONE RABID. AND GIRDER'S DOWN. DOWN HARD.
PUT MAGENTA OUT OF HER MISERY, MIRROR MASTER.
PLEASURE'S MINE.
SHAZZZ
HELL.
DAMN. TRAITORS.
PIED PIPER, HEAT WAVE, THE FIRST TRICKSTER. ALL FORMER ROGUES THAT WENT SOFT ON US, TOO. SOME WORDS OF ADVICE AXEL.
YO?

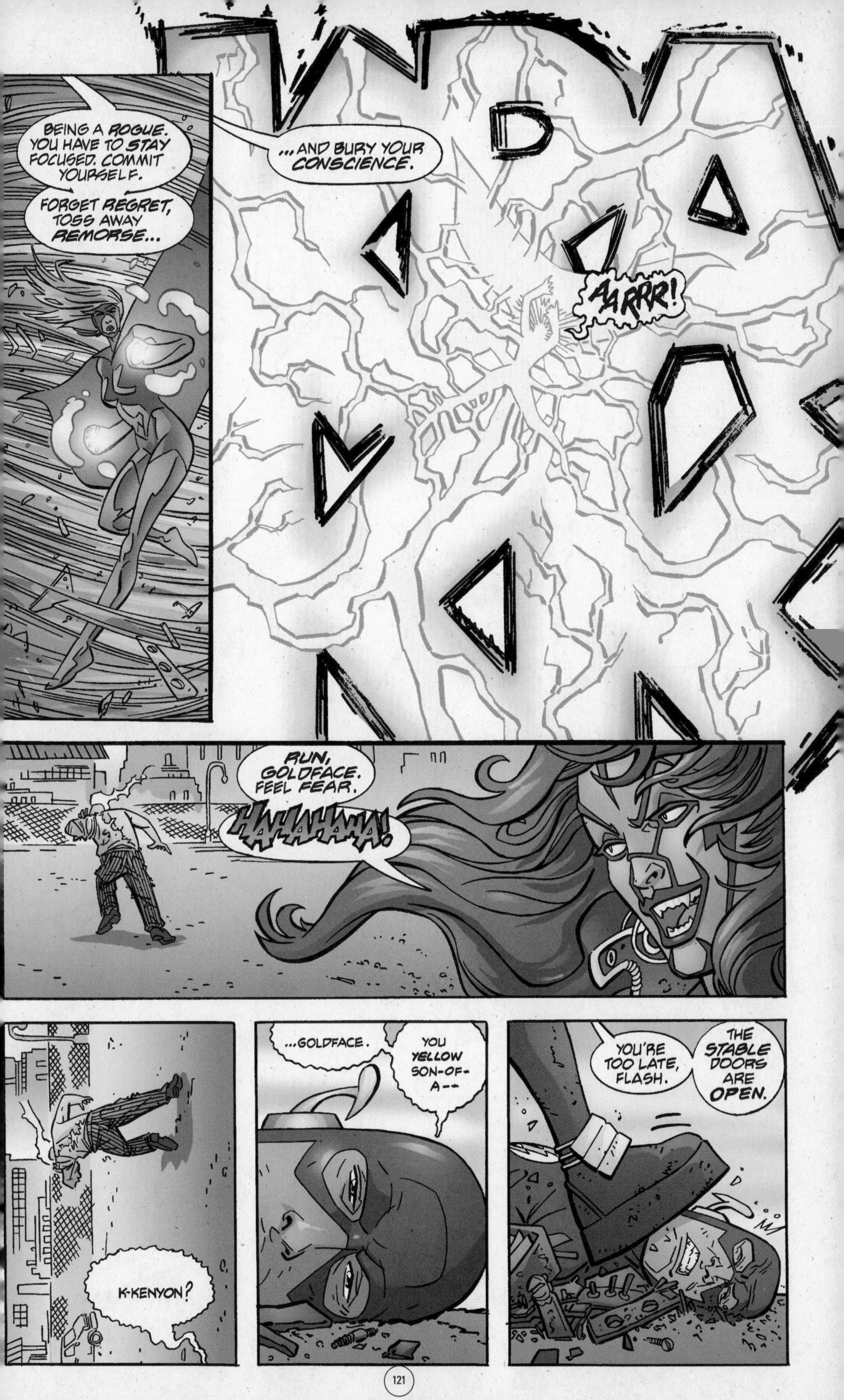
BEING A ROGUE. YOU HAVE TO STAY FOCUSED. COMMIT YOURSELF.
FORGET REGRET, TOSS AWAY REMORSE...
...AND BURY YOUR CONSCIENCE.
AARRR!
RUN, GOLDFACE. FEEL FEAR.
HAHAHAHA!
K-KENYON?
...GOLDFACE.
YOU YELLOW SON-OF-A--
YOU'RE TOO LATE, FLASH.
THE STABLE DOORS ARE OPEN.

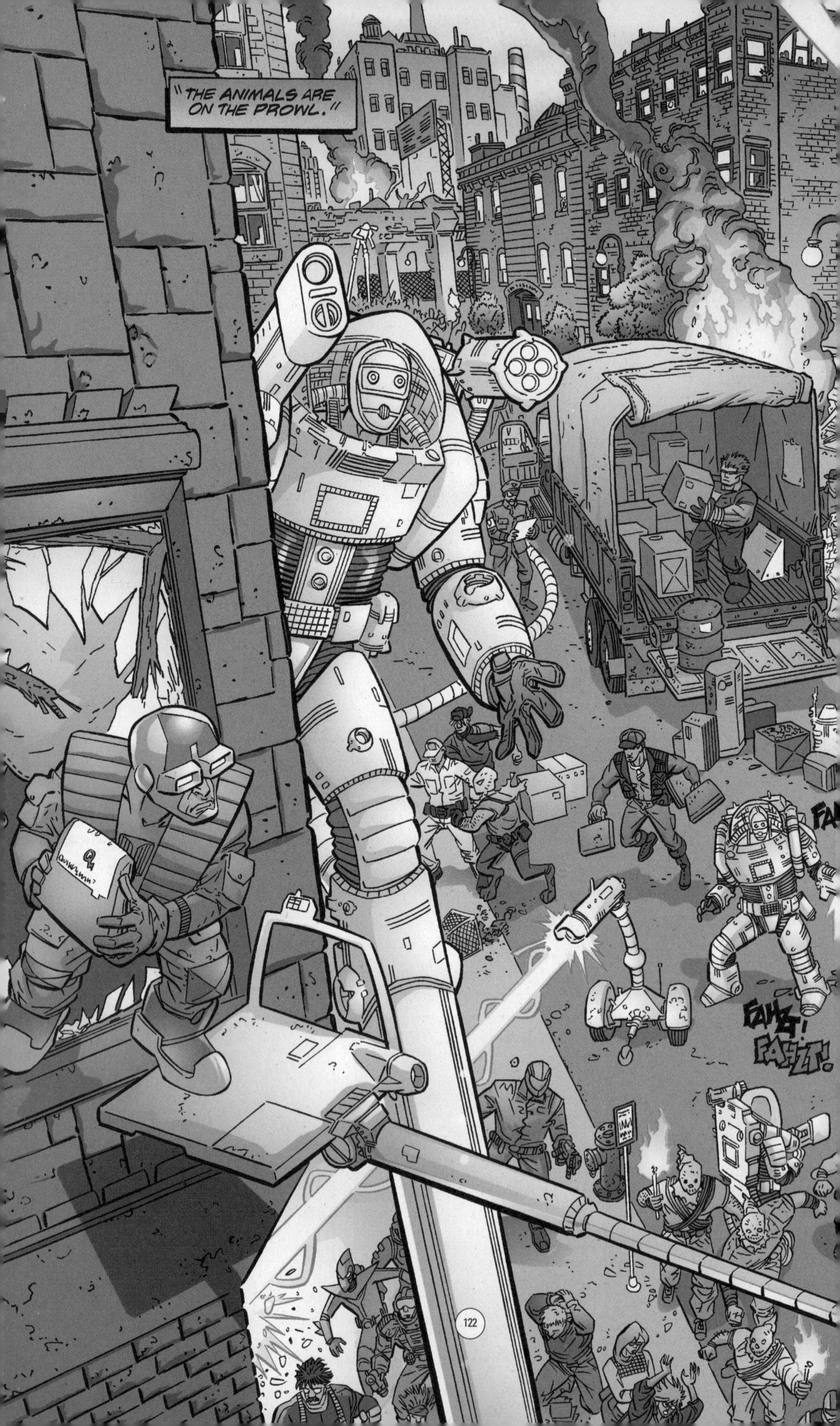
"THE ANIMALS ARE ON THE PROWL."
FAHZT!
FAHZT!

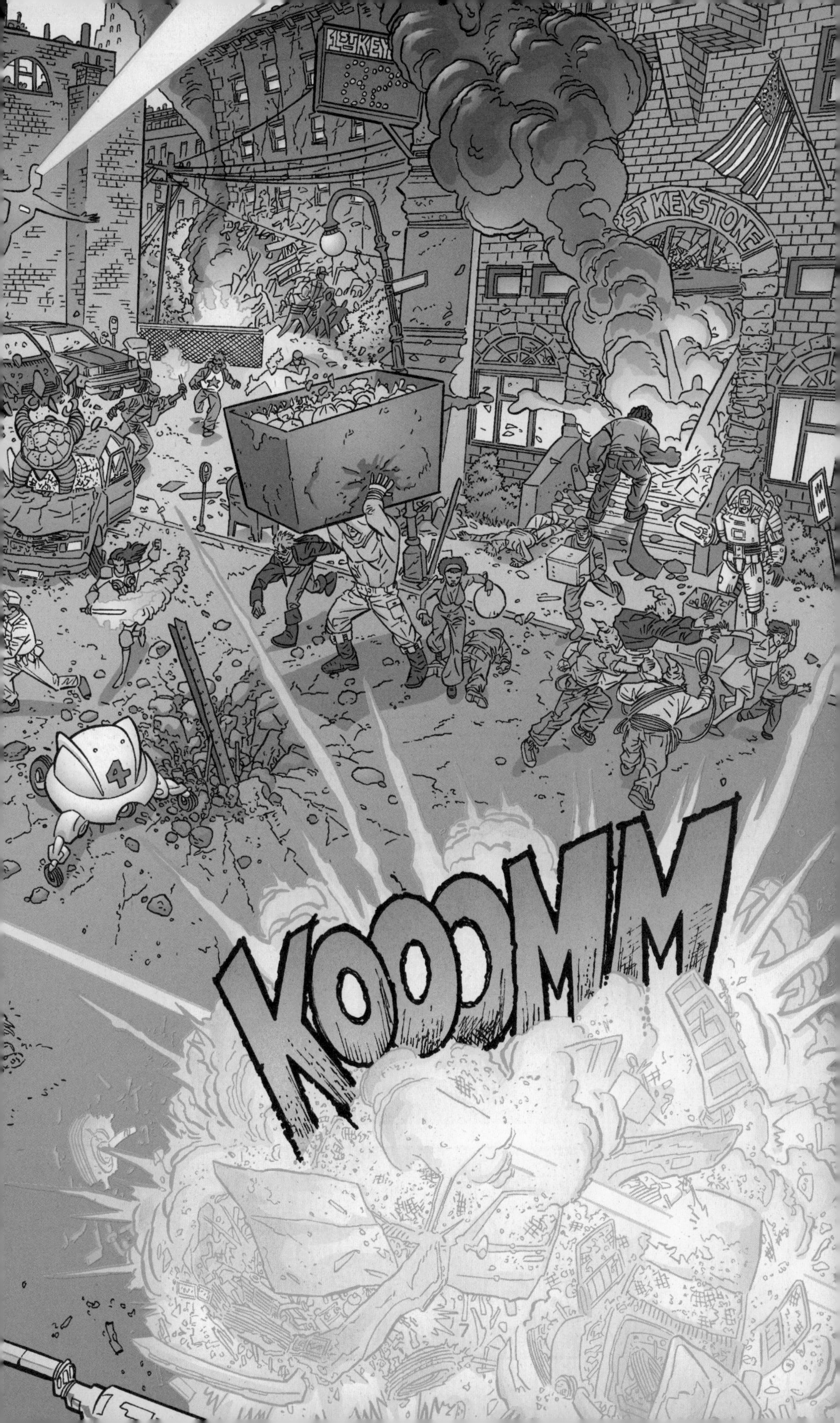
1ST KEY
82
ST KEYSTONE
4
KOOOMM

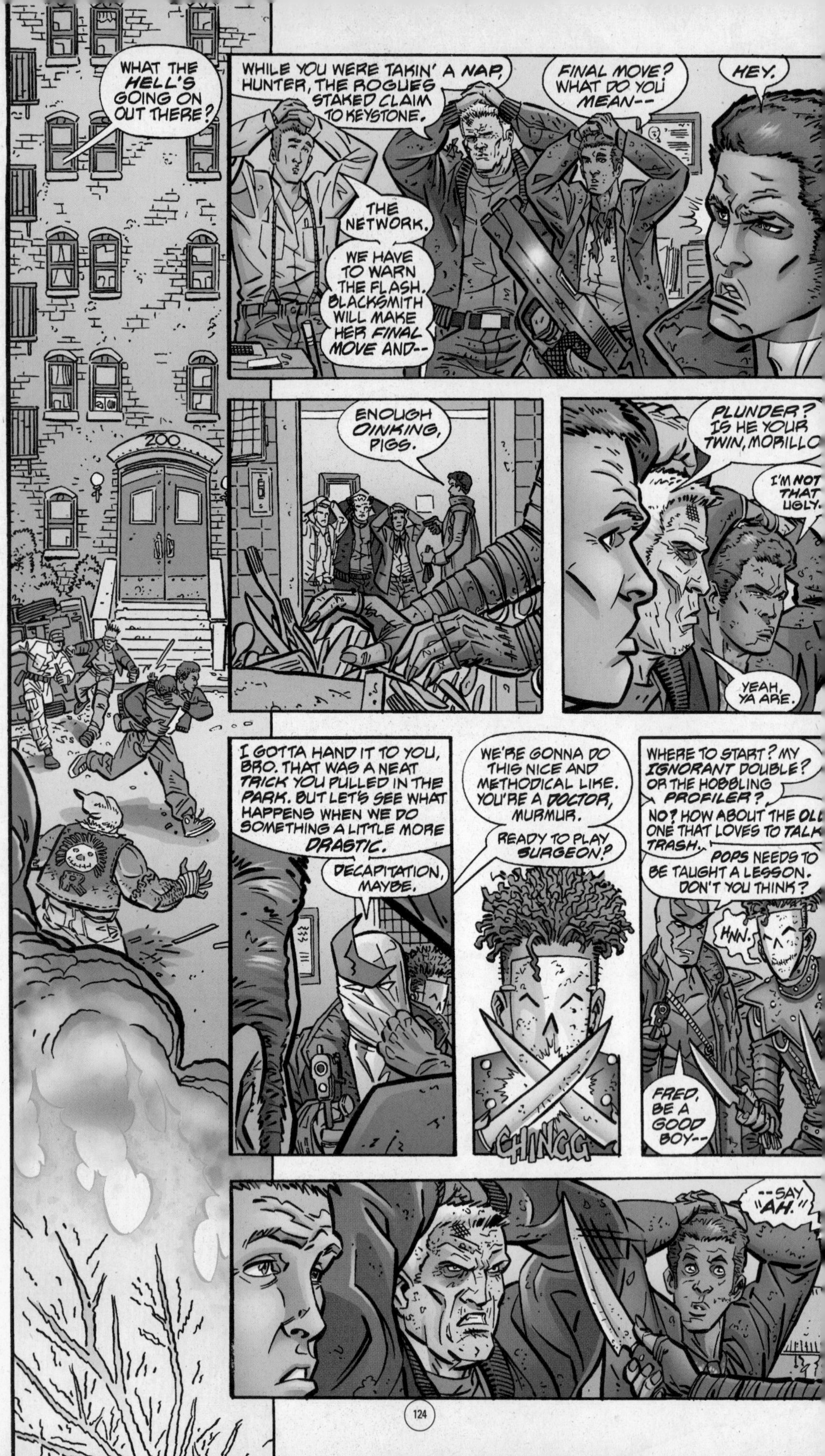
WHAT THE HELL'S GOING ON OUT THERE?
WHILE YOU WERE TAKIN' A NAP, HUNTER, THE ROGUES STAKED CLAIM TO KEYSTONE.
THE NETWORK.
WE HAVE TO WARN THE FLASH. BLACKSMITH WILL MAKE HER FINAL MOVE AND--
FINAL MOVE? WHAT DO YOU MEAN--
HEY.
ENOUGH OINKING, PIGS.
PLUNDER? IS HE YOUR TWIN, MORILLO
I'M NOT THAT UGLY.
YEAH, YA ARE.
I GOTTA HAND IT TO YOU, BRO. THAT WAS A NEAT TRICK YOU PULLED IN THE PARK. BUT LET'S SEE WHAT HAPPENS WHEN WE DO SOMETHING A LITTLE MORE DRASTIC.
DECAPITATION, MAYBE.
WE'RE GONNA DO THIS NICE AND METHODICAL LIKE. YOU'RE A DOCTOR, MURMUR.
READY TO PLAY SURGEON?
CHINGG
WHERE TO START? MY IGNORANT DOUBLE? OR THE HOBBLING PROFILER?
NO? HOW ABOUT THE OL ONE THAT LOVES TO TALK TRASH.
POPS NEEDS TO BE TAUGHT A LESSON. DON'T YOU THINK?
HNN.
FRED, BE A GOOD BOY--
--SAY "AH."

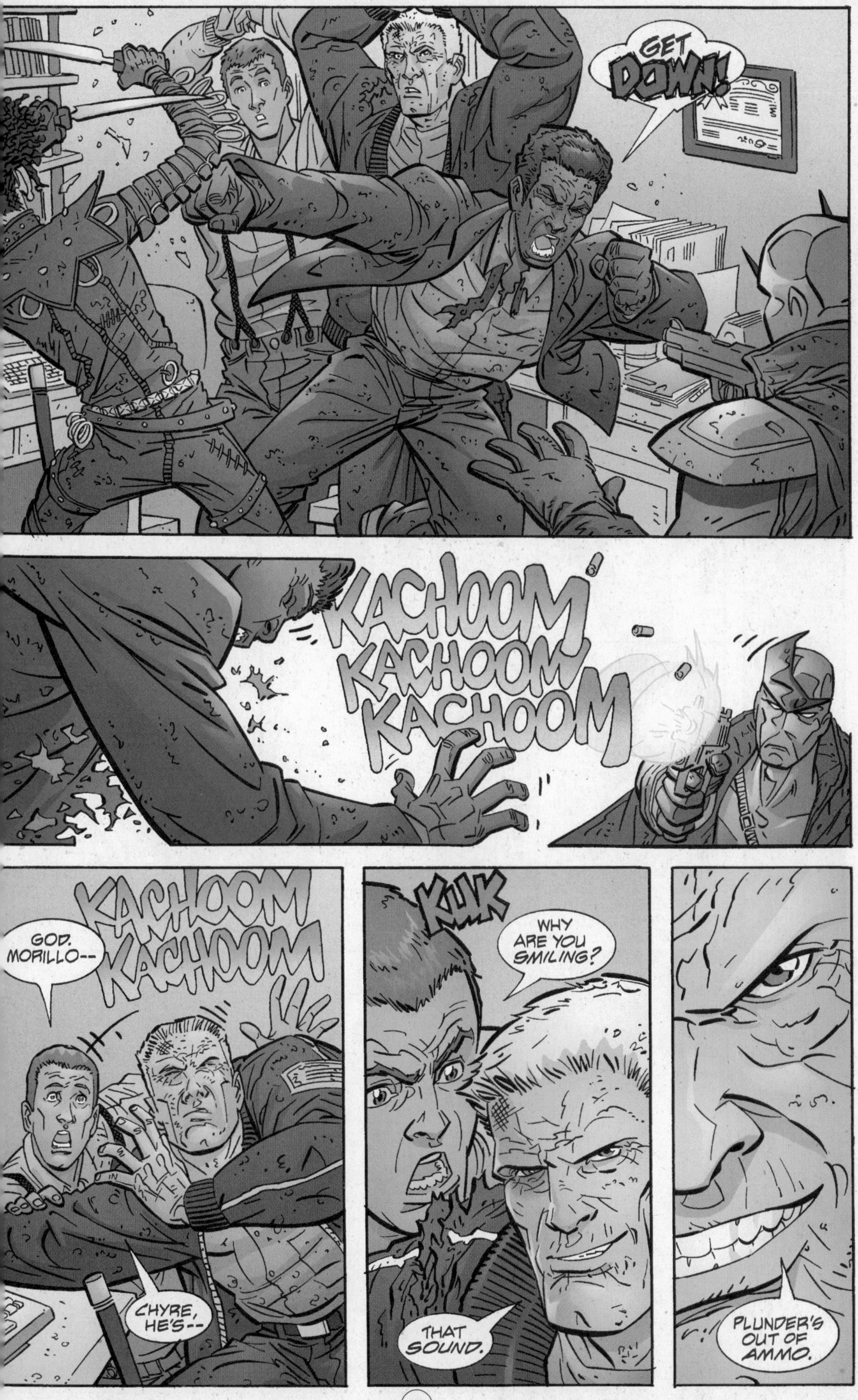

GET DOWN!
KACHOOM
KACHOOM
KACHOOM
KACHOOM
KACHOOM
GOD. MORILLO--
CHYRE, HE'S--
KLIK
WHY ARE YOU SMILING?
THAT SOUND.
PLUNDER'S OUT OF AMMO.

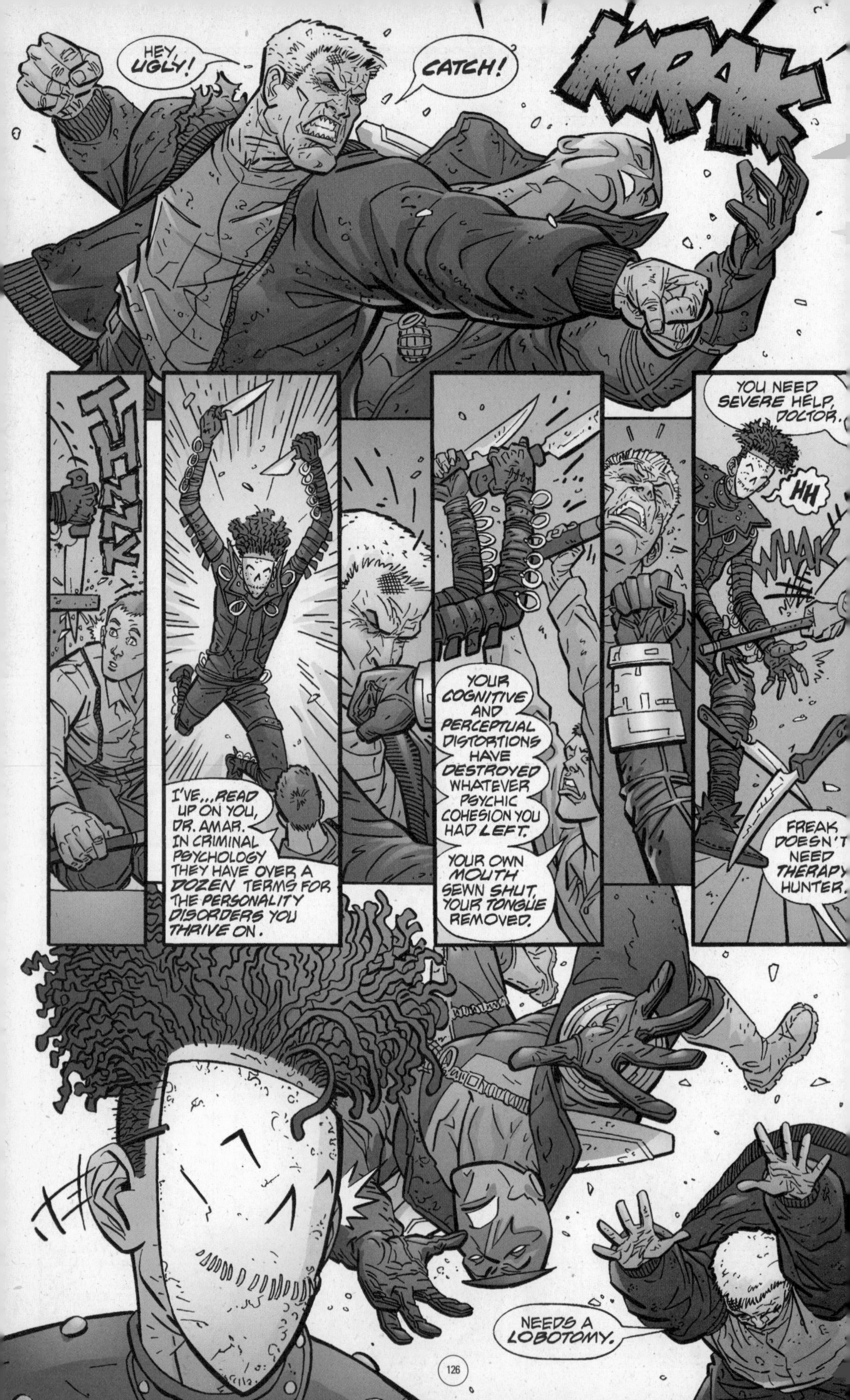
HEY, UGLY!
CATCH!
KRAK
THOCK
I'VE... READ UP ON YOU, DR. AMAR. IN CRIMINAL PSYCHOLOGY THEY HAVE OVER A DOZEN TERMS FOR THE PERSONALITY DISORDERS YOU THRIVE ON.
YOUR COGNITIVE AND PERCEPTUAL DISTORTIONS HAVE DESTROYED WHATEVER PSYCHIC COHESION YOU HAD LEFT.
YOUR OWN MOUTH SEWN SHUT, YOUR TONGUE REMOVED.
YOU NEED SEVERE HELP, DOCTOR.
HH
WHAK
FREAK DOESN'T NEED THERAPY HUNTER.
NEEDS A LOBOTOMY.

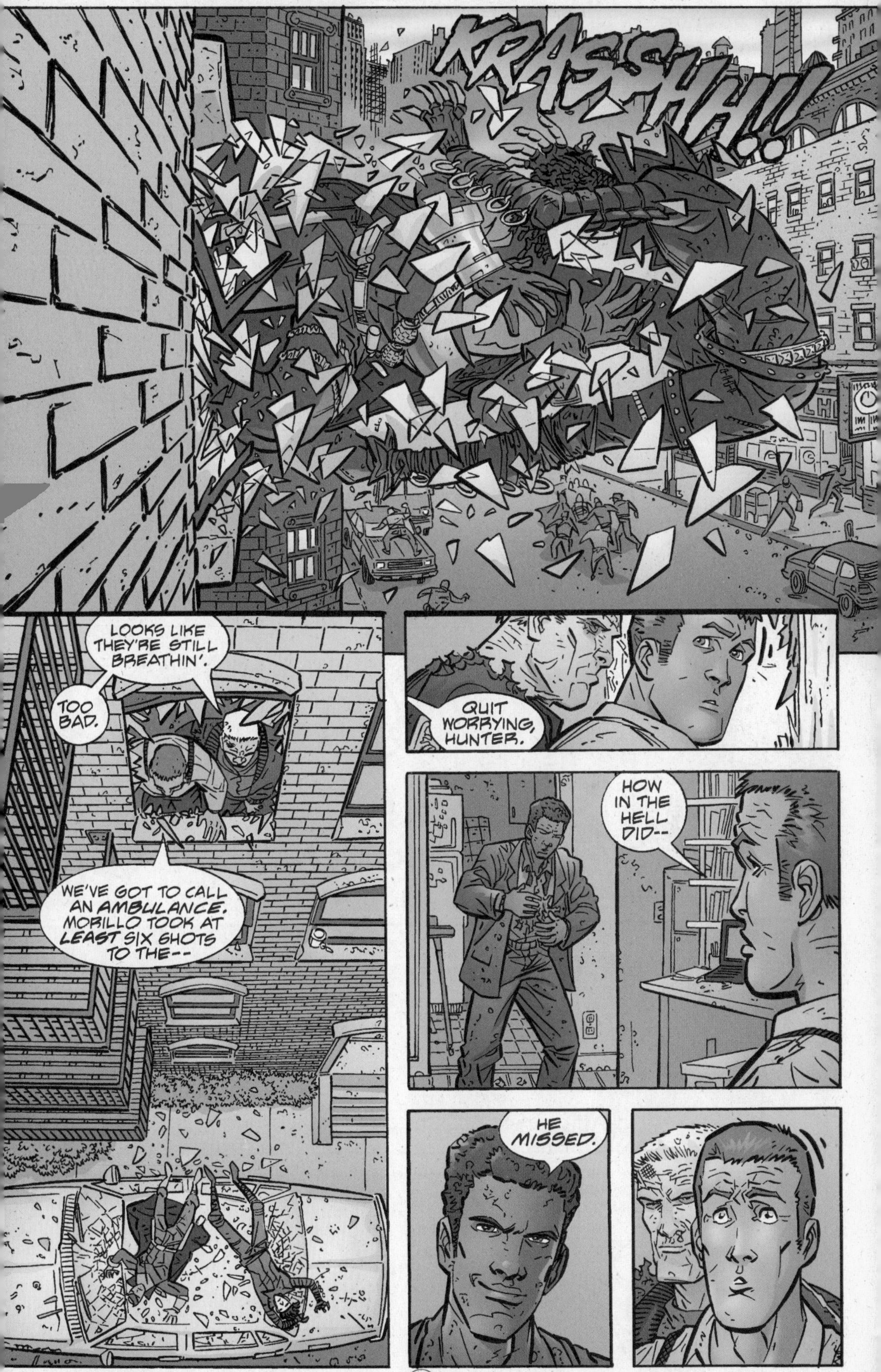
KRASSHH!!
LOOKS LIKE THEY'RE STILL BREATHIN'.
TOO BAD.
WE'VE GOT TO CALL AN AMBULANCE. MORILLO TOOK AT LEAST SIX SHOTS TO THE--
QUIT WORRYING, HUNTER.
HOW IN THE HELL DID--
HE MISSED.

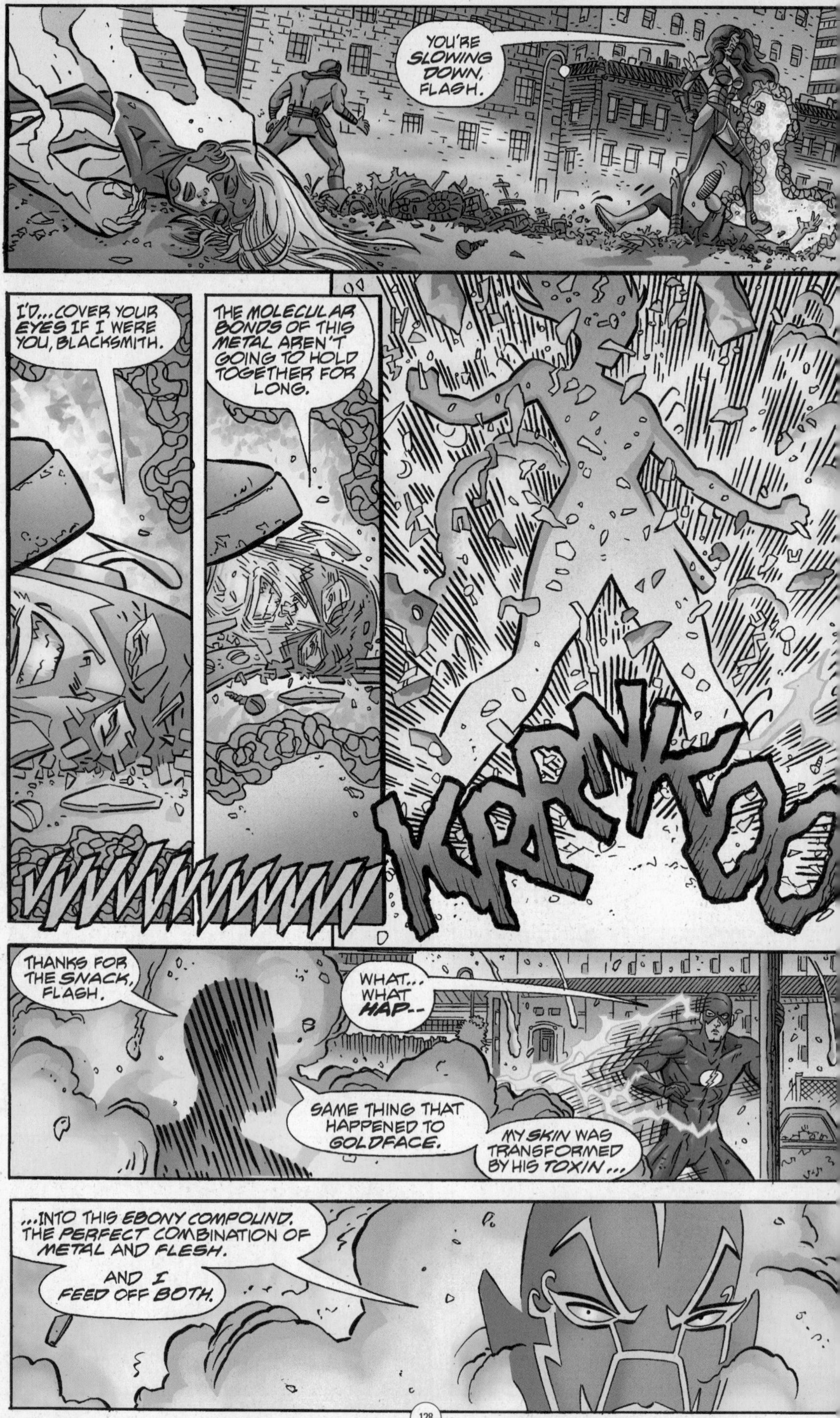
YOU'RE SLOWING DOWN, FLASH.
I'D... COVER YOUR EYES IF I WERE YOU, BLACKSMITH.
THE MOLECULAR BONDS OF THIS METAL AREN'T GOING TO HOLD TOGETHER FOR LONG.
VVVVVVVVVVVVVVVVVV
KRRNKOO
THANKS FOR THE SNACK, FLASH.
WHAT... WHAT HAP--
SAME THING THAT HAPPENED TO GOLDFACE.
MY SKIN WAS TRANSFORMED BY HIS TOXIN...
...INTO THIS EBONY COMPOUND. THE PERFECT COMBINATION OF METAL AND FLESH.
AND I FEED OFF BOTH.

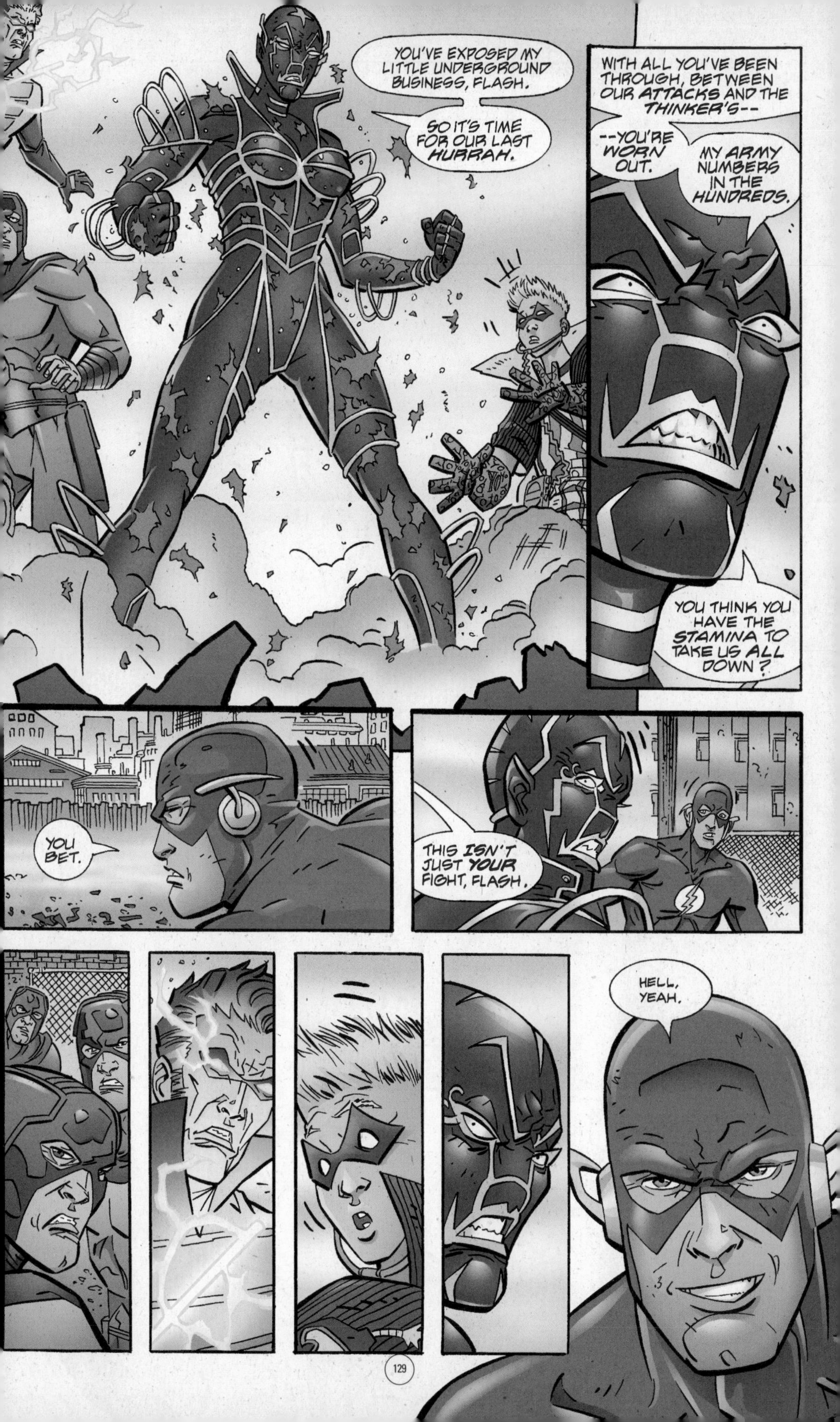

YOU'VE EXPOSED MY LITTLE UNDERGROUND BUSINESS, FLASH.
SO IT'S TIME FOR OUR LAST HURRAH.
WITH ALL YOU'VE BEEN THROUGH, BETWEEN OUR ATTACKS AND THE THINKER'S--
--YOU'RE WORN OUT.
MY ARMY NUMBERS IN THE HUNDREDS.
YOU THINK YOU HAVE THE STAMINA TO TAKE US ALL DOWN?
YOU BET.
THIS ISN'T JUST YOUR FIGHT, FLASH.
HELL, YEAH.

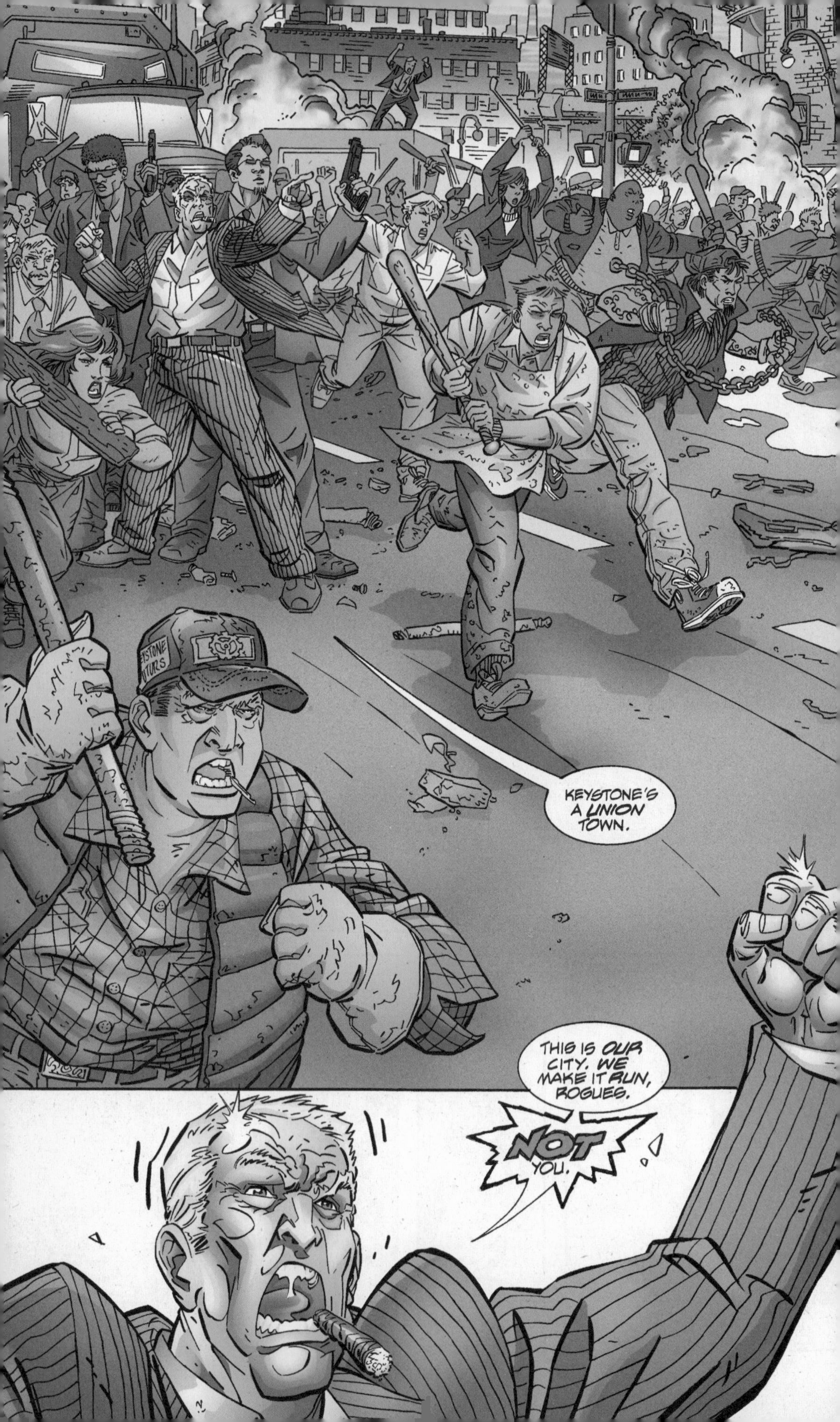
KEYSTONE'S A UNION TOWN.
THIS IS OUR CITY. WE MAKE IT RUN, ROGUES.
NOT YOU.

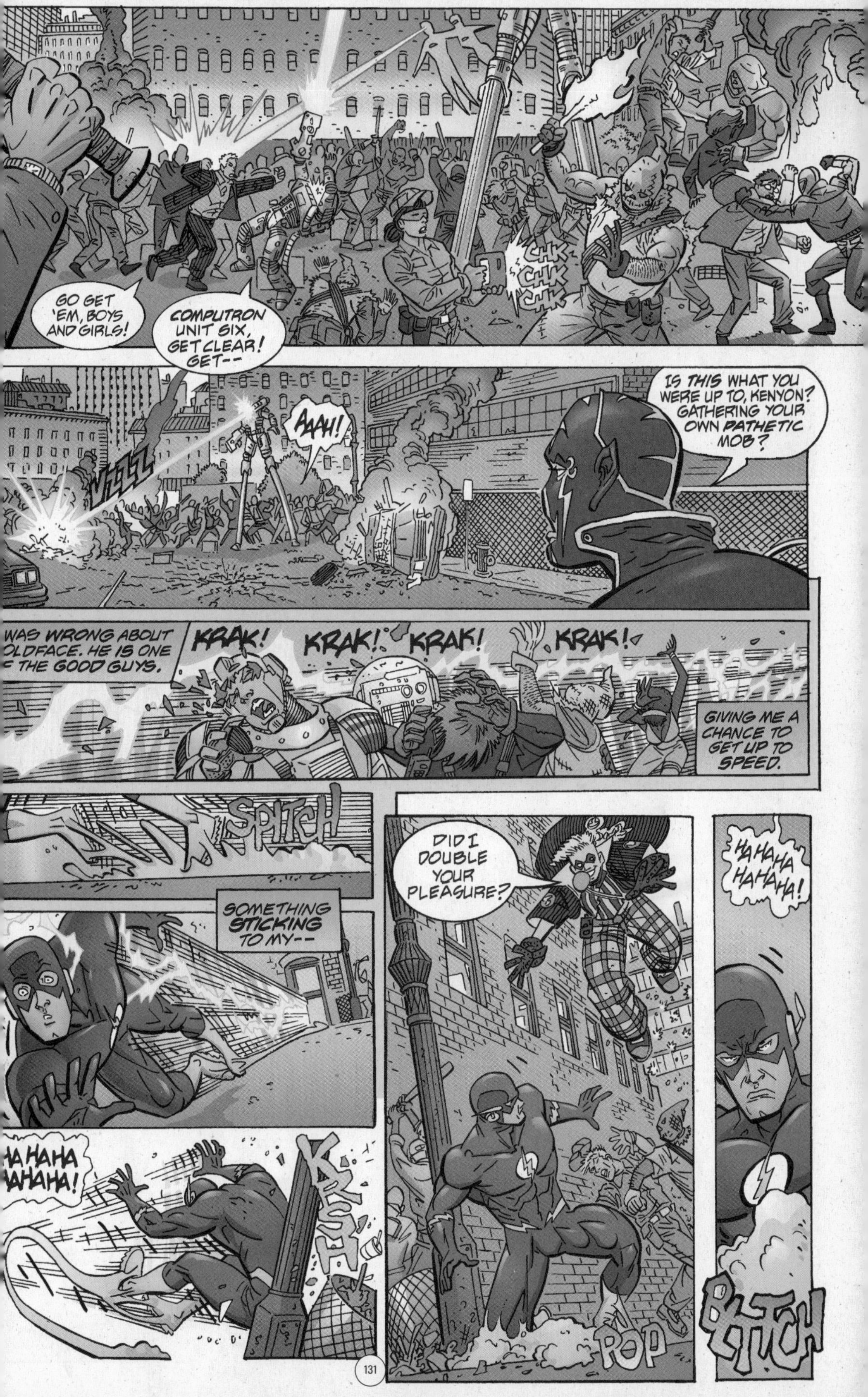
GO GET 'EM, BOYS AND GIRLS!
COMPUTRON UNIT SIX, GET CLEAR! GET--
CHK CHK CHK
VIZZZ
AAAH!
IS THIS WHAT YOU WERE UP TO, KENYON? GATHERING YOUR OWN PATHETIC MOB?
WAS WRONG ABOUT OLDFACE. HE IS ONE OF THE GOOD GUYS.
KRAK! KRAK! KRAK! KRAK!
GIVING ME A CHANCE TO GET UP TO SPEED.
SPITCH
SOMETHING STICKING TO MY--
HAHAHA HAHAHA!
KRSH
DID I DOUBLE YOUR PLEASURE?
POP
HAHAHA HAHAHA!
BLTCH

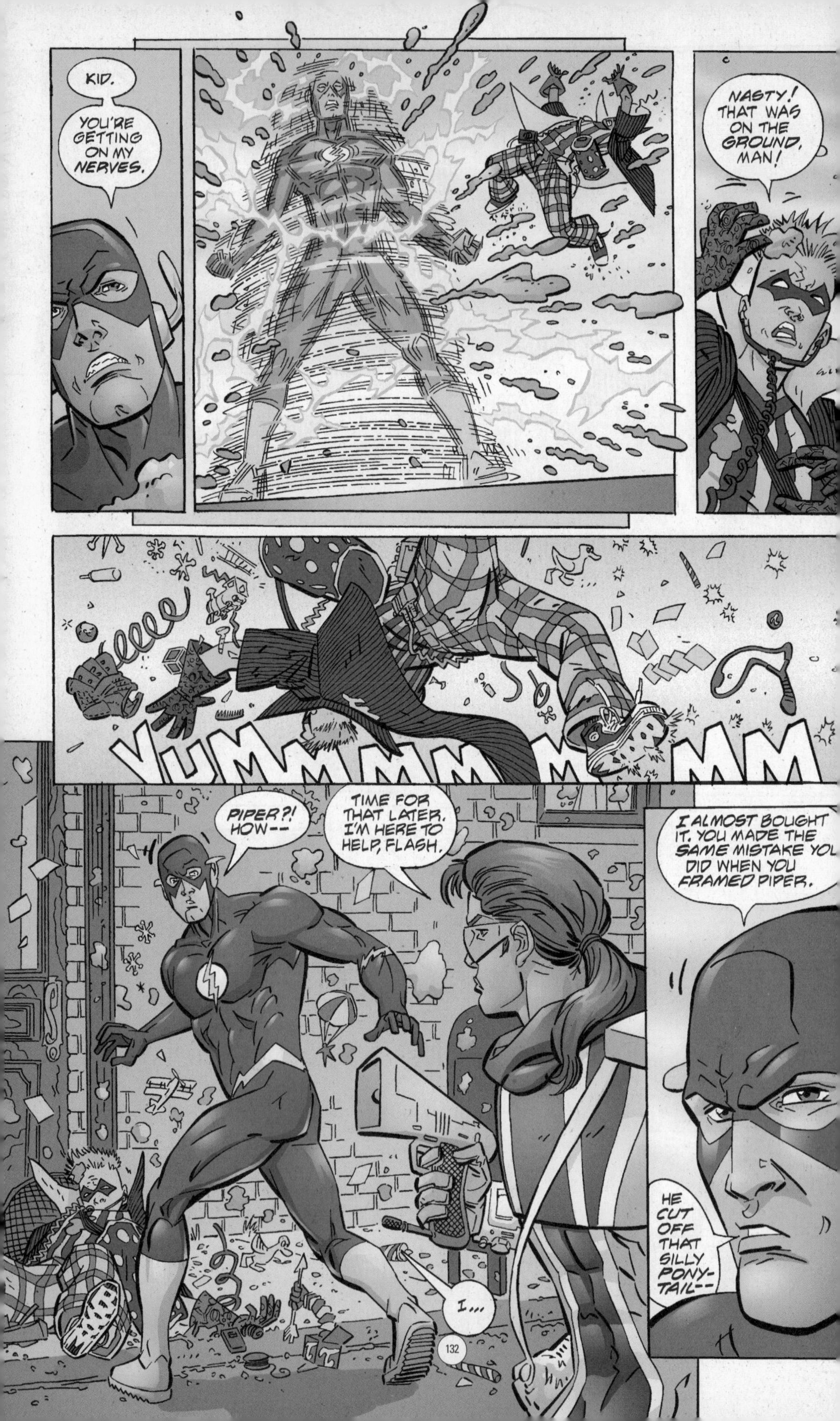
KID.
YOU'RE GETTING ON MY NERVES.
NASTY! THAT WAS ON THE GROUND, MAN!
VUMMMMMMMMMM
PIPER?! HOW--
TIME FOR THAT LATER. I'M HERE TO HELP, FLASH.
I...
I ALMOST BOUGHT IT. YOU MADE THE SAME MISTAKE YOU DID WHEN YOU FRAMED PIPER.
HE CUT OFF THAT SILLY PONY-TAIL--

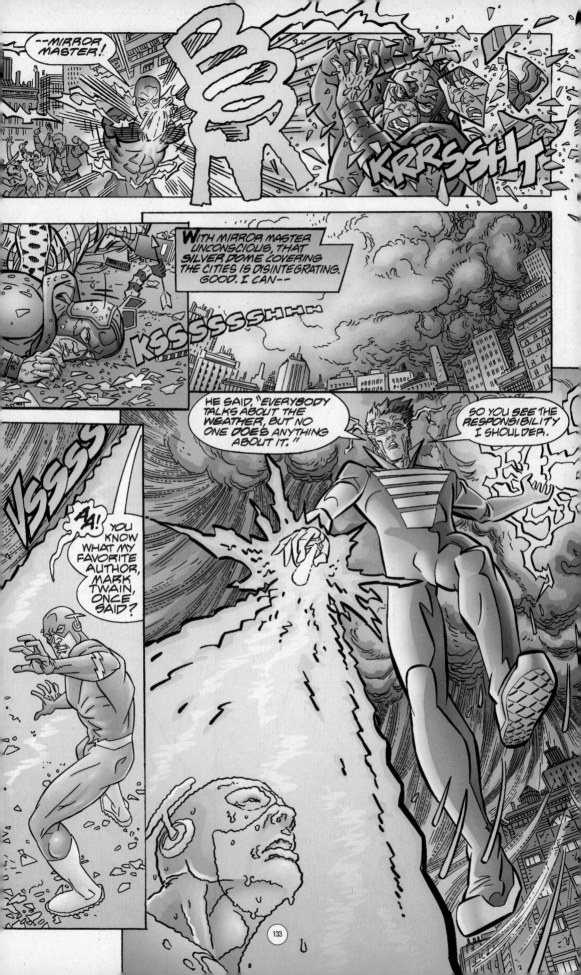

--MIRROR MASTER!

BOOR

KRRSSH.T

WITH MIRROR MASTER UNCONSCIOUS, THAT SILVER DOME COVERING THE CITIES IS DISINTEGRATING. GOOD. I CAN--

KSSSSSSHHH

HE SAID, "EVERYBODY TALKS ABOUT THE WEATHER, BUT NO ONE DOES ANYTHING ABOUT IT."

SO YOU SEE THE RESPONSIBILITY I SHOULDER.

VSSSSS

AA! YOU KNOW WHAT MY FAVORITE AUTHOR, MARK TWAIN, ONCE SAID?

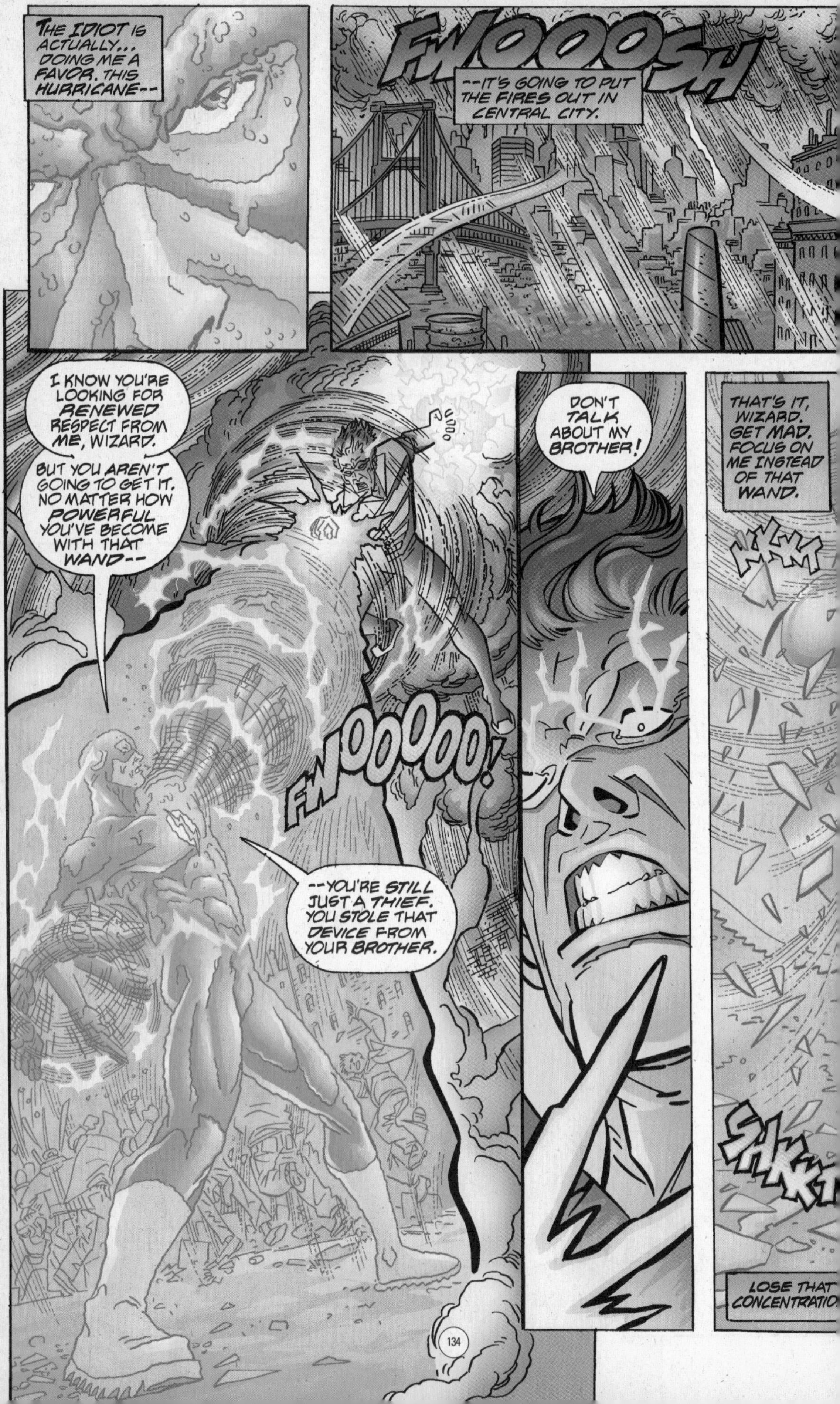

THE IDIOT IS ACTUALLY... DOING ME A FAVOR. THIS HURRICANE--
FWOOOOSH
--IT'S GOING TO PUT THE FIRES OUT IN CENTRAL CITY.
I KNOW YOU'RE LOOKING FOR RENEWED RESPECT FROM ME, WIZARD.
BUT YOU AREN'T GOING TO GET IT. NO MATTER HOW POWERFUL YOU'VE BECOME WITH THAT WAND--
FWOOOOOO!
--YOU'RE STILL JUST A THIEF. YOU STOLE THAT DEVICE FROM YOUR BROTHER.
DON'T TALK ABOUT MY BROTHER!
THAT'S IT, WIZARD. GET MAD. FOCUS ON ME INSTEAD OF THAT WAND.
LOSE THAT CONCENTRATIO

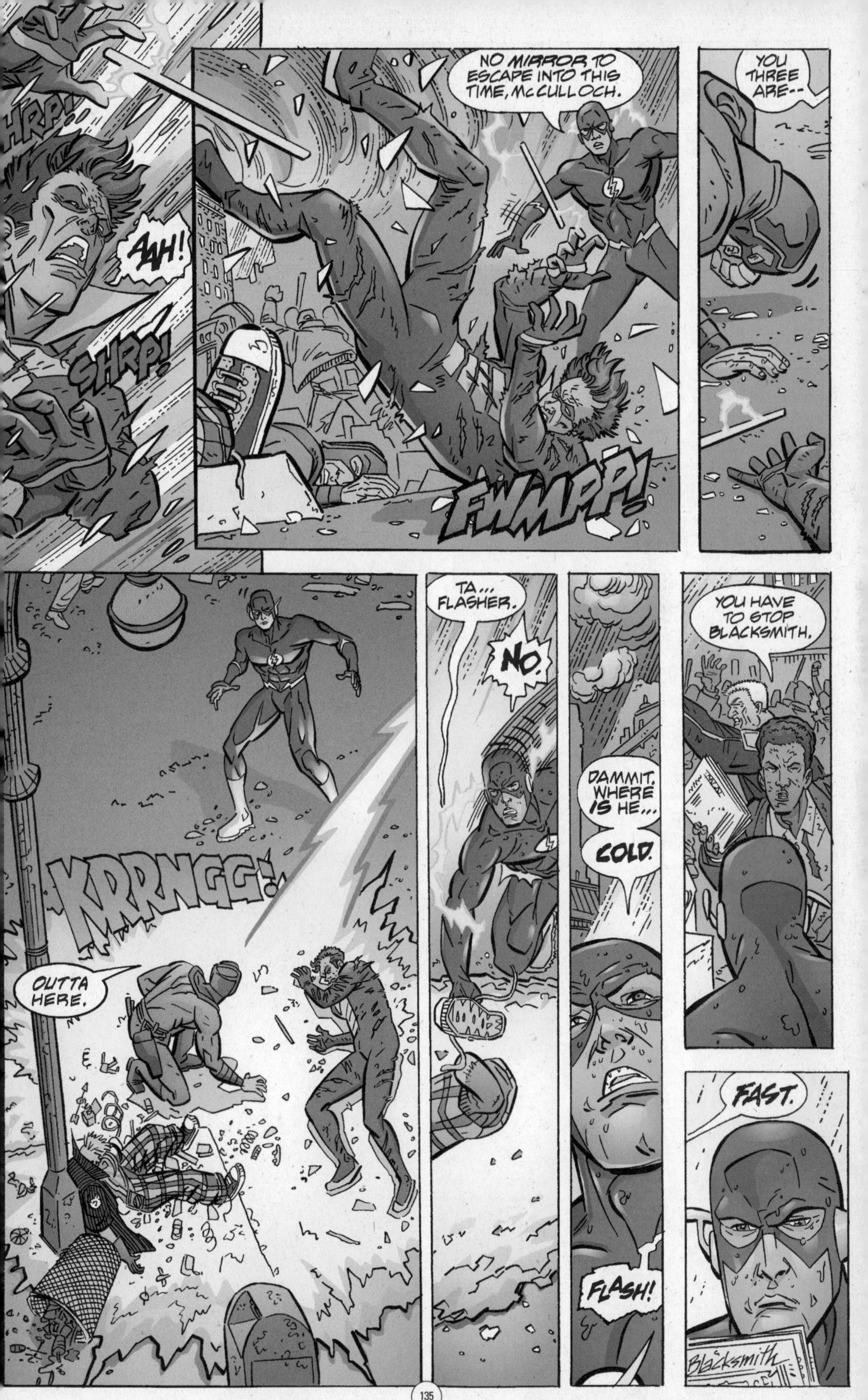
SHRP!
AAH!
SHRP!
NO MIRROR TO ESCAPE INTO THIS TIME, McCULLOCH.
FWMPP!
YOU THREE ARE--
KRRNGG!
OUTTA HERE.
TA... FLASHER.
NO.
DAMMIT. WHERE IS HE...
COLD.
FLASH!
YOU HAVE TO STOP BLACKSMITH.
FAST.
Blacksmith

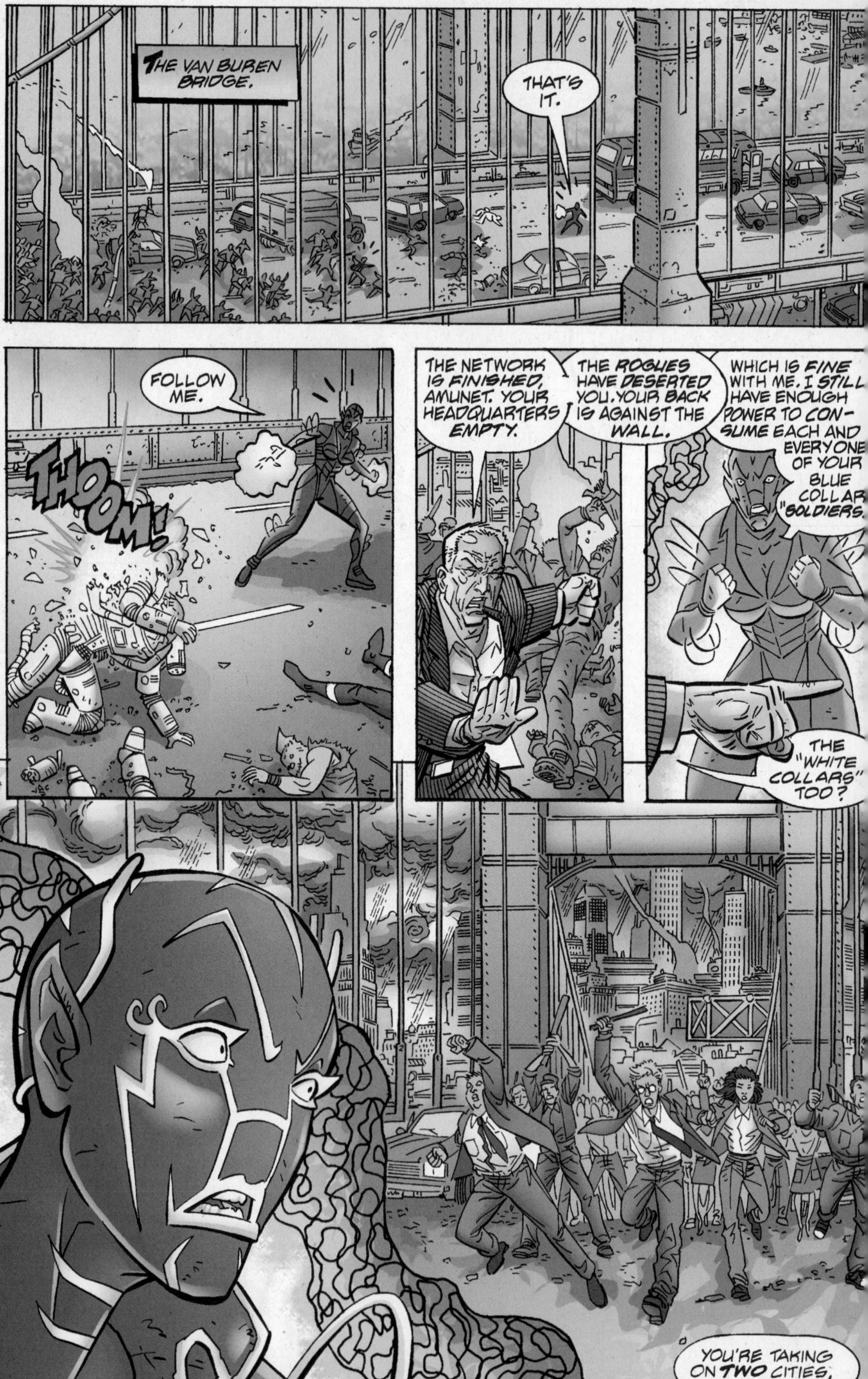
THE VAN BUREN BRIDGE.
THAT'S IT.
FOLLOW ME.
THOOOM!
THE NETWORK IS FINISHED, AMUNET. YOUR HEADQUARTERS EMPTY.
THE ROGUES HAVE DESERTED YOU. YOUR BACK IS AGAINST THE WALL.
WHICH IS FINE WITH ME. I STILL HAVE ENOUGH POWER TO CONSUME EACH AND EVERYONE OF YOUR BLUE COLLAR "SOLDIERS."
THE "WHITE COLLARS" TOO?
YOU'RE TAKING ON TWO CITIES, BLACKSMITH.

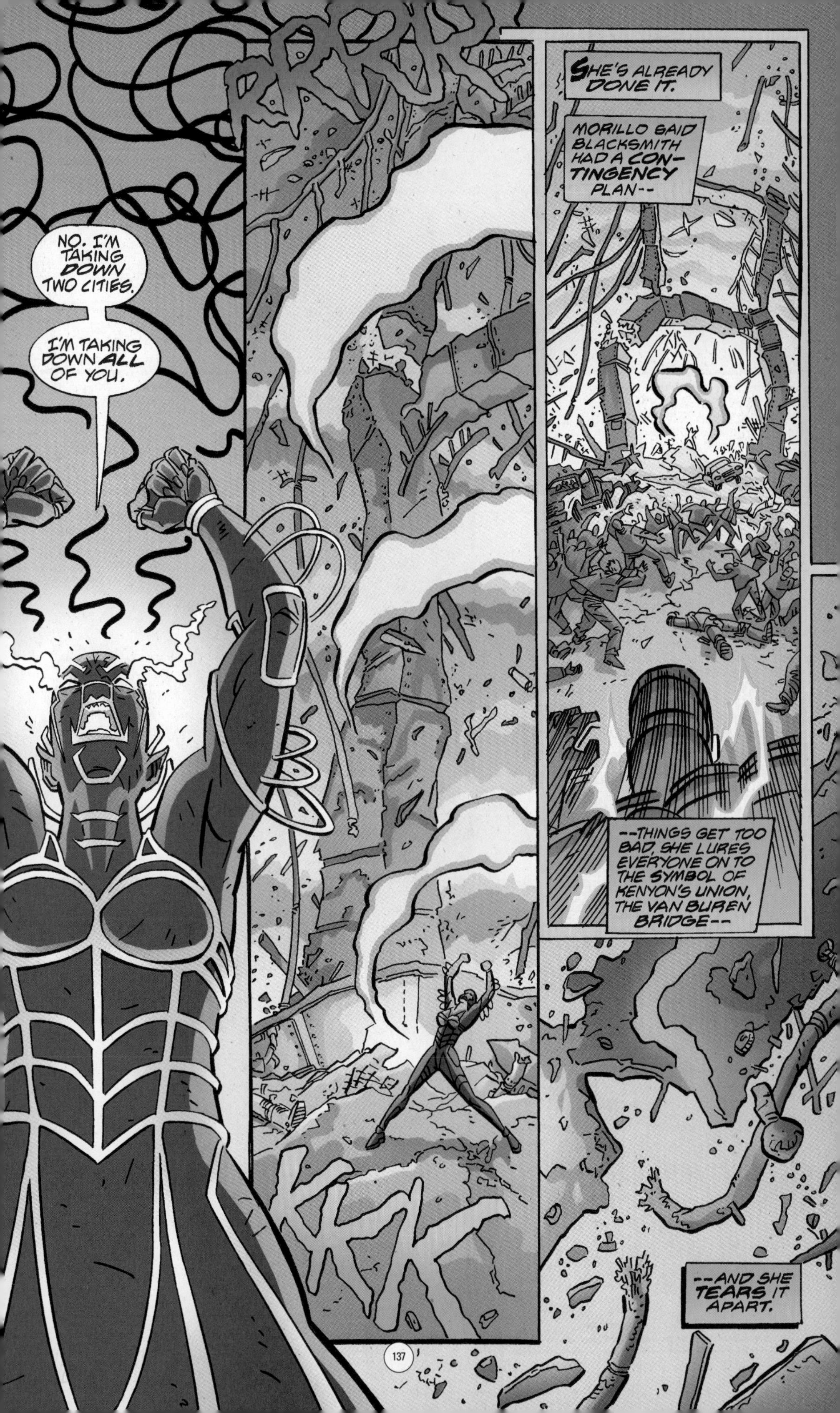

RRRRR
NO. I'M TAKING DOWN TWO CITIES.
I'M TAKING DOWN ALL OF YOU.
SHE'S ALREADY DONE IT.
MORILLO SAID BLACKSMITH HAD A CONTINGENCY PLAN--
--THINGS GET TOO BAD, SHE LURES EVERYONE ON TO THE SYMBOL OF KENYON'S UNION, THE VAN BUREN BRIDGE--
--AND SHE TEARS IT APART.

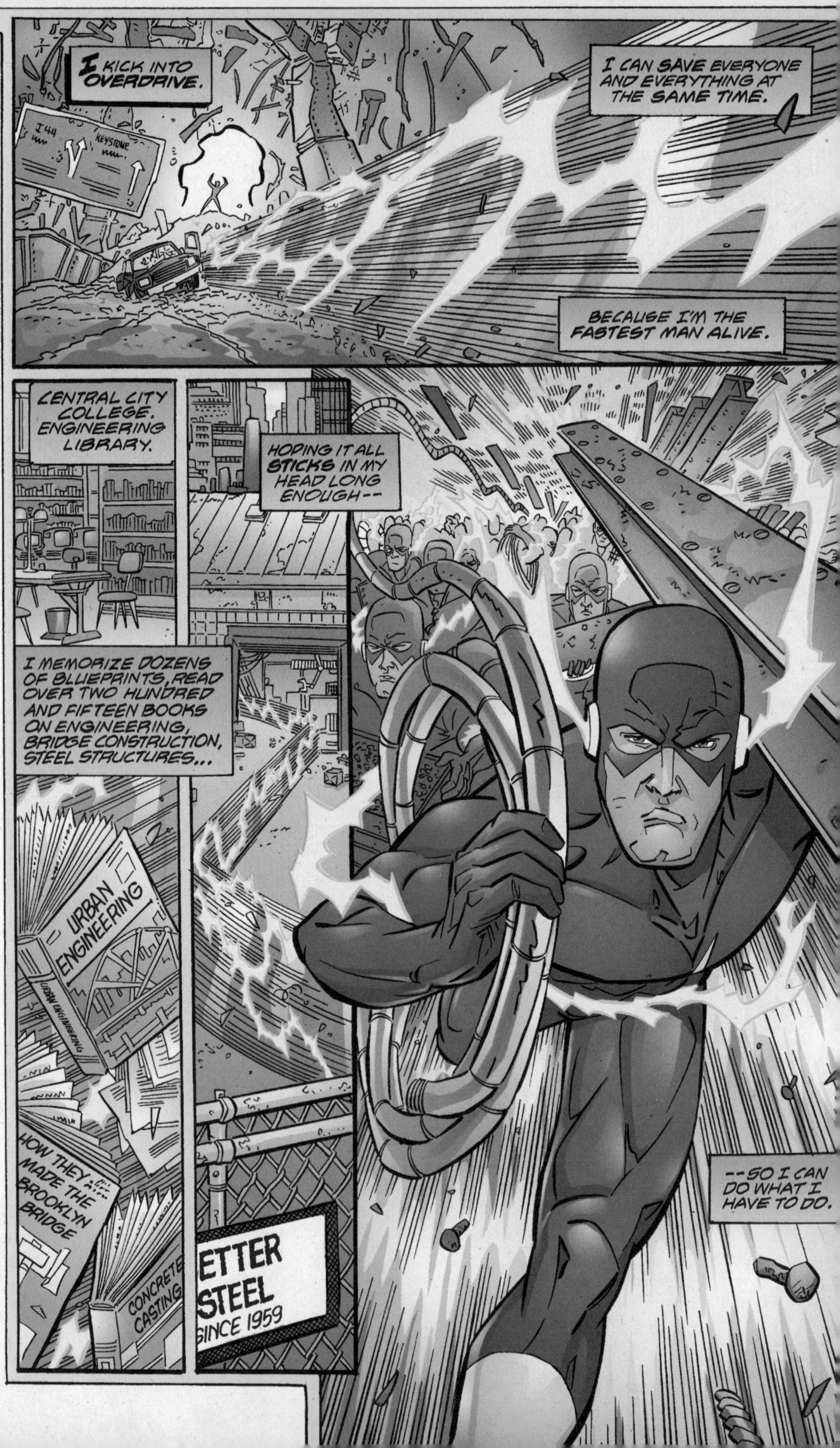
I KICK INTO OVERDRIVE.
I 44
KEYSTONE
I CAN SAVE EVERYONE AND EVERYTHING AT THE SAME TIME.
BECAUSE I'M THE FASTEST MAN ALIVE.
CENTRAL CITY COLLEGE. ENGINEERING LIBRARY.
HOPING IT ALL STICKS IN MY HEAD LONG ENOUGH--
I MEMORIZE DOZENS OF BLUEPRINTS, READ OVER TWO HUNDRED AND FIFTEEN BOOKS ON ENGINEERING, BRIDGE CONSTRUCTION, STEEL STRUCTURES...
URBAN ENGINEERING
URBAN ENGINEERING
HOW THEY MADE THE BROOKLYN BRIDGE
CONCRETE CASTING
ETTER STEEL SINCE 1959
--SO I CAN DO WHAT I HAVE TO DO.

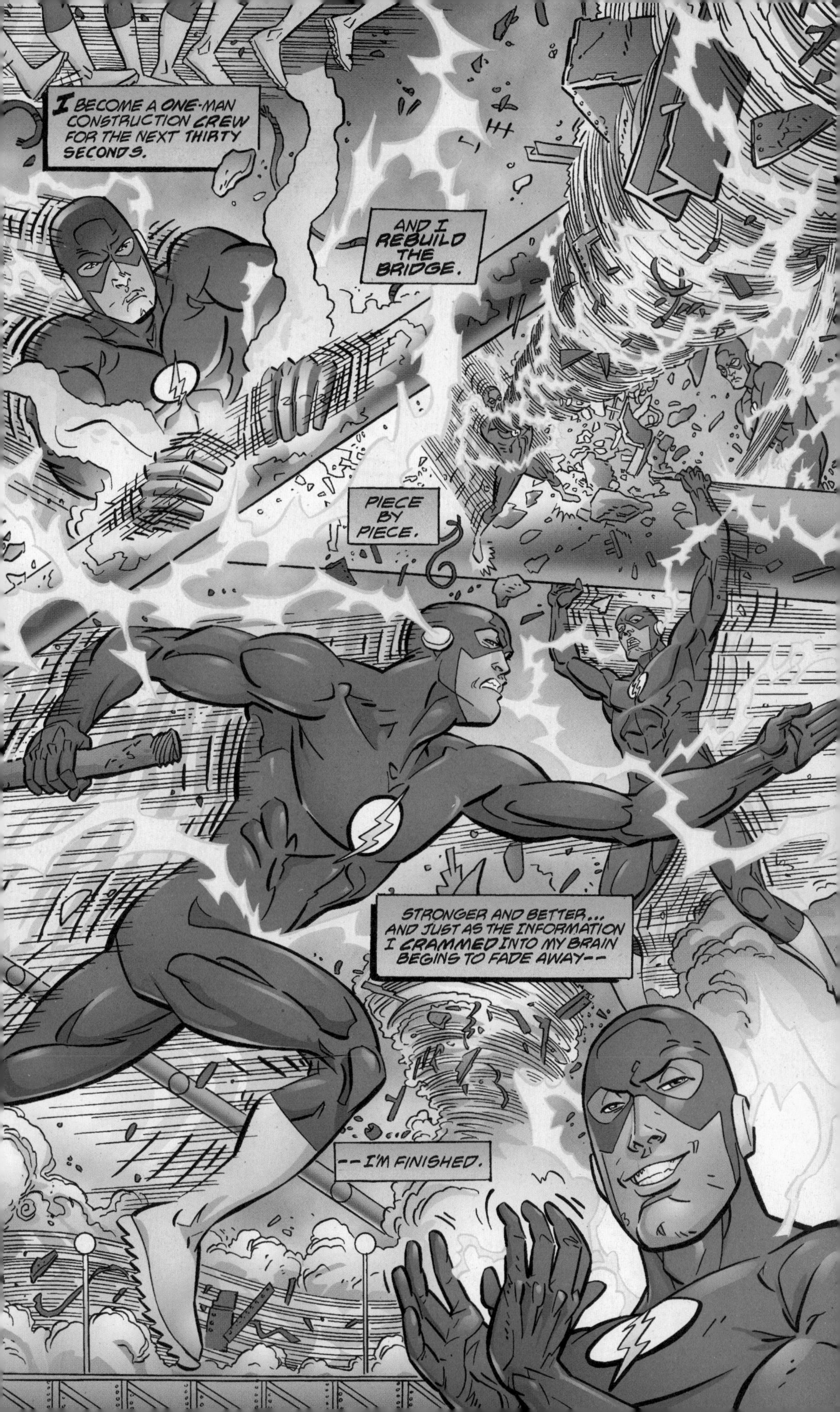
I BECOME A ONE-MAN CONSTRUCTION CREW FOR THE NEXT THIRTY SECONDS.
AND I REBUILD THE BRIDGE.
PIECE BY PIECE.
STRONGER AND BETTER... AND JUST AS THE INFORMATION I CRAMMED INTO MY BRAIN BEGINS TO FADE AWAY--
--I'M FINISHED.

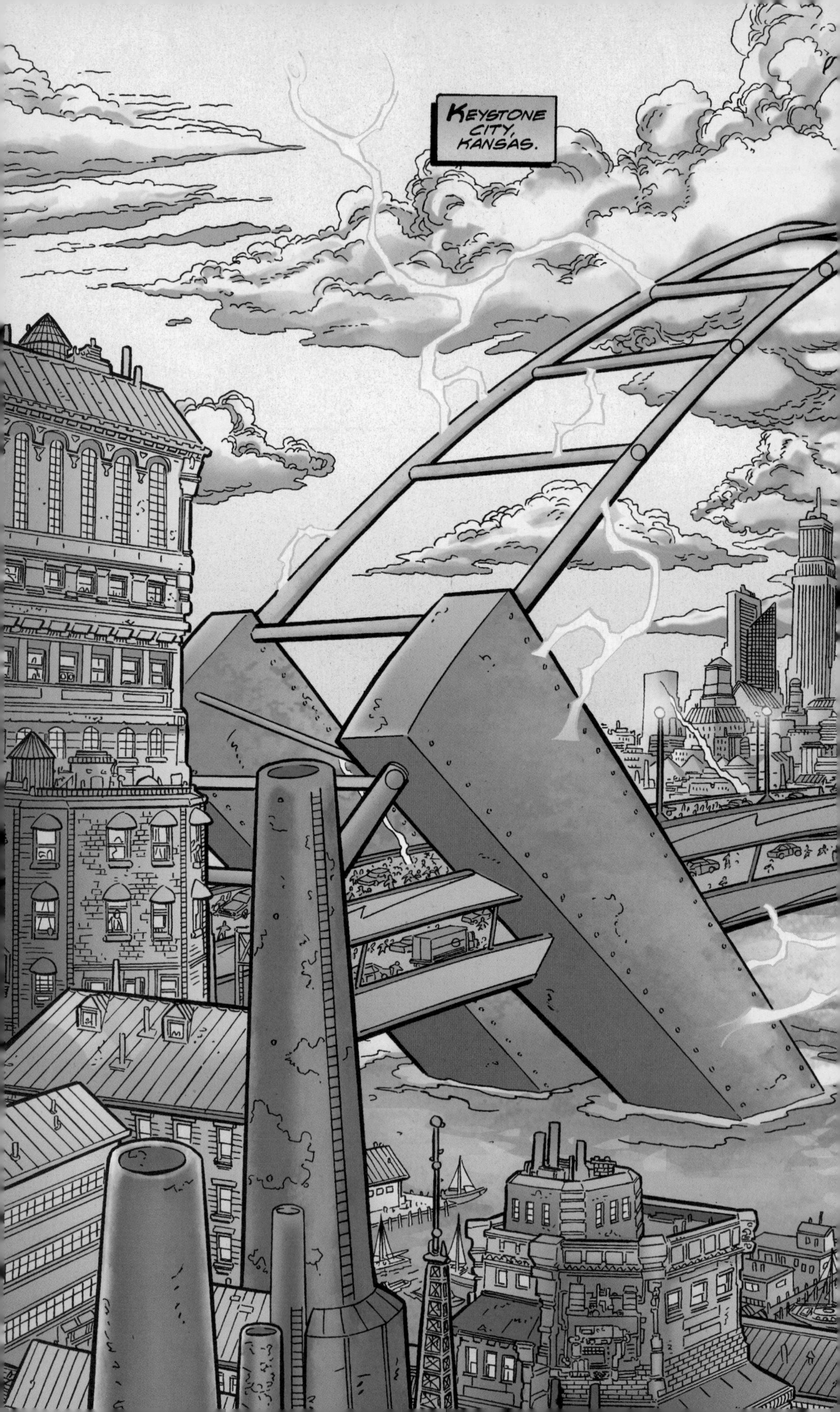
KEYSTONE CITY, KANSAS.

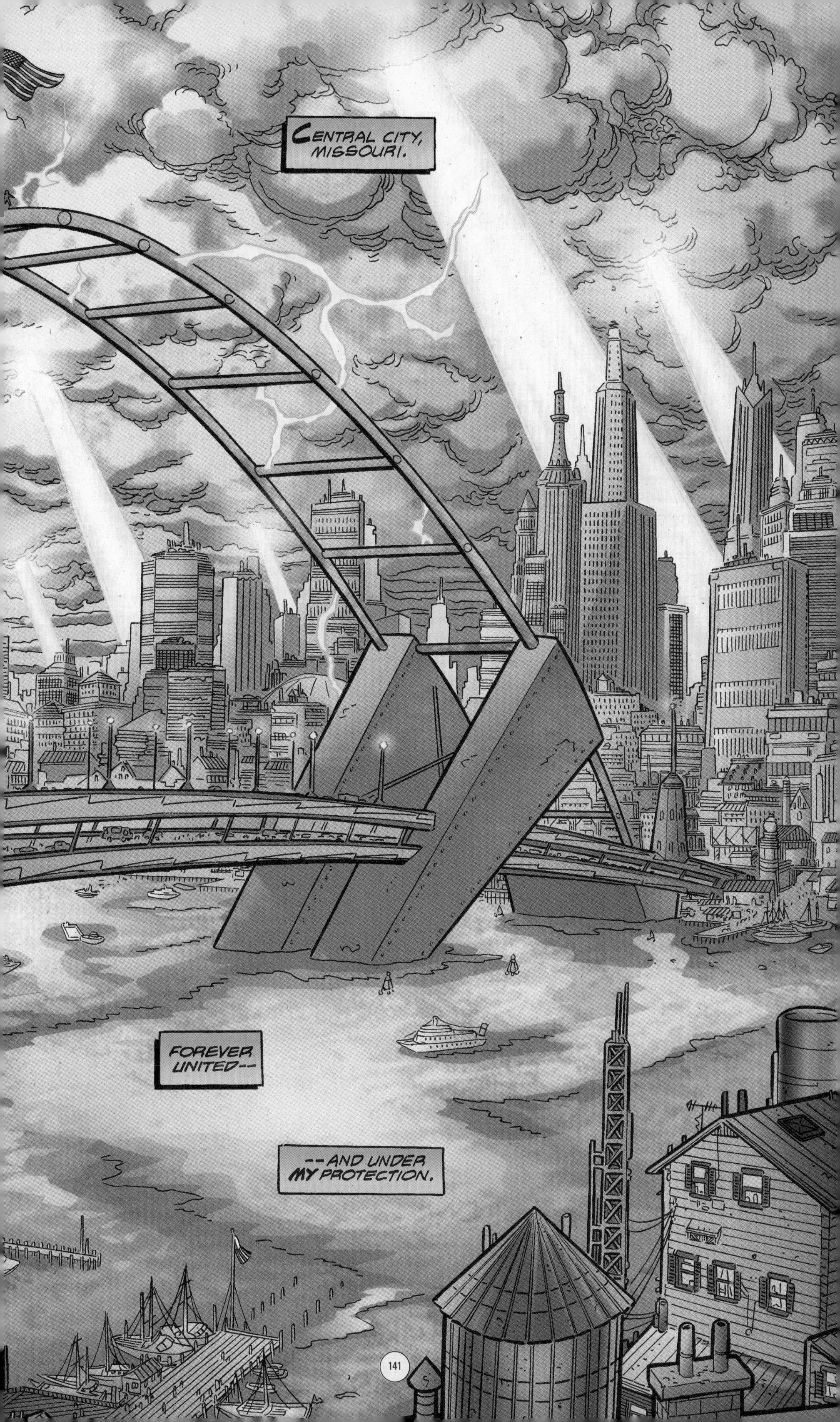
CENTRAL CITY, MISSOURI.
FOREVER UNITED--
--AND UNDER MY PROTECTION.

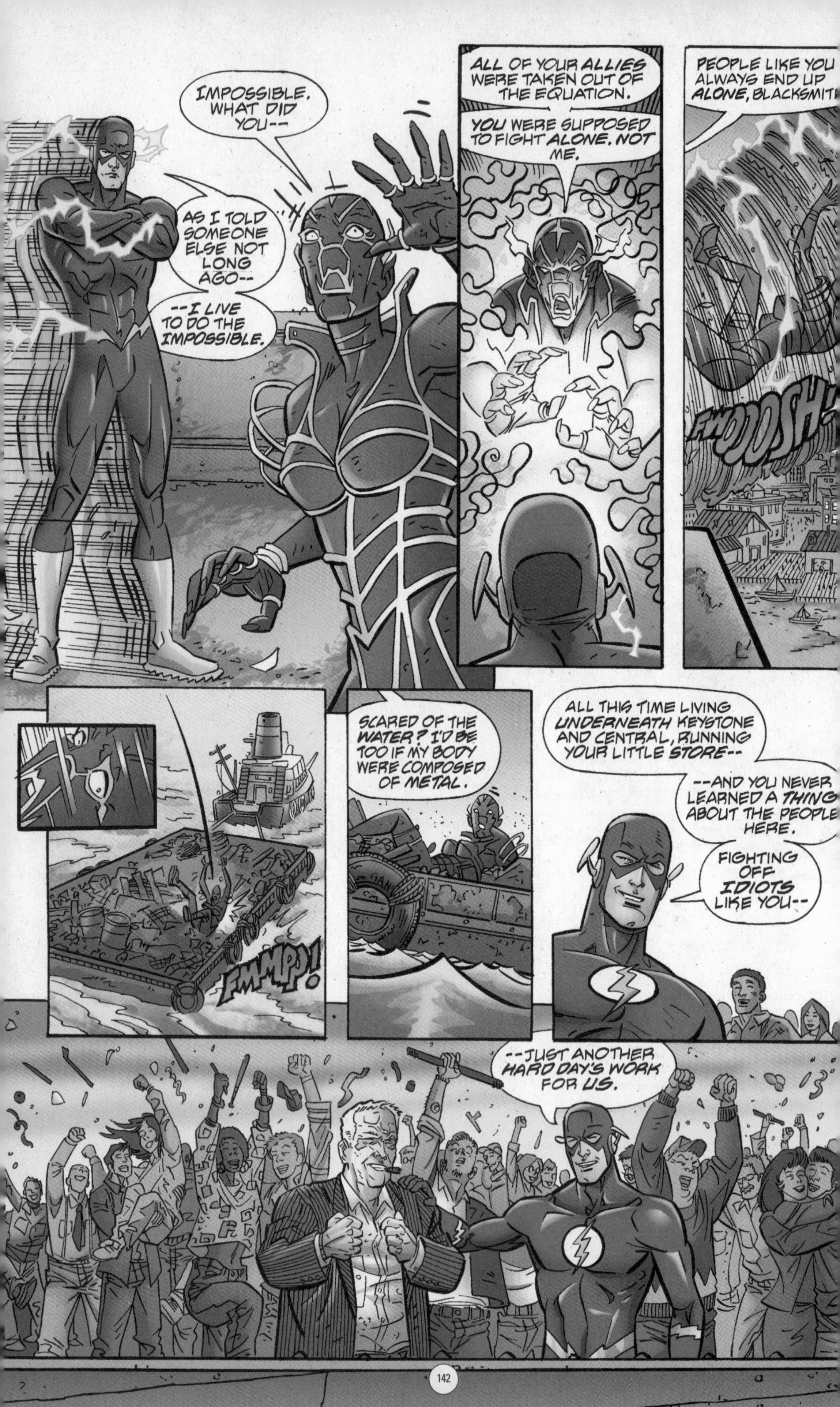
IMPOSSIBLE. WHAT DID YOU--
AS I TOLD SOMEONE ELSE NOT LONG AGO--
--I LIVE TO DO THE IMPOSSIBLE.
ALL OF YOUR ALLIES WERE TAKEN OUT OF THE EQUATION.
YOU WERE SUPPOSED TO FIGHT ALONE. NOT ME.
PEOPLE LIKE YOU ALWAYS END UP ALONE, BLACKSMITH
FWOOOSH!
FMMPP!
SCARED OF THE WATER? I'D BE TOO IF MY BODY WERE COMPOSED OF METAL.
ALL THIS TIME LIVING UNDERNEATH KEYSTONE AND CENTRAL, RUNNING YOUR LITTLE STORE--
--AND YOU NEVER LEARNED A THING ABOUT THE PEOPLE HERE.
FIGHTING OFF IDIOTS LIKE YOU--
--JUST ANOTHER HARD DAY'S WORK FOR US.

EPILOGUE ONE

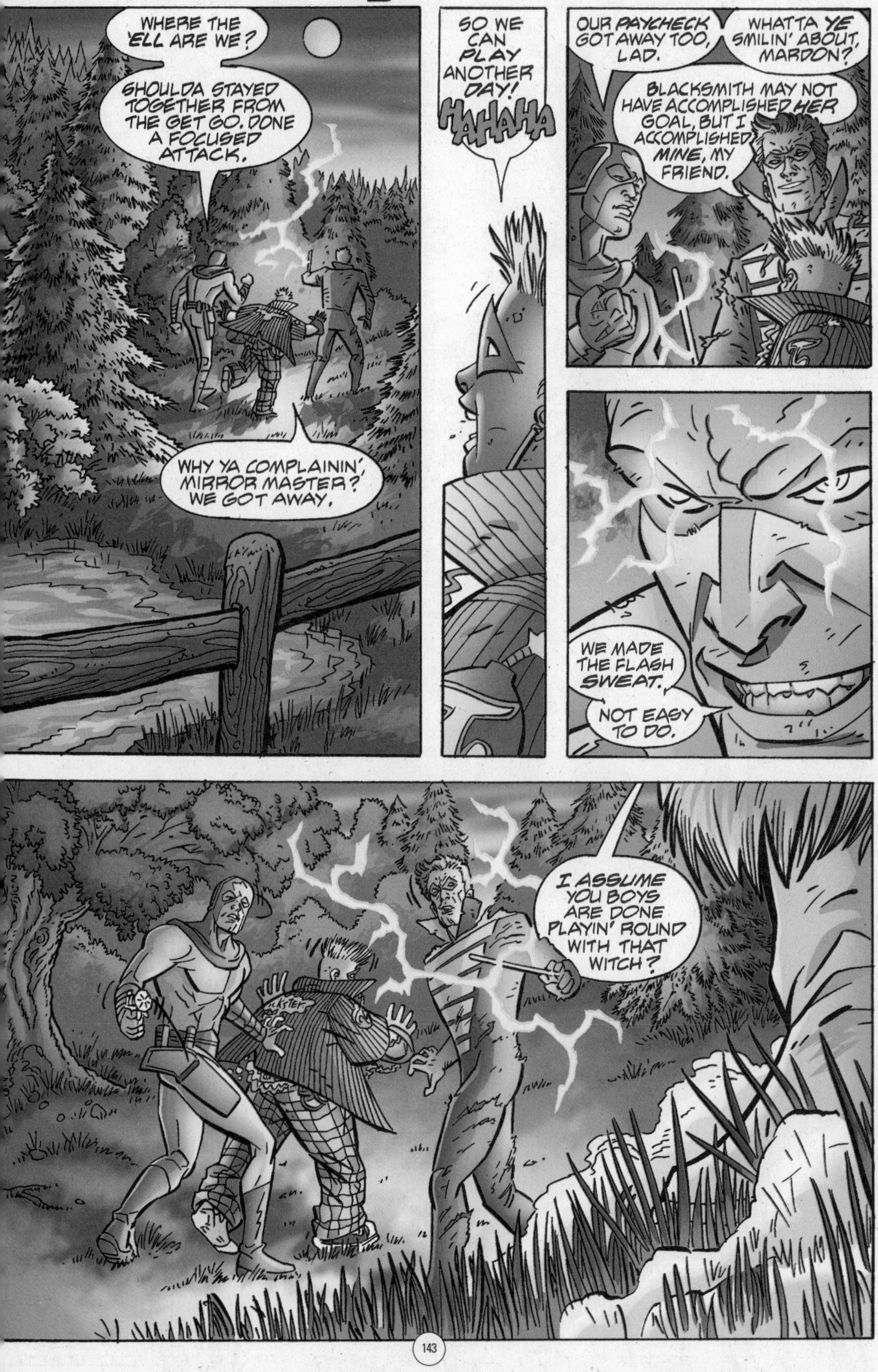
WHERE THE 'ELL ARE WE?
SHOULDA STAYED TOGETHER FROM THE GET GO. DONE A FOCUSED ATTACK.
WHY YA COMPLAININ', MIRROR MASTER? WE GOT AWAY.
SO WE CAN PLAY ANOTHER DAY!
HAHAHA
OUR PAYCHECK GOT AWAY TOO, LAD.
WHATTA YE SMILIN' ABOUT, MARDON?
BLACKSMITH MAY NOT HAVE ACCOMPLISHED HER GOAL, BUT I ACCOMPLISHED MINE, MY FRIEND.
WE MADE THE FLASH SWEAT.
NOT EASY TO DO.
I ASSUME YOU BOYS ARE DONE PLAYIN' ROUND WITH THAT WITCH?

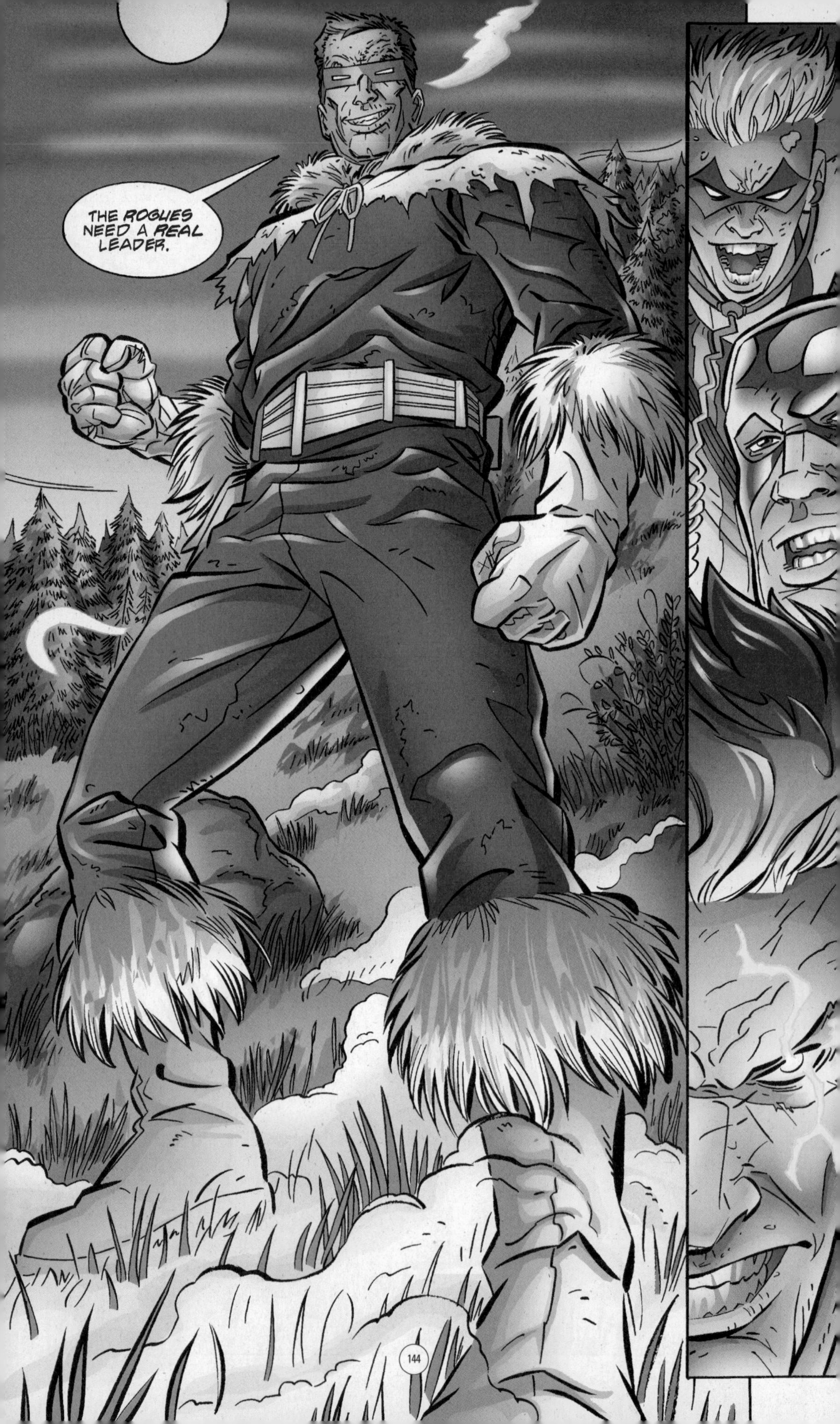
THE *ROGUES* NEED A *REAL* LEADER.

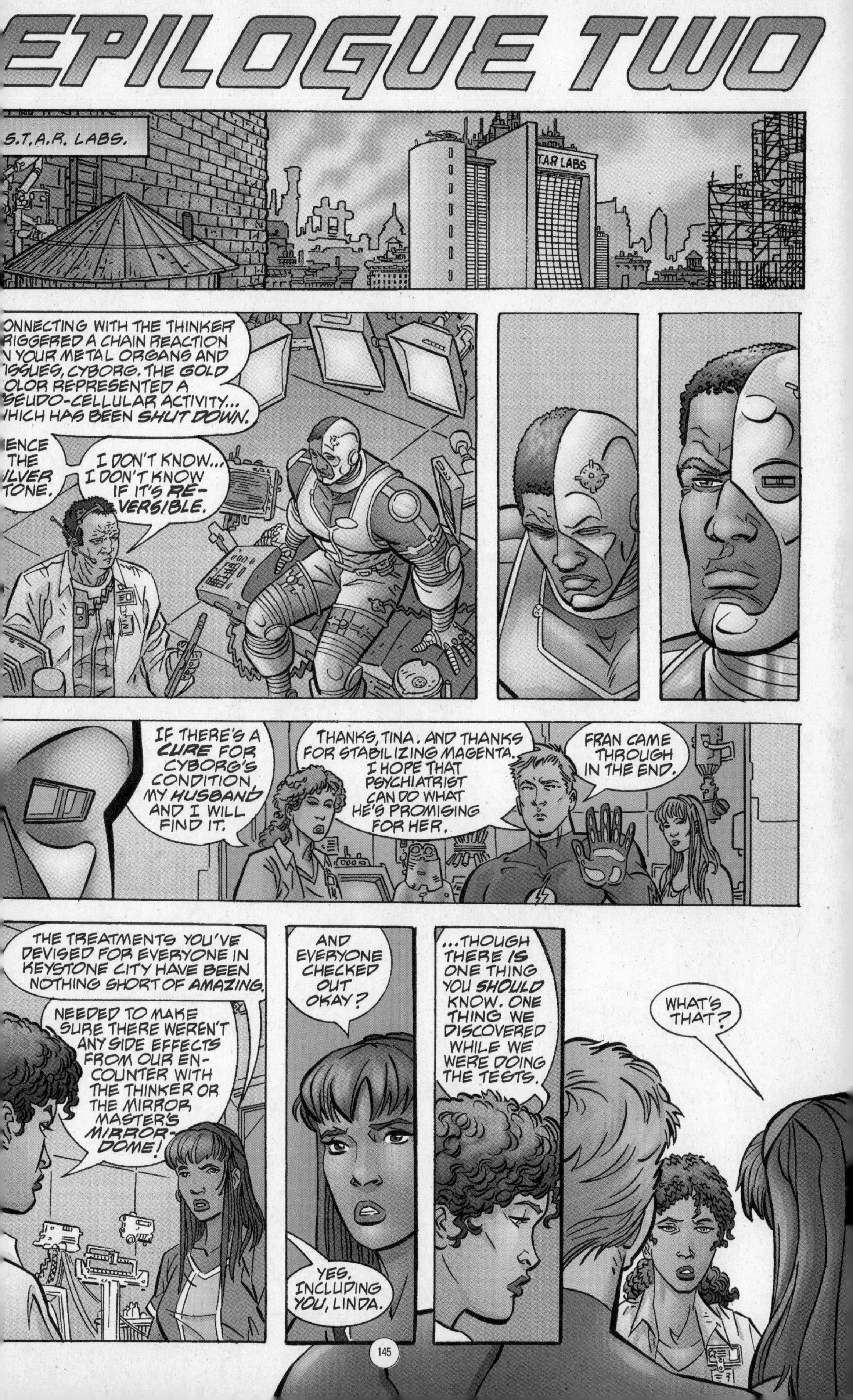

EPILOGUE TWO
S.T.A.R. LABS.
.T.A.R LABS
ONNECTING WITH THE THINKER RIGGERED A CHAIN REACTION N YOUR METAL ORGANS AND ISSUES, CYBORG. THE GOLD OLOR REPRESENTED A SEUDO-CELLULAR ACTIVITY... WHICH HAS BEEN SHUT DOWN.
ENCE THE ILVER TONE.
I DON'T KNOW... I DON'T KNOW IF IT'S RE-VERSIBLE.
IF THERE'S A CURE FOR CYBORG'S CONDITION, MY HUSBAND AND I WILL FIND IT.
THANKS, TINA. AND THANKS FOR STABILIZING MAGENTA. I HOPE THAT PSYCHIATRIST CAN DO WHAT HE'S PROMISING FOR HER.
FRAN CAME THROUGH IN THE END.
THE TREATMENTS YOU'VE DEVISED FOR EVERYONE IN KEYSTONE CITY HAVE BEEN NOTHING SHORT OF AMAZING.
NEEDED TO MAKE SURE THERE WEREN'T ANY SIDE EFFECTS FROM OUR EN-COUNTER WITH THE THINKER OR THE MIRROR MASTER'S MIRROR-DOME!
AND EVERYONE CHECKED OUT OKAY?
YES. INCLUDING YOU, LINDA.
...THOUGH THERE IS ONE THING YOU SHOULD KNOW. ONE THING WE DISCOVERED WHILE WE WERE DOING THE TESTS.
WHAT'S THAT?

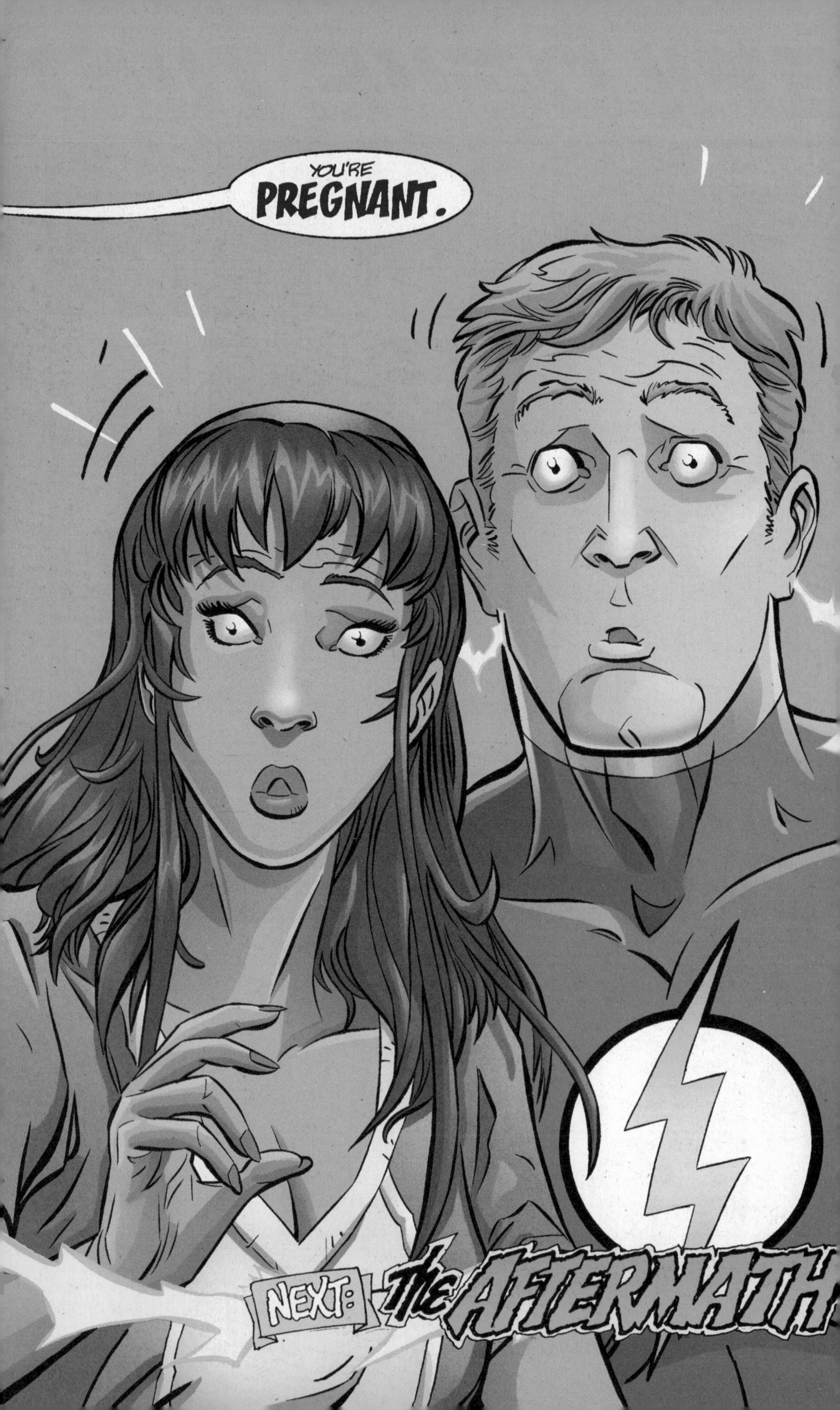

YOU'RE PREGNANT.
NEXT: THE AFTERMATH

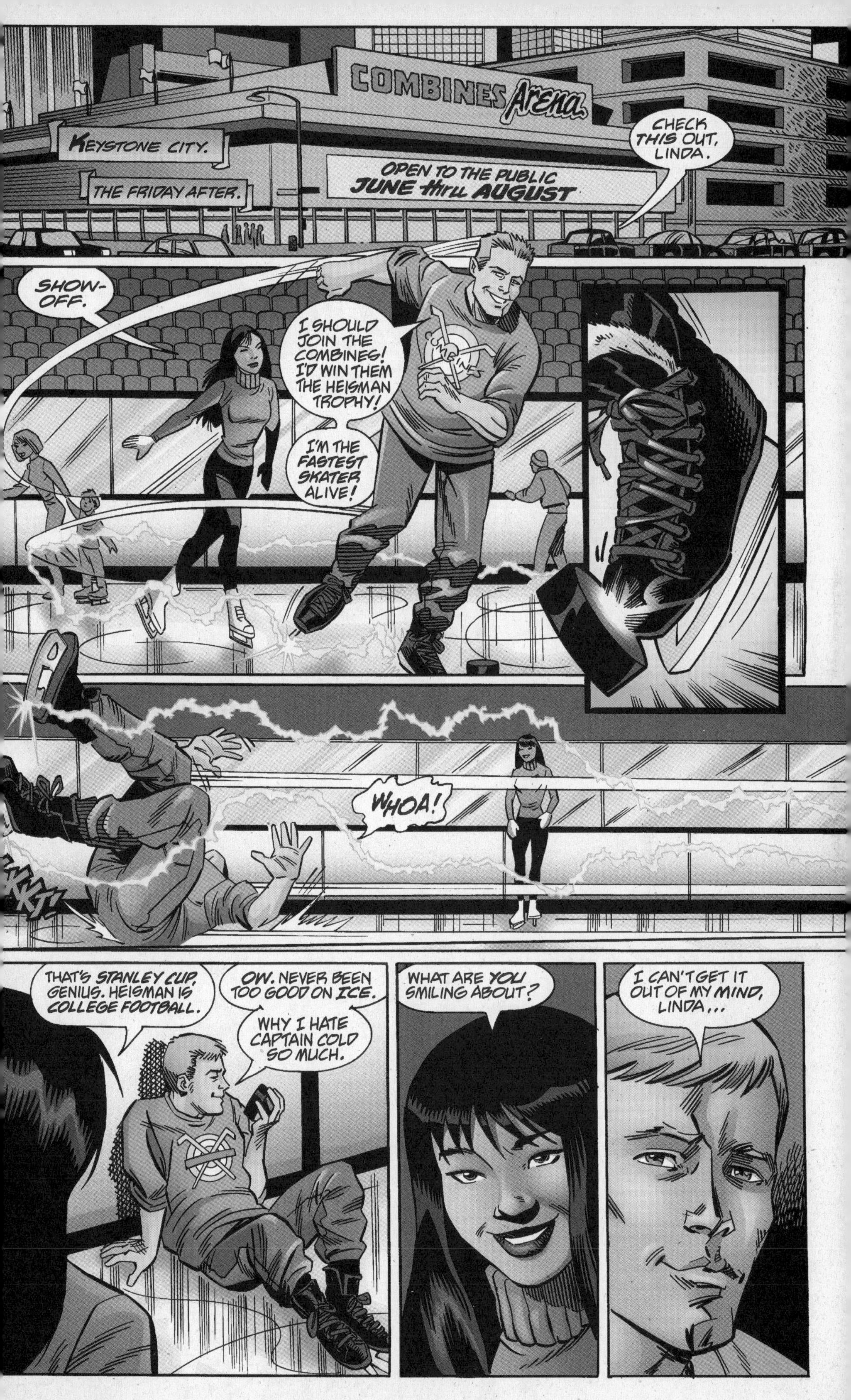
COMBINES Arena
KEYSTONE CITY.
THE FRIDAY AFTER.
OPEN TO THE PUBLIC JUNE thru AUGUST
CHECK THIS OUT, LINDA.
SHOW-OFF.
I SHOULD JOIN THE COMBINES! I'D WIN THEM THE HEISMAN TROPHY!
I'M THE FASTEST SKATER ALIVE!
WHOA!
THAT'S STANLEY CUP, GENIUS. HEISMAN IS COLLEGE FOOTBALL.
OW. NEVER BEEN TOO GOOD ON ICE.
WHY I HATE CAPTAIN COLD SO MUCH.
WHAT ARE YOU SMILING ABOUT?
I CAN'T GET IT OUT OF MY MIND, LINDA...

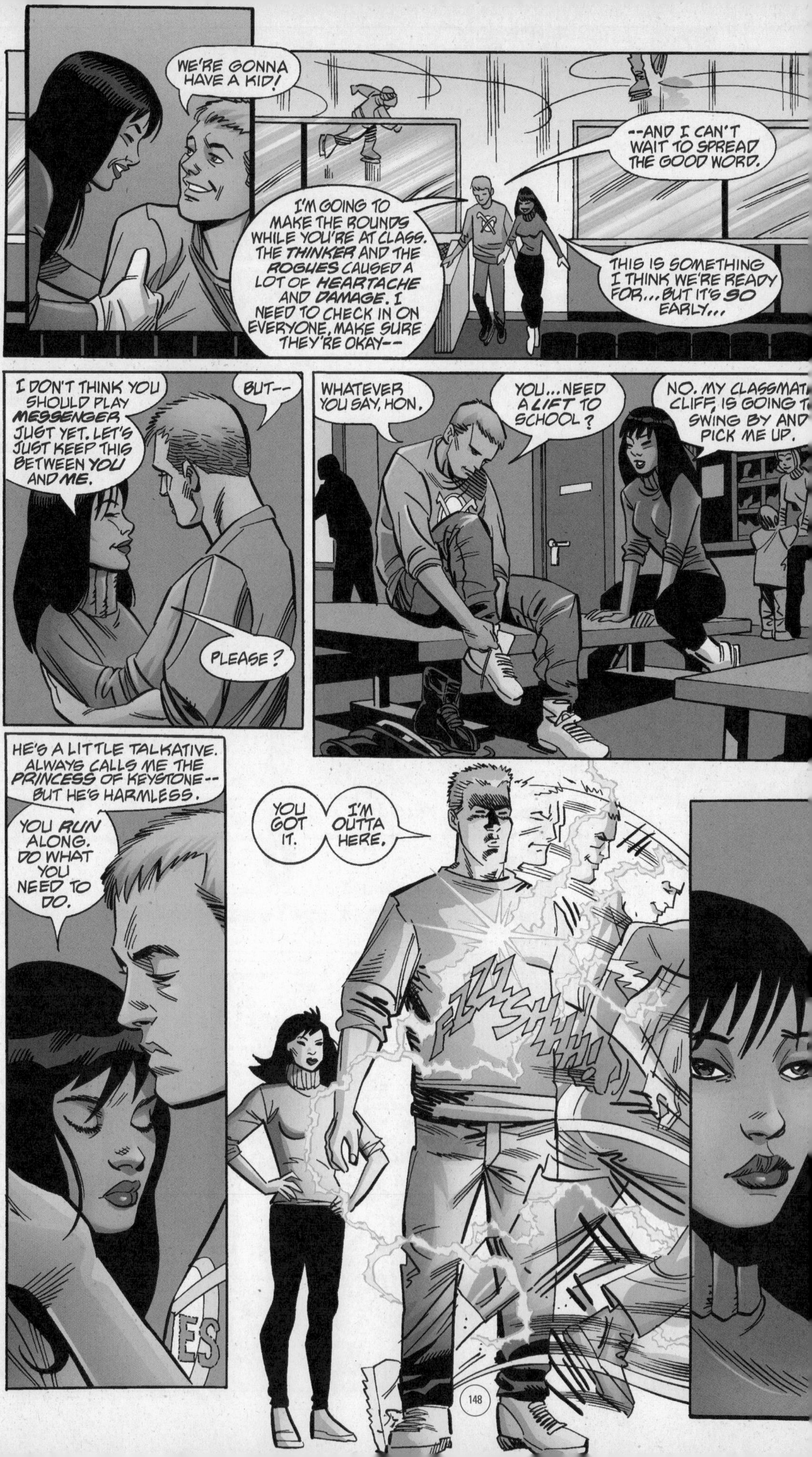
WE'RE GONNA HAVE A KID!
--AND I CAN'T WAIT TO SPREAD THE GOOD WORD.
I'M GOING TO MAKE THE ROUNDS WHILE YOU'RE AT CLASS. THE THINKER AND THE ROGUES CAUSED A LOT OF HEARTACHE AND DAMAGE. I NEED TO CHECK IN ON EVERYONE, MAKE SURE THEY'RE OKAY--
THIS IS SOMETHING I THINK WE'RE READY FOR... BUT IT'S SO EARLY...
I DON'T THINK YOU SHOULD PLAY MESSENGER JUST YET. LET'S JUST KEEP THIS BETWEEN YOU AND ME.
BUT--
PLEASE?
WHATEVER YOU SAY, HON.
YOU... NEED A LIFT TO SCHOOL?
NO. MY CLASSMAT CLIFF, IS GOING T SWING BY AND PICK ME UP.
HE'S A LITTLE TALKATIVE. ALWAYS CALLS ME THE PRINCESS OF KEYSTONE-- BUT HE'S HARMLESS.
YOU RUN ALONG. DO WHAT YOU NEED TO DO.
YOU GOT IT.
I'M OUTTA HERE.
FZZZSHHH

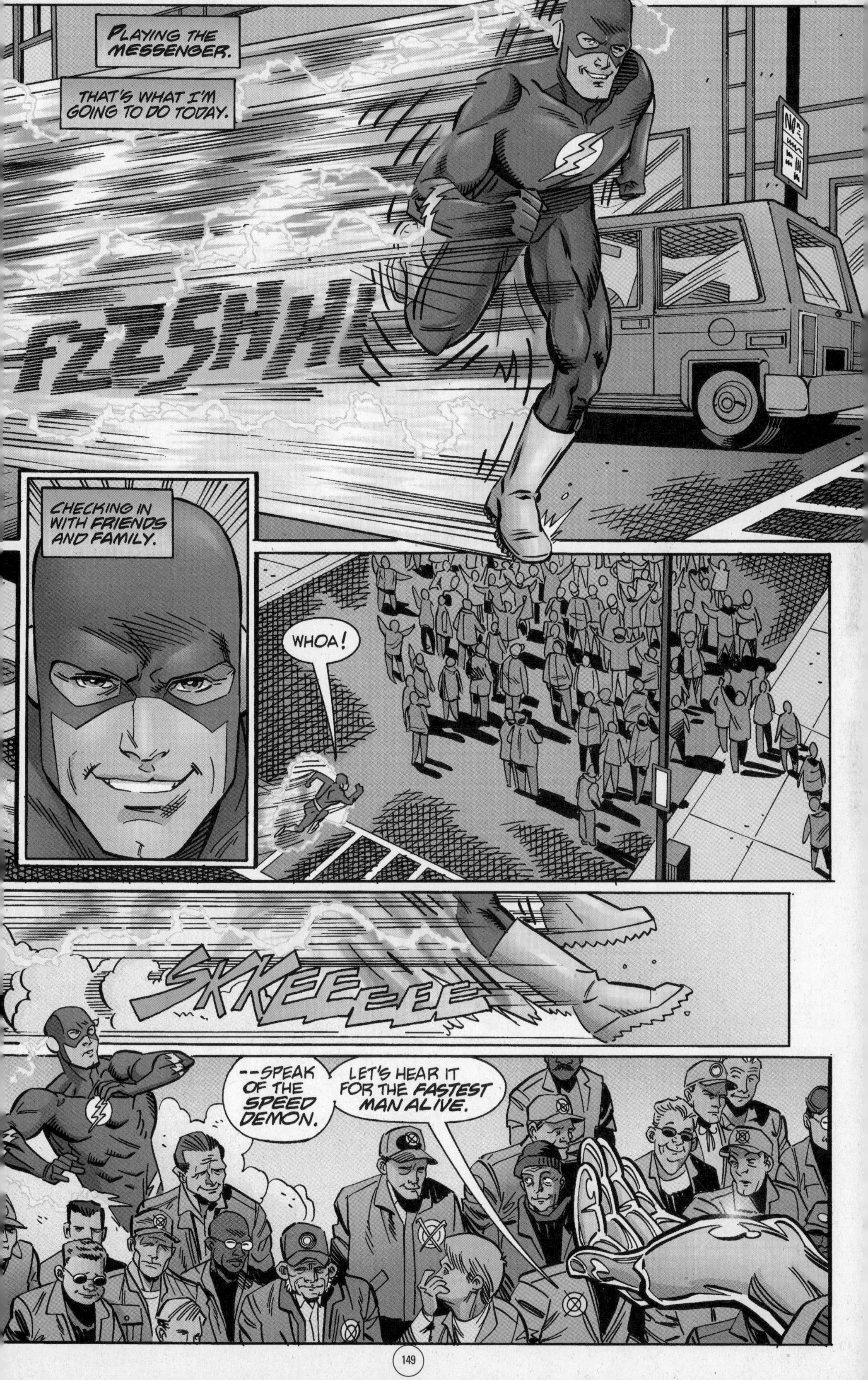

PLAYING THE MESSENGER.
THAT'S WHAT I'M GOING TO DO TODAY.
FZZSHHH!
CHECKING IN WITH FRIENDS AND FAMILY.
WHOA!
SKREEEEEE
--SPEAK OF THE SPEED DEMON.
LET'S HEAR IT FOR THE FASTEST MAN ALIVE.

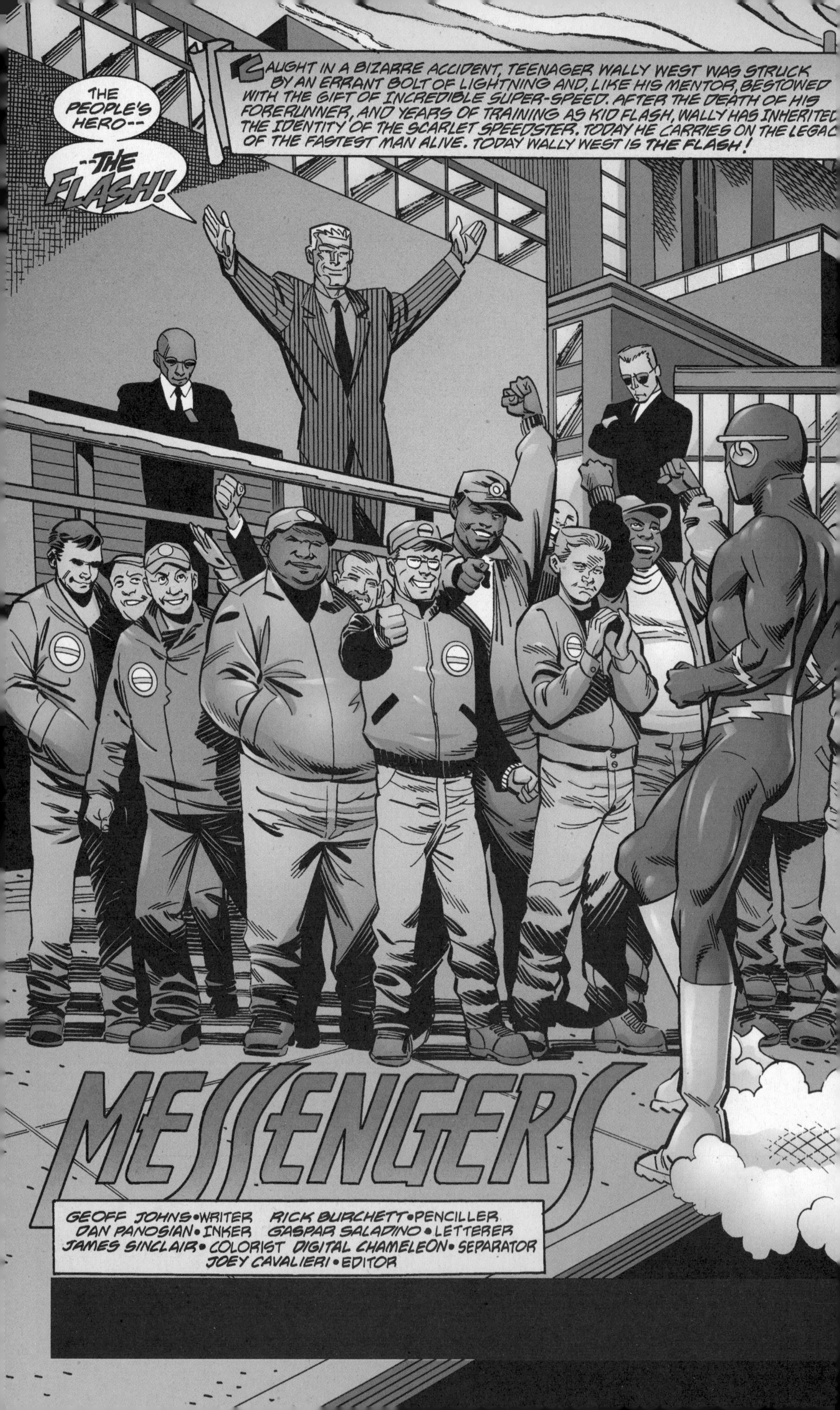
CAUGHT IN A BIZARRE ACCIDENT, TEENAGER WALLY WEST WAS STRUCK BY AN ERRANT BOLT OF LIGHTNING AND, LIKE HIS MENTOR, BESTOWED WITH THE GIFT OF INCREDIBLE SUPER-SPEED. AFTER THE DEATH OF HIS FORERUNNER, AND YEARS OF TRAINING AS KID FLASH, WALLY HAS INHERITED THE IDENTITY OF THE SCARLET SPEEDSTER. TODAY HE CARRIES ON THE LEGAC OF THE FASTEST MAN ALIVE. TODAY WALLY WEST IS THE FLASH!
THE PEOPLE'S HERO--
--THE FLASH!
MESSENGERS
GEOFF JOHNS•WRITER RICK BURCHETT•PENCILLER
DAN PANOSIAN•INKER GASPAR SALADINO•LETTERER
JAMES SINCLAIR•COLORIST DIGITAL CHAMELEON•SEPARATOR
JOEY CAVALIERI•EDITOR

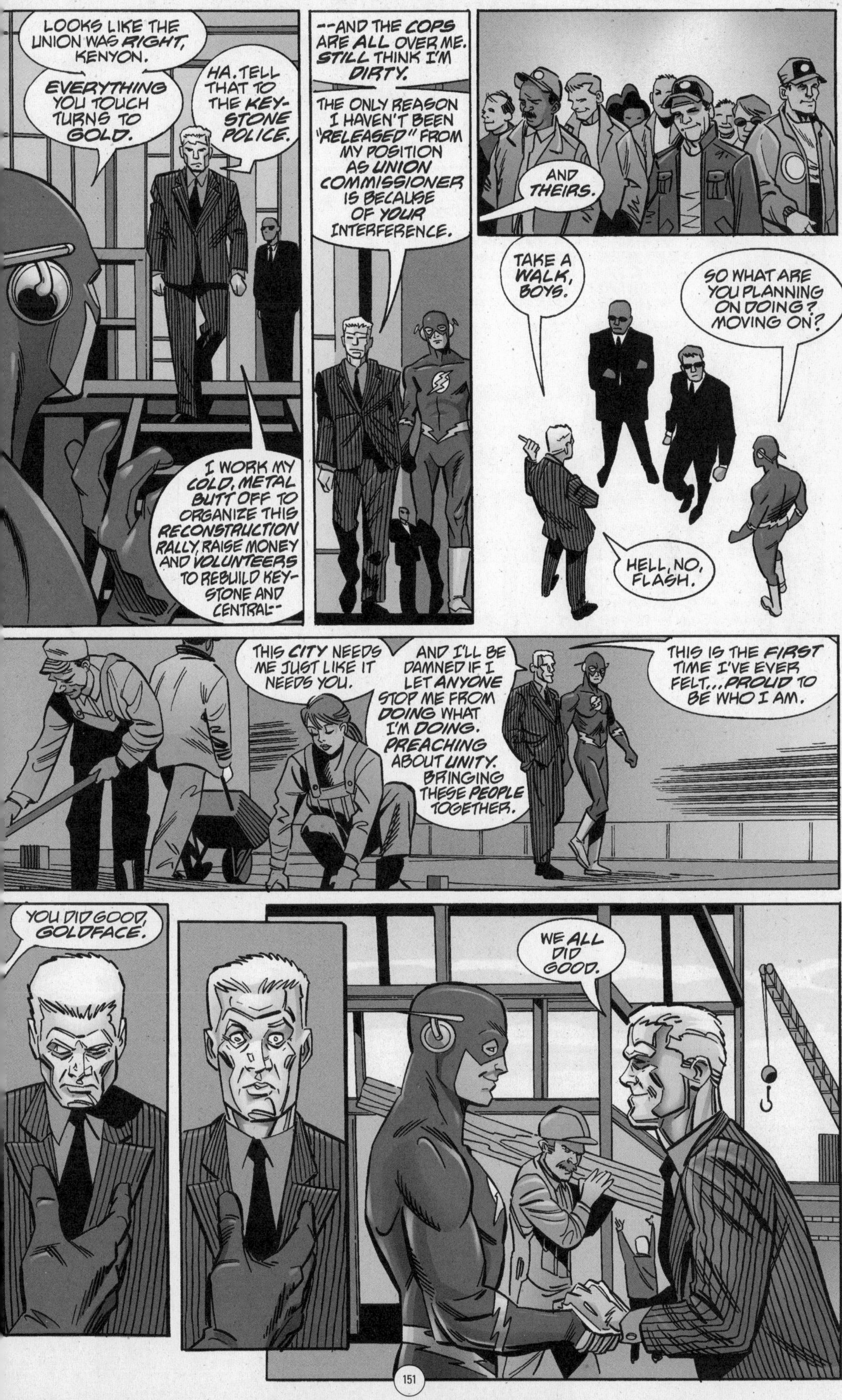
LOOKS LIKE THE UNION WAS RIGHT, KENYON.
EVERYTHING YOU TOUCH TURNS TO GOLD.
HA. TELL THAT TO THE KEY-STONE POLICE.
I WORK MY COLD, METAL BUTT OFF TO ORGANIZE THIS RECONSTRUCTION RALLY, RAISE MONEY AND VOLUNTEERS TO REBUILD KEY-STONE AND CENTRAL--
--AND THE COPS ARE ALL OVER ME. STILL THINK I'M DIRTY.
THE ONLY REASON I HAVEN'T BEEN "RELEASED" FROM MY POSITION AS UNION COMMISSIONER IS BECAUSE OF YOUR INTERFERENCE.
AND THEIRS.
TAKE A WALK, BOYS.
SO WHAT ARE YOU PLANNING ON DOING? MOVING ON?
HELL, NO, FLASH.
THIS CITY NEEDS ME JUST LIKE IT NEEDS YOU.
AND I'LL BE DAMNED IF I LET ANYONE STOP ME FROM DOING WHAT I'M DOING. PREACHING ABOUT UNITY. BRINGING THESE PEOPLE TOGETHER.
THIS IS THE FIRST TIME I'VE EVER FELT... PROUD TO BE WHO I AM.
YOU DID GOOD, GOLDFACE.
WE ALL DID GOOD.

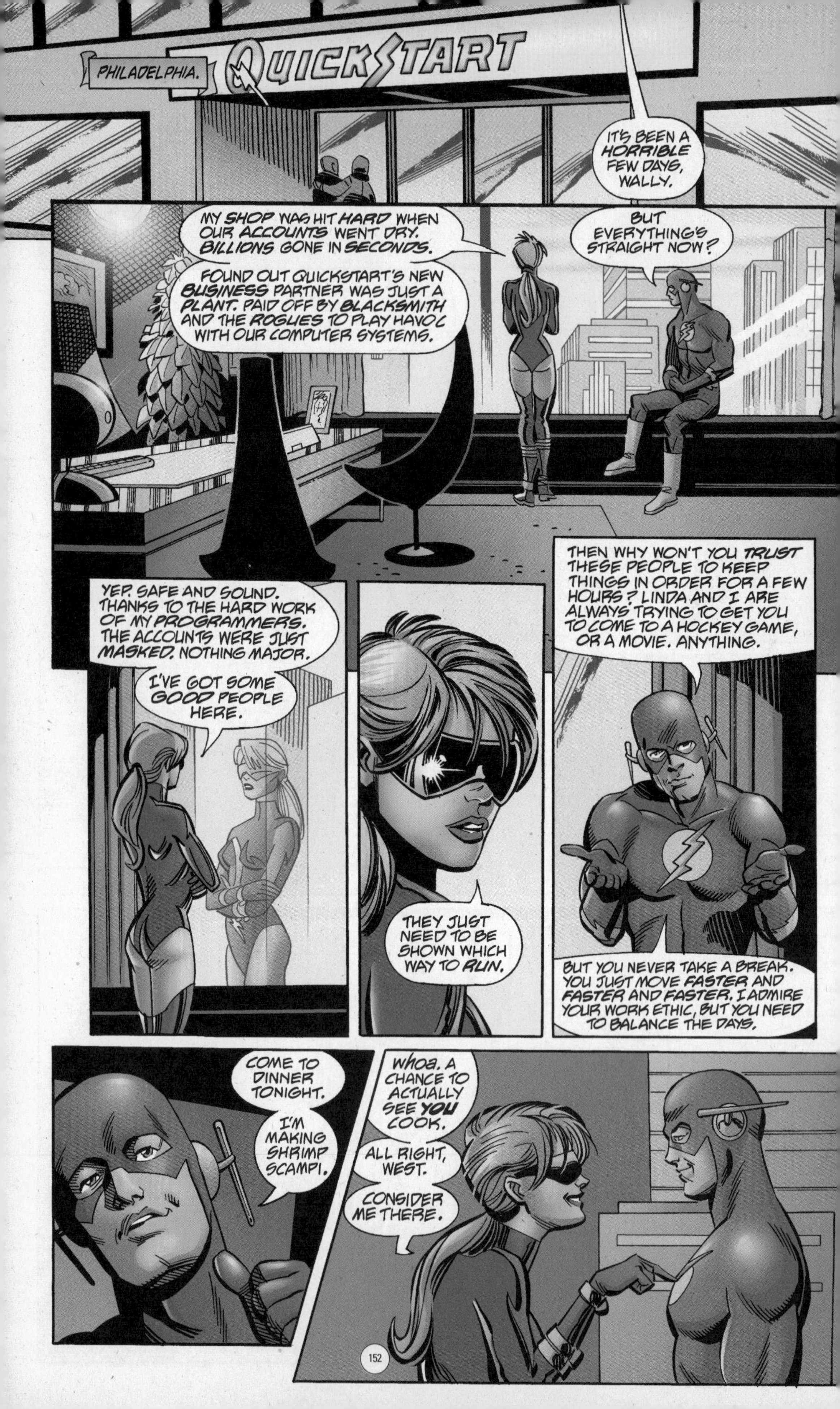

QUICKSTART
PHILADELPHIA.
IT'S BEEN A HORRIBLE FEW DAYS, WALLY.
MY SHOP WAS HIT HARD WHEN OUR ACCOUNTS WENT DRY. BILLIONS GONE IN SECONDS.
FOUND OUT QUICKSTART'S NEW BUSINESS PARTNER WAS JUST A PLANT. PAID OFF BY BLACKSMITH AND THE ROGUES TO PLAY HAVOC WITH OUR COMPUTER SYSTEMS.
BUT EVERYTHING'S STRAIGHT NOW?
YEP. SAFE AND SOUND. THANKS TO THE HARD WORK OF MY PROGRAMMERS. THE ACCOUNTS WERE JUST MASKED. NOTHING MAJOR.
I'VE GOT SOME GOOD PEOPLE HERE.
THEY JUST NEED TO BE SHOWN WHICH WAY TO RUN.
THEN WHY WON'T YOU TRUST THESE PEOPLE TO KEEP THINGS IN ORDER FOR A FEW HOURS? LINDA AND I ARE ALWAYS TRYING TO GET YOU TO COME TO A HOCKEY GAME, OR A MOVIE. ANYTHING.
BUT YOU NEVER TAKE A BREAK. YOU JUST MOVE FASTER AND FASTER AND FASTER. I ADMIRE YOUR WORK ETHIC, BUT YOU NEED TO BALANCE THE DAYS.
COME TO DINNER TONIGHT.
I'M MAKING SHRIMP SCAMPI.
WHOA. A CHANCE TO ACTUALLY SEE YOU COOK.
ALL RIGHT, WEST.
CONSIDER ME THERE.

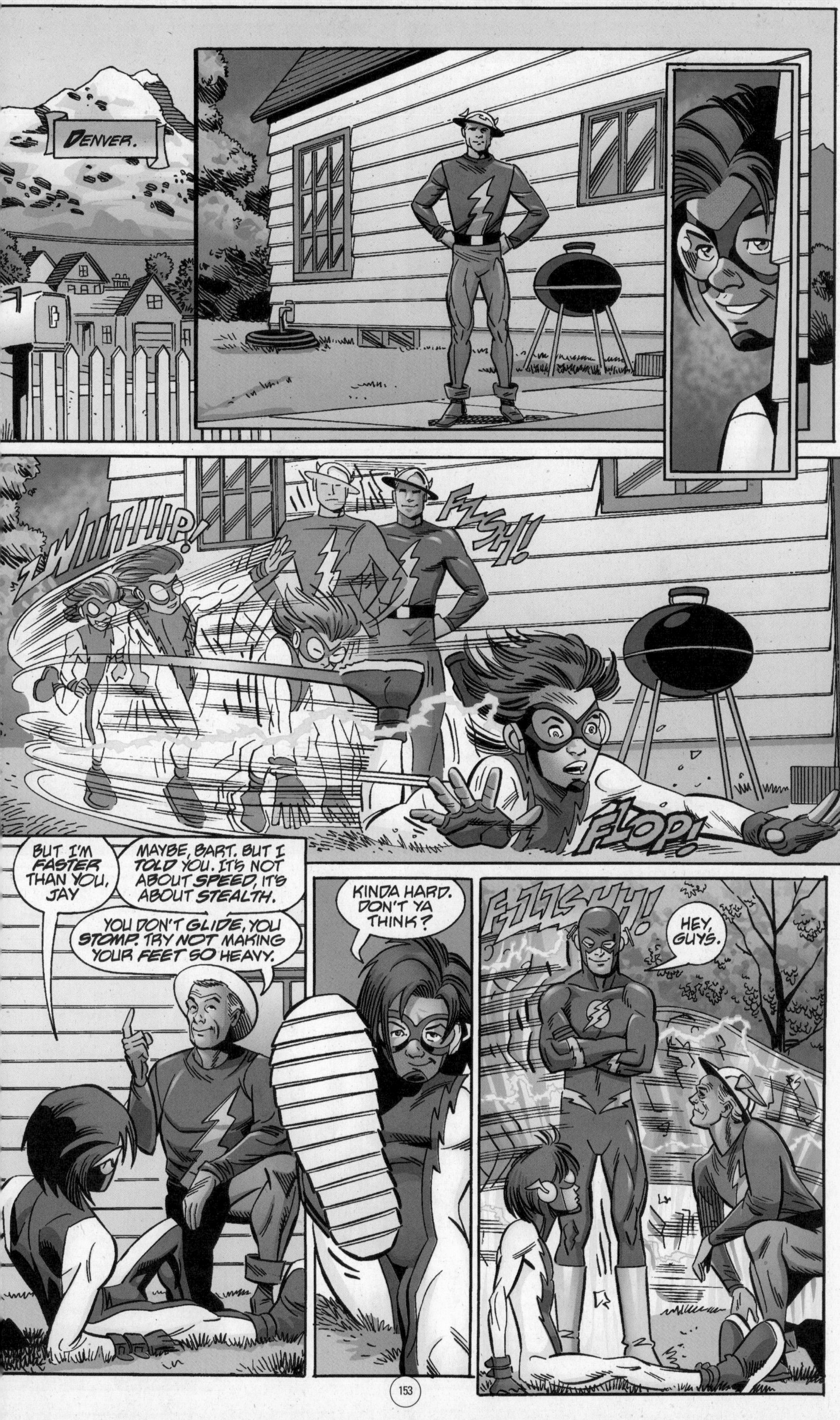
DENVER.
ZWIIIIIIP!
FZSH!
FLOP!
BUT I'M FASTER THAN YOU, JAY
MAYBE, BART. BUT I TOLD YOU. IT'S NOT ABOUT SPEED, IT'S ABOUT STEALTH.
YOU DON'T GLIDE, YOU STOMP. TRY NOT MAKING YOUR FEET SO HEAVY.
KINDA HARD. DON'T YA THINK?
FZZSHH!
HEY, GUYS.

WALLY!

IMPULSE. HOW YOU *TWO SPEEDSTERS* GETTING ALONG, JAY?

ALL RIGHT.

ZHWP!

YES! GOT IT!

REALLY ALL RIGHT, ACTUALLY.

THIS WHOLE *MESS*. IT'S LIKE WAKING UP FROM A *NIGHTMARE*.

WE *FELL* FOR ALL OF *RIVAL'S* LIES. THOUGHT JOAN'S *CANCER* WAS *UNTREATABLE*.

WHEN WE FOUND OUT THE *TRUTH*, THAT IT WASN'T AS *DIRE* AS HE TOLD US...I'VE NEVER BEEN *HAPPIER* IN MY LIFE.

WE'RE GOING TO STAY IN DENVER FOR A WHILE, WALLY. JOAN STILL HAS TREATMENT SHE NEEDS TO GO THROUGH.

PLUS--

--THIS *BOY* STILL NEEDS *TRAINING*.

I'VE GOT IT!

HEY! DIDN'T MR. TERRIFIC TEACH YA *FAIR PLAY*?! I WAS *NOT READY*.

HOW'S JOAN DOING?

NEVER BETTER, WALLY.

NEVER BETTER.

COOKIE?

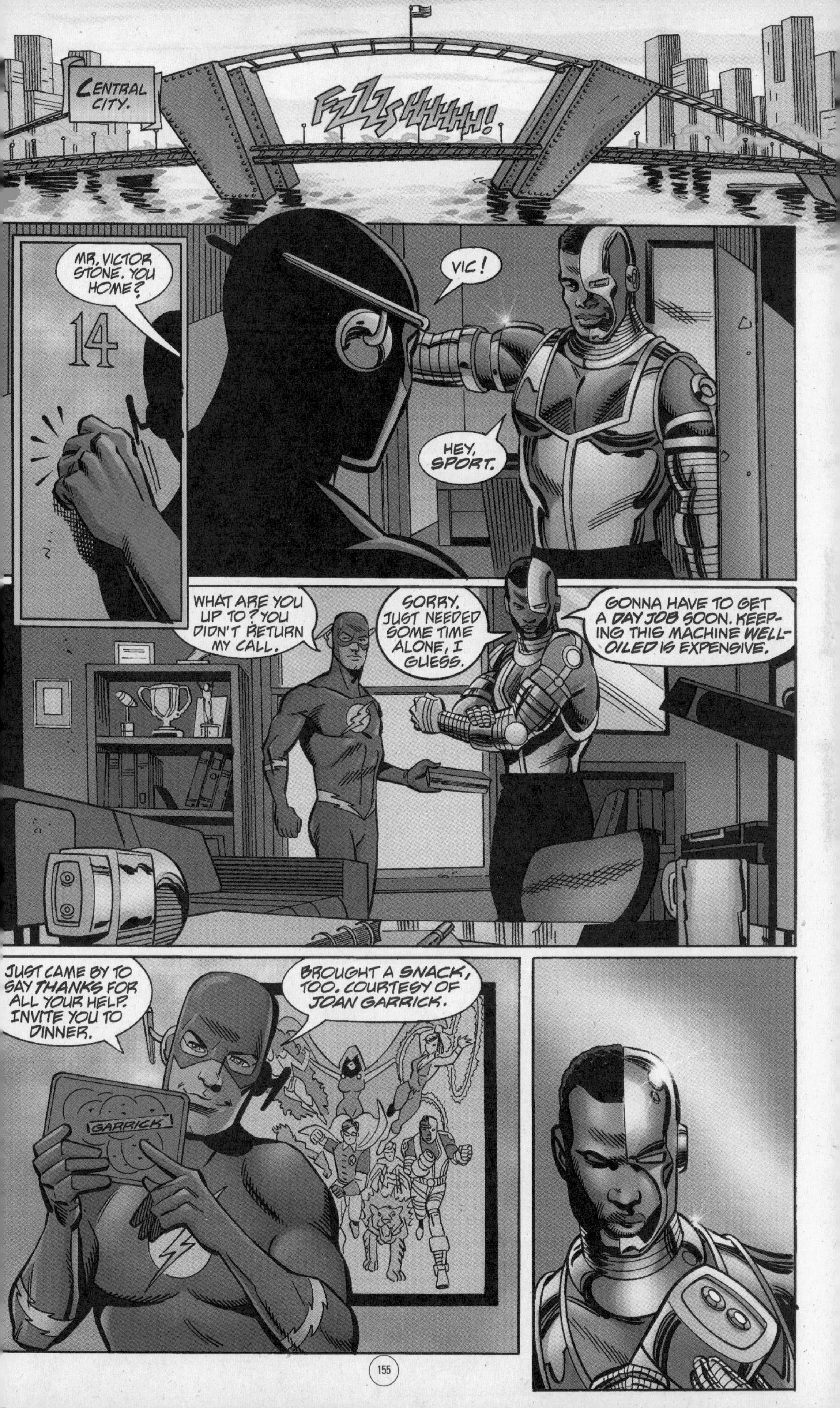
CENTRAL CITY.
FZZZSHHHHH!
MR. VICTOR STONE. YOU HOME?
14
VIC!
HEY, SPORT.
WHAT ARE YOU UP TO? YOU DIDN'T RETURN MY CALL.
SORRY. JUST NEEDED SOME TIME ALONE, I GUESS.
GONNA HAVE TO GET A DAY JOB SOON. KEEPING THIS MACHINE WELL-OILED IS EXPENSIVE.
JUST CAME BY TO SAY THANKS FOR ALL YOUR HELP. INVITE YOU TO DINNER.
BROUGHT A SNACK, TOO. COURTESY OF JOAN GARRICK.
GARRICK

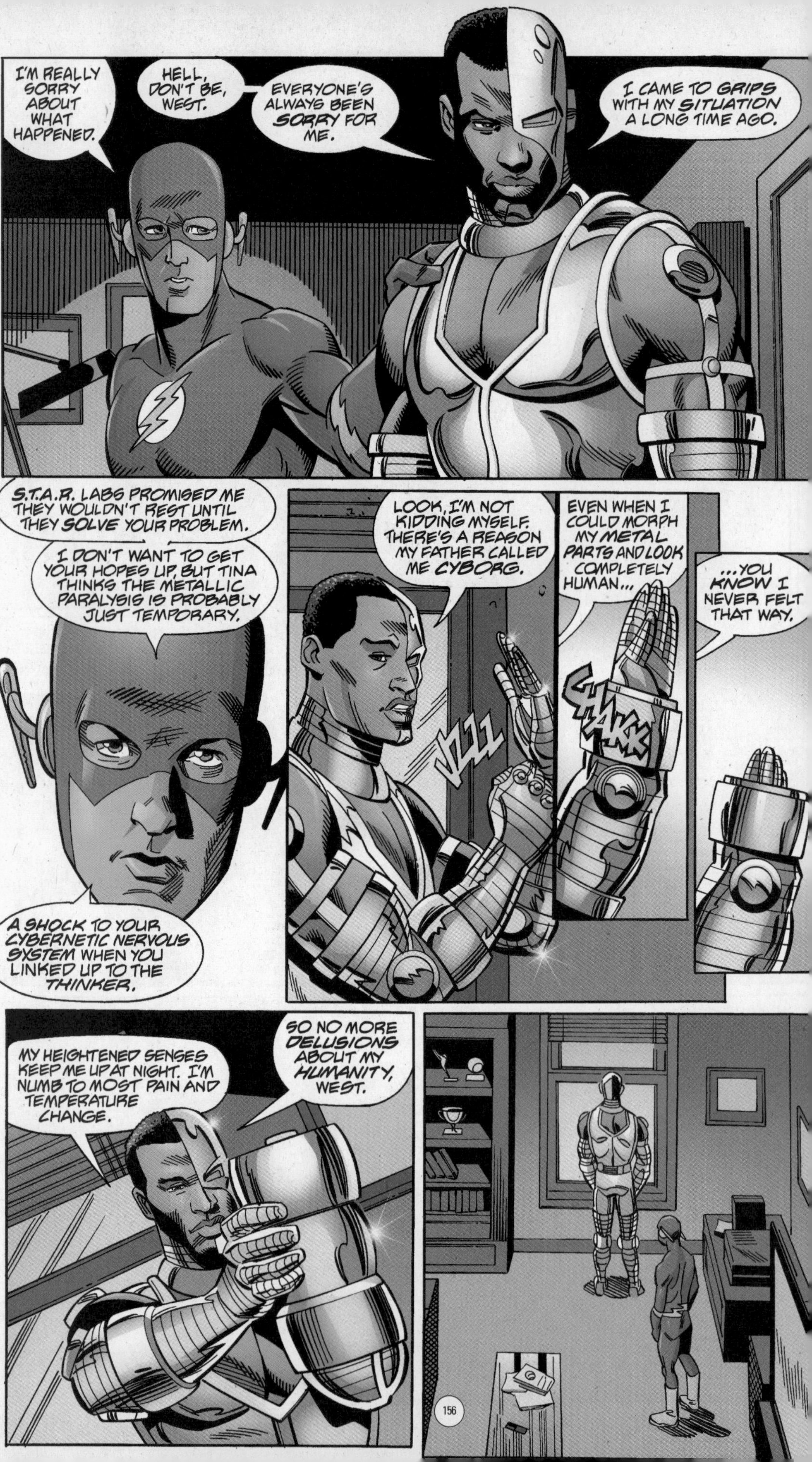
I'M REALLY SORRY ABOUT WHAT HAPPENED.
HELL, DON'T BE, WEST.
EVERYONE'S ALWAYS BEEN SORRY FOR ME.
I CAME TO GRIPS WITH MY SITUATION A LONG TIME AGO.
S.T.A.R. LABS PROMISED ME THEY WOULDN'T REST UNTIL THEY SOLVE YOUR PROBLEM.
I DON'T WANT TO GET YOUR HOPES UP, BUT TINA THINKS THE METALLIC PARALYSIS IS PROBABLY JUST TEMPORARY.
A SHOCK TO YOUR CYBERNETIC NERVOUS SYSTEM WHEN YOU LINKED UP TO THE THINKER.
LOOK, I'M NOT KIDDING MYSELF. THERE'S A REASON MY FATHER CALLED ME CYBORG.
JZZT
EVEN WHEN I COULD MORPH MY METAL PARTS AND LOOK COMPLETELY HUMAN...
CHAKK
...YOU KNOW I NEVER FELT THAT WAY.
MY HEIGHTENED SENSES KEEP ME UP AT NIGHT. I'M NUMB TO MOST PAIN AND TEMPERATURE CHANGE.
SO NO MORE DELUSIONS ABOUT MY HUMANITY, WEST.

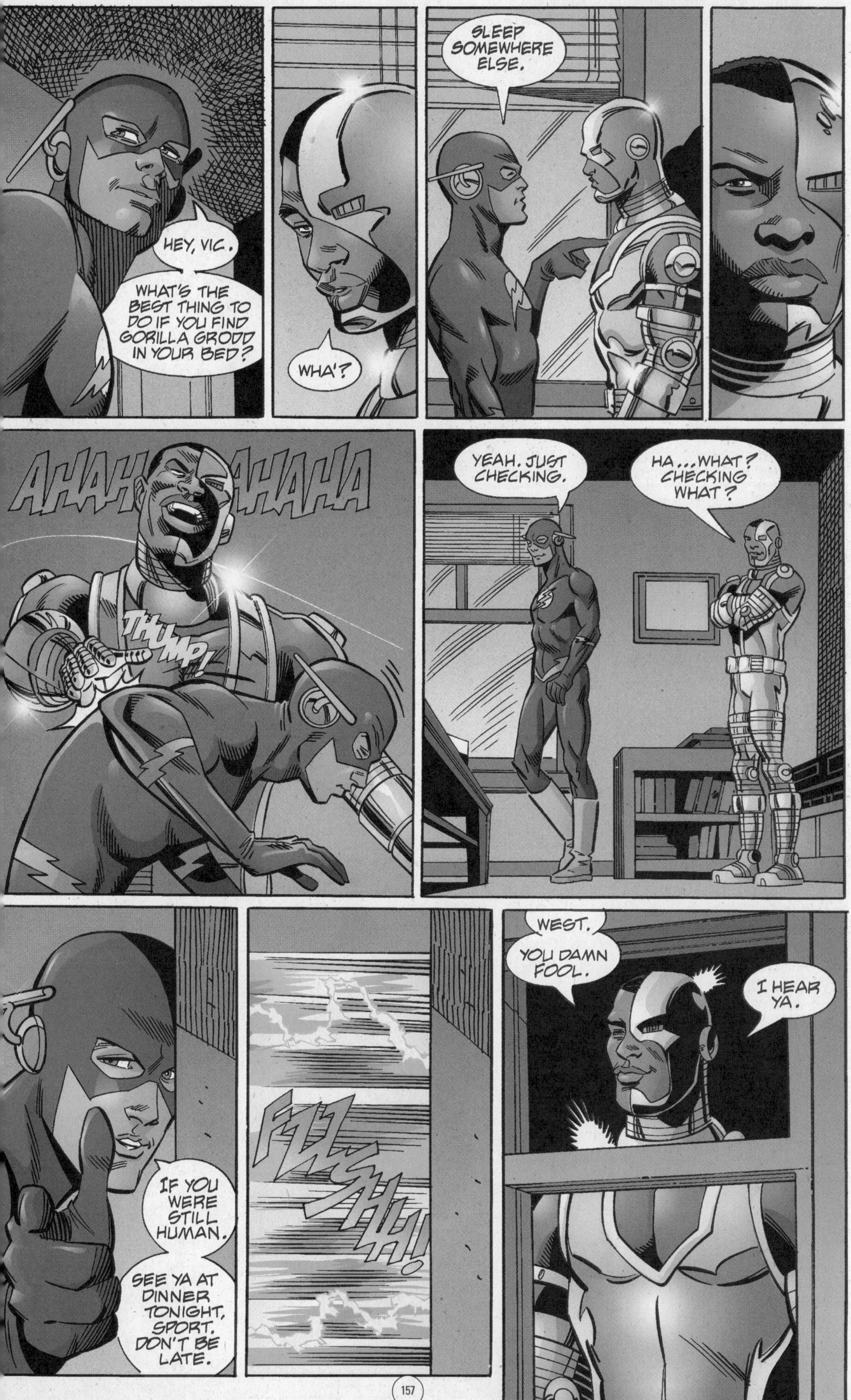
HEY, VIC.
WHAT'S THE BEST THING TO DO IF YOU FIND GORILLA GRODD IN YOUR BED?
WHA'?
SLEEP SOMEWHERE ELSE.
AHAHAHAHAHA
THUMP!
YEAH. JUST CHECKING.
HA...WHAT? CHECKING WHAT?
IF YOU WERE STILL HUMAN.
SEE YA AT DINNER TONIGHT, SPORT. DON'T BE LATE.
FZZSHH!
WEST.
YOU DAMN FOOL.
I HEAR YA.

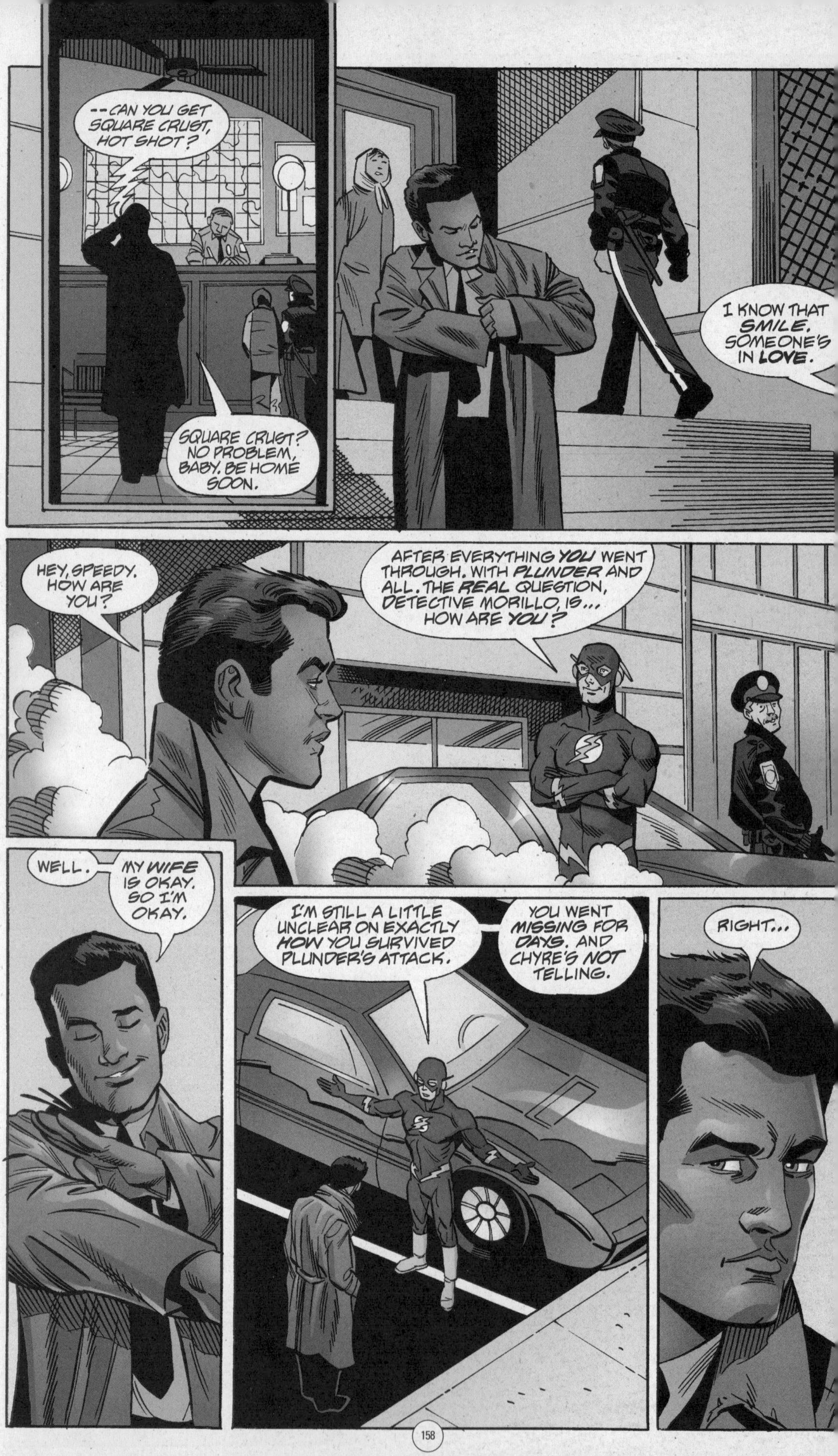
--CAN YOU GET SQUARE CRUST, HOT SHOT?
SQUARE CRUST? NO PROBLEM, BABY. BE HOME SOON.
I KNOW THAT SMILE. SOMEONE'S IN LOVE.
HEY, SPEEDY. HOW ARE YOU?
AFTER EVERYTHING YOU WENT THROUGH. WITH PLUNDER AND ALL. THE REAL QUESTION, DETECTIVE MORILLO, IS... HOW ARE YOU?
WELL.
MY WIFE IS OKAY. SO I'M OKAY.
I'M STILL A LITTLE UNCLEAR ON EXACTLY HOW YOU SURVIVED PLUNDER'S ATTACK.
YOU WENT MISSING FOR DAYS. AND CHYRE'S NOT TELLING.
RIGHT...

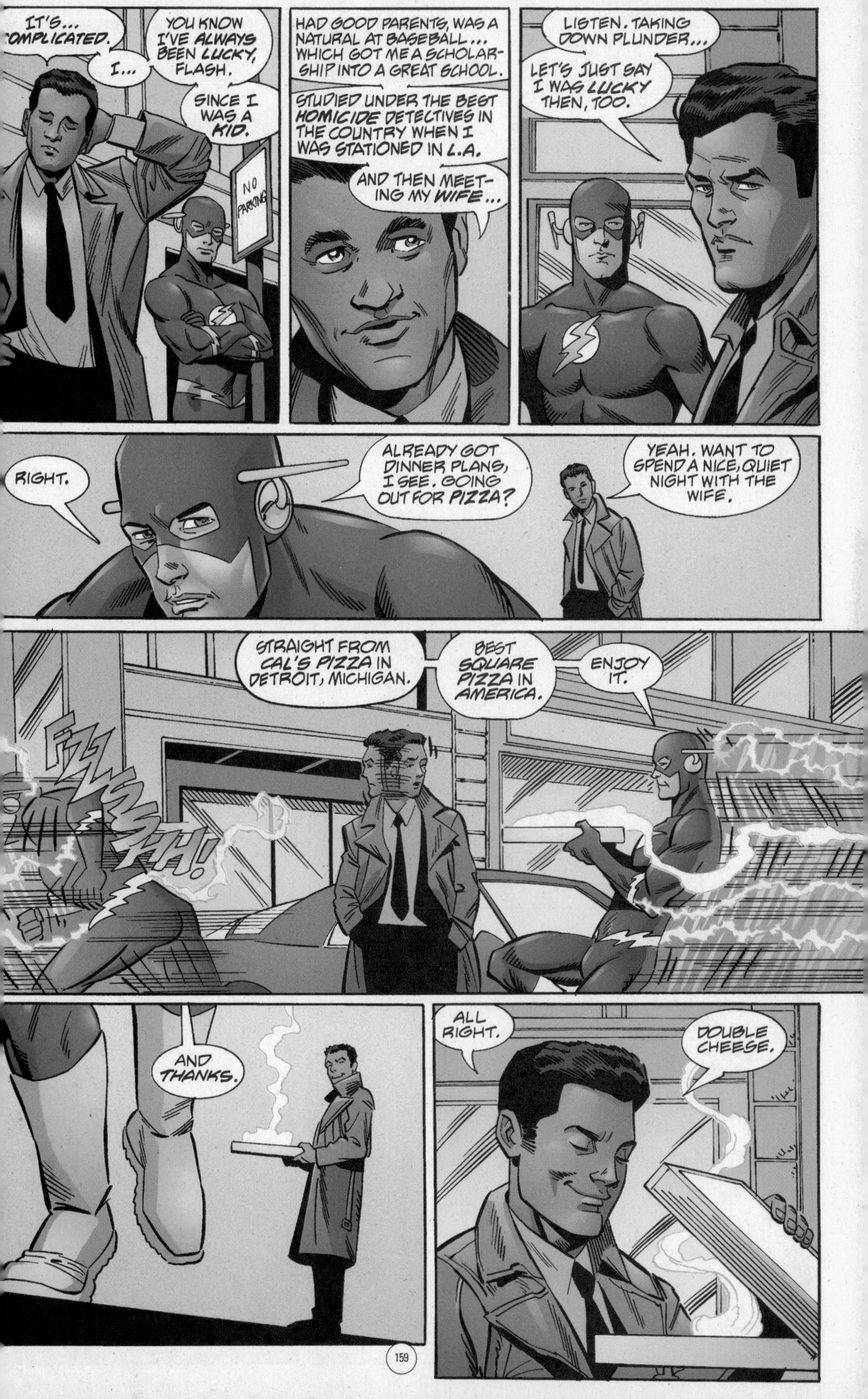
IT'S... COMPLICATED.
I...
YOU KNOW I'VE ALWAYS BEEN LUCKY, FLASH.
SINCE I WAS A KID.
NO PARKING
HAD GOOD PARENTS, WAS A NATURAL AT BASEBALL... WHICH GOT ME A SCHOLARSHIP INTO A GREAT SCHOOL.
STUDIED UNDER THE BEST HOMICIDE DETECTIVES IN THE COUNTRY WHEN I WAS STATIONED IN L.A.
AND THEN MEETING MY WIFE...
LISTEN. TAKING DOWN PLUNDER...
LET'S JUST SAY I WAS LUCKY THEN, TOO.
RIGHT.
ALREADY GOT DINNER PLANS, I SEE. GOING OUT FOR PIZZA?
YEAH. WANT TO SPEND A NICE, QUIET NIGHT WITH THE WIFE.
STRAIGHT FROM CAL'S PIZZA IN DETROIT, MICHIGAN.
BEST SQUARE PIZZA IN AMERICA.
ENJOY IT.
FZZWSSHH!
AND THANKS.
ALL RIGHT.
DOUBLE CHEESE.

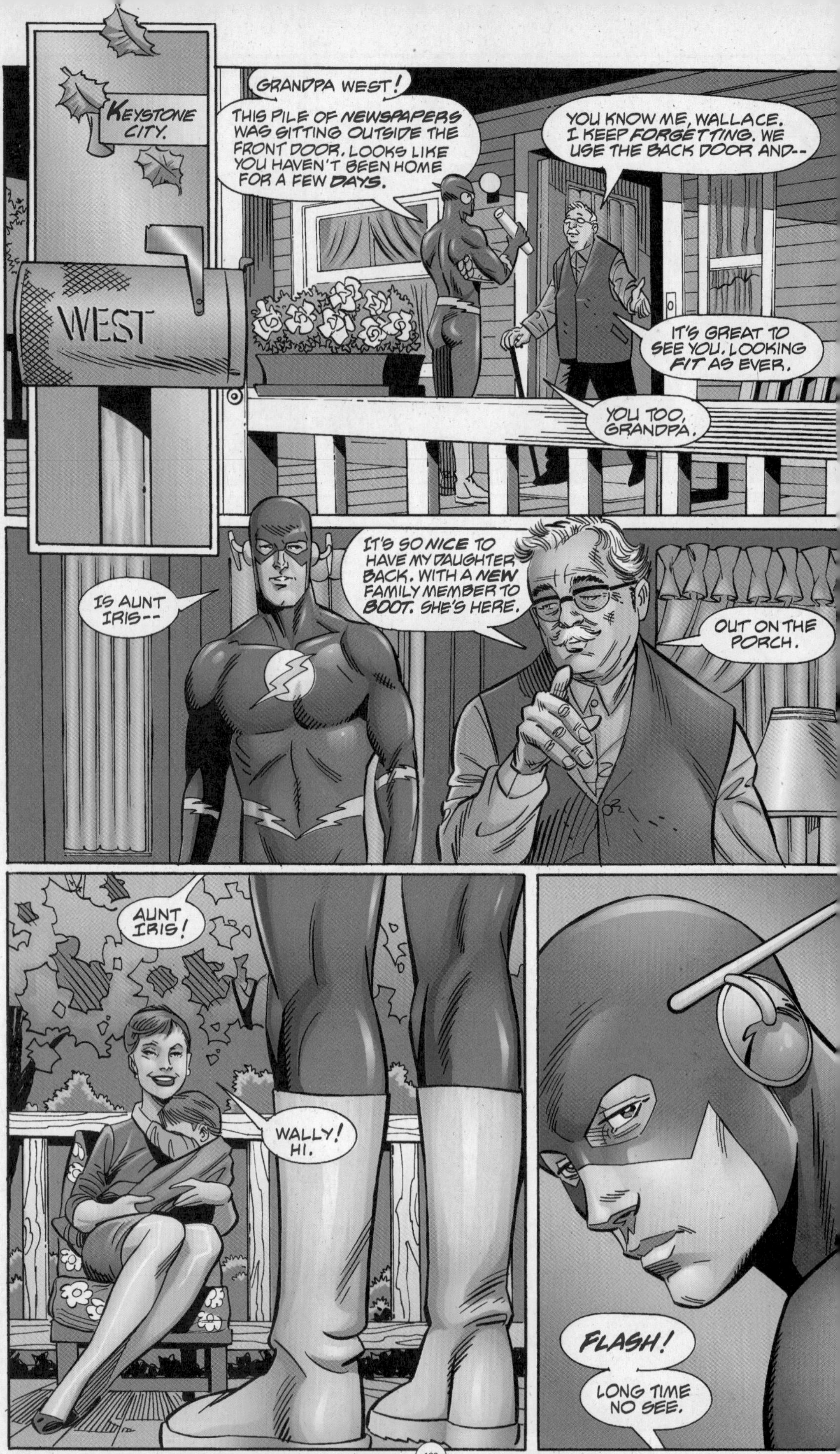
KEYSTONE CITY.
WEST
GRANDPA WEST!
THIS PILE OF NEWSPAPERS WAS SITTING OUTSIDE THE FRONT DOOR. LOOKS LIKE YOU HAVEN'T BEEN HOME FOR A FEW DAYS.
YOU KNOW ME, WALLACE. I KEEP FORGETTING. WE USE THE BACK DOOR AND--
IT'S GREAT TO SEE YOU. LOOKING FIT AS EVER.
YOU TOO, GRANDPA.
IS AUNT IRIS--
IT'S SO NICE TO HAVE MY DAUGHTER BACK. WITH A NEW FAMILY MEMBER TO BOOT. SHE'S HERE.
OUT ON THE PORCH.
AUNT IRIS!
WALLY! HI.
FLASH!
LONG TIME NO SEE.

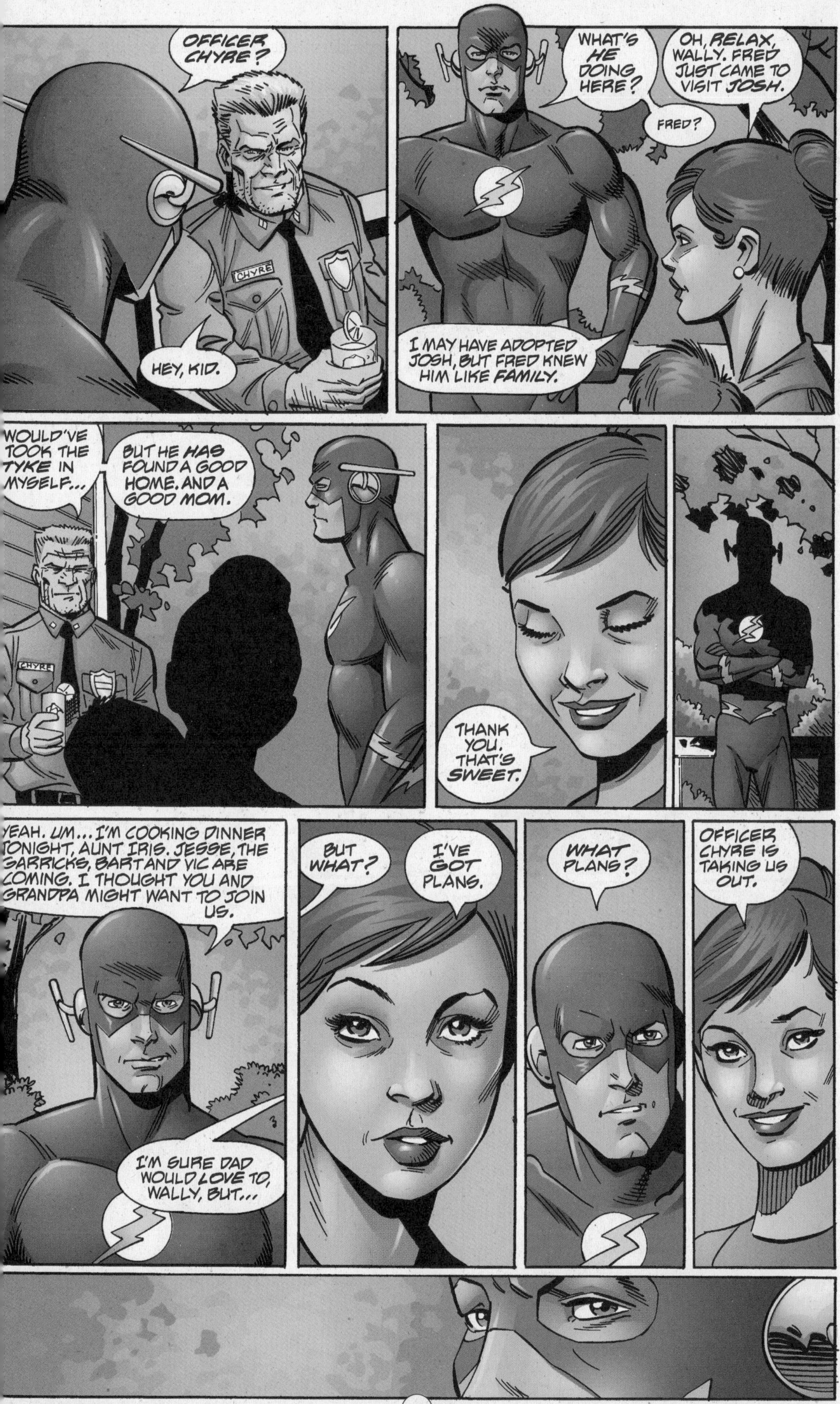
OFFICER CHYRE?
HEY, KID.
WHAT'S HE DOING HERE?
OH, RELAX, WALLY. FRED JUST CAME TO VISIT JOSH.
FRED?
I MAY HAVE ADOPTED JOSH, BUT FRED KNEW HIM LIKE FAMILY.
WOULD'VE TOOK THE TYKE IN MYSELF...
BUT HE HAS FOUND A GOOD HOME. AND A GOOD MOM.
THANK YOU. THAT'S SWEET.
YEAH. UM... I'M COOKING DINNER TONIGHT, AUNT IRIS. JESSE, THE GARRICKS, BART AND VIC ARE COMING. I THOUGHT YOU AND GRANDPA MIGHT WANT TO JOIN US.
I'M SURE DAD WOULD LOVE TO, WALLY, BUT...
BUT WHAT?
I'VE GOT PLANS.
WHAT PLANS?
OFFICER CHYRE IS TAKING US OUT.

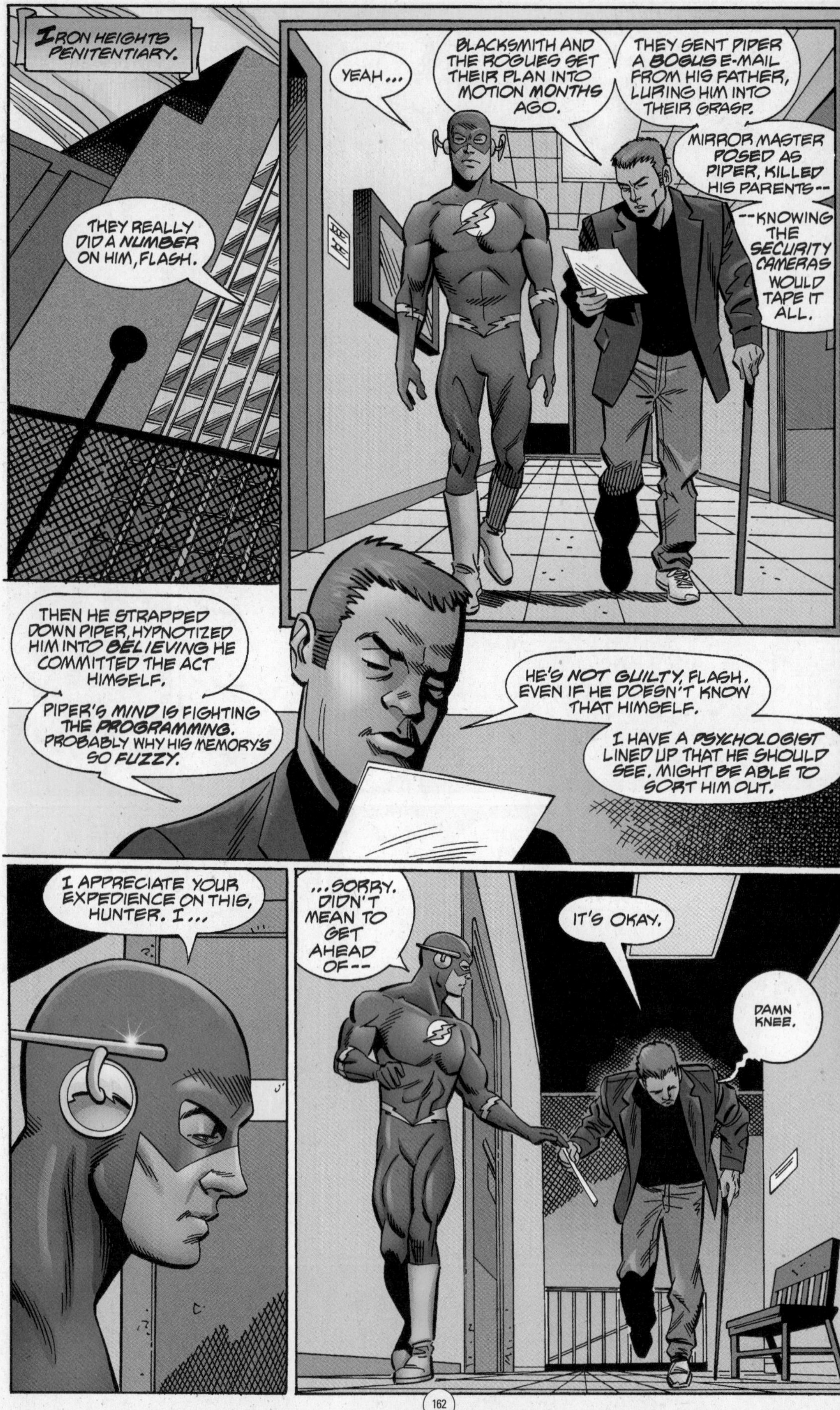
IRON HEIGHTS PENITENTIARY.
THEY REALLY DID A NUMBER ON HIM, FLASH.
YEAH...
BLACKSMITH AND THE ROGUES SET THEIR PLAN INTO MOTION MONTHS AGO.
THEY SENT PIPER A BOGUS E-MAIL FROM HIS FATHER, LURING HIM INTO THEIR GRASP.
MIRROR MASTER POSED AS PIPER, KILLED HIS PARENTS--
--KNOWING THE SECURITY CAMERAS WOULD TAPE IT ALL.
THEN HE STRAPPED DOWN PIPER, HYPNOTIZED HIM INTO BELIEVING HE COMMITTED THE ACT HIMSELF.
PIPER'S MIND IS FIGHTING THE PROGRAMMING. PROBABLY WHY HIS MEMORY'S SO FUZZY.
HE'S NOT GUILTY, FLASH. EVEN IF HE DOESN'T KNOW THAT HIMSELF.
I HAVE A PSYCHOLOGIST LINED UP THAT HE SHOULD SEE. MIGHT BE ABLE TO SORT HIM OUT.
I APPRECIATE YOUR EXPEDIENCE ON THIS, HUNTER. I...
...SORRY. DIDN'T MEAN TO GET AHEAD OF--
IT'S OKAY.
DAMN KNEE.

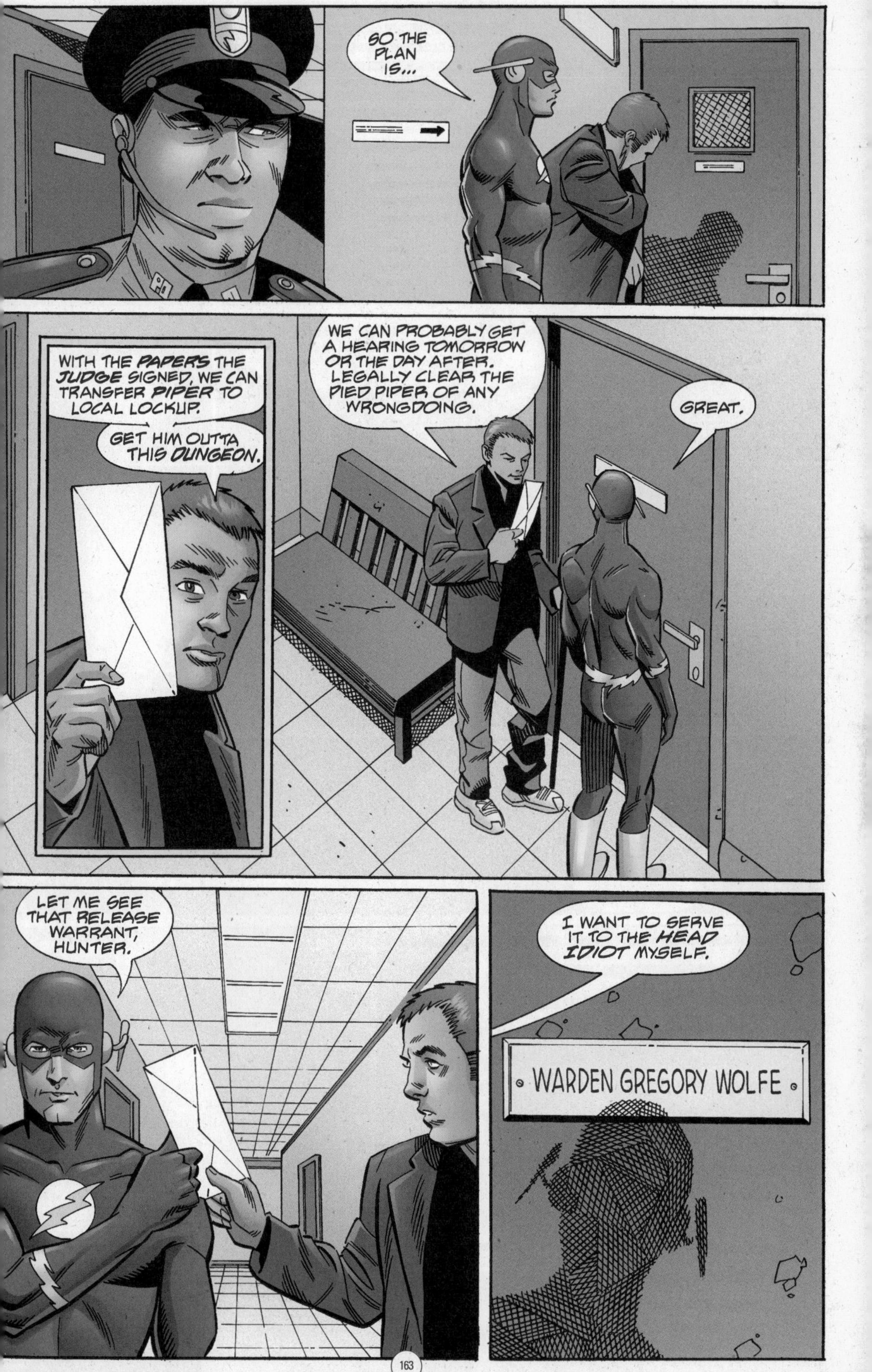
SO THE PLAN IS...
WITH THE PAPERS THE JUDGE SIGNED, WE CAN TRANSFER PIPER TO LOCAL LOCKUP.
GET HIM OUTTA THIS DUNGEON.
WE CAN PROBABLY GET A HEARING TOMORROW OR THE DAY AFTER. LEGALLY CLEAR THE PIED PIPER OF ANY WRONGDOING.
GREAT.
LET ME SEE THAT RELEASE WARRANT, HUNTER.
I WANT TO SERVE IT TO THE HEAD IDIOT MYSELF.
WARDEN GREGORY WOLFE

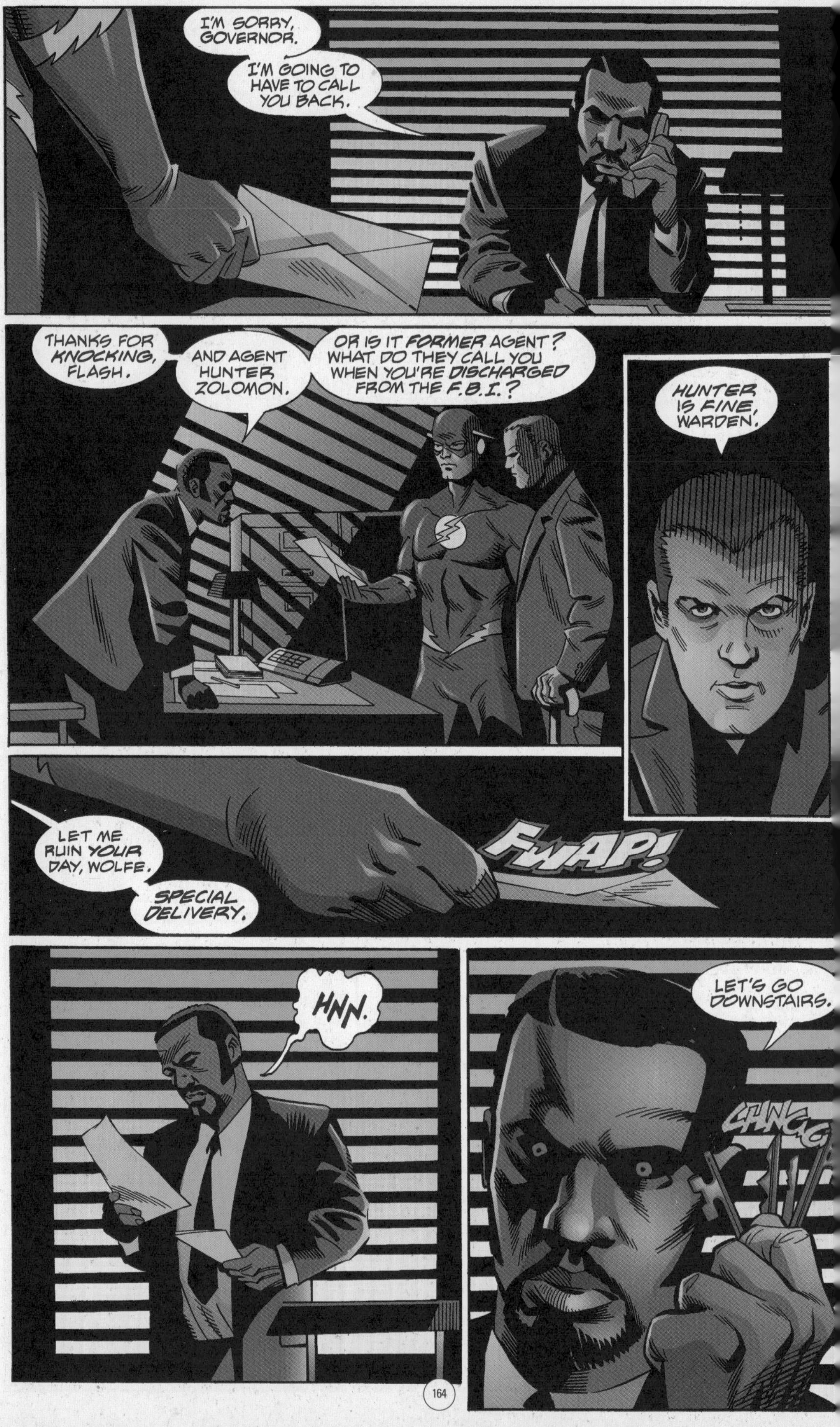
I'M SORRY, GOVERNOR.
I'M GOING TO HAVE TO CALL YOU BACK.
THANKS FOR KNOCKING, FLASH.
AND AGENT HUNTER ZOLOMON.
OR IS IT FORMER AGENT? WHAT DO THEY CALL YOU WHEN YOU'RE DISCHARGED FROM THE F.B.I.?
HUNTER IS FINE, WARDEN.
LET ME RUIN YOUR DAY, WOLFE.
SPECIAL DELIVERY.
FWAP!
HNN.
LET'S GO DOWNSTAIRS.

THE PIPELINE.

NOTHING ELSE TO *SAY*, WOLFE?

LOTS OF NEW *FACES* DOWN HERE. *MURMUR*, *PLUNDER*, *PEEK-A-BOO*.

ABRA KADABRA, BLACKSMITH...AND *GIRDER. MAGENTA RIPPED* HIM IN *HALF*. I'M TRYING TO HELP MAGENTA OUT. SHE'S BEEN TRANSFERRED TO A *PSYCHIATRIC WARD* UPSTATE.

DON'T KNOW HOW THEY *DID* IT, BUT *S.T.A.R.* LABS *WELDED* GIRDER RIGHT *BACK TOGETHER.*

HUNDREDS OF *THUGS* ON THE UPPER LEVELS *TOO*, HUNTER. LEFT OVER FROM THE NETWORK.

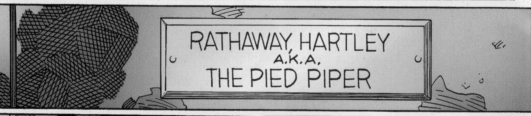

RATHAWAY, HARTLEY
A.K.A.
THE PIED PIPER

KLANK!

PIPER?

165

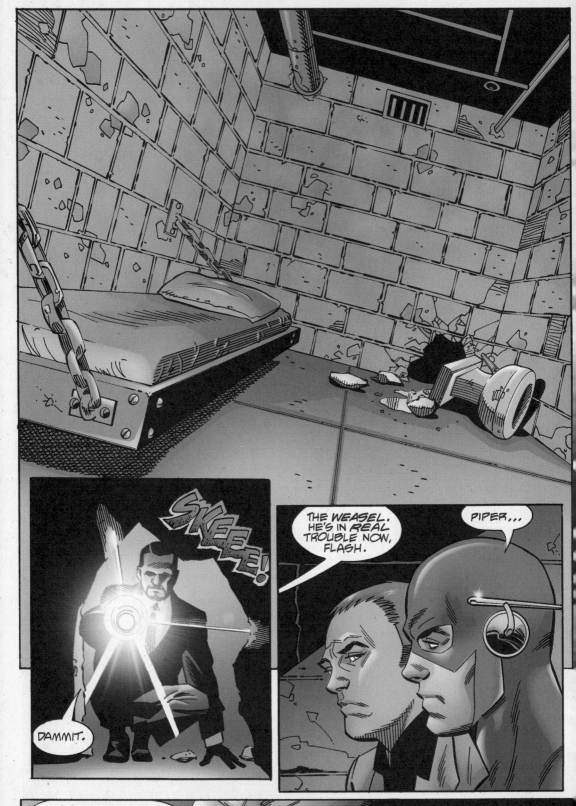

SKEEE!

THE WEASEL. HE'S IN *REAL* TROUBLE NOW, FLASH.

PIPER...

DAMMIT.

GET EVERY *LAW* ENFORCEMENT AGENCY YOU *CAN* ON THE *HORN*--

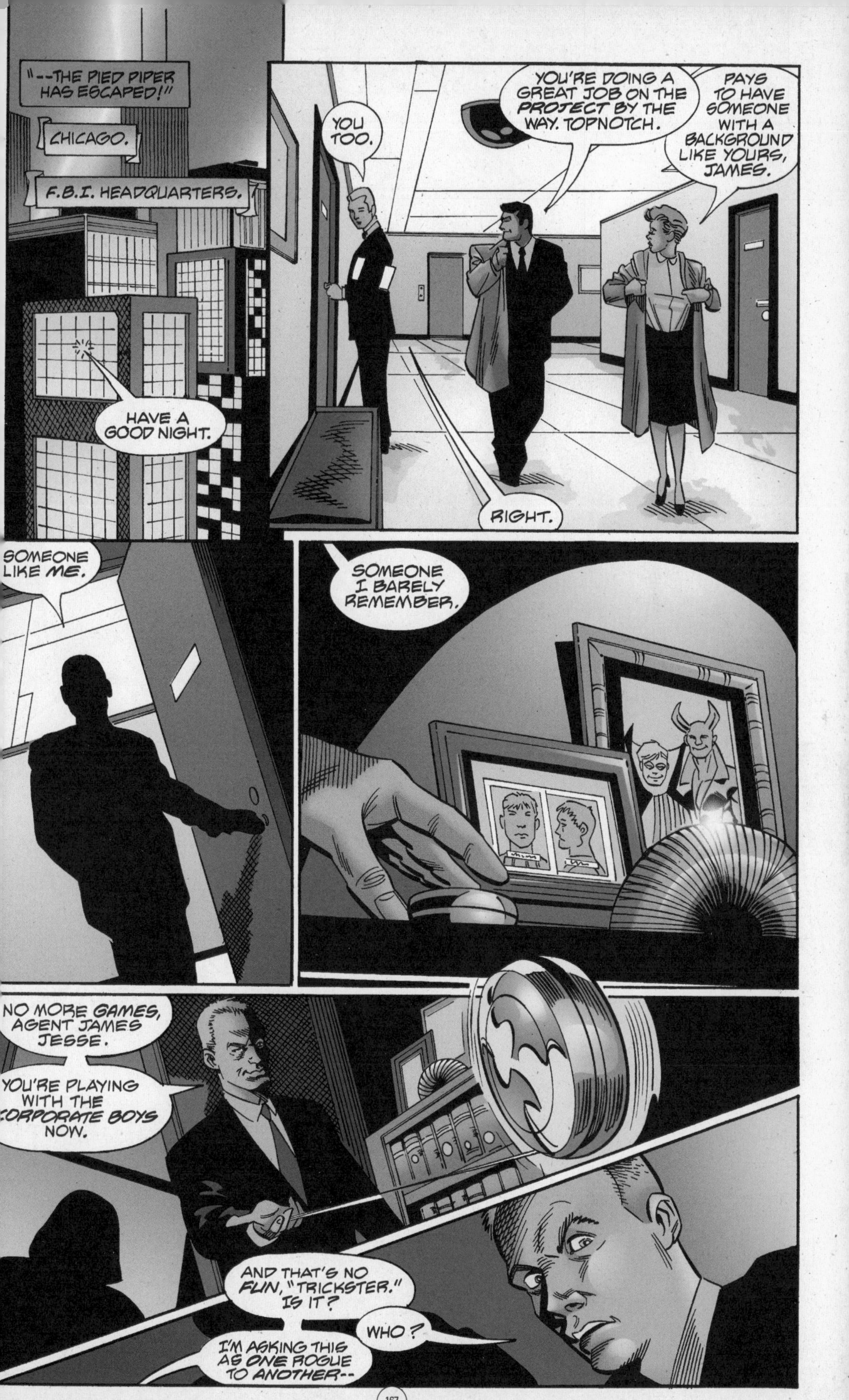
"--THE PIED PIPER HAS ESCAPED!"
CHICAGO.
F.B.I. HEADQUARTERS.
HAVE A GOOD NIGHT.
YOU TOO.
YOU'RE DOING A GREAT JOB ON THE PROJECT BY THE WAY. TOPNOTCH.
PAYS TO HAVE SOMEONE WITH A BACKGROUND LIKE YOURS, JAMES.
RIGHT.
SOMEONE LIKE ME.
SOMEONE I BARELY REMEMBER.
NO MORE GAMES, AGENT JAMES JESSE.
YOU'RE PLAYING WITH THE CORPORATE BOYS NOW.
AND THAT'S NO FUN, "TRICKSTER." IS IT?
WHO?
I'M ASKING THIS AS ONE ROGUE TO ANOTHER--

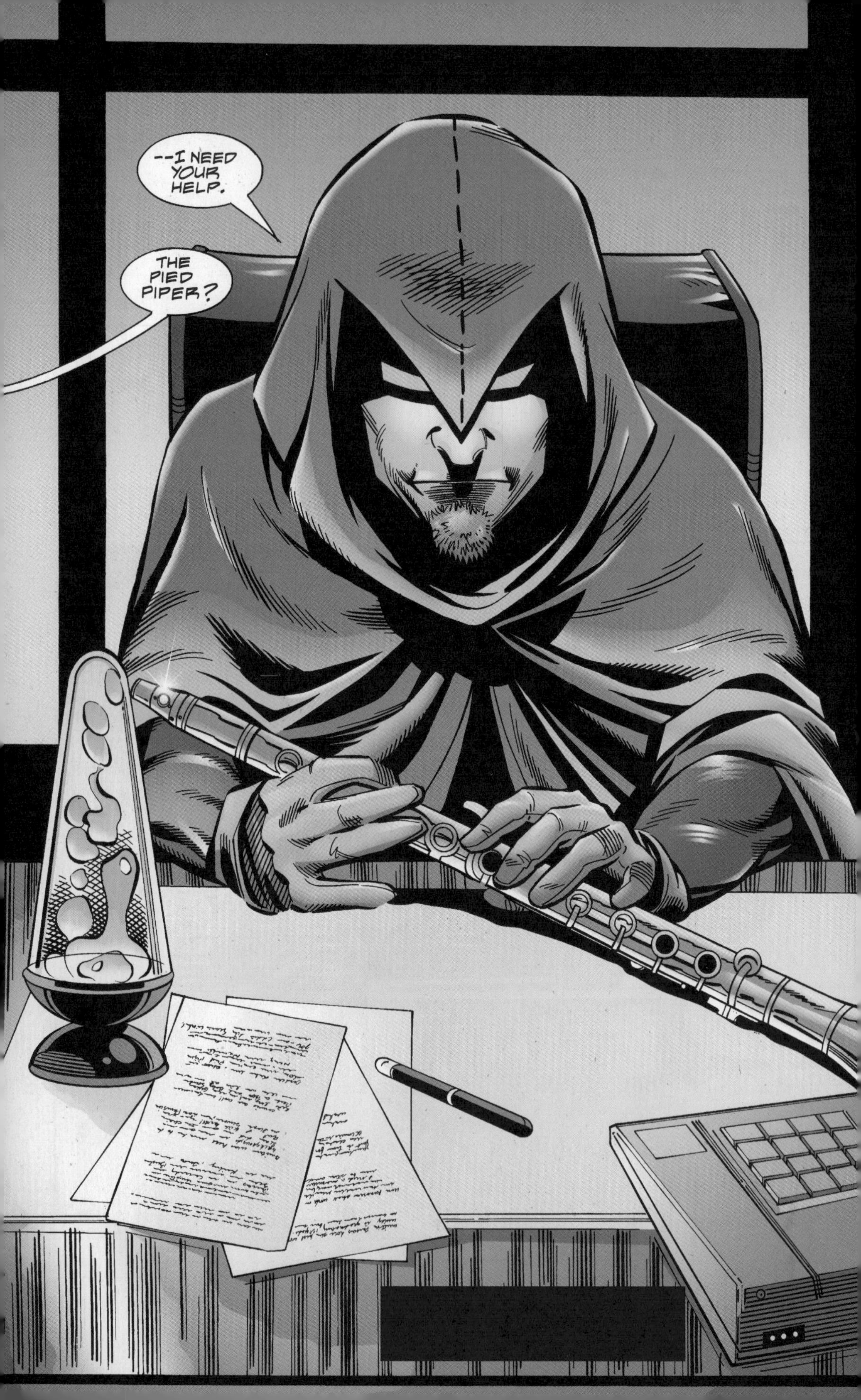
--I NEED YOUR HELP.
THE PIED PIPER?

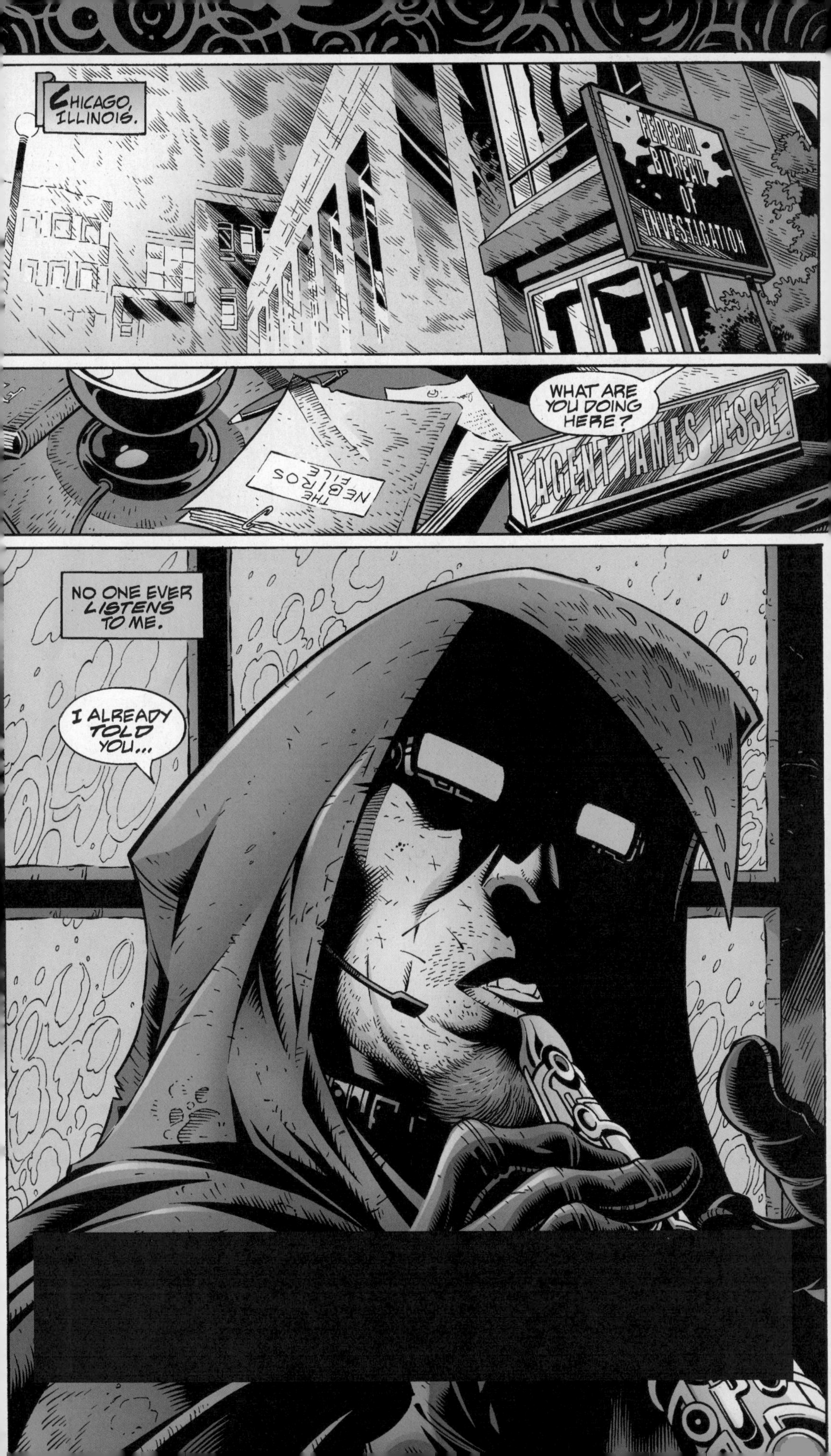
CHICAGO, ILLINOIS.
FEDERAL BUREAU OF INVESTIGATION
WHAT ARE YOU DOING HERE?
AGENT JAMES JESSE
THE NEGIROS FILE
NO ONE EVER LISTENS TO ME.
I ALREADY TOLD YOU...
[redacted]

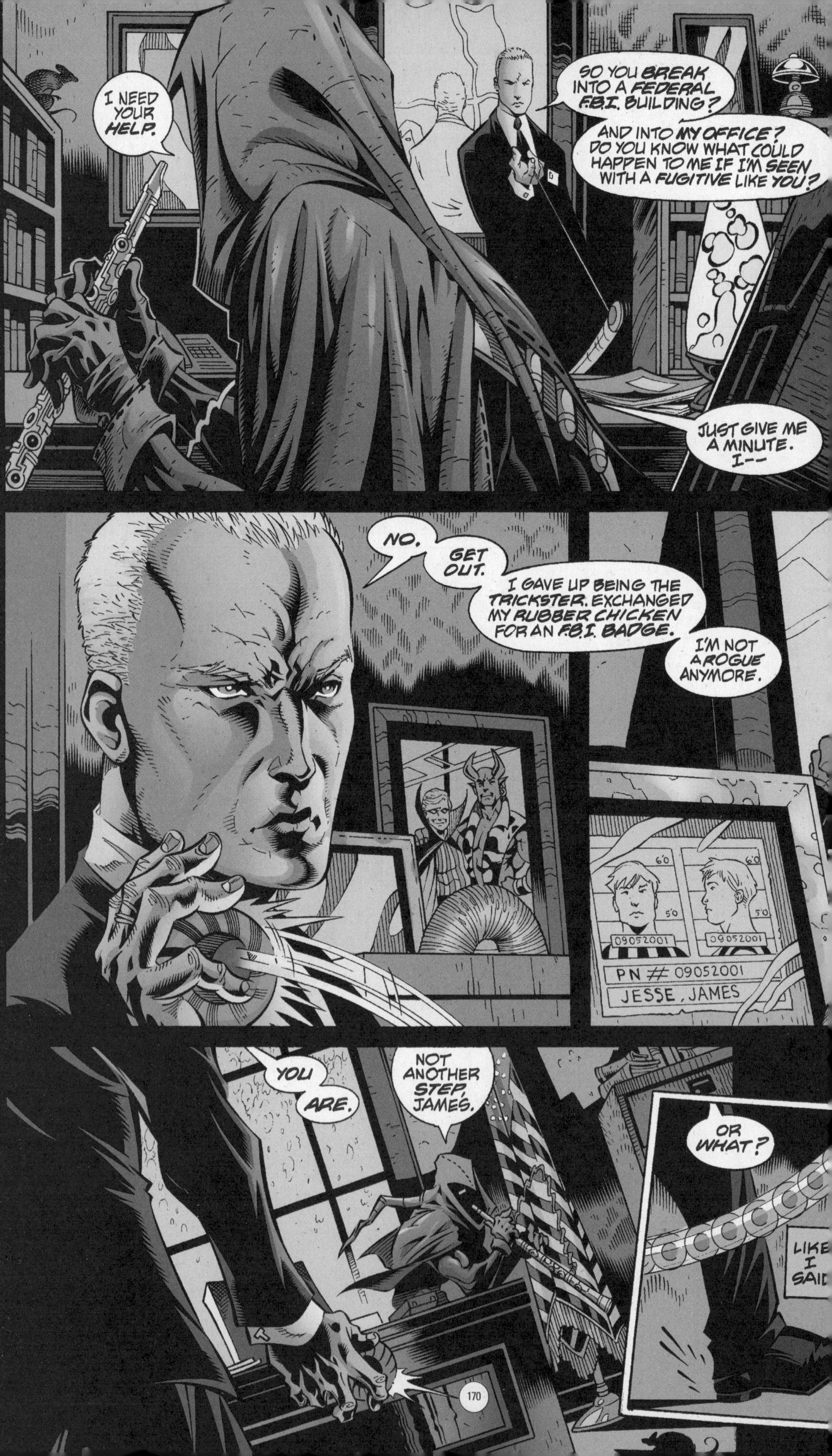
I NEED YOUR HELP.
SO YOU BREAK INTO A FEDERAL F.B.I. BUILDING?
AND INTO MY OFFICE? DO YOU KNOW WHAT COULD HAPPEN TO ME IF I'M SEEN WITH A FUGITIVE LIKE YOU?
JUST GIVE ME A MINUTE. I--
NO.
GET OUT.
I GAVE UP BEING THE TRICKSTER. EXCHANGED MY RUBBER CHICKEN FOR AN F.B.I. BADGE.
I'M NOT A ROGUE ANYMORE.
PN # 09052001
JESSE, JAMES
YOU ARE.
NOT ANOTHER STEP, JAMES.
OR WHAT?
LIKE I SAID

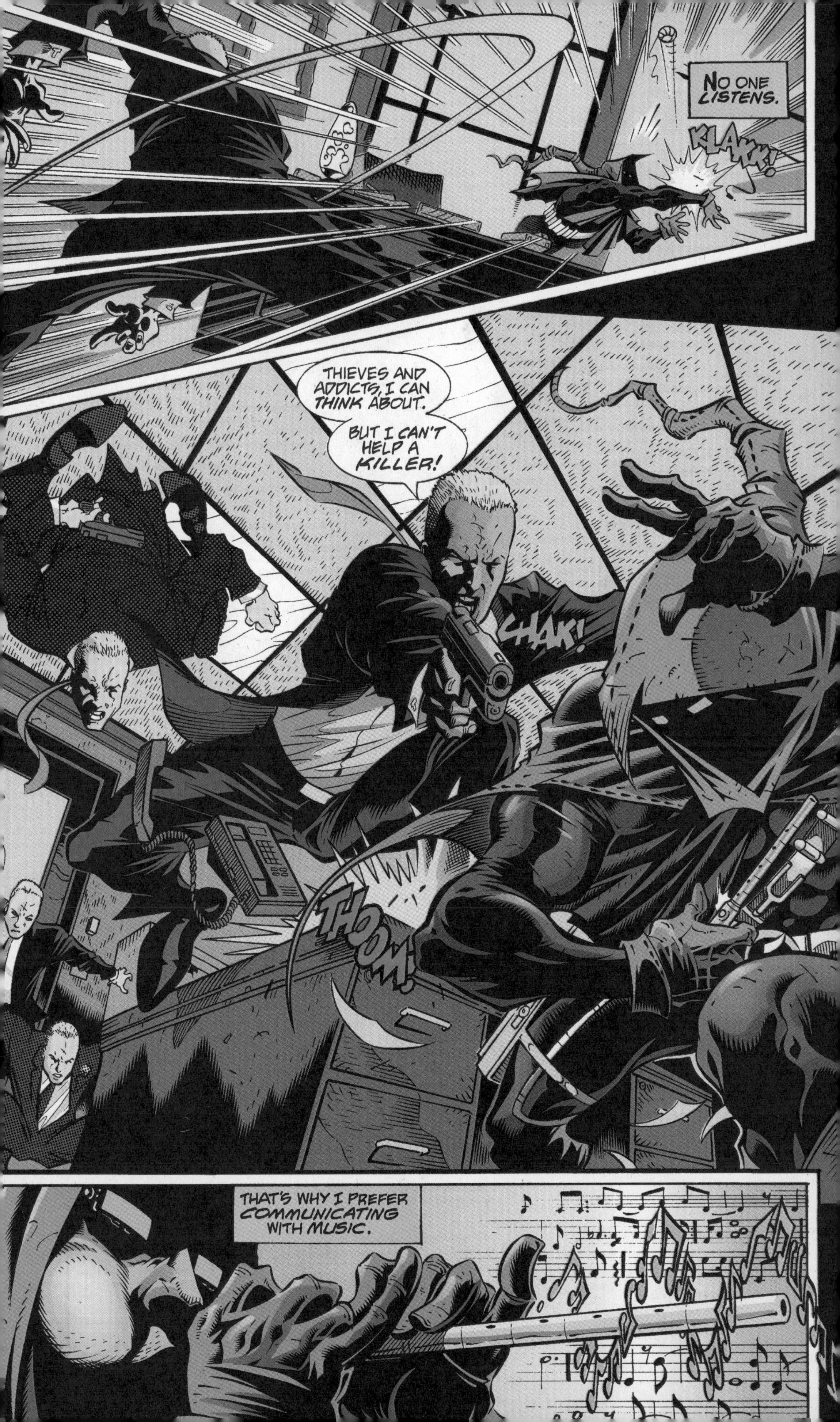
NO ONE LISTENS.
KLAKK!
THIEVES AND ADDICTS, I CAN THINK ABOUT.
BUT I CAN'T HELP A KILLER!
CHAK!
THOOM!
THAT'S WHY I PREFER COMMUNICATING WITH MUSIC.

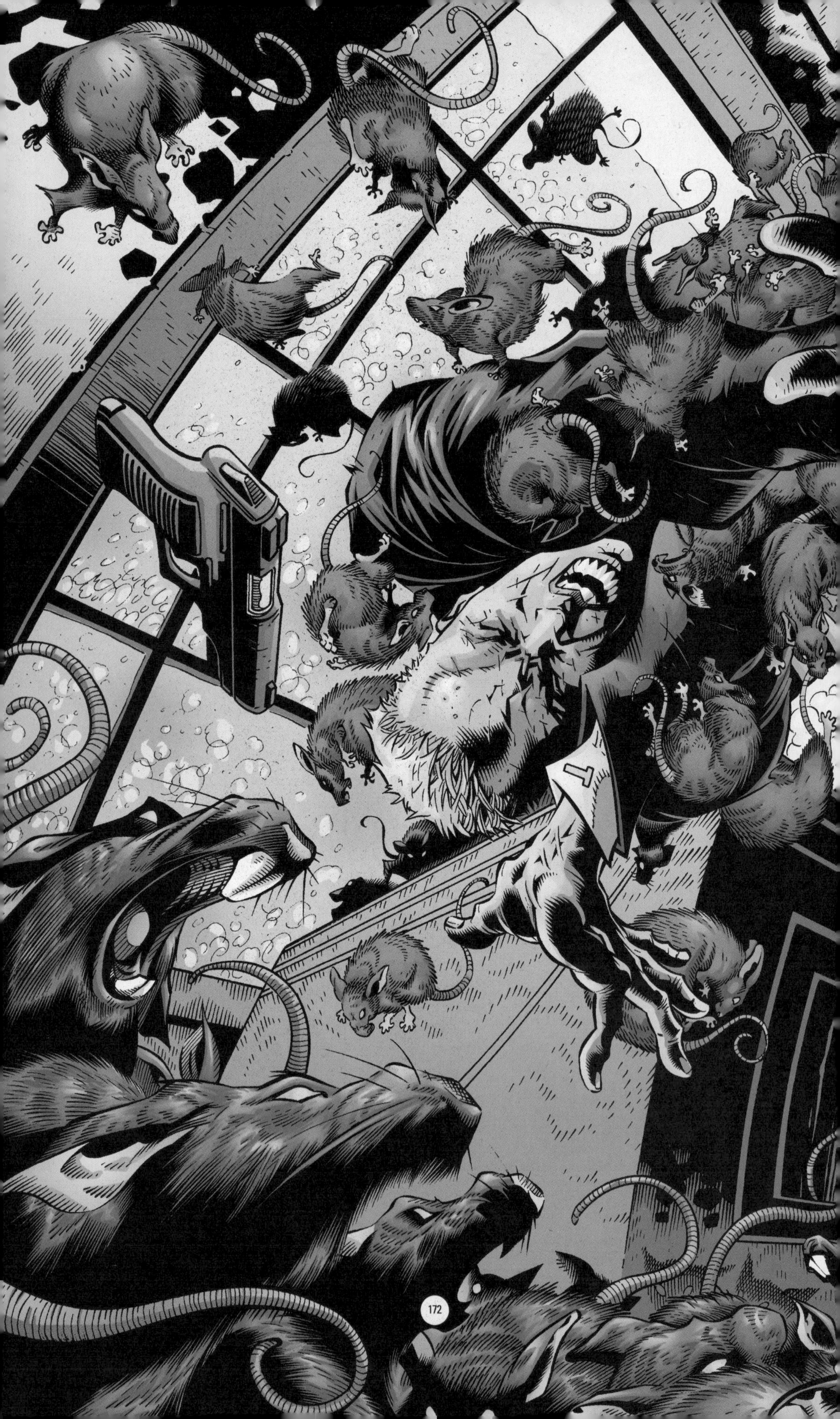

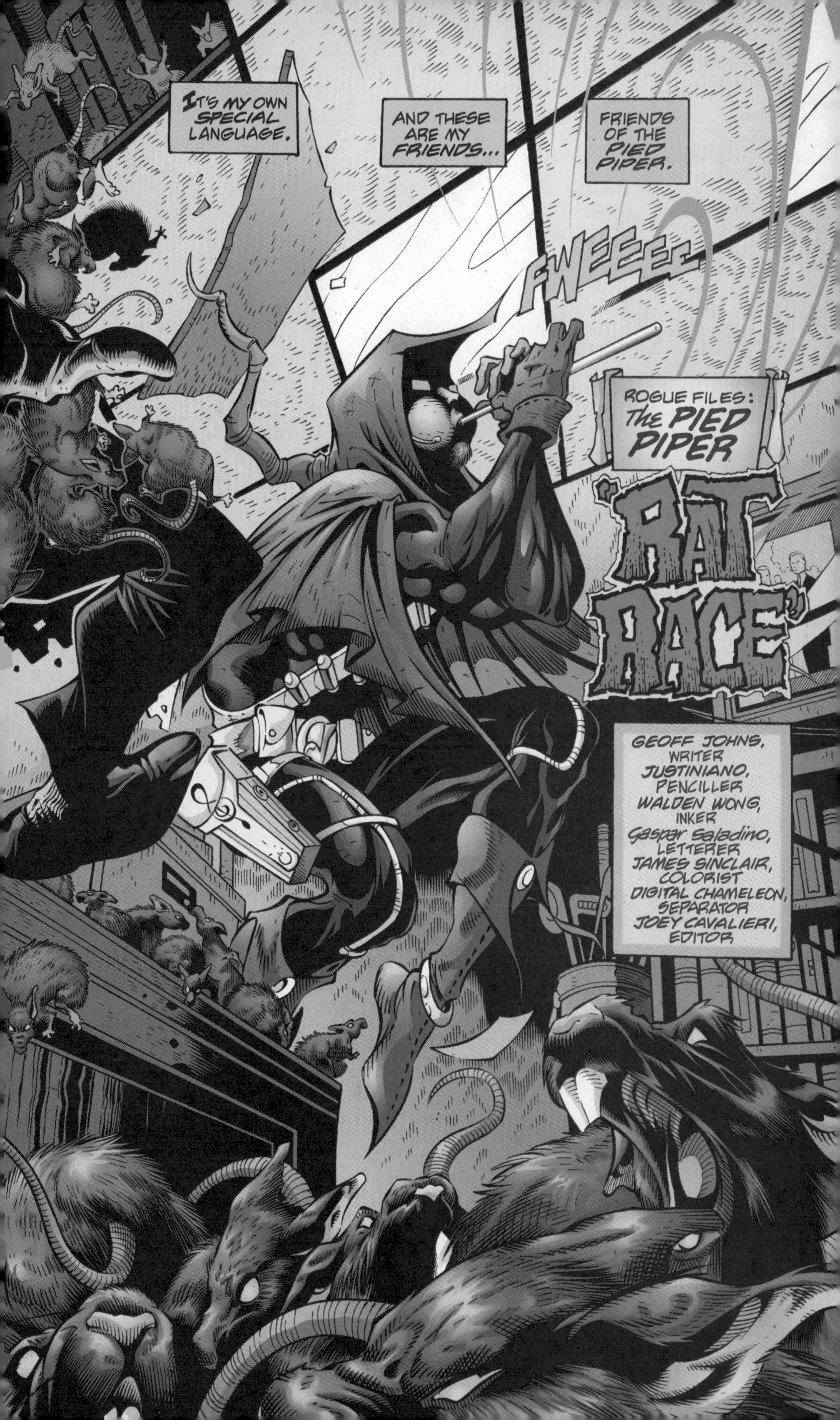
IT'S MY OWN SPECIAL LANGUAGE.
AND THESE ARE MY FRIENDS...
FRIENDS OF THE PIED PIPER.
FWEEEEE
ROGUE FILES: The PIED PIPER
'RAT RACE'
GEOFF JOHNS, WRITER
JUSTINIANO, PENCILLER
WALDEN WONG, INKER
Gaspar Saladino, LETTERER
JAMES SINCLAIR, COLORIST
DIGITAL CHAMELEON, SEPARATOR
JOEY CAVALIERI, EDITOR

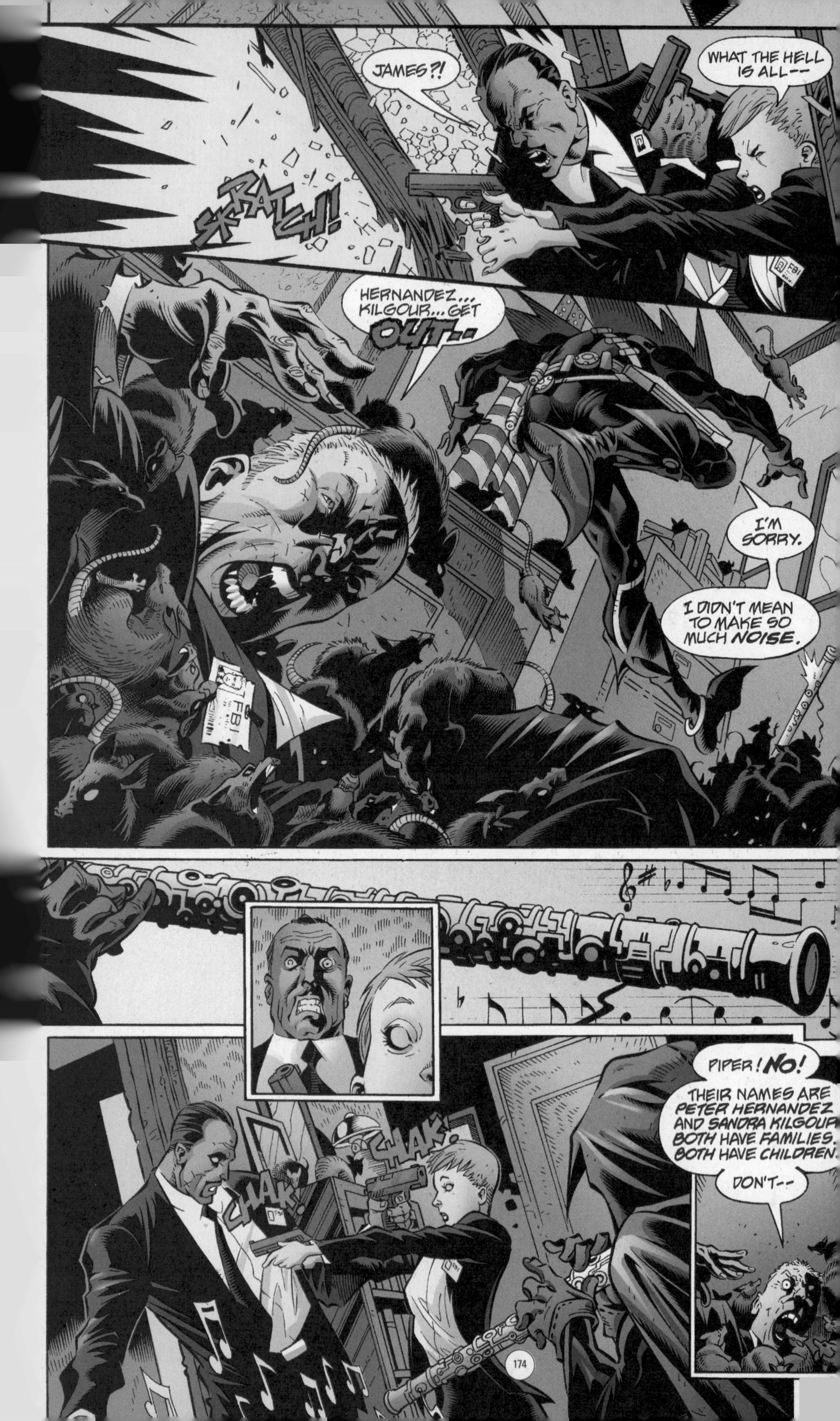
JAMES?!
WHAT THE HELL IS ALL--
SKRATCH!
HERNANDEZ... KILGOUR... GET OUT..
I'M SORRY.
I DIDN'T MEAN TO MAKE SO MUCH NOISE.
PIPER! NO!
THEIR NAMES ARE PETER HERNANDEZ AND SANDRA KILGOUR. BOTH HAVE FAMILIES. BOTH HAVE CHILDREN.
DON'T--
CHAK!
CHAK!

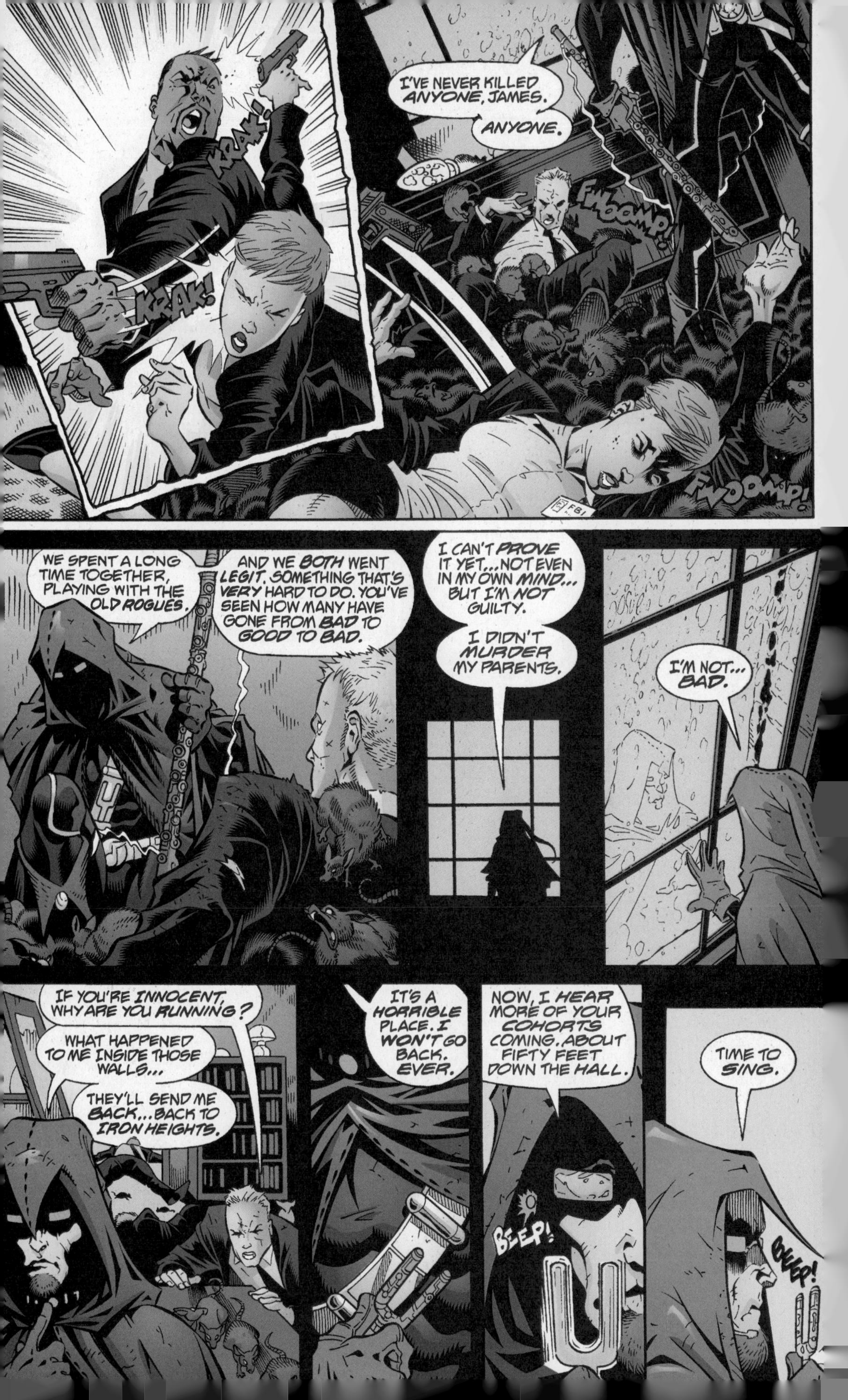
KRAK!
KRAK!
I'VE NEVER KILLED ANYONE, JAMES.
ANYONE.
FWOOMP!
FWOOMP!
WE SPENT A LONG TIME TOGETHER, PLAYING WITH THE OLD ROGUES.
AND WE BOTH WENT LEGIT. SOMETHING THAT'S VERY HARD TO DO. YOU'VE SEEN HOW MANY HAVE GONE FROM BAD TO GOOD TO BAD.
I CAN'T PROVE IT YET... NOT EVEN IN MY OWN MIND... BUT I'M NOT GUILTY.
I DIDN'T MURDER MY PARENTS.
I'M NOT... BAD.
IF YOU'RE INNOCENT, WHY ARE YOU RUNNING?
WHAT HAPPENED TO ME INSIDE THOSE WALLS...
THEY'LL SEND ME BACK... BACK TO IRON HEIGHTS.
IT'S A HORRIBLE PLACE. I WON'T GO BACK. EVER.
NOW, I HEAR MORE OF YOUR COHORTS COMING. ABOUT FIFTY FEET DOWN THE HALL.
BEEP!
TIME TO SING.
BWEEP!

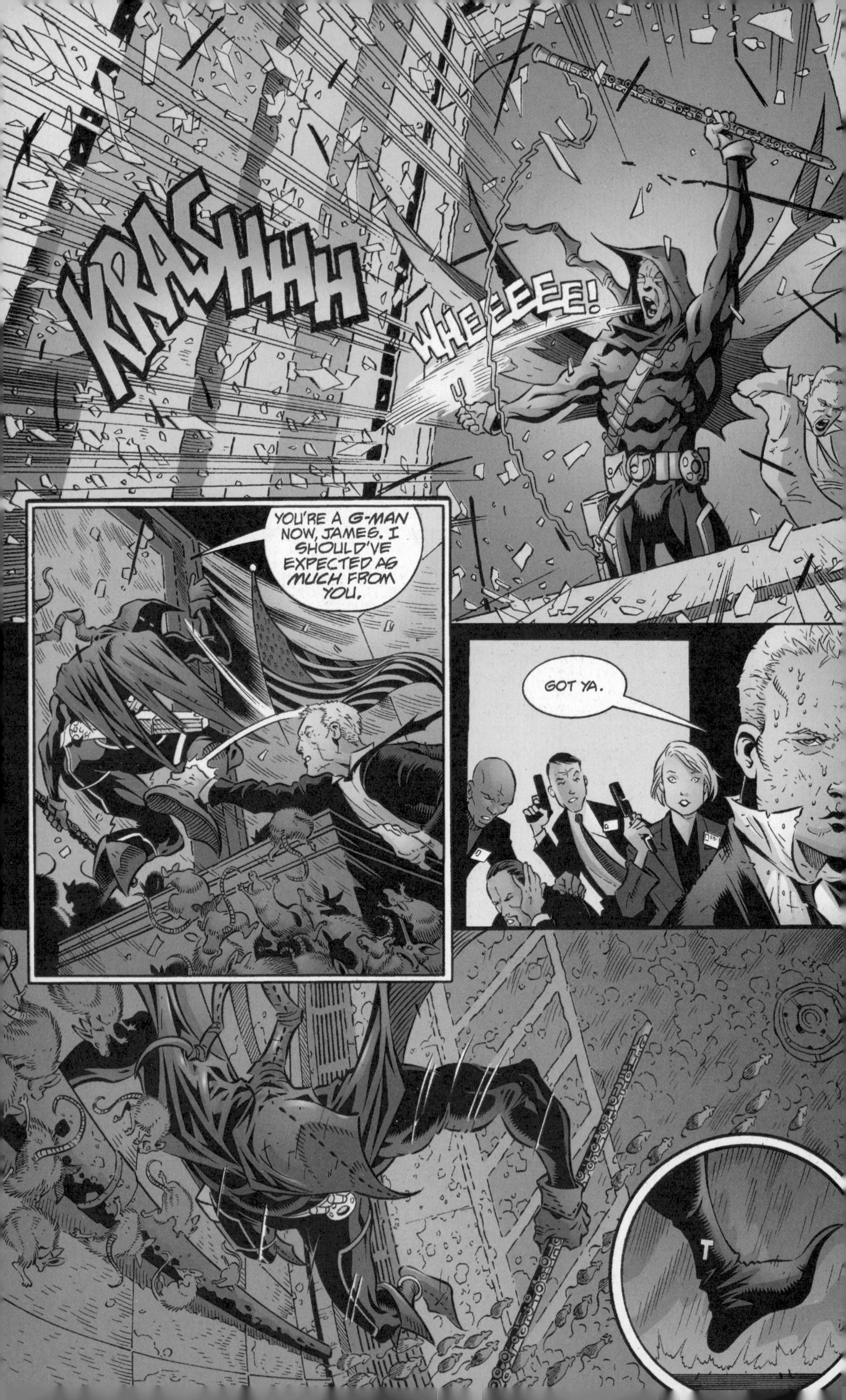
KRASHHH
WHEEEEE!
YOU'RE A G-MAN NOW, JAMES. I SHOULD'VE EXPECTED AS MUCH FROM YOU.
GOT YA.
T

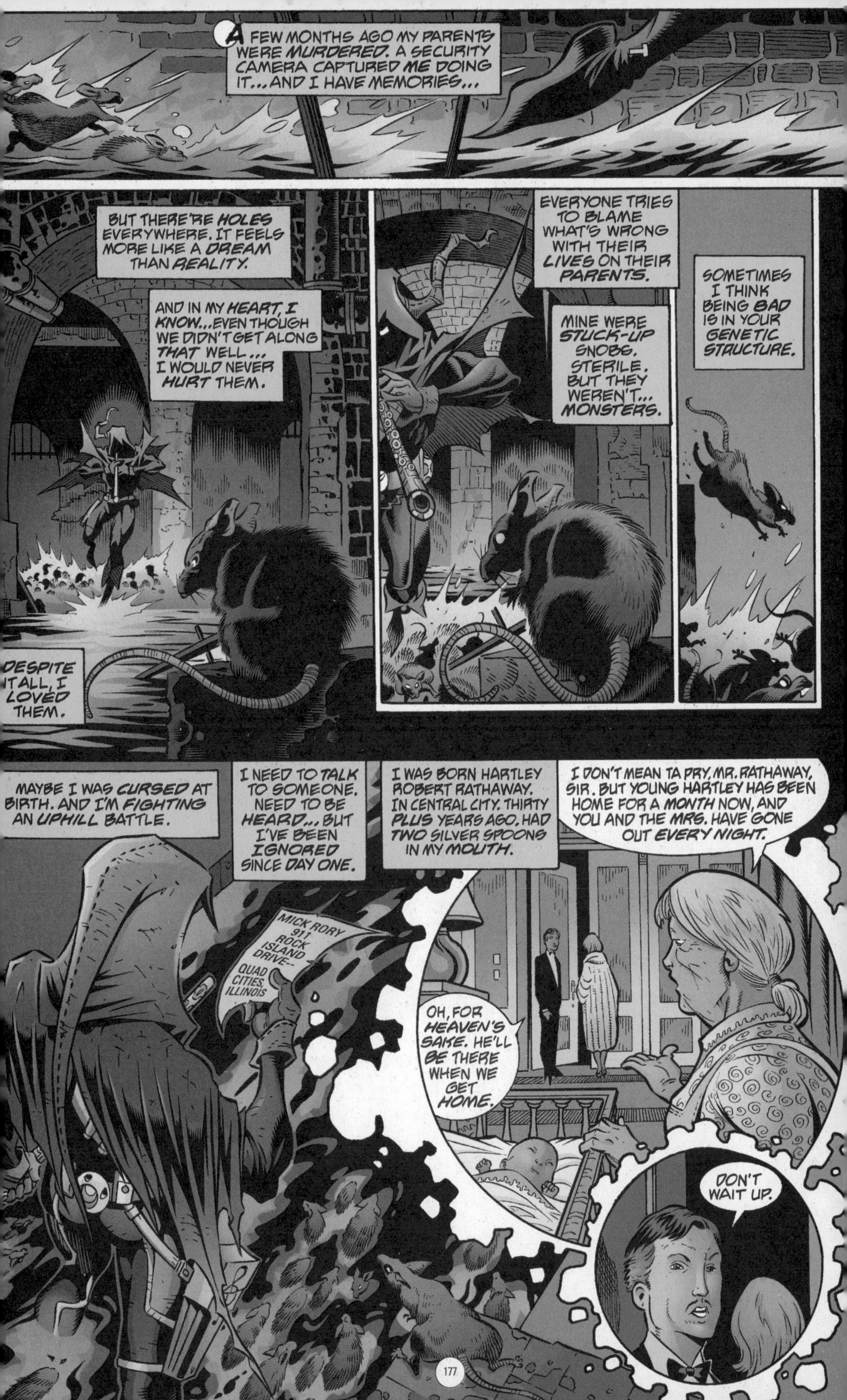

A FEW MONTHS AGO MY PARENTS WERE MURDERED. A SECURITY CAMERA CAPTURED ME DOING IT... AND I HAVE MEMORIES...
BUT THERE'RE HOLES EVERYWHERE. IT FEELS MORE LIKE A DREAM THAN REALITY.
AND IN MY HEART, I KNOW... EVEN THOUGH WE DIDN'T GET ALONG THAT WELL... I WOULD NEVER HURT THEM.
DESPITE IT ALL, I LOVED THEM.
EVERYONE TRIES TO BLAME WHAT'S WRONG WITH THEIR LIVES ON THEIR PARENTS.
MINE WERE STUCK-UP SNOBS. STERILE. BUT THEY WEREN'T... MONSTERS.
SOMETIMES I THINK BEING BAD IS IN YOUR GENETIC STRUCTURE.
MAYBE I WAS CURSED AT BIRTH. AND I'M FIGHTING AN UPHILL BATTLE.
I NEED TO TALK TO SOMEONE. NEED TO BE HEARD... BUT I'VE BEEN IGNORED SINCE DAY ONE.
I WAS BORN HARTLEY ROBERT RATHAWAY. IN CENTRAL CITY. THIRTY PLUS YEARS AGO. HAD TWO SILVER SPOONS IN MY MOUTH.
I DON'T MEAN TA PRY, MR. RATHAWAY, SIR. BUT YOUNG HARTLEY HAS BEEN HOME FOR A MONTH NOW, AND YOU AND THE MRS. HAVE GONE OUT EVERY NIGHT.
MICK RORY 911 ROCK ISLAND DRIVE-- QUAD CITIES, ILLINOIS
OH, FOR HEAVEN'S SAKE. HE'LL BE THERE WHEN WE GET HOME.
DON'T WAIT UP.

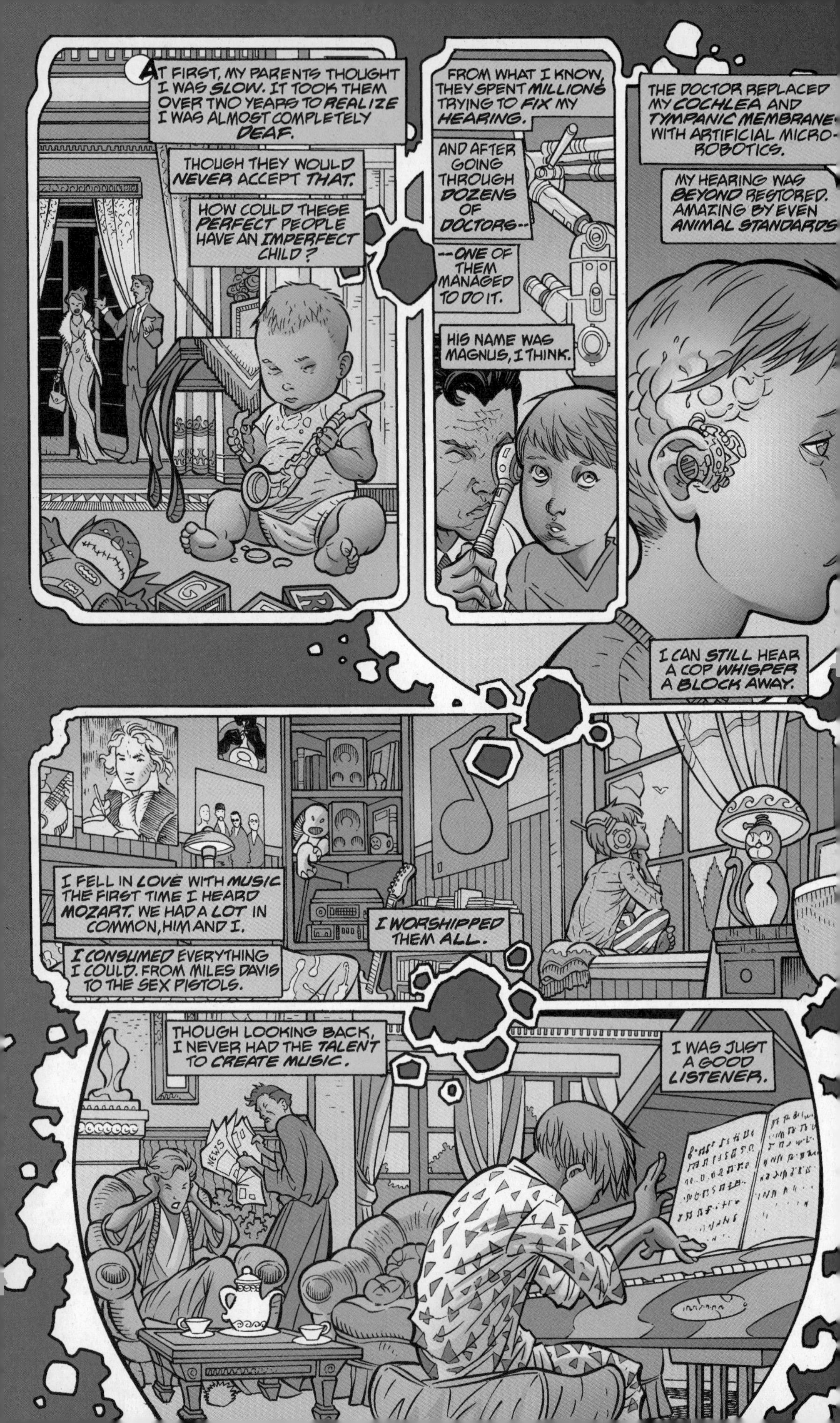

AT FIRST, MY PARENTS THOUGHT I WAS SLOW. IT TOOK THEM OVER TWO YEARS TO REALIZE I WAS ALMOST COMPLETELY DEAF.
THOUGH THEY WOULD NEVER ACCEPT THAT.
HOW COULD THESE PERFECT PEOPLE HAVE AN IMPERFECT CHILD?
FROM WHAT I KNOW, THEY SPENT MILLIONS TRYING TO FIX MY HEARING.
AND AFTER GOING THROUGH DOZENS OF DOCTORS--
--ONE OF THEM MANAGED TO DO IT.
HIS NAME WAS MAGNUS, I THINK.
THE DOCTOR REPLACED MY COCHLEA AND TYMPANIC MEMBRANE WITH ARTIFICIAL MICRO-ROBOTICS.
MY HEARING WAS BEYOND RESTORED. AMAZING BY EVEN ANIMAL STANDARDS.
I CAN STILL HEAR A COP WHISPER A BLOCK AWAY.
I FELL IN LOVE WITH MUSIC THE FIRST TIME I HEARD MOZART. WE HAD A LOT IN COMMON, HIM AND I.
I CONSUMED EVERYTHING I COULD. FROM MILES DAVIS TO THE SEX PISTOLS.
I WORSHIPPED THEM ALL.
THOUGH LOOKING BACK, I NEVER HAD THE TALENT TO CREATE MUSIC.
I WAS JUST A GOOD LISTENER.
NEWS

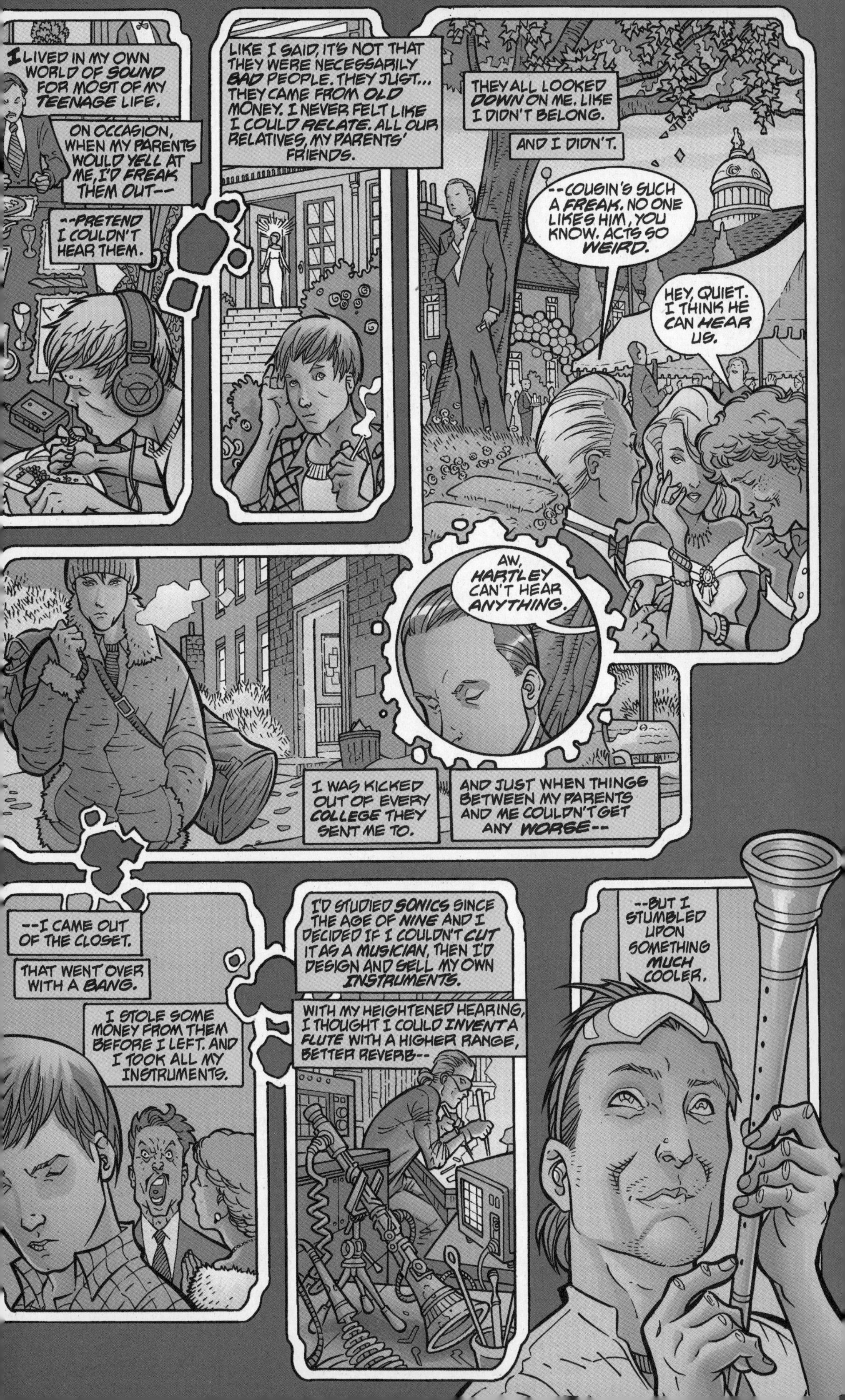
I LIVED IN MY OWN WORLD OF SOUND FOR MOST OF MY TEENAGE LIFE.
ON OCCASION, WHEN MY PARENTS WOULD YELL AT ME, I'D FREAK THEM OUT--
--PRETEND I COULDN'T HEAR THEM.
LIKE I SAID, IT'S NOT THAT THEY WERE NECESSARILY BAD PEOPLE. THEY JUST... THEY CAME FROM OLD MONEY. I NEVER FELT LIKE I COULD RELATE. ALL OUR RELATIVES, MY PARENTS' FRIENDS.
THEY ALL LOOKED DOWN ON ME. LIKE I DIDN'T BELONG.
AND I DIDN'T.
--COUSIN'S SUCH A FREAK. NO ONE LIKES HIM, YOU KNOW. ACTS SO WEIRD.
HEY, QUIET. I THINK HE CAN HEAR US.
AW, HARTLEY CAN'T HEAR ANYTHING.
I WAS KICKED OUT OF EVERY COLLEGE THEY SENT ME TO.
AND JUST WHEN THINGS BETWEEN MY PARENTS AND ME COULDN'T GET ANY WORSE--
--I CAME OUT OF THE CLOSET.
THAT WENT OVER WITH A BANG.
I STOLE SOME MONEY FROM THEM BEFORE I LEFT. AND I TOOK ALL MY INSTRUMENTS.
I'D STUDIED SONICS SINCE THE AGE OF NINE AND I DECIDED IF I COULDN'T CUT IT AS A MUSICIAN, THEN I'D DESIGN AND SELL MY OWN INSTRUMENTS.
WITH MY HEIGHTENED HEARING, I THOUGHT I COULD INVENT A FLUTE WITH A HIGHER RANGE, BETTER REVERB--
--BUT I STUMBLED UPON SOMETHING MUCH COOLER.

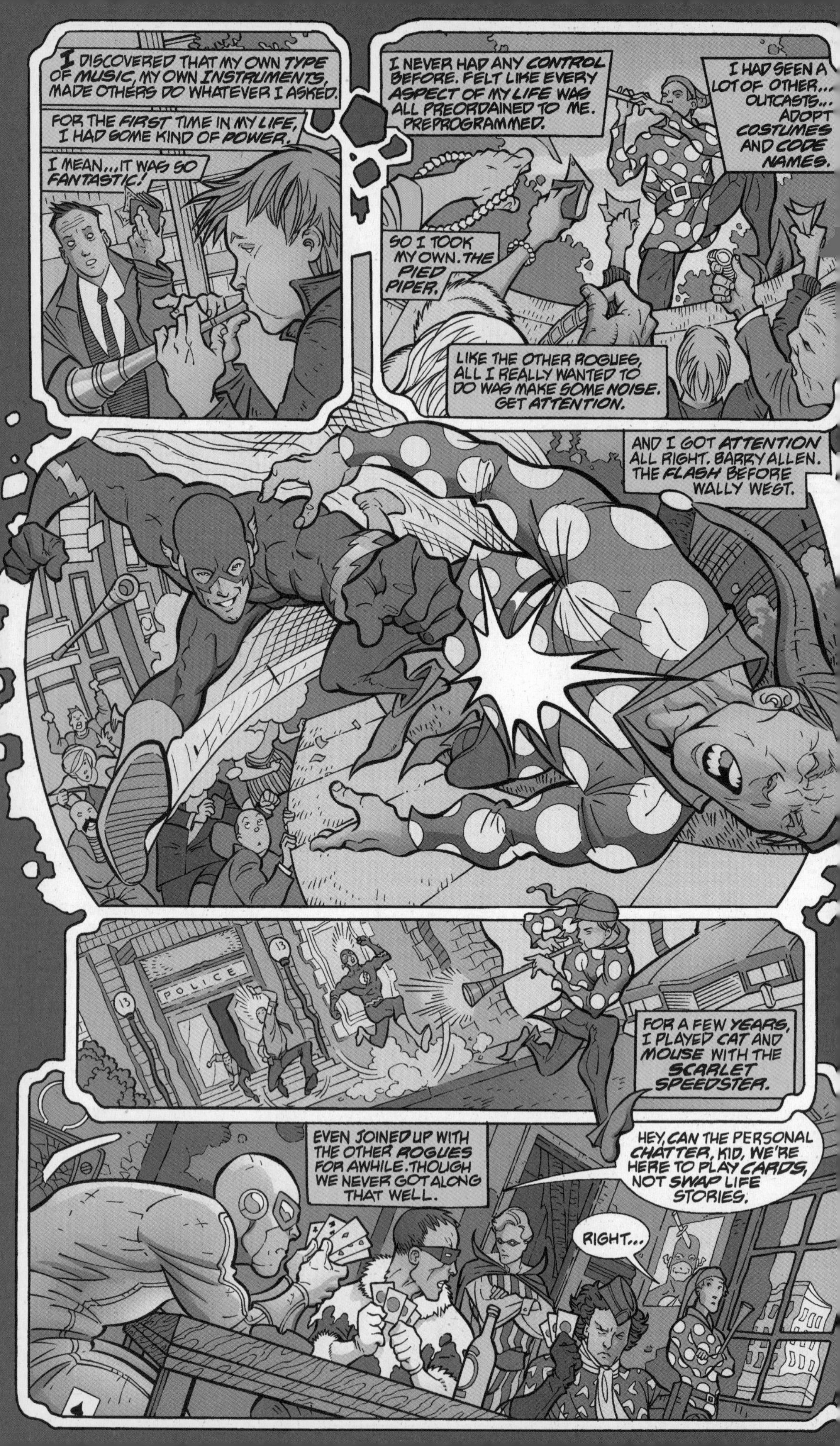
I DISCOVERED THAT MY OWN TYPE OF MUSIC, MY OWN INSTRUMENTS, MADE OTHERS DO WHATEVER I ASKED.
FOR THE FIRST TIME IN MY LIFE, I HAD SOME KIND OF POWER.
I MEAN... IT WAS SO FANTASTIC!
I NEVER HAD ANY CONTROL BEFORE. FELT LIKE EVERY ASPECT OF MY LIFE WAS ALL PREORDAINED TO ME. PREPROGRAMMED.
I HAD SEEN A LOT OF OTHER... OUTCASTS... ADOPT COSTUMES AND CODE NAMES.
SO I TOOK MY OWN. THE PIED PIPER.
LIKE THE OTHER ROGUES, ALL I REALLY WANTED TO DO WAS MAKE SOME NOISE. GET ATTENTION.
AND I GOT ATTENTION ALL RIGHT. BARRY ALLEN. THE FLASH BEFORE WALLY WEST.
POLICE
13
13
FOR A FEW YEARS, I PLAYED CAT AND MOUSE WITH THE SCARLET SPEEDSTER.
EVEN JOINED UP WITH THE OTHER ROGUES FOR AWHILE. THOUGH WE NEVER GOT ALONG THAT WELL.
HEY, CAN THE PERSONAL CHATTER, KID, WE'RE HERE TO PLAY CARDS, NOT SWAP LIFE STORIES.
RIGHT...

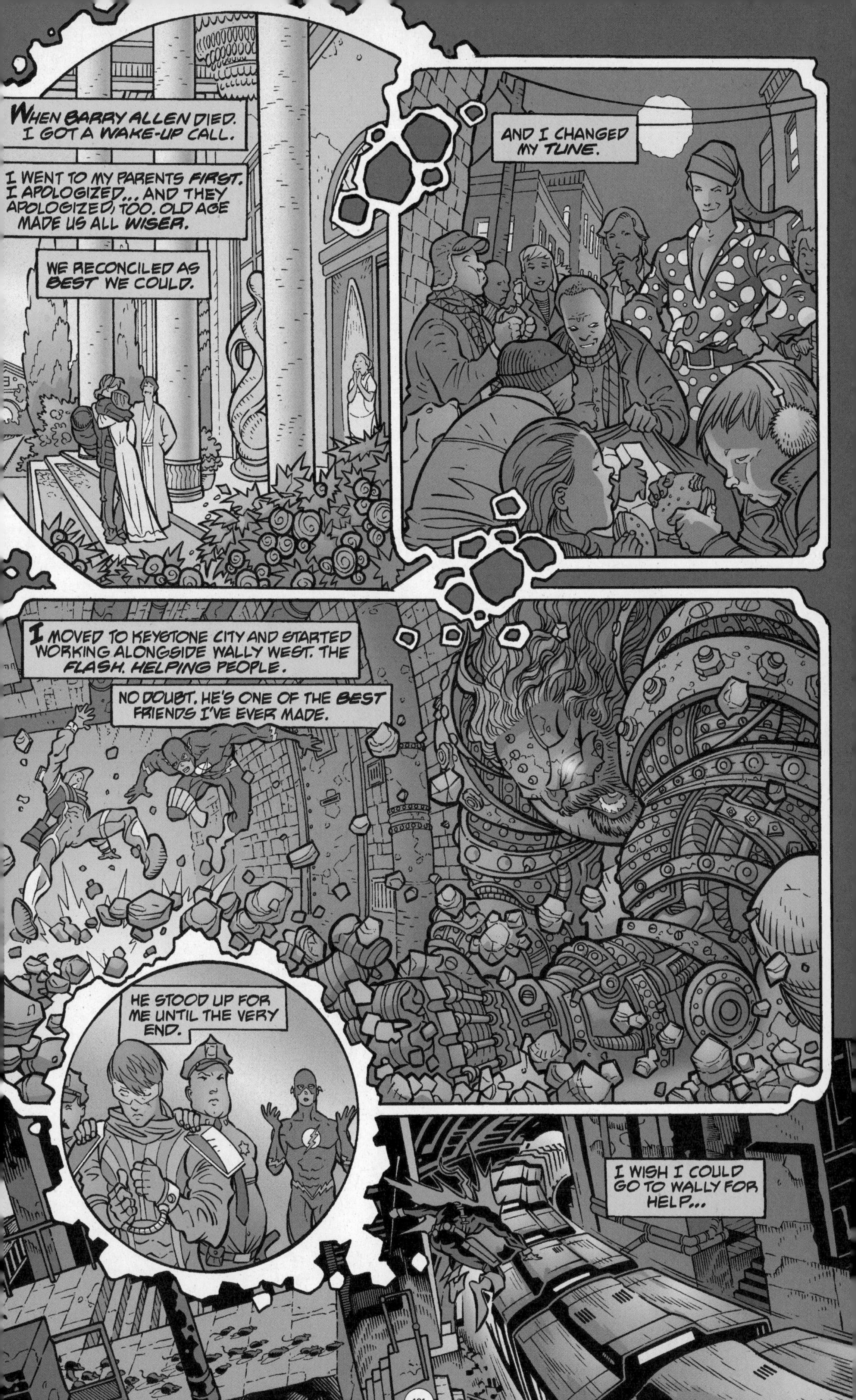
WHEN BARRY ALLEN DIED, I GOT A WAKE-UP CALL.
I WENT TO MY PARENTS FIRST. I APOLOGIZED... AND THEY APOLOGIZED, TOO. OLD AGE MADE US ALL WISER.
WE RECONCILED AS BEST WE COULD.
AND I CHANGED MY TUNE.
I MOVED TO KEYSTONE CITY AND STARTED WORKING ALONGSIDE WALLY WEST, THE FLASH. HELPING PEOPLE.
NO DOUBT, HE'S ONE OF THE BEST FRIENDS I'VE EVER MADE.
HE STOOD UP FOR ME UNTIL THE VERY END.
I WISH I COULD GO TO WALLY FOR HELP...

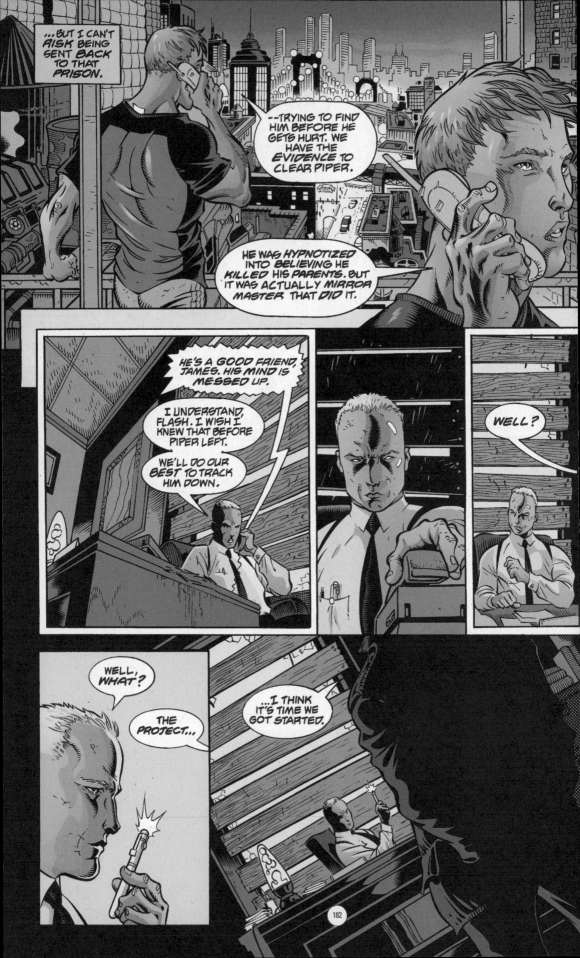

...BUT I CAN'T RISK BEING SENT BACK TO THAT PRISON.

--TRYING TO FIND HIM BEFORE HE GETS HURT. WE HAVE THE EVIDENCE TO CLEAR PIPER.

HE WAS HYPNOTIZED INTO BELIEVING HE KILLED HIS PARENTS. BUT IT WAS ACTUALLY MIRROR MASTER THAT DID IT.

HE'S A GOOD FRIEND, JAMES. HIS MIND IS MESSED UP.

I UNDERSTAND, FLASH. I WISH I KNEW THAT BEFORE PIPER LEFT.

WE'LL DO OUR BEST TO TRACK HIM DOWN.

WELL?

WELL, WHAT?

THE PROJECT...

...I THINK IT'S TIME WE GOT STARTED.

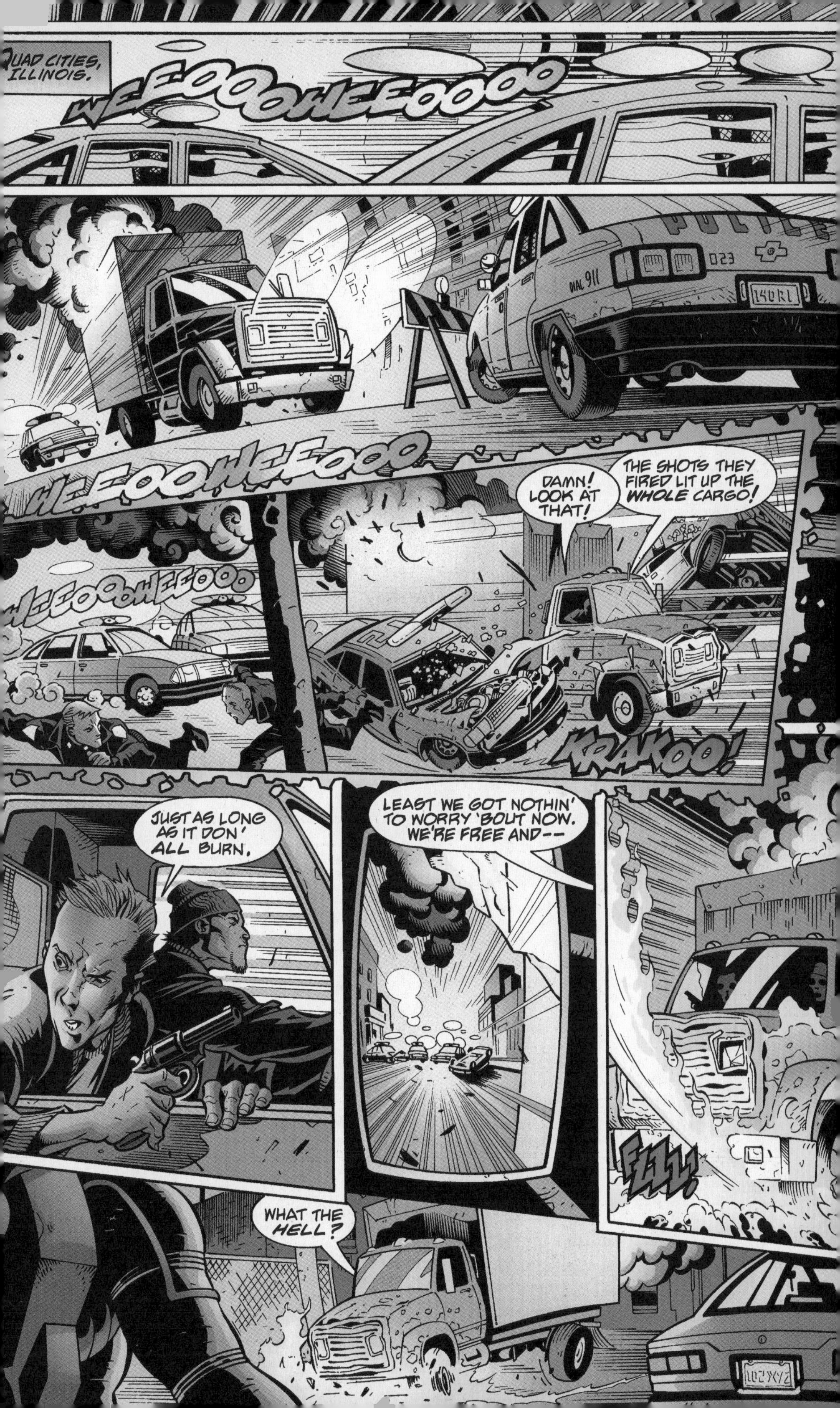
QUAD CITIES, ILLINOIS.
WEEOOOWHEEOOOO
WEEOOWHEEOOO
WEEOOWHEEOOO
DAMN! LOOK AT THAT!
THE SHOTS THEY FIRED LIT UP THE WHOLE CARGO!
KRAKOO!
JUST AS LONG AS IT DON' ALL BURN.
LEAST WE GOT NOTHIN' TO WORRY 'BOUT NOW. WE'RE FREE AND--
FZZZ!
WHAT THE HELL?

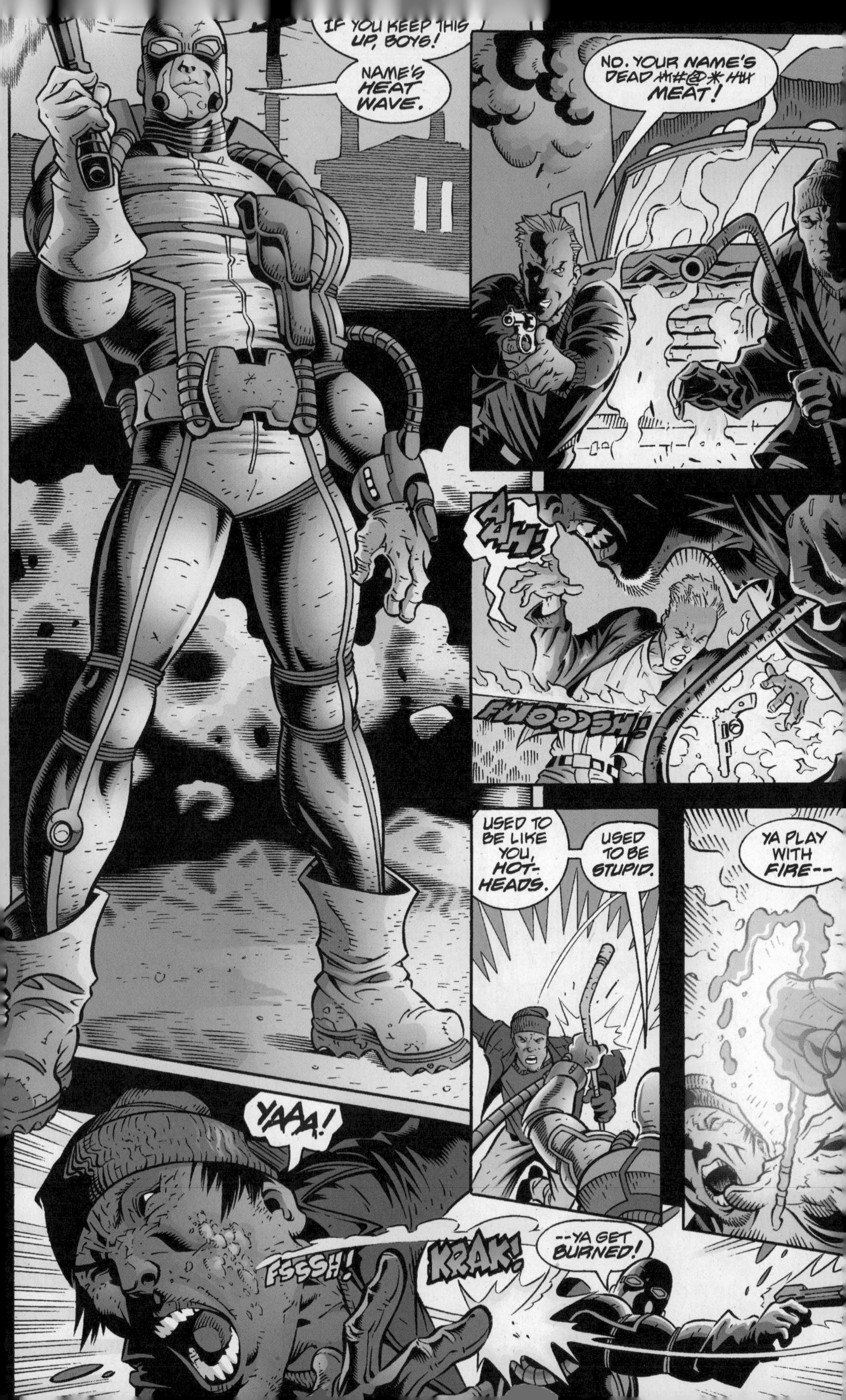

IF YOU KEEP THIS UP, BOYS!
NAME'S HEAT WAVE.
NO. YOUR NAME'S DEAD #!#@*#!# MEAT!
AAH!
FWOOOSH!
USED TO BE LIKE YOU, HOT-HEADS.
USED TO BE STUPID.
YA PLAY WITH FIRE--
YAAA!
FSSSH!
KRAK!
--YA GET BURNED!

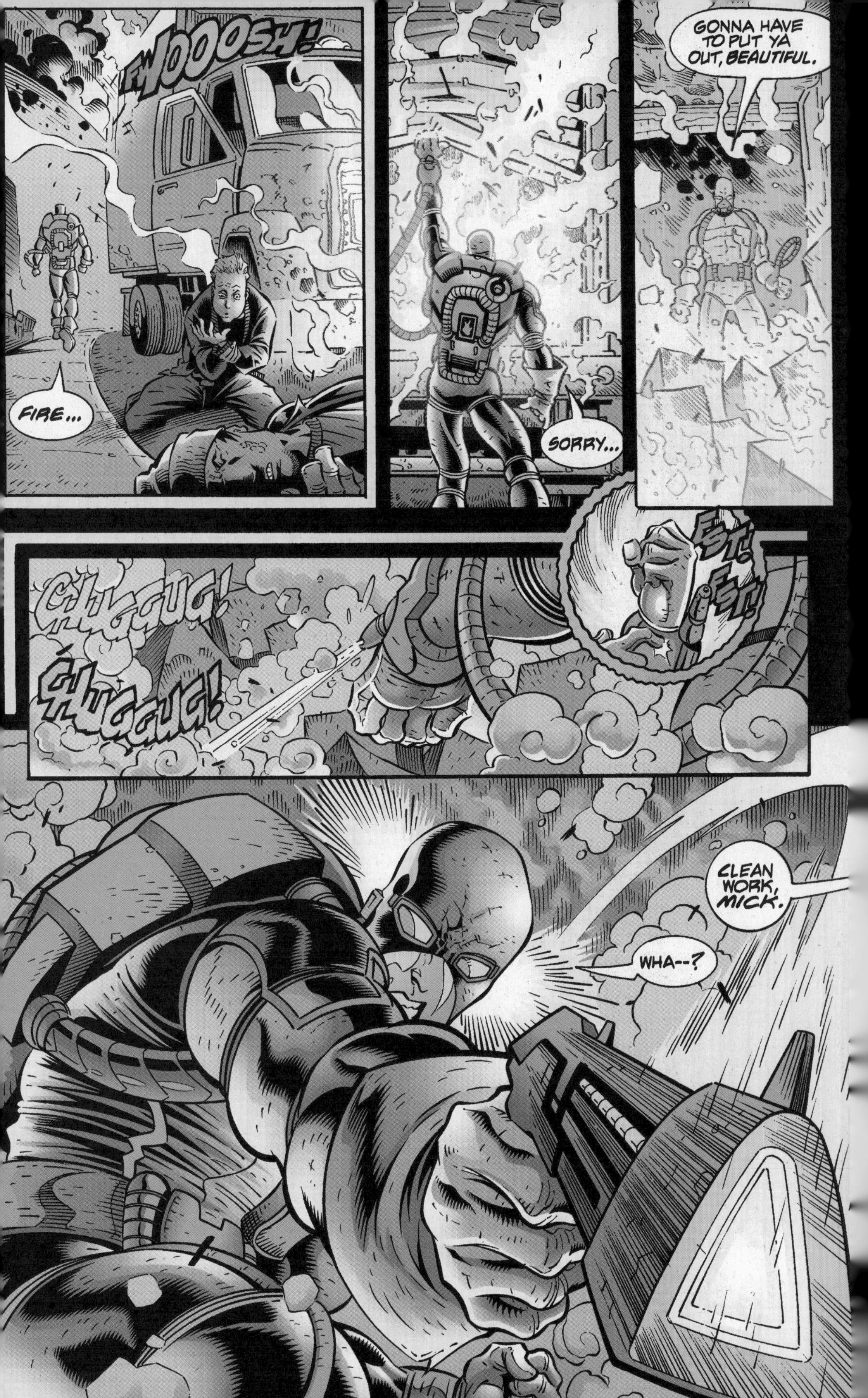
FWOOOSH!
FIRE...
SORRY...
GONNA HAVE TO PUT YA OUT, BEAUTIFUL.
CHUGGUG!
CHUGGUG!
FST! FST!
CLEAN WORK, MICK.
WHA--?

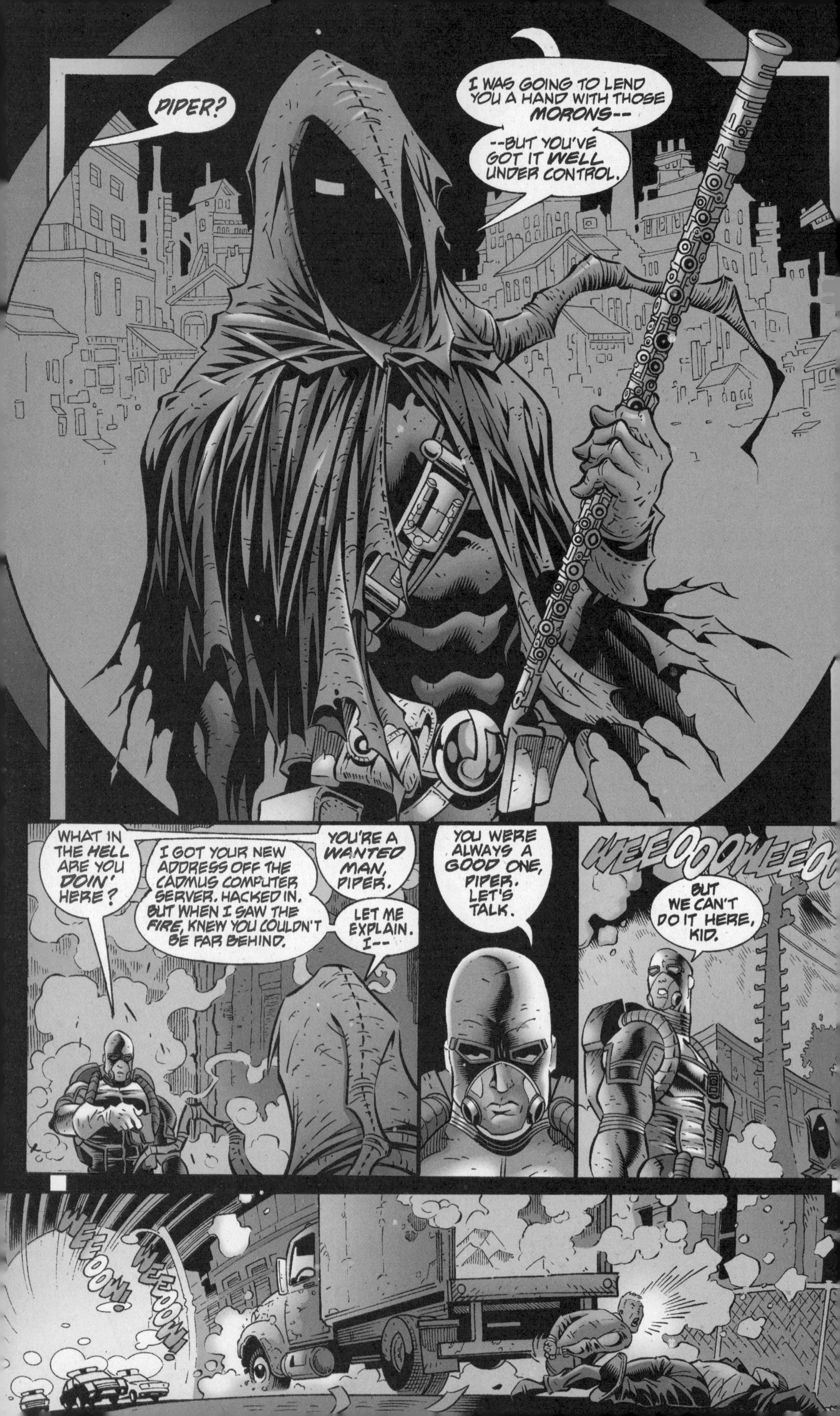
PIPER?
I WAS GOING TO LEND YOU A HAND WITH THOSE MORONS--
--BUT YOU'VE GOT IT WELL UNDER CONTROL.
WHAT IN THE HELL ARE YOU DOIN' HERE?
I GOT YOUR NEW ADDRESS OFF THE CADMUS COMPUTER SERVER. HACKED IN. BUT WHEN I SAW THE FIRE, KNEW YOU COULDN'T BE FAR BEHIND.
YOU'RE A WANTED MAN, PIPER.
LET ME EXPLAIN. I--
YOU WERE ALWAYS A GOOD ONE, PIPER. LET'S TALK.
WEEOOOOWEEOO
BUT WE CAN'T DO IT HERE, KID.
WEEOOW! WEEOOW!

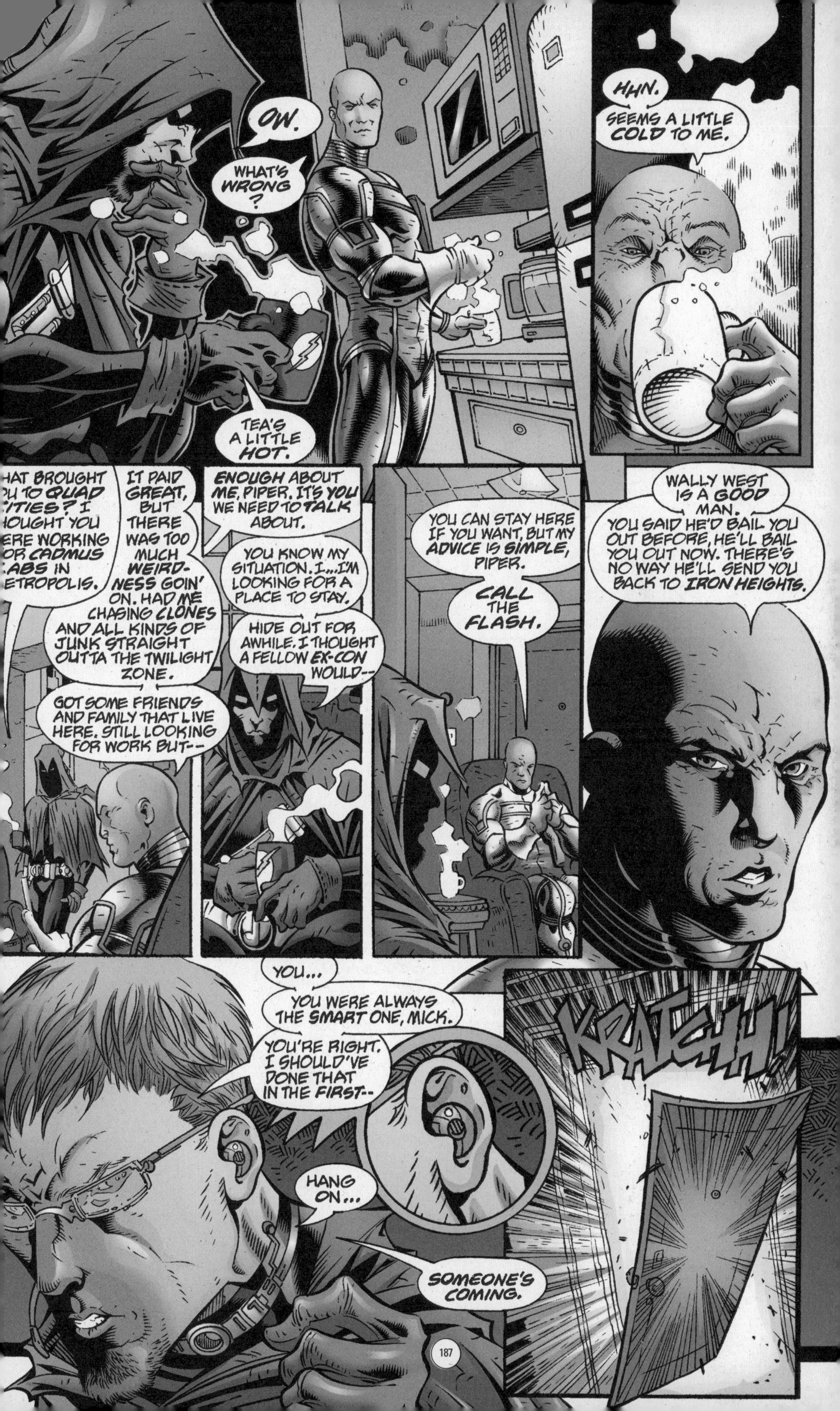
OW.
WHAT'S WRONG?
TEA'S A LITTLE HOT.
HHN.
SEEMS A LITTLE COLD TO ME.
HAT BROUGHT OU TO QUAD CITIES? I HOUGHT YOU ERE WORKING OR CADMUS ABS IN ETROPOLIS.
IT PAID GREAT, BUT THERE WAS TOO MUCH WEIRD-NESS GOIN' ON. HAD ME CHASING CLONES AND ALL KINDS OF JUNK STRAIGHT OUTTA THE TWILIGHT ZONE.
GOT SOME FRIENDS AND FAMILY THAT LIVE HERE. STILL LOOKING FOR WORK BUT--
ENOUGH ABOUT ME, PIPER. IT'S YOU WE NEED TO TALK ABOUT.
YOU KNOW MY SITUATION. I...I'M LOOKING FOR A PLACE TO STAY.
HIDE OUT FOR AWHILE. I THOUGHT A FELLOW EX-CON WOULD--
YOU CAN STAY HERE IF YOU WANT, BUT MY ADVICE IS SIMPLE, PIPER.
CALL THE FLASH.
WALLY WEST IS A GOOD MAN.
YOU SAID HE'D BAIL YOU OUT BEFORE, HE'LL BAIL YOU OUT NOW. THERE'S NO WAY HE'LL SEND YOU BACK TO IRON HEIGHTS.
YOU...
YOU WERE ALWAYS THE SMART ONE, MICK.
YOU'RE RIGHT. I SHOULD'VE DONE THAT IN THE FIRST--
HANG ON...
SOMEONE'S COMING.
KRATCHH!

CHAK! CHAK! CHAK! CHAK!

EXIT

JAMES JESSE.

HOW DID YOU--

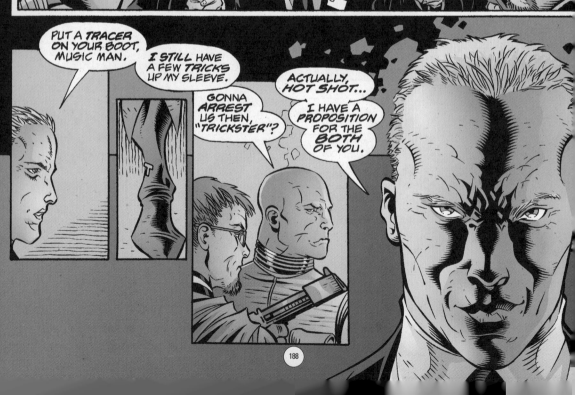

PUT A *TRACER* ON YOUR BOOT, MUSIC MAN.

I STILL HAVE A FEW *TRICKS* UP MY SLEEVE.

GONNA *ARREST* US THEN, "*TRICKSTER*"?

ACTUALLY, *HOT SHOT*... I HAVE A PROPOSITION FOR THE *BOTH* OF YOU.

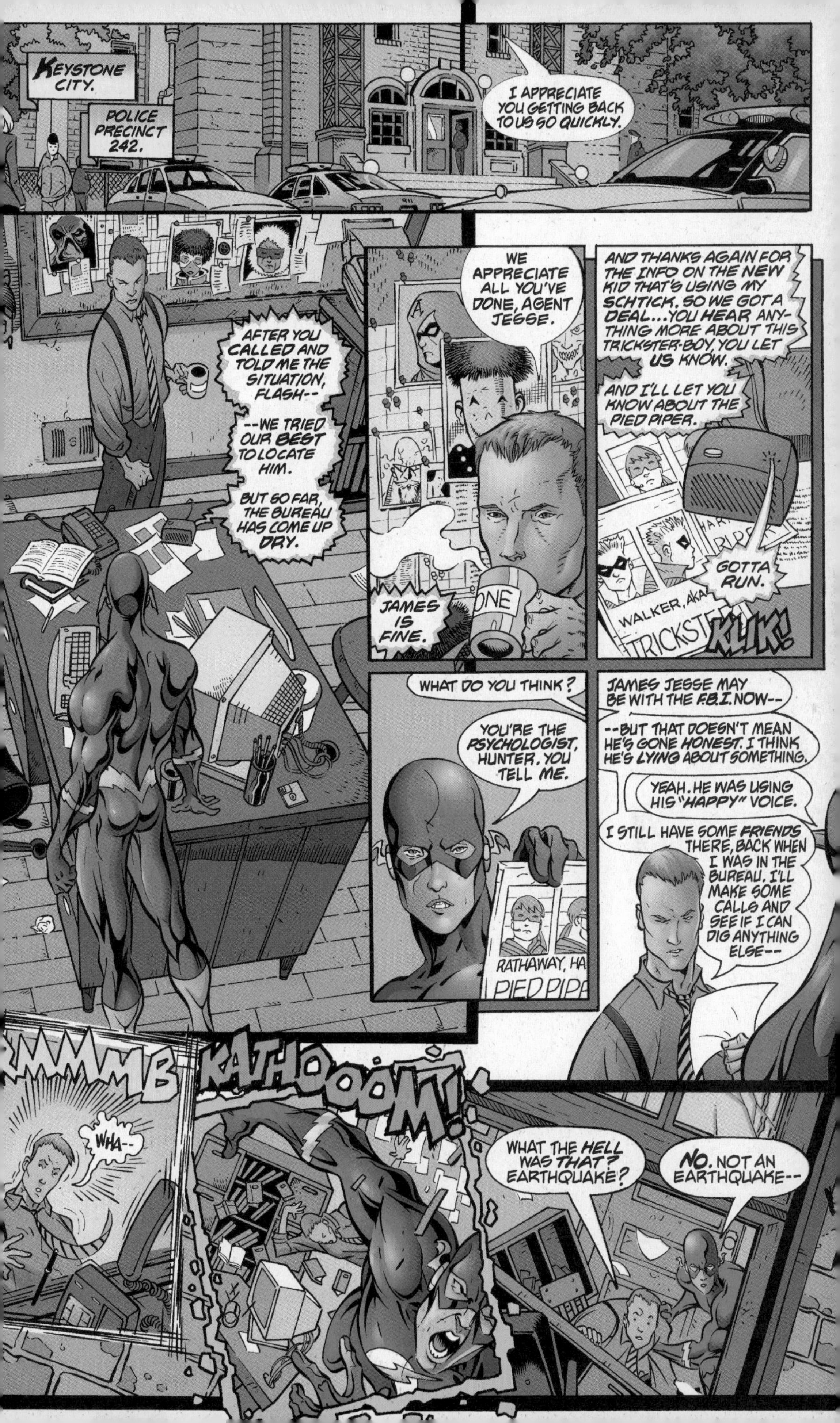
KEYSTONE CITY.
POLICE PRECINCT 242.
I APPRECIATE YOU GETTING BACK TO US SO QUICKLY.
AFTER YOU CALLED AND TOLD ME THE SITUATION, FLASH--
--WE TRIED OUR BEST TO LOCATE HIM.
BUT SO FAR, THE BUREAU HAS COME UP DRY.
JAMES IS FINE.
WE APPRECIATE ALL YOU'VE DONE, AGENT JESSE.
ONE
AND THANKS AGAIN FOR THE INFO ON THE NEW KID THAT'S USING MY SCHTICK. SO WE GOT A DEAL... YOU HEAR ANYTHING MORE ABOUT THIS TRICKSTER-BOY, YOU LET US KNOW.
AND I'LL LET YOU KNOW ABOUT THE PIED PIPER.
GOTTA RUN.
WALKER, AKA
TRICKST
KLIK!
WHAT DO YOU THINK?
YOU'RE THE PSYCHOLOGIST, HUNTER. YOU TELL ME.
RATHAWAY, HA
PIED PIP
JAMES JESSE MAY BE WITH THE F.B.I. NOW--
--BUT THAT DOESN'T MEAN HE'S GONE HONEST. I THINK HE'S LYING ABOUT SOMETHING.
YEAH. HE WAS USING HIS "HAPPY" VOICE.
I STILL HAVE SOME FRIENDS THERE, BACK WHEN I WAS IN THE BUREAU. I'LL MAKE SOME CALLS AND SEE IF I CAN DIG ANYTHING ELSE--
WHAMMB
KATHOOOOM!!
WHA--
WHAT THE HELL WAS THAT? EARTHQUAKE?
NO. NOT AN EARTHQUAKE--

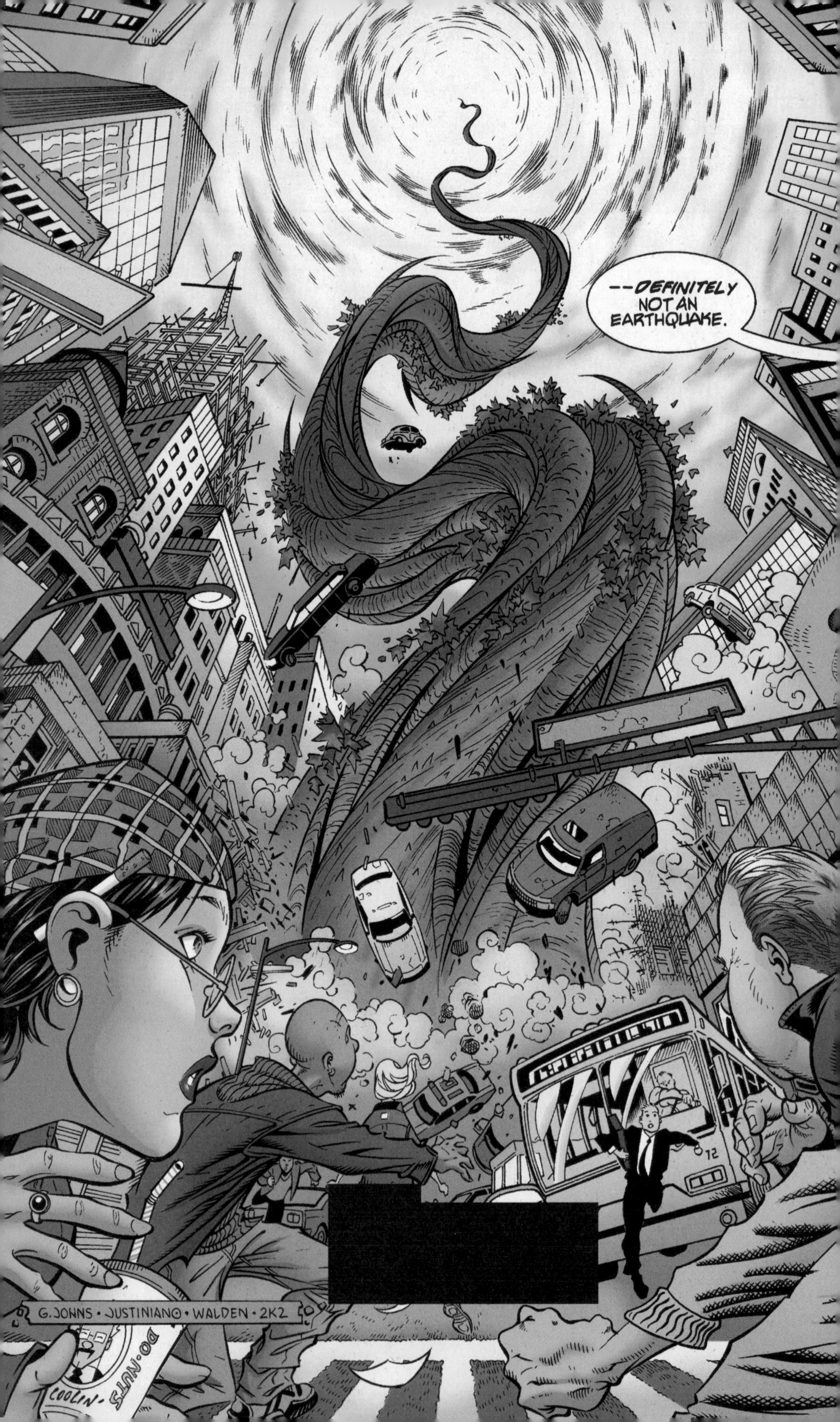
--DEFINITELY NOT AN EARTHQUAKE.
[redacted]
G. JOHNS • JUSTINIANO • WALDEN • 2K2
DO-NUTS

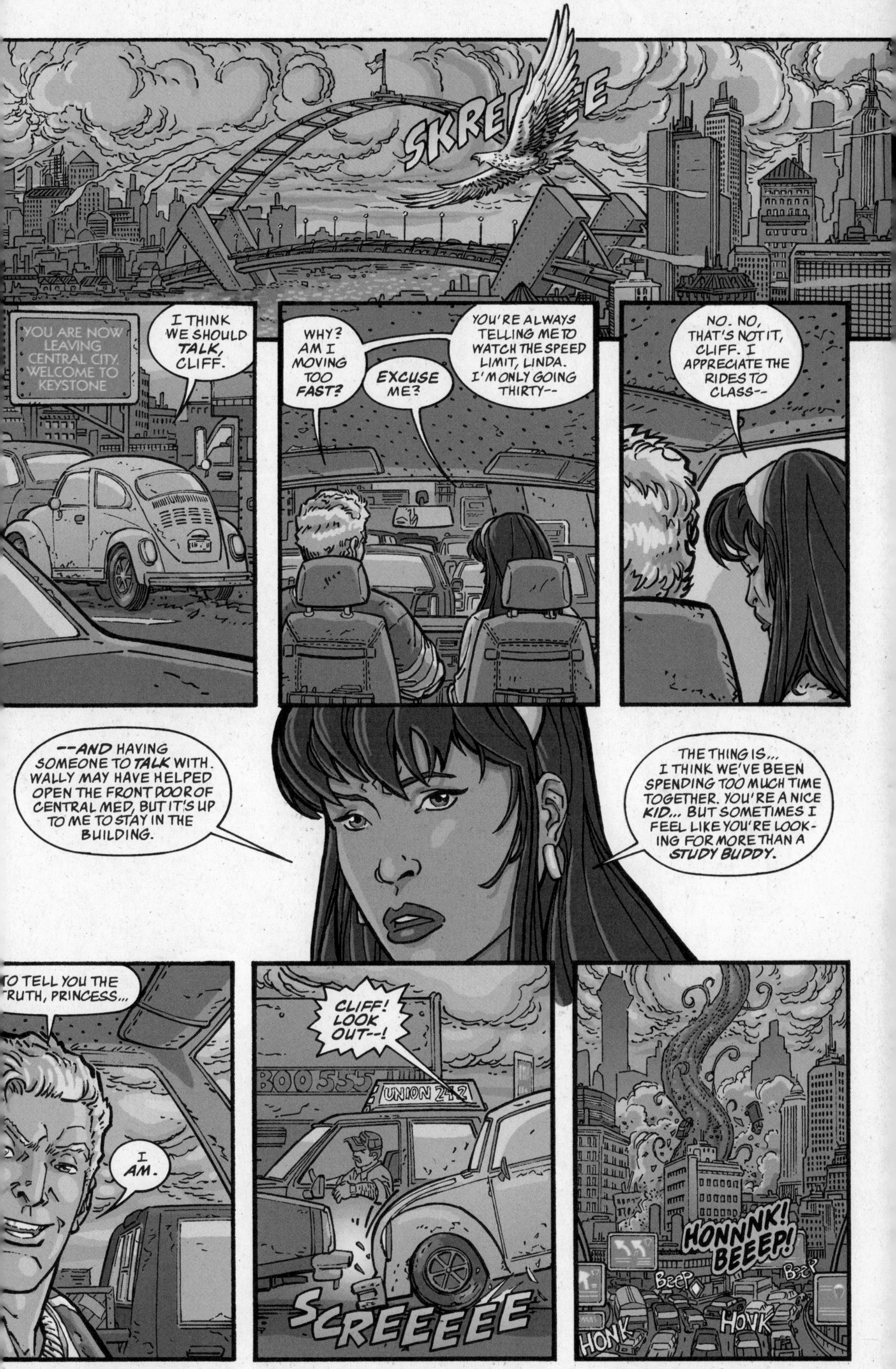
SKREEEEE
YOU ARE NOW LEAVING CENTRAL CITY. WELCOME TO KEYSTONE
I THINK WE SHOULD TALK, CLIFF.
WHY? AM I MOVING TOO FAST?
EXCUSE ME?
YOU'RE ALWAYS TELLING ME TO WATCH THE SPEED LIMIT, LINDA. I'M ONLY GOING THIRTY--
NO. NO, THAT'S NOT IT, CLIFF. I APPRECIATE THE RIDES TO CLASS--
--AND HAVING SOMEONE TO TALK WITH. WALLY MAY HAVE HELPED OPEN THE FRONT DOOR OF CENTRAL MED, BUT IT'S UP TO ME TO STAY IN THE BUILDING.
THE THING IS... I THINK WE'VE BEEN SPENDING TOO MUCH TIME TOGETHER. YOU'RE A NICE KID... BUT SOMETIMES I FEEL LIKE YOU'RE LOOKING FOR MORE THAN A STUDY BUDDY.
TO TELL YOU THE TRUTH, PRINCESS...
I AM.
CLIFF! LOOK OUT--!
UNION 242
SCREEEEEE
HONNNK! BEEEP!
Beep
Beep
HONK
HONK

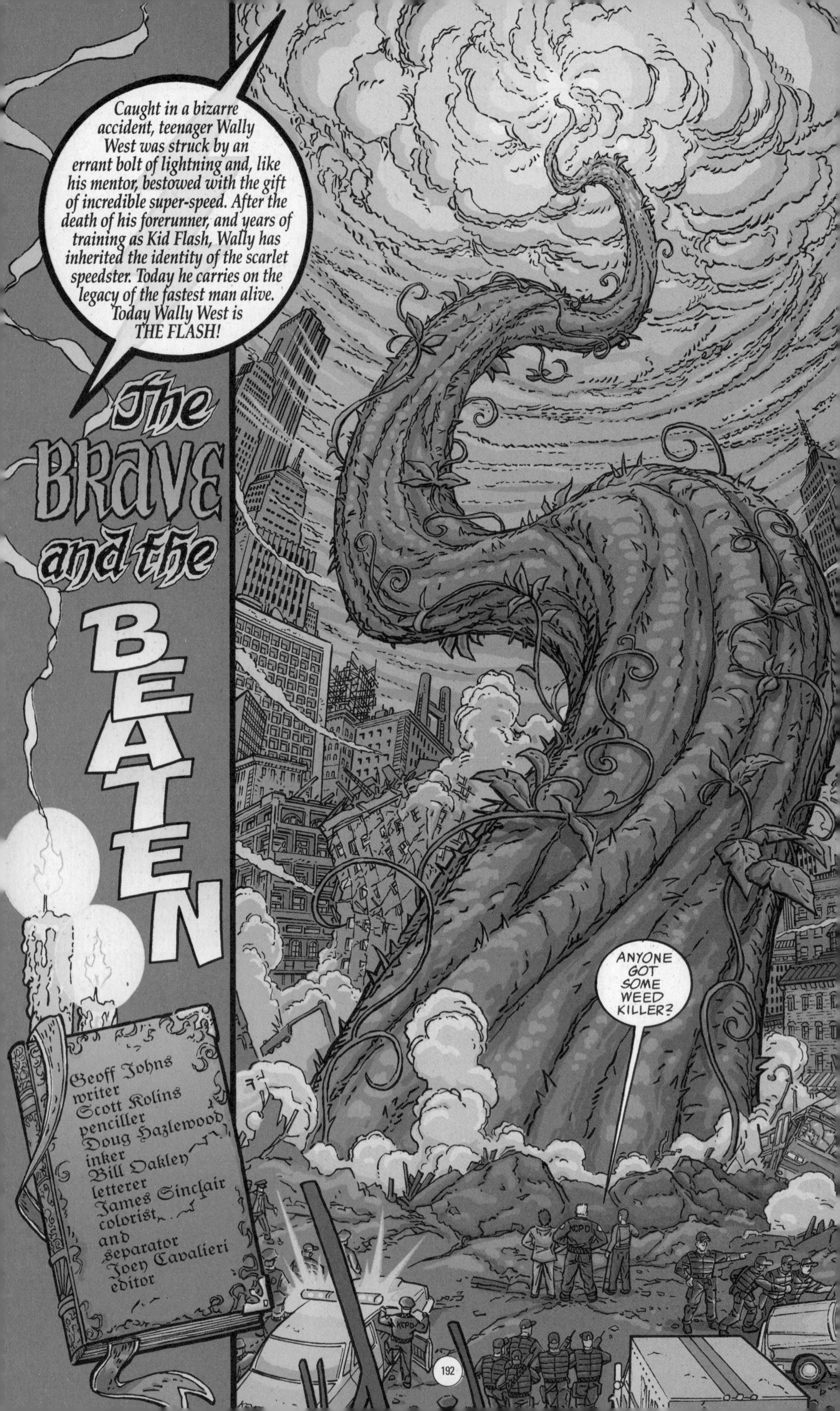
Caught in a bizarre accident, teenager Wally West was struck by an errant bolt of lightning and, like his mentor, bestowed with the gift of incredible super-speed. After the death of his forerunner, and years of training as Kid Flash, Wally has inherited the identity of the scarlet speedster. Today he carries on the legacy of the fastest man alive. Today Wally West is THE FLASH!
The BRAVE and the BEATEN
Geoff Johns writer
Scott Kolins penciller
Doug Hazlewood inker
Bill Oakley letterer
James Sinclair colorist and separator
Joey Cavalieri editor
ANYONE GOT SOME WEED KILLER?

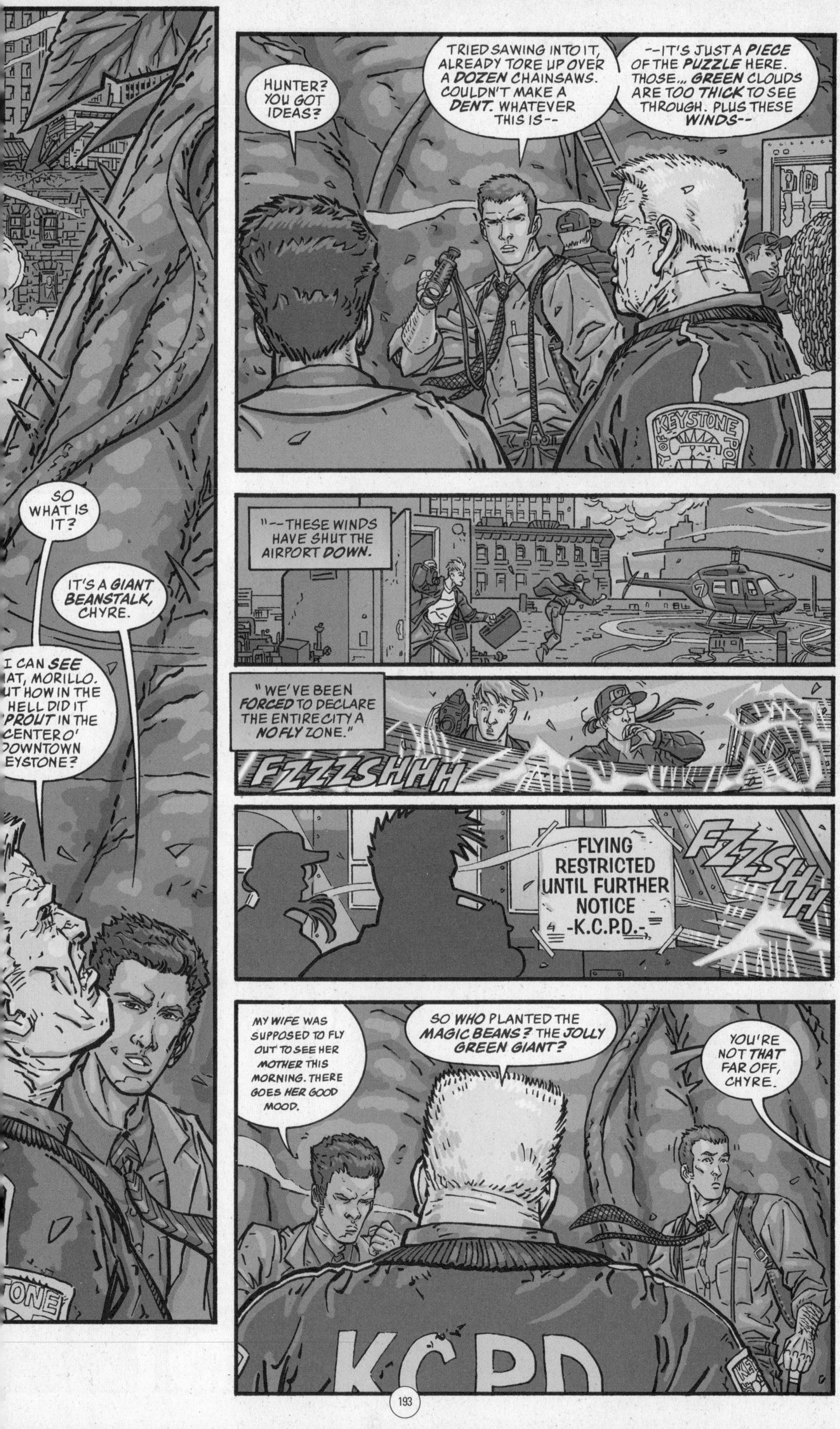
SO WHAT IS IT?
IT'S A GIANT BEANSTALK, CHYRE.
I CAN SEE AT, MORILLO. UT HOW IN THE HELL DID IT PROUT IN THE CENTER O' OWNTOWN EYSTONE?
HUNTER? YOU GOT IDEAS?
TRIED SAWING INTO IT, ALREADY TORE UP OVER A DOZEN CHAINSAWS. COULDN'T MAKE A DENT. WHATEVER THIS IS--
--IT'S JUST A PIECE OF THE PUZZLE HERE. THOSE... GREEN CLOUDS ARE TOO THICK TO SEE THROUGH. PLUS THESE WINDS--
KEYSTONE
"--THESE WINDS HAVE SHUT THE AIRPORT DOWN.
"WE'VE BEEN FORCED TO DECLARE THE ENTIRE CITY A NO FLY ZONE."
FZZZSHHH
FLYING RESTRICTED UNTIL FURTHER NOTICE -K.C.P.D.-
FZZSHH
MY WIFE WAS SUPPOSED TO FLY OUT TO SEE HER MOTHER THIS MORNING. THERE GOES HER GOOD MOOD.
SO WHO PLANTED THE MAGIC BEANS? THE JOLLY GREEN GIANT?
YOU'RE NOT THAT FAR OFF, CHYRE.
KCPD

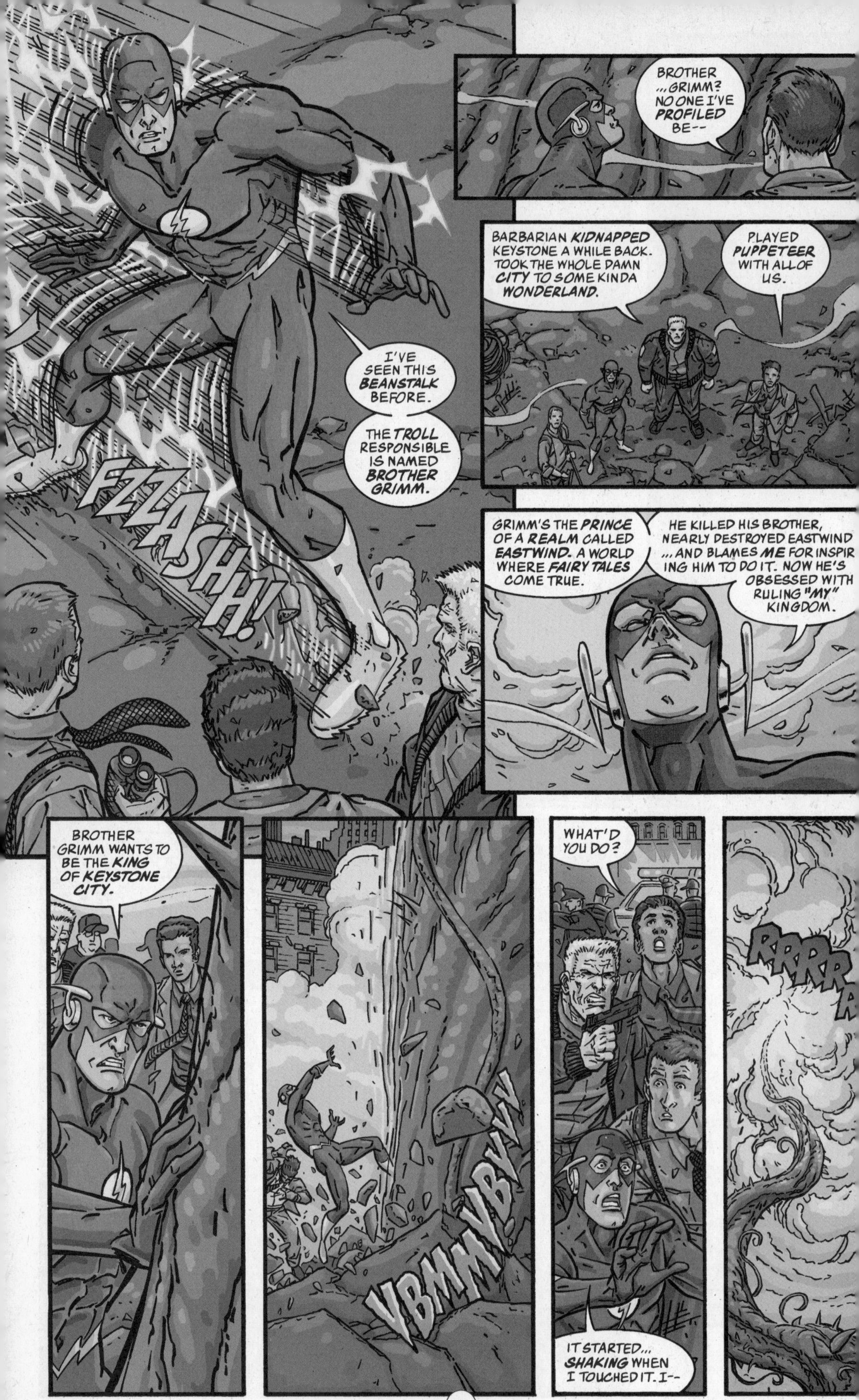
I'VE SEEN THIS BEANSTALK BEFORE.
THE TROLL RESPONSIBLE IS NAMED BROTHER GRIMM.
FZZASHH!
BROTHER ...GRIMM? NO ONE I'VE PROFILED BE--
BARBARIAN KIDNAPPED KEYSTONE A WHILE BACK. TOOK THE WHOLE DAMN CITY TO SOME KINDA WONDERLAND.
PLAYED PUPPETEER WITH ALL OF US.
GRIMM'S THE PRINCE OF A REALM CALLED EASTWIND. A WORLD WHERE FAIRY TALES COME TRUE.
HE KILLED HIS BROTHER, NEARLY DESTROYED EASTWIND ...AND BLAMES ME FOR INSPIRING HIM TO DO IT. NOW HE'S OBSESSED WITH RULING "MY" KINGDOM.
BROTHER GRIMM WANTS TO BE THE KING OF KEYSTONE CITY.
VBMMVBVV
WHAT'D YOU DO?
IT STARTED... SHAKING WHEN I TOUCHED IT. I--
RRRRR

RRAAA AAA

KRKOOM! FWOOOOOO

RRAAAAAA

TAKE A *DEEP BREATH.* I'M GETTING YOU ALL OUT OF--

STAND YOUR GROUND, FLASH.

195

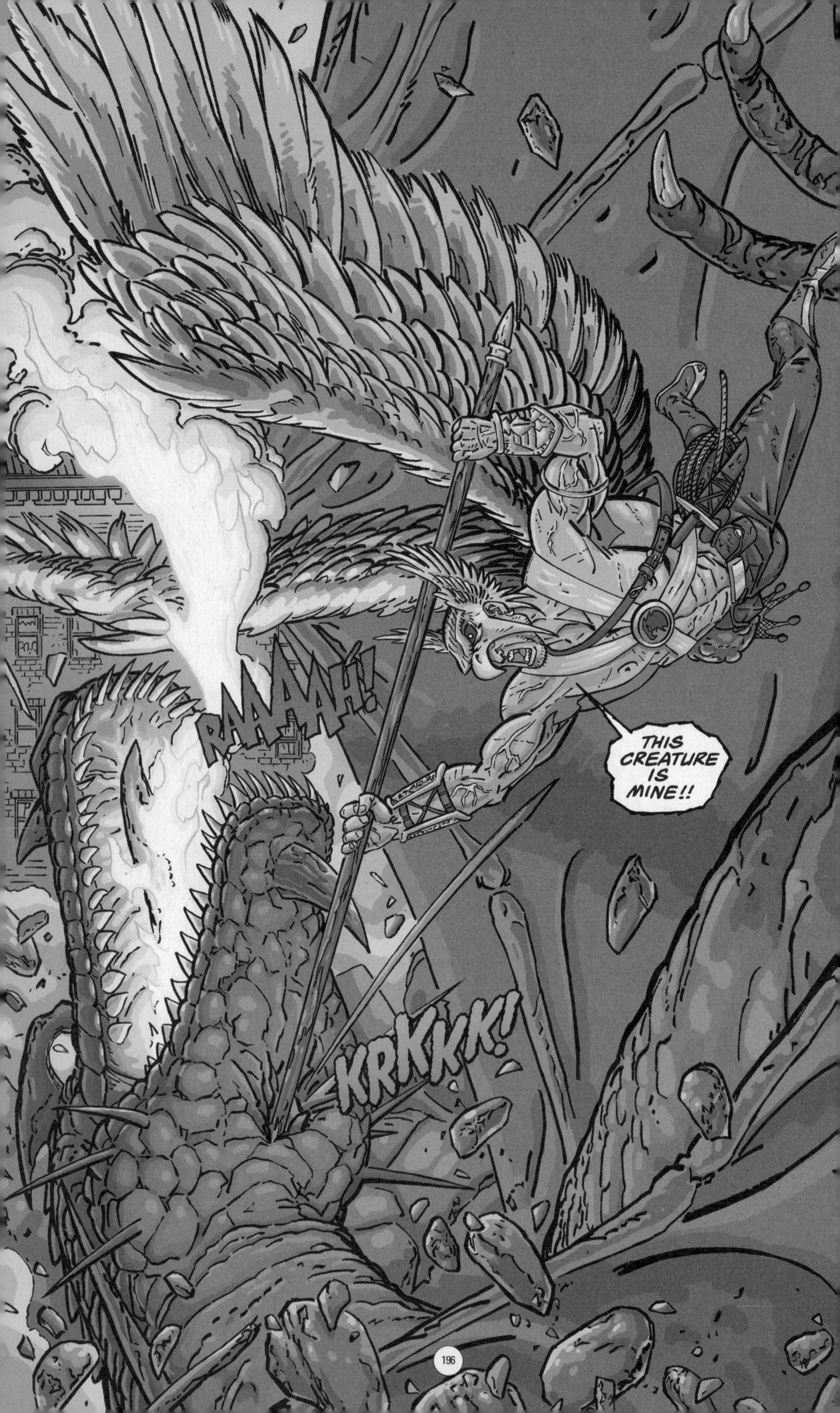
RAAAAAH!
THIS CREATURE IS MINE!!
KRKKK!

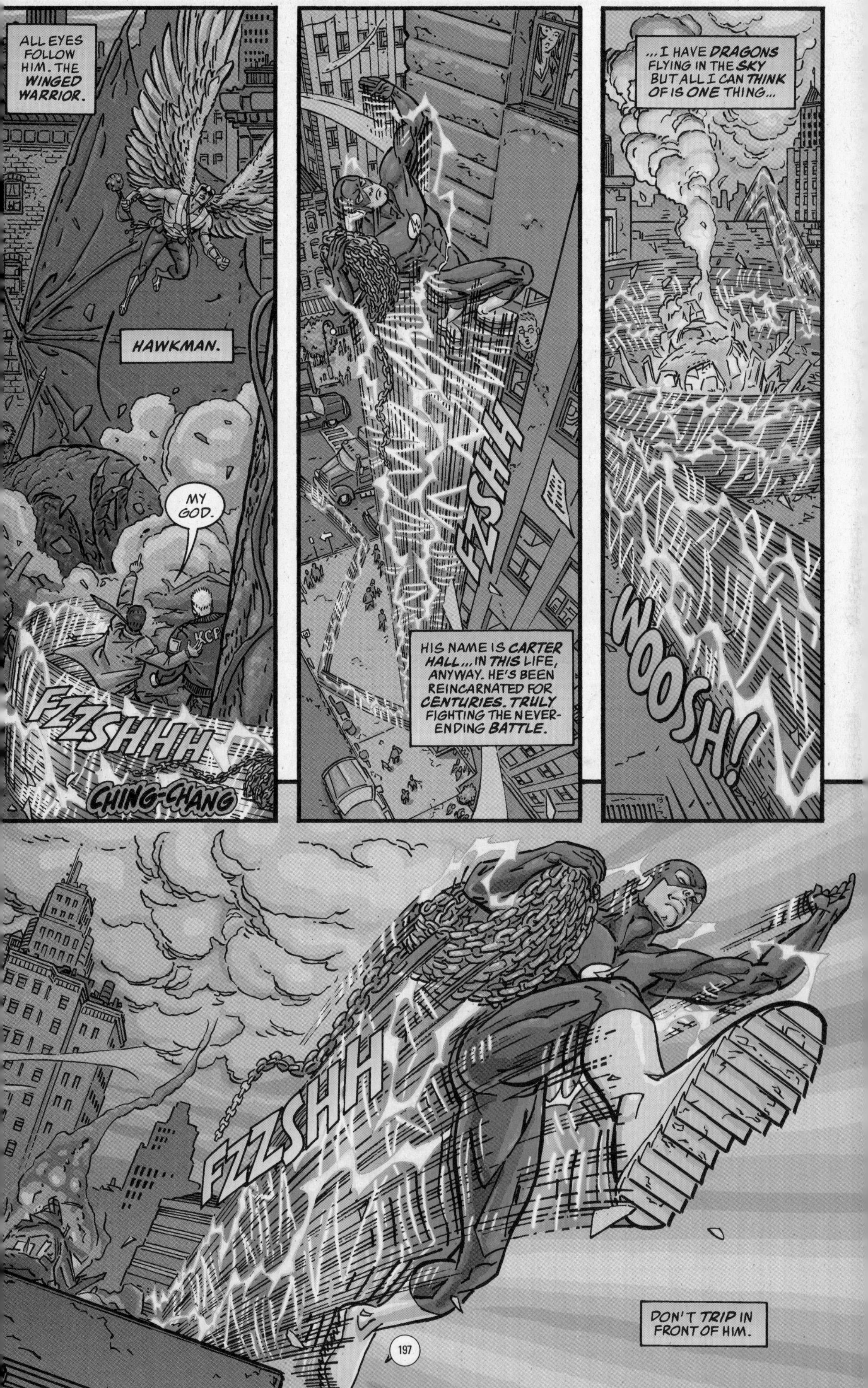
ALL EYES FOLLOW HIM. THE WINGED WARRIOR.
HAWKMAN.
MY GOD.
FZZSHHH
CHING-CHANG
FZZSHH
HIS NAME IS CARTER HALL... IN THIS LIFE, ANYWAY. HE'S BEEN REINCARNATED FOR CENTURIES. TRULY FIGHTING THE NEVER-ENDING BATTLE.
...I HAVE DRAGONS FLYING IN THE SKY BUT ALL I CAN THINK OF IS ONE THING...
WOOSH!
FZZSHH
DON'T TRIP IN FRONT OF HIM.

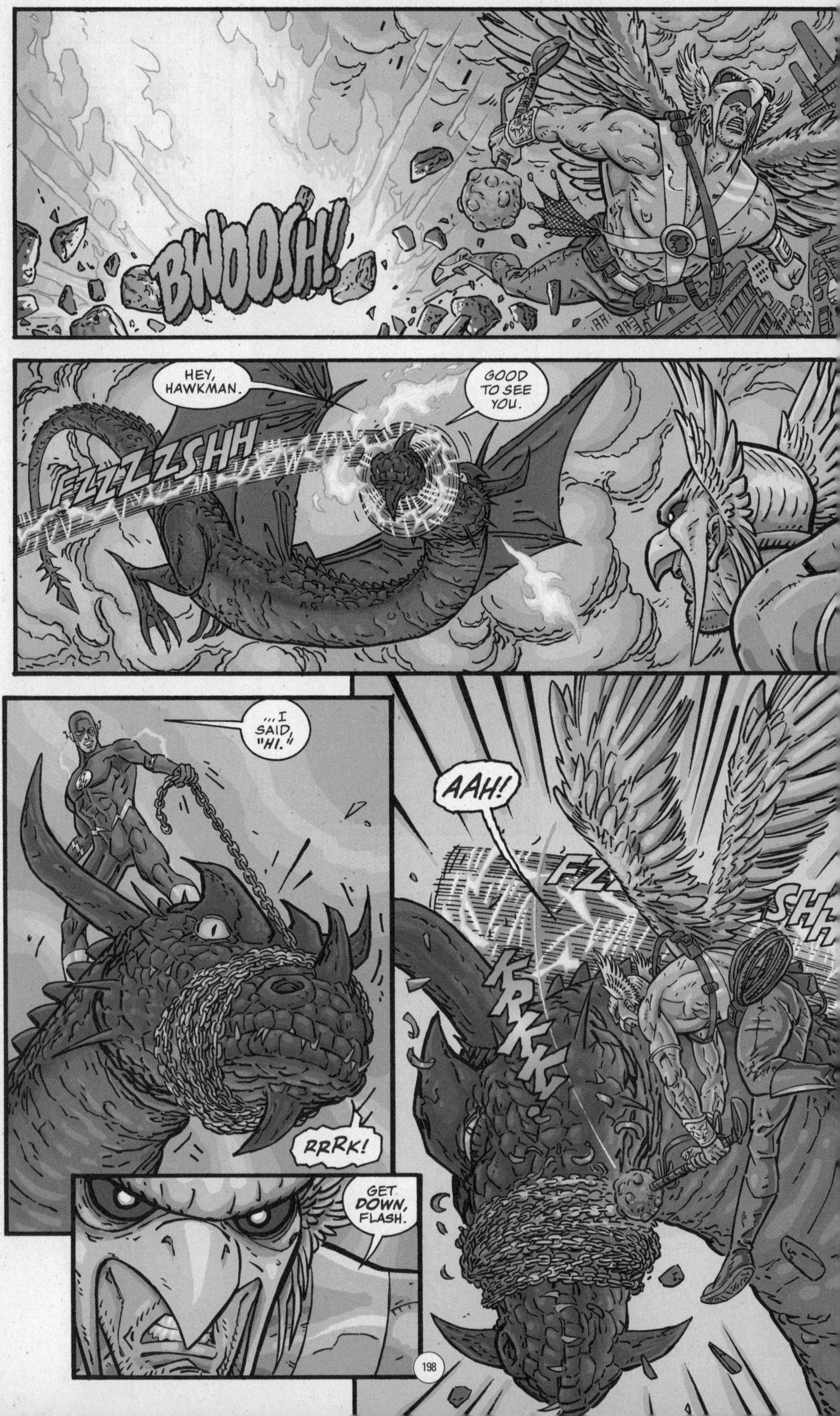
BWOOSH!
HEY, HAWKMAN.
GOOD TO SEE YOU.
FZZZZZSHH
...I SAID, "HI."
RRRK!
GET DOWN, FLASH.
AAH!
FZZ
SHH
KRKK

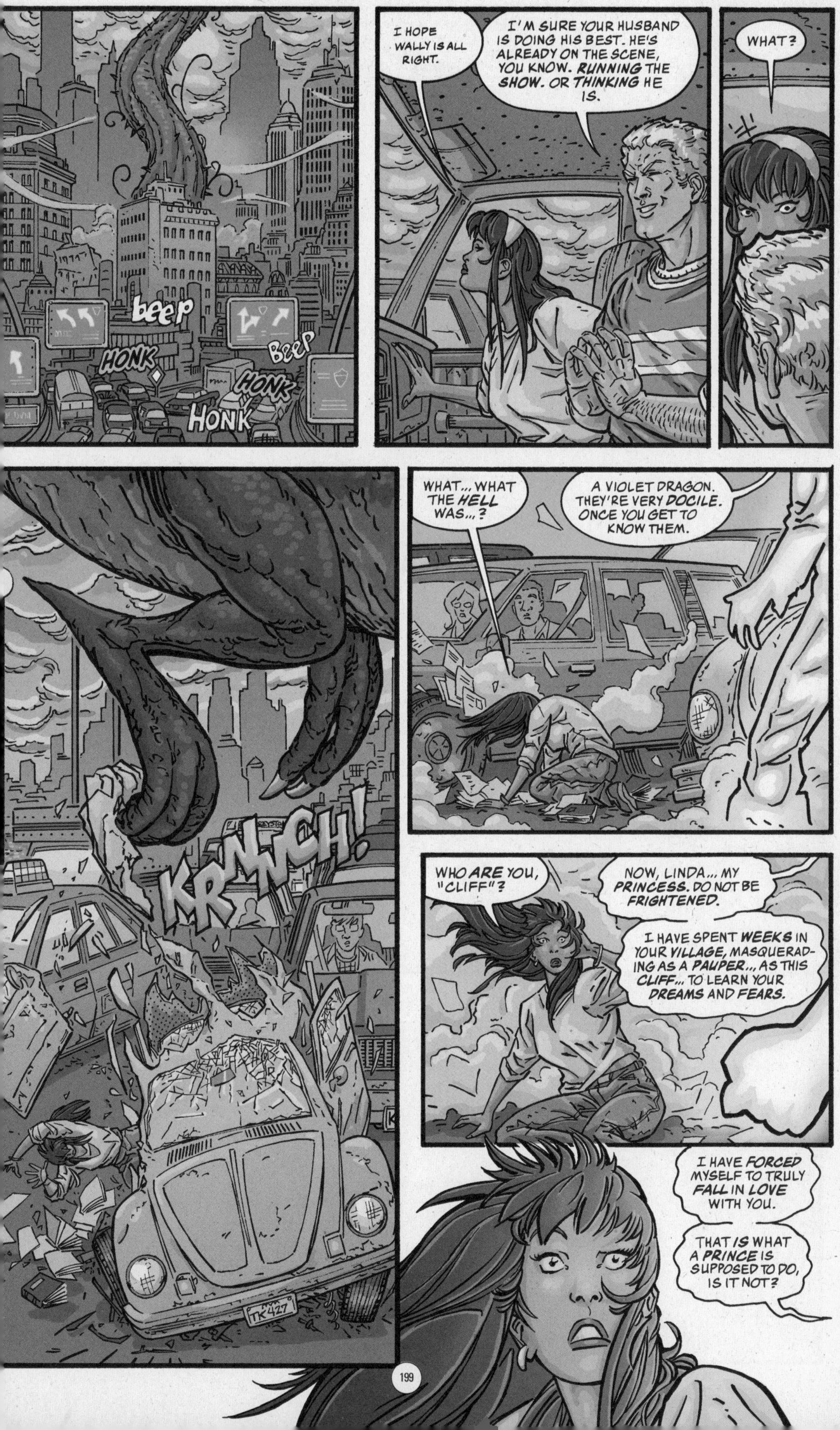
beep
HONK
Beep
HONK
HONK
I HOPE WALLY IS ALL RIGHT.
I'M SURE YOUR HUSBAND IS DOING HIS BEST. HE'S ALREADY ON THE SCENE, YOU KNOW. RUNNING THE SHOW. OR THINKING HE IS.
WHAT?
KRNNCH!
WHAT... WHAT THE HELL WAS...?
A VIOLET DRAGON. THEY'RE VERY DOCILE. ONCE YOU GET TO KNOW THEM.
WHO ARE YOU, "CLIFF"?
NOW, LINDA... MY PRINCESS. DO NOT BE FRIGHTENED.
I HAVE SPENT WEEKS IN YOUR VILLAGE, MASQUERADING AS A PAUPER... AS THIS CLIFF... TO LEARN YOUR DREAMS AND FEARS.
I HAVE FORCED MYSELF TO TRULY FALL IN LOVE WITH YOU.
THAT IS WHAT A PRINCE IS SUPPOSED TO DO, IS IT NOT?

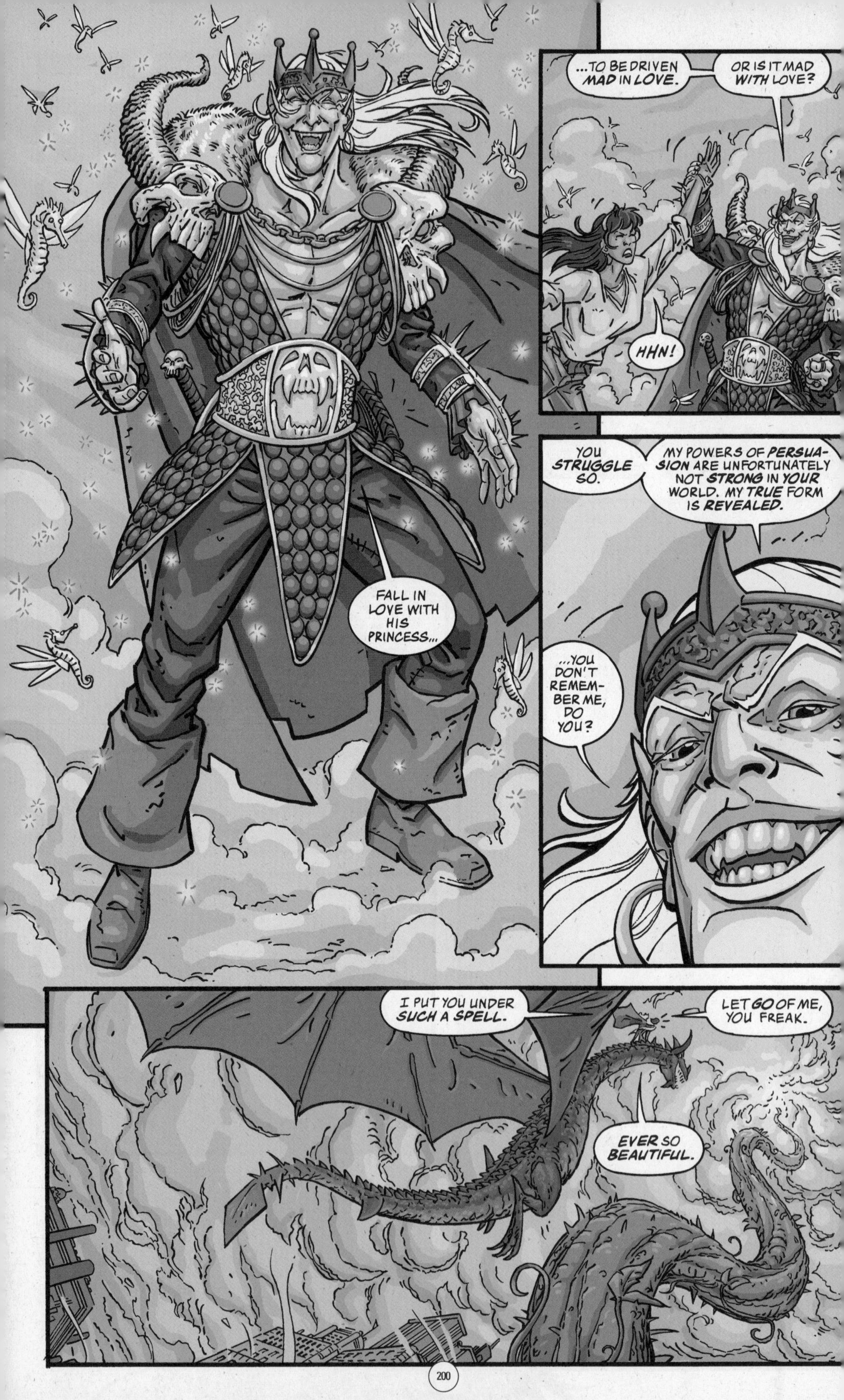
FALL IN LOVE WITH HIS PRINCESS...
...TO BE DRIVEN MAD IN LOVE.
OR IS IT MAD WITH LOVE?
HHN!
YOU STRUGGLE SO.
MY POWERS OF PERSUASION ARE UNFORTUNATELY NOT STRONG IN YOUR WORLD. MY TRUE FORM IS REVEALED.
...YOU DON'T REMEMBER ME, DO YOU?
I PUT YOU UNDER SUCH A SPELL.
LET GO OF ME, YOU FREAK.
EVER SO BEAUTIFUL.

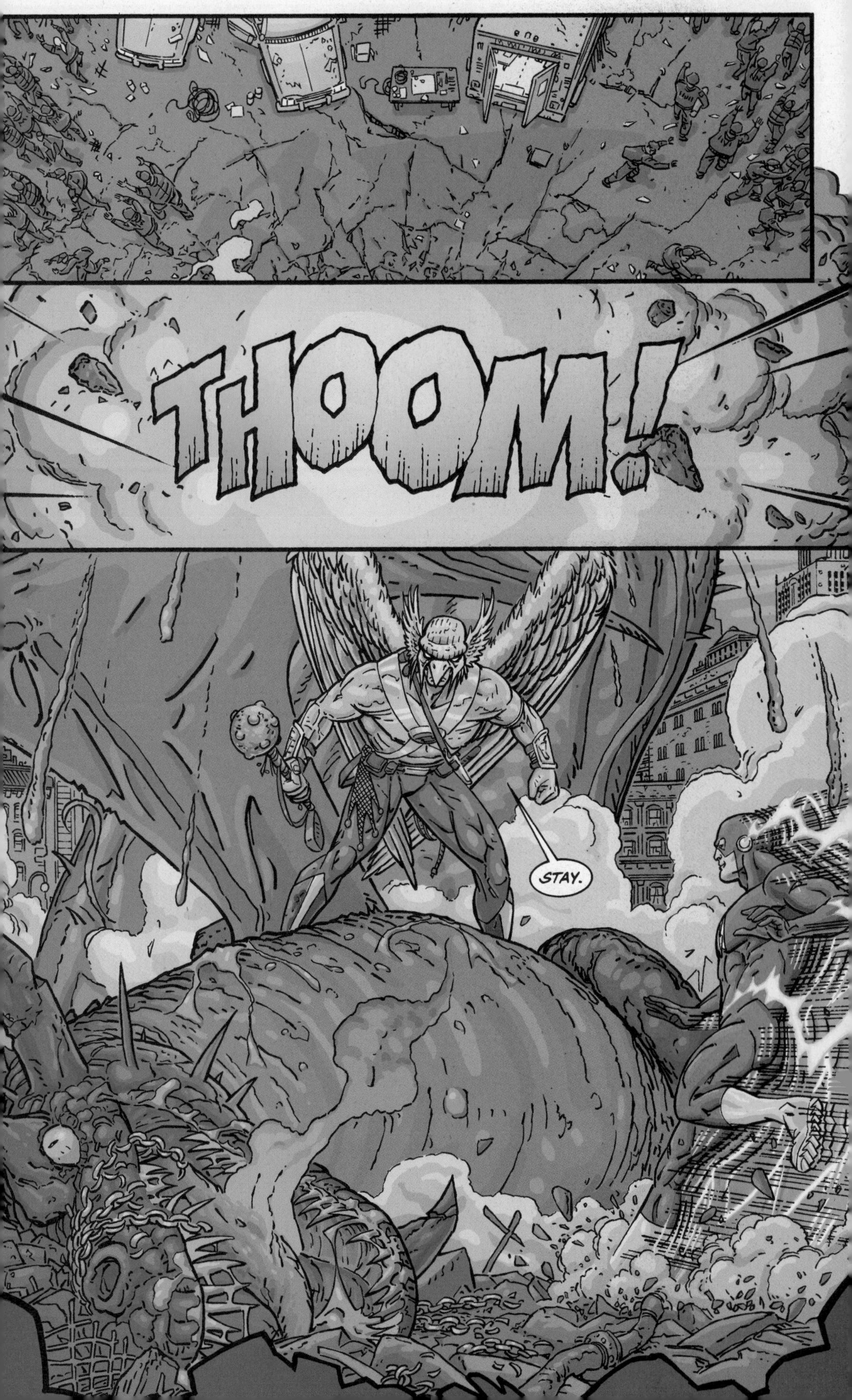
THOOM!
STAY.

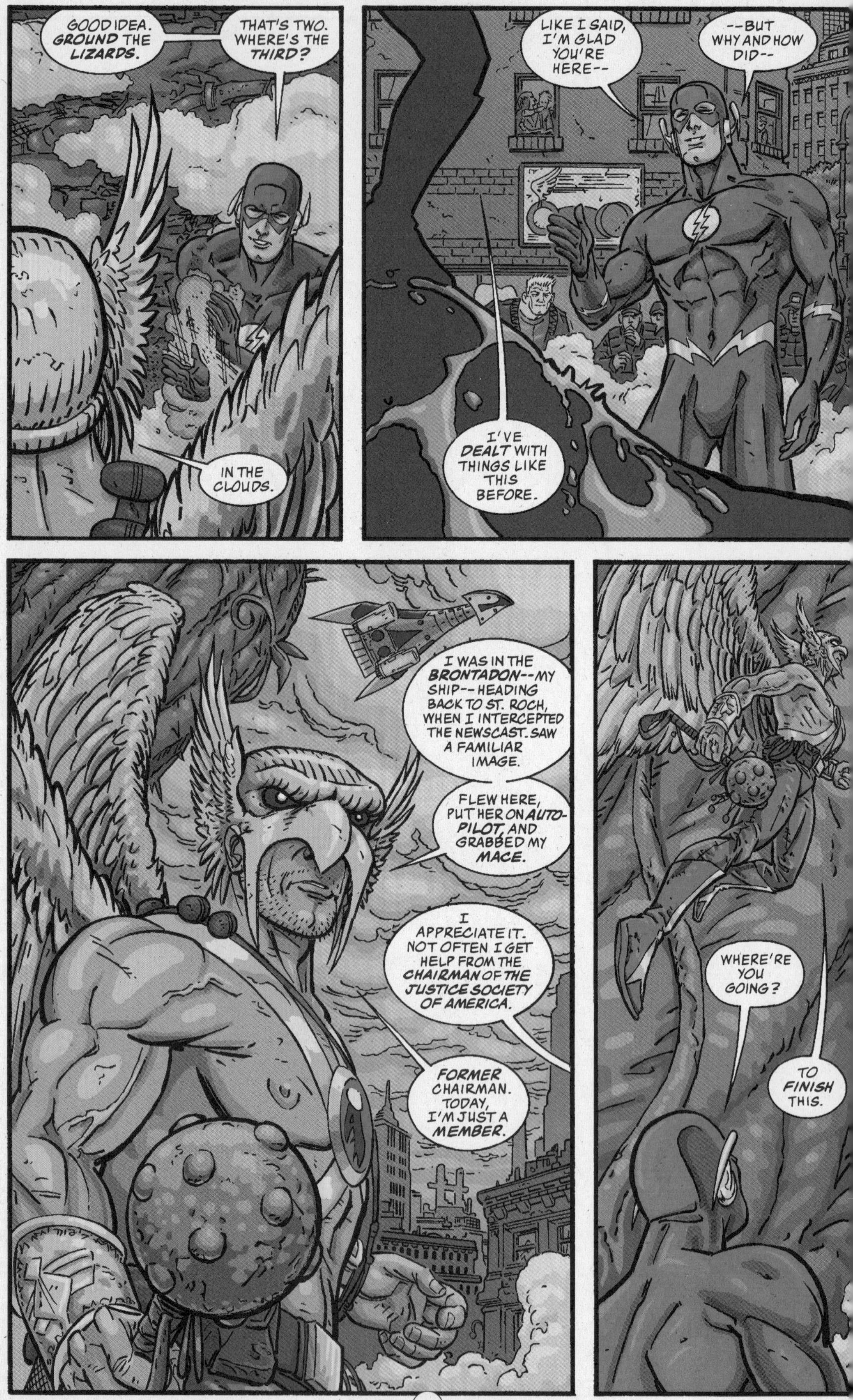
GOOD IDEA. GROUND THE LIZARDS.
THAT'S TWO. WHERE'S THE THIRD?
IN THE CLOUDS.
LIKE I SAID, I'M GLAD YOU'RE HERE--
--BUT WHY AND HOW DID--
I'VE DEALT WITH THINGS LIKE THIS BEFORE.
I WAS IN THE BRONTADON--MY SHIP--HEADING BACK TO ST. ROCH, WHEN I INTERCEPTED THE NEWSCAST. SAW A FAMILIAR IMAGE.
FLEW HERE, PUT HER ON AUTO-PILOT, AND GRABBED MY MACE.
I APPRECIATE IT. NOT OFTEN I GET HELP FROM THE CHAIRMAN OF THE JUSTICE SOCIETY OF AMERICA.
FORMER CHAIRMAN. TODAY, I'M JUST A MEMBER.
WHERE'RE YOU GOING?
TO FINISH THIS.

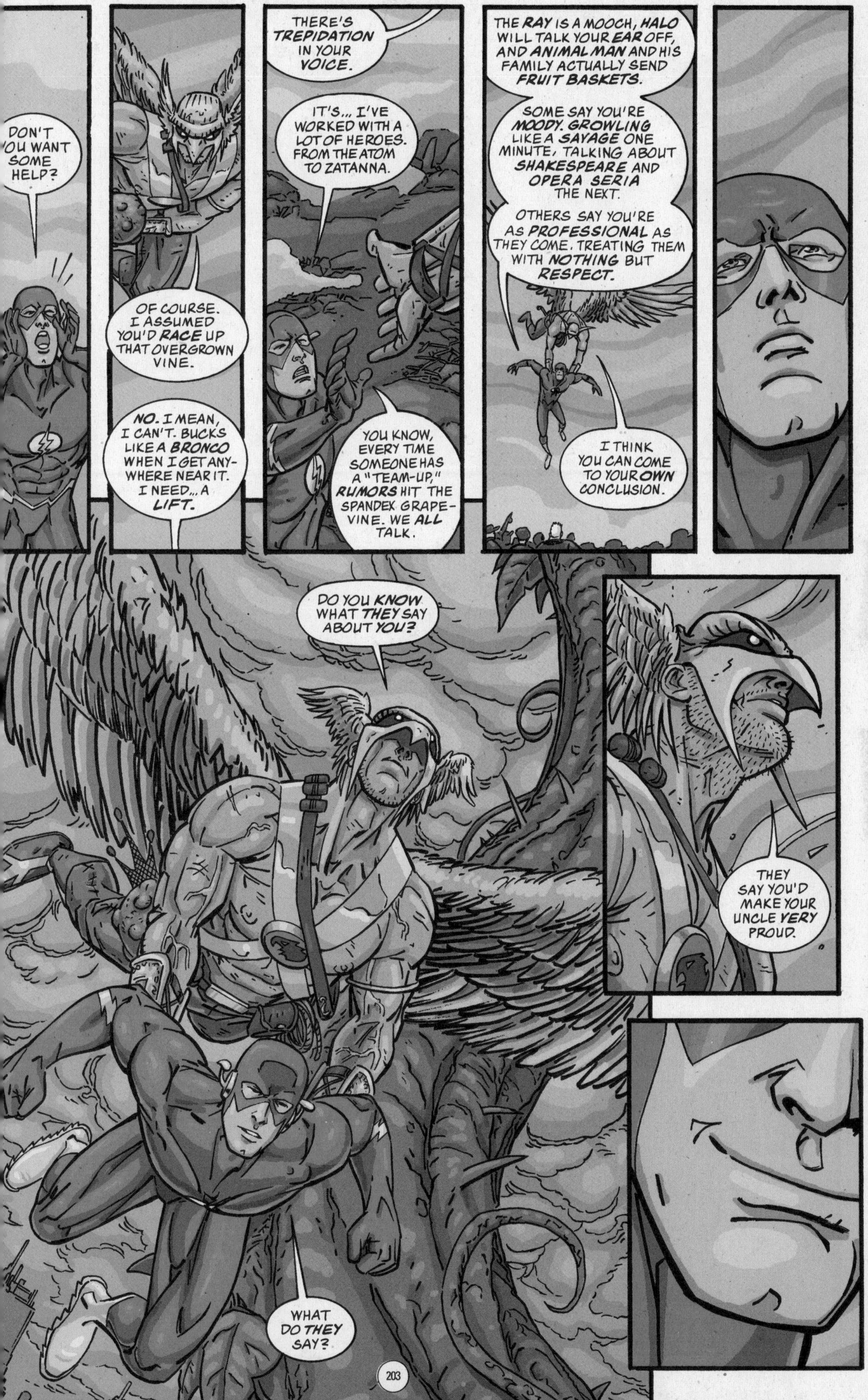
DON'T YOU WANT SOME HELP?
OF COURSE. I ASSUMED YOU'D RACE UP THAT OVERGROWN VINE.
NO. I MEAN, I CAN'T. BUCKS LIKE A BRONCO WHEN I GET ANYWHERE NEAR IT. I NEED... A LIFT.
THERE'S TREPIDATION IN YOUR VOICE.
IT'S... I'VE WORKED WITH A LOT OF HEROES. FROM THE ATOM TO ZATANNA.
YOU KNOW, EVERY TIME SOMEONE HAS A "TEAM-UP," RUMORS HIT THE SPANDEX GRAPEVINE. WE ALL TALK.
THE RAY IS A MOOCH, HALO WILL TALK YOUR EAR OFF, AND ANIMAL MAN AND HIS FAMILY ACTUALLY SEND FRUIT BASKETS.
SOME SAY YOU'RE MOODY. GROWLING LIKE A SAVAGE ONE MINUTE, TALKING ABOUT SHAKESPEARE AND OPERA SERIA THE NEXT.
OTHERS SAY YOU'RE AS PROFESSIONAL AS THEY COME. TREATING THEM WITH NOTHING BUT RESPECT.
I THINK YOU CAN COME TO YOUR OWN CONCLUSION.
DO YOU KNOW WHAT THEY SAY ABOUT YOU?
WHAT DO THEY SAY?
THEY SAY YOU'D MAKE YOUR UNCLE VERY PROUD.

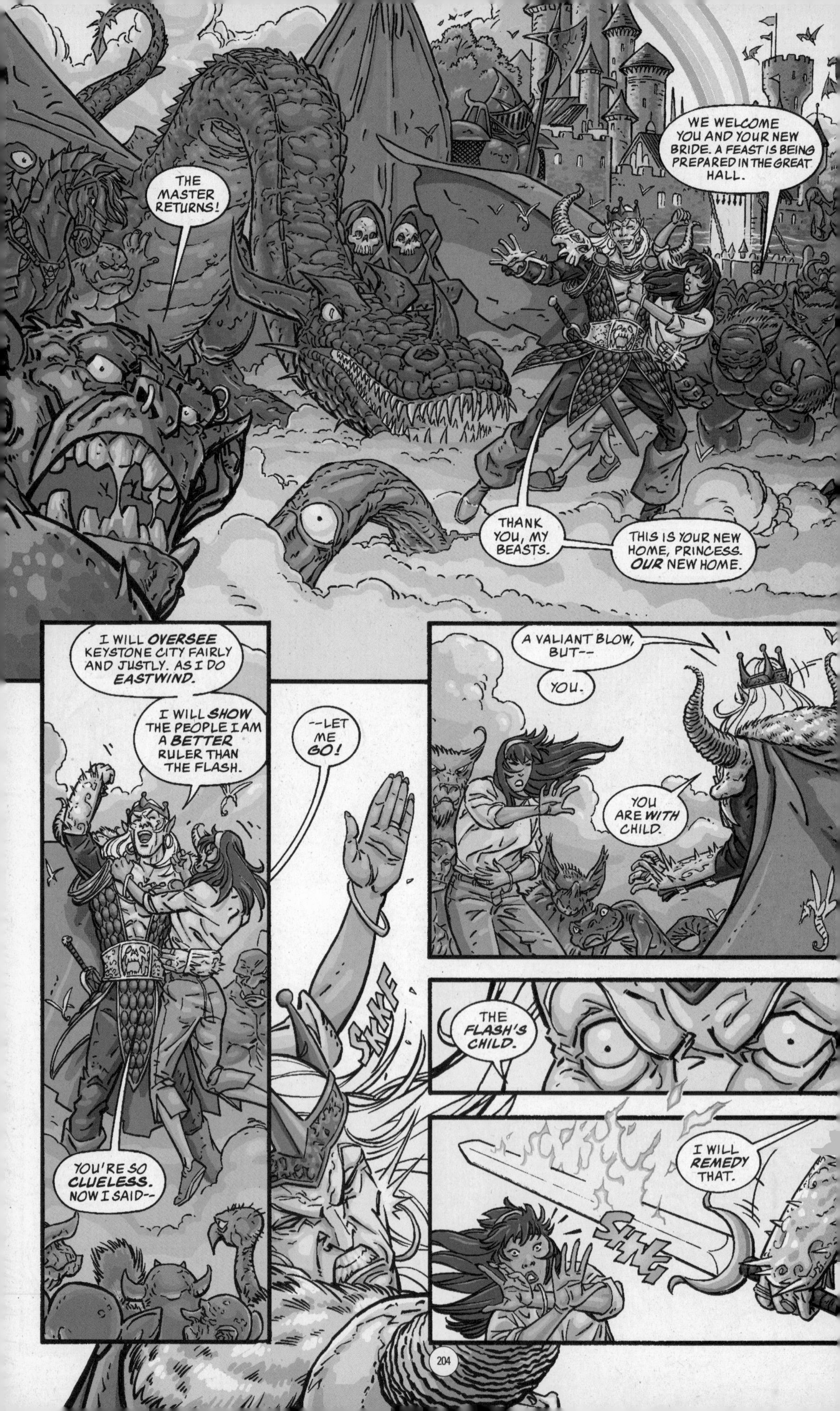
THE MASTER RETURNS!
WE WELCOME YOU AND YOUR NEW BRIDE. A FEAST IS BEING PREPARED IN THE GREAT HALL.
THANK YOU, MY BEASTS.
THIS IS YOUR NEW HOME, PRINCESS. **OUR** NEW HOME.
I WILL **OVERSEE** KEYSTONE CITY FAIRLY AND JUSTLY. AS I DO **EASTWIND**.
I WILL **SHOW** THE PEOPLE I AM A **BETTER** RULER THAN THE FLASH.
YOU'RE SO **CLUELESS**. NOW I SAID--
--LET ME **GO**!
SKRAK
A VALIANT BLOW, BUT--
YOU.
YOU ARE **WITH** CHILD.
THE **FLASH'S** CHILD.
I WILL **REMEDY** THAT.
SHING

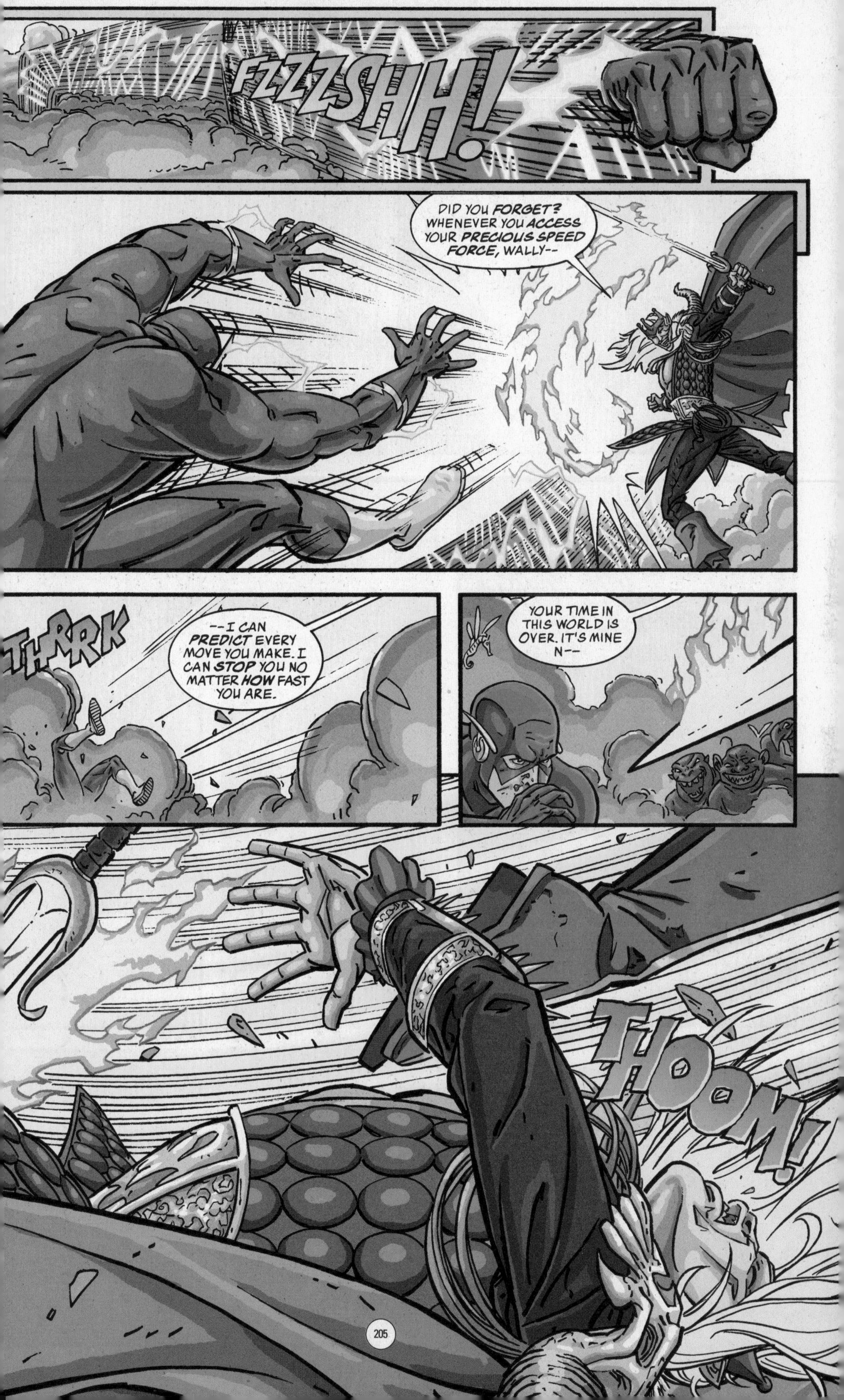
FZZZSHH!
DID YOU FORGET? WHENEVER YOU ACCESS YOUR PRECIOUS SPEED FORCE, WALLY--
THRRK
--I CAN PREDICT EVERY MOVE YOU MAKE. I CAN STOP YOU NO MATTER HOW FAST YOU ARE.
YOUR TIME IN THIS WORLD IS OVER. IT'S MINE N--
THOOM!

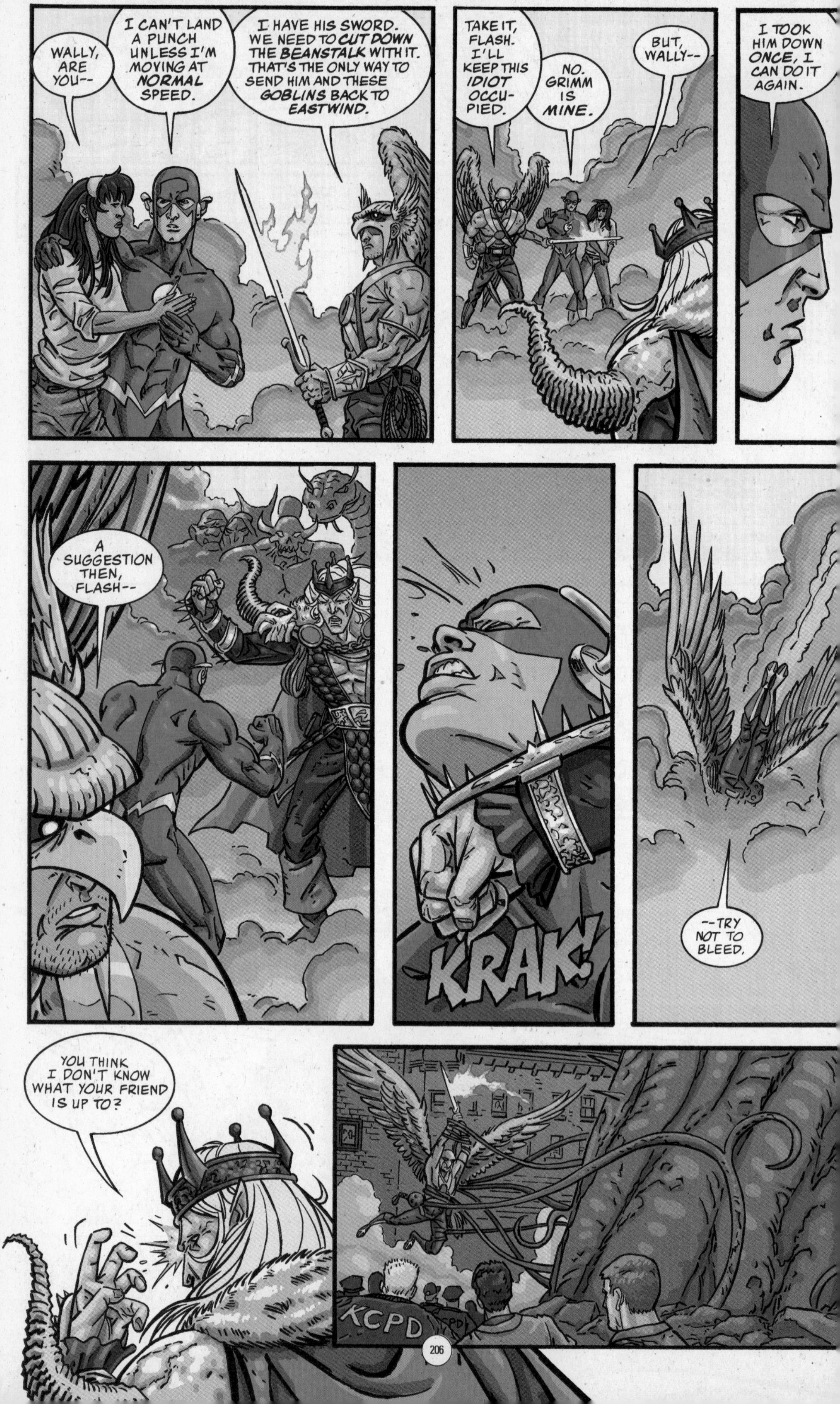

WALLY, ARE YOU--
I CAN'T LAND A PUNCH UNLESS I'M MOVING AT NORMAL SPEED.
I HAVE HIS SWORD. WE NEED TO CUT DOWN THE BEANSTALK WITH IT. THAT'S THE ONLY WAY TO SEND HIM AND THESE GOBLINS BACK TO EASTWIND.
TAKE IT, FLASH. I'LL KEEP THIS IDIOT OCCU-PIED.
NO. GRIMM IS MINE.
BUT, WALLY--
I TOOK HIM DOWN ONCE, I CAN DO IT AGAIN.
A SUGGESTION THEN, FLASH--
KRAK!
--TRY NOT TO BLEED.
YOU THINK I DON'T KNOW WHAT YOUR FRIEND IS UP TO?
KCPD

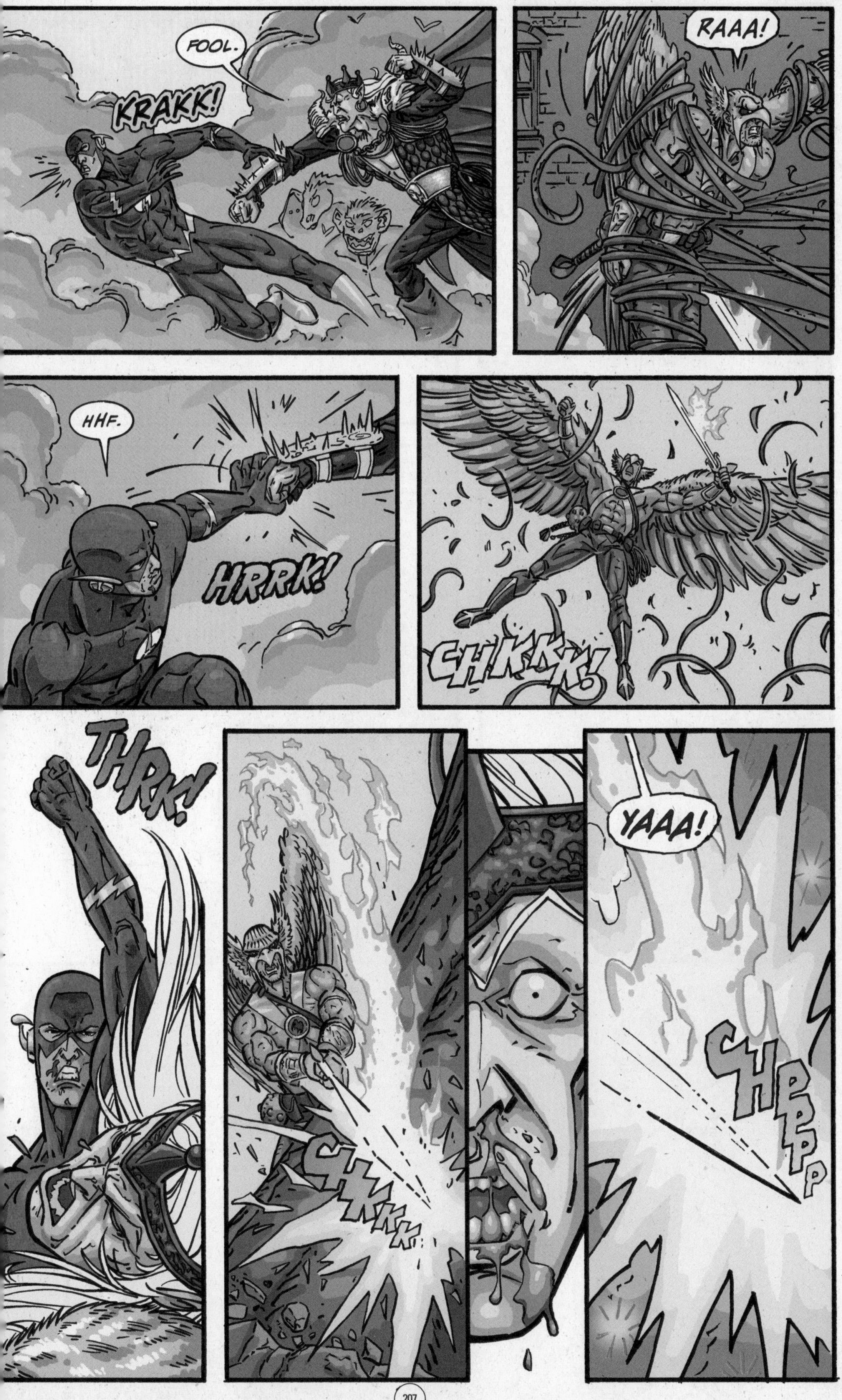
FOOL.
KRAKK!
RAAA!
HHF.
HRRK!
CHKKKK!
THRK!
CHKKKK
YAAA!
CHPPPP

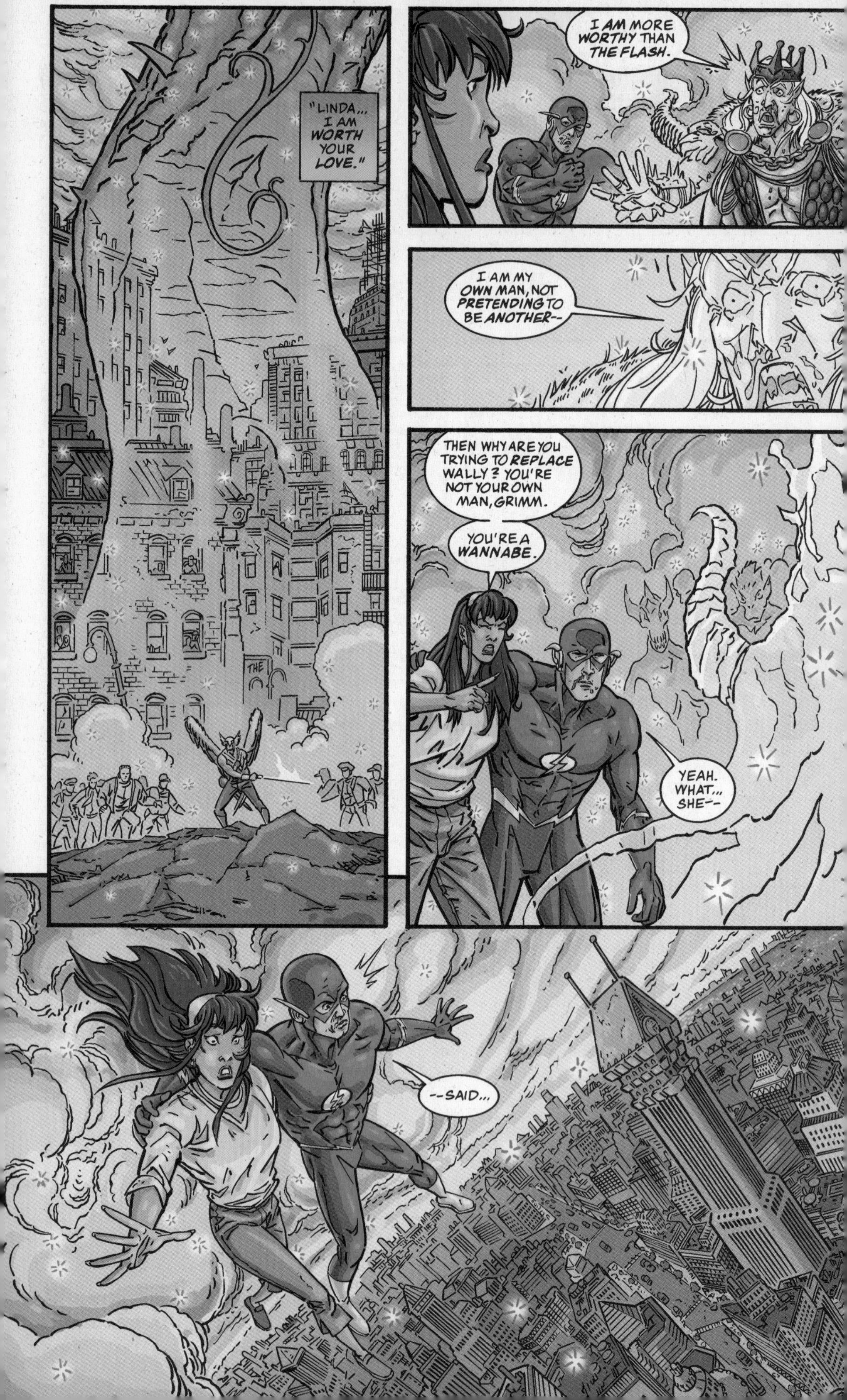
"LINDA... I AM WORTH YOUR LOVE."
I AM MORE WORTHY THAN THE FLASH.
I AM MY OWN MAN, NOT PRETENDING TO BE ANOTHER--
THEN WHY ARE YOU TRYING TO REPLACE WALLY? YOU'RE NOT YOUR OWN MAN, GRIMM.
YOU'RE A WANNABE.
YEAH. WHAT... SHE--
--SAID...

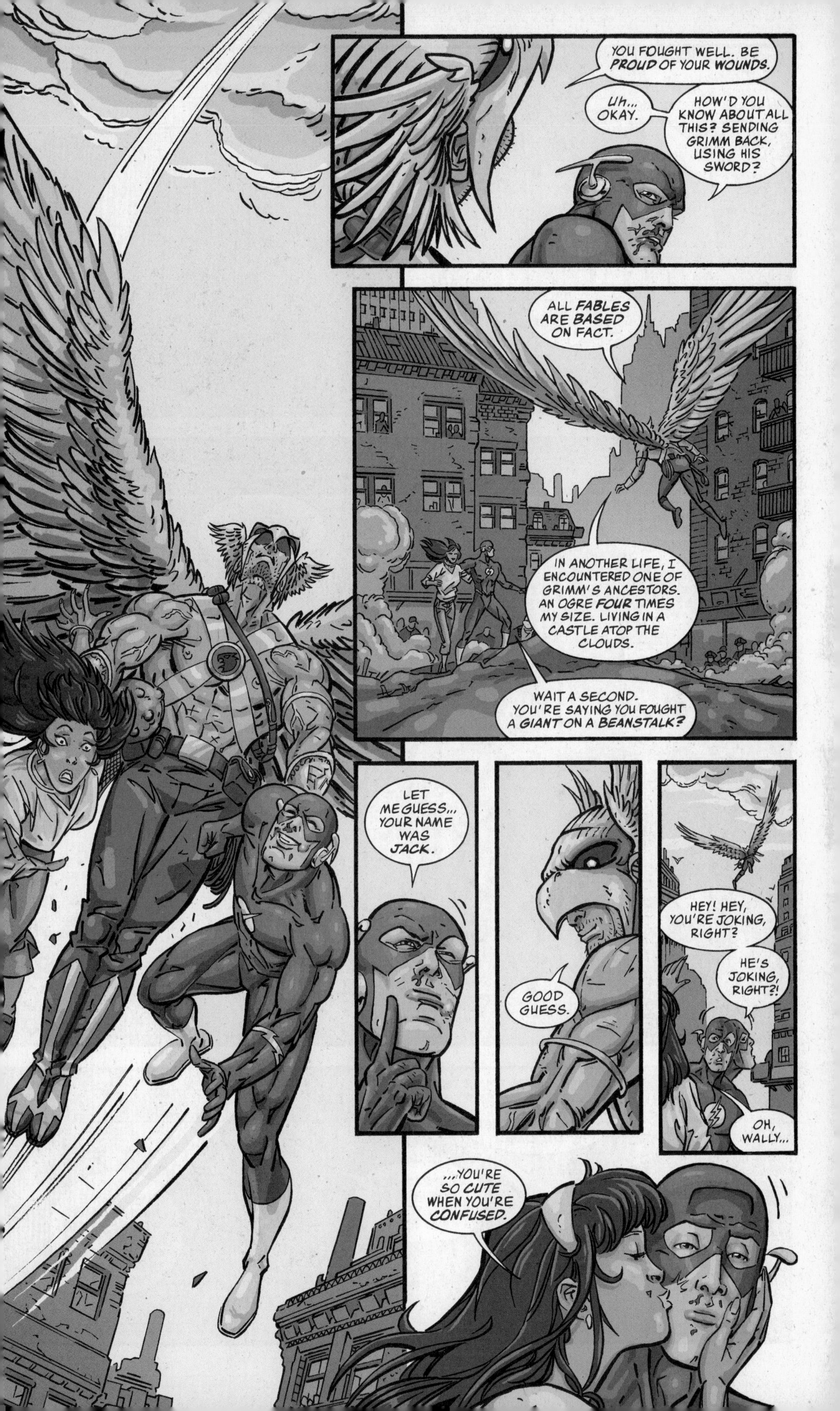
YOU FOUGHT WELL. BE PROUD OF YOUR WOUNDS.
UH... OKAY.
HOW'D YOU KNOW ABOUT ALL THIS? SENDING GRIMM BACK, USING HIS SWORD?
ALL FABLES ARE BASED ON FACT.
IN ANOTHER LIFE, I ENCOUNTERED ONE OF GRIMM'S ANCESTORS. AN OGRE FOUR TIMES MY SIZE. LIVING IN A CASTLE ATOP THE CLOUDS.
WAIT A SECOND. YOU'RE SAYING YOU FOUGHT A GIANT ON A BEANSTALK?
LET ME GUESS... YOUR NAME WAS JACK.
GOOD GUESS.
HEY! HEY, YOU'RE JOKING, RIGHT?
HE'S JOKING, RIGHT?!
OH, WALLY...
...YOU'RE SO CUTE WHEN YOU'RE CONFUSED.

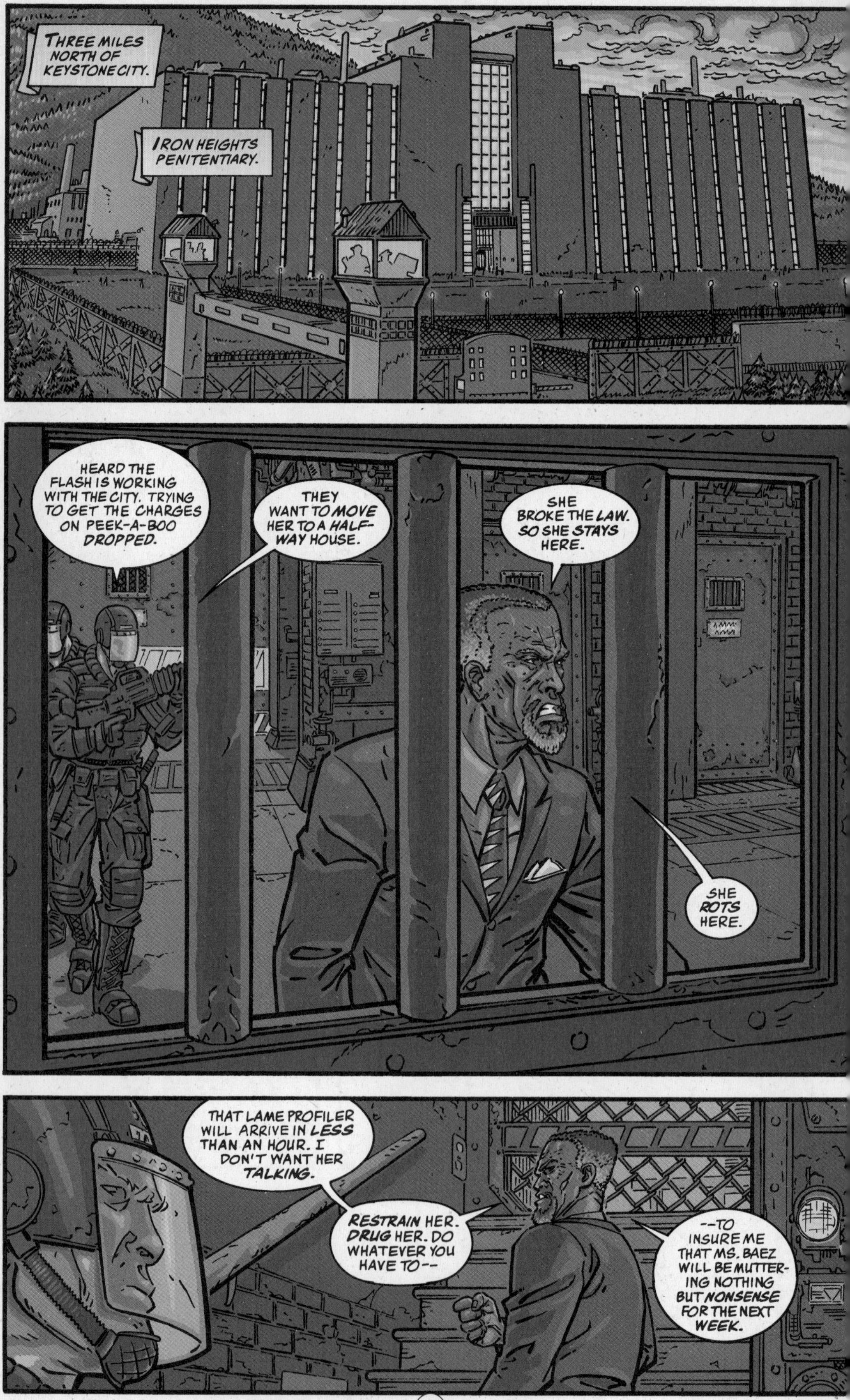
THREE MILES NORTH OF KEYSTONE CITY.
IRON HEIGHTS PENITENTIARY.
HEARD THE FLASH IS WORKING WITH THE CITY. TRYING TO GET THE CHARGES ON PEEK-A-BOO DROPPED.
THEY WANT TO MOVE HER TO A HALF-WAY HOUSE.
SHE BROKE THE LAW. SO SHE STAYS HERE.
SHE ROTS HERE.
THAT LAME PROFILER WILL ARRIVE IN LESS THAN AN HOUR. I DON'T WANT HER TALKING.
RESTRAIN HER. DRUG HER. DO WHATEVER YOU HAVE TO--
--TO INSURE ME THAT MS. BAEZ WILL BE MUTTER-ING NOTHING BUT NONSENSE FOR THE NEXT WEEK.

WE'VE HAD ENOUGH SCREW-UPS OF LATE. I WON'T TOLERATE ANY MORE.
GORILLA GRODD
DANGER
YES, WARDEN.

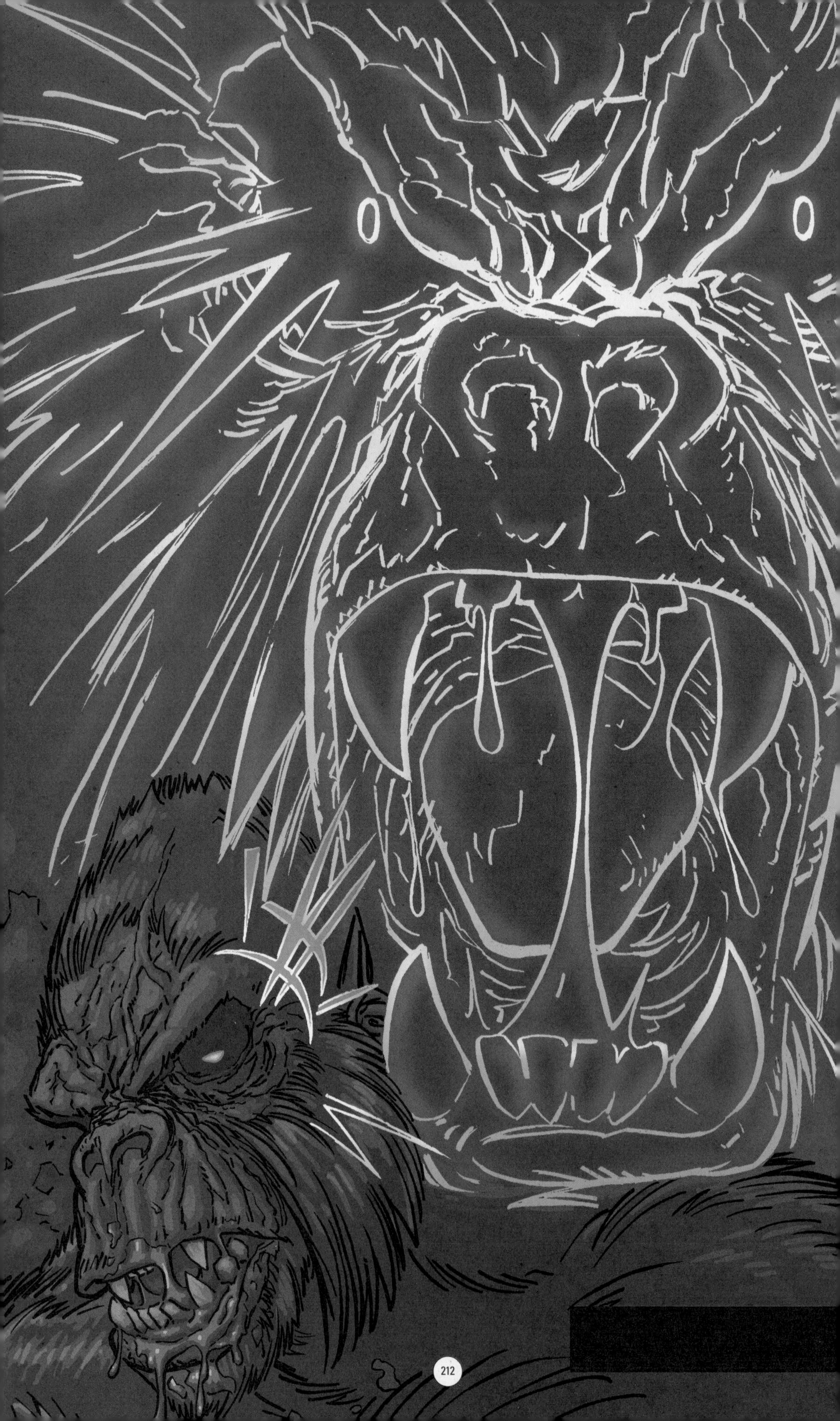
[redacted]

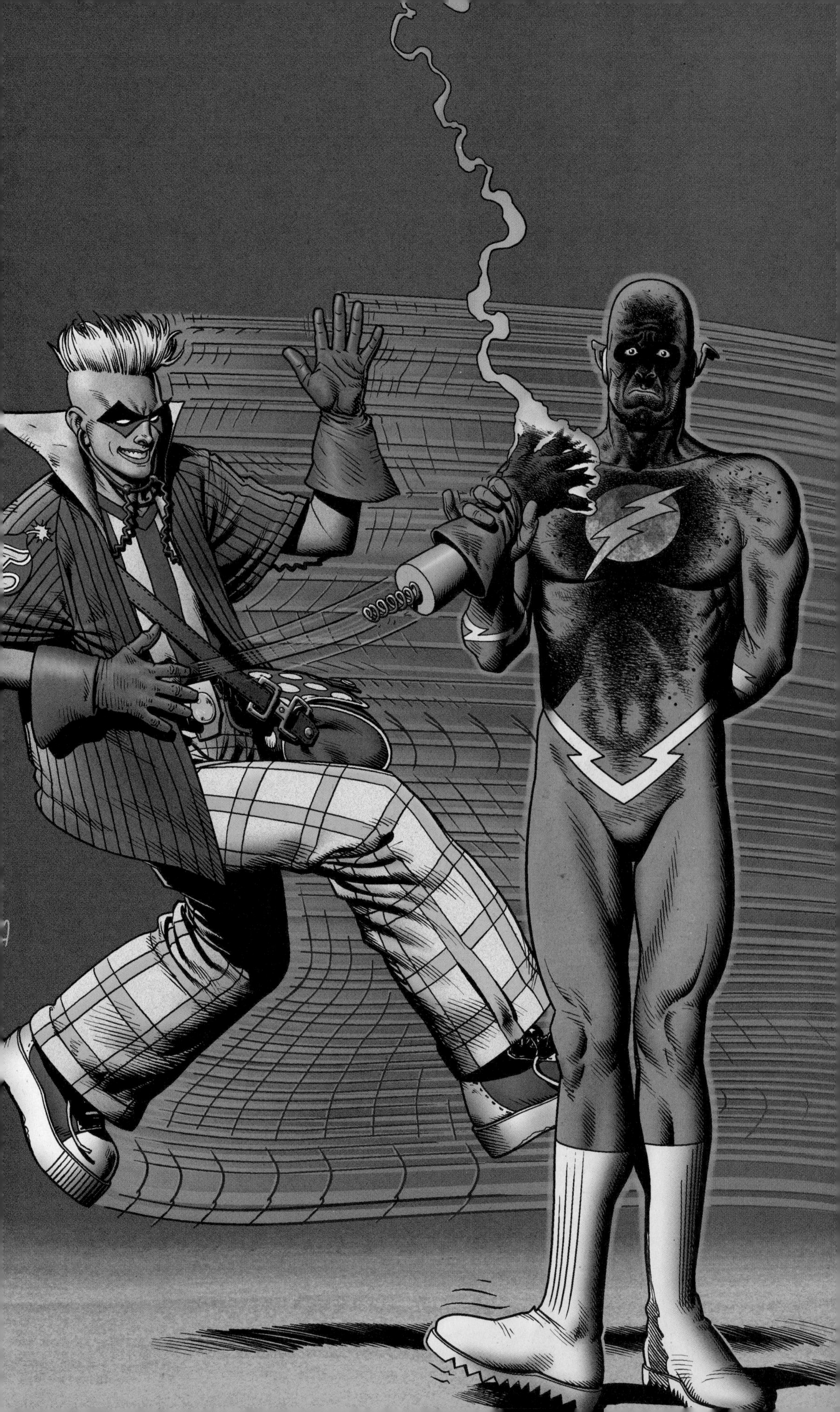

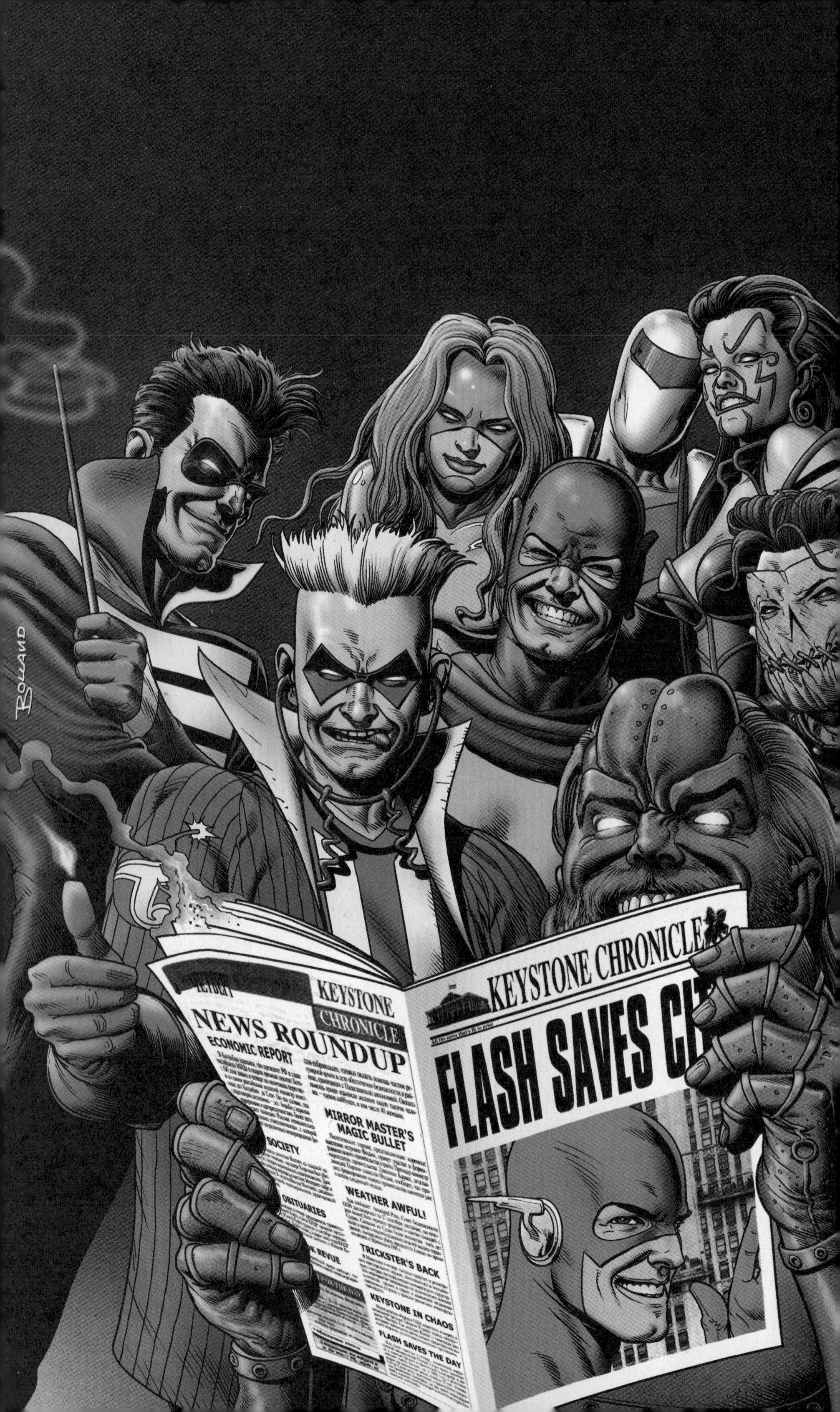
BOLLAND
KEYSTONE CHRONICLE
NEWS ROUNDUP
ECONOMIC REPORT
MIRROR MASTER'S MAGIC BULLET
SOCIETY
WEATHER AWFUL!
OBITUARIES
TRICKSTER'S BACK
KEYSTONE IN CHAOS
FLASH SAVES THE DAY
KEYSTONE CHRONICLE
FLASH SAVES CI

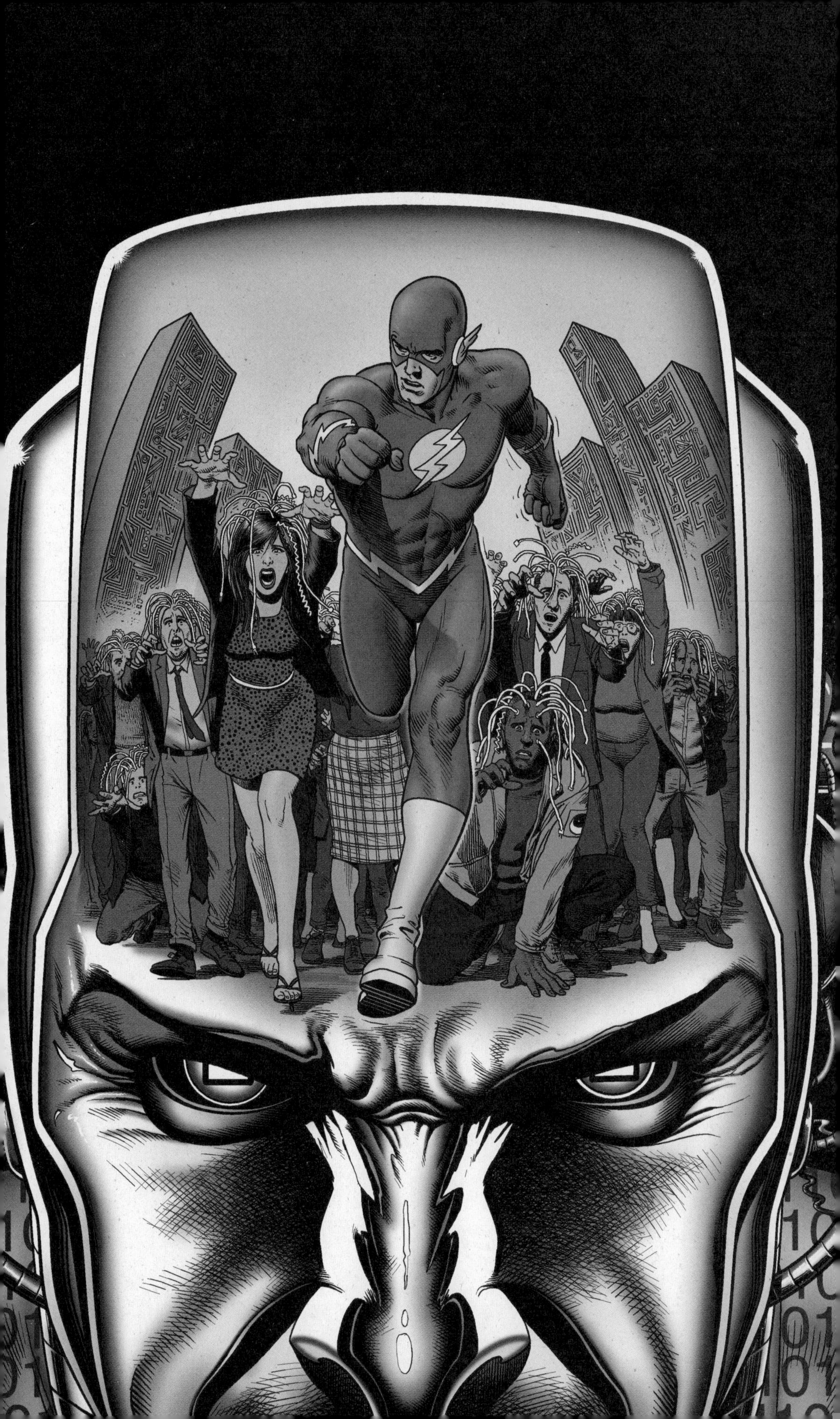

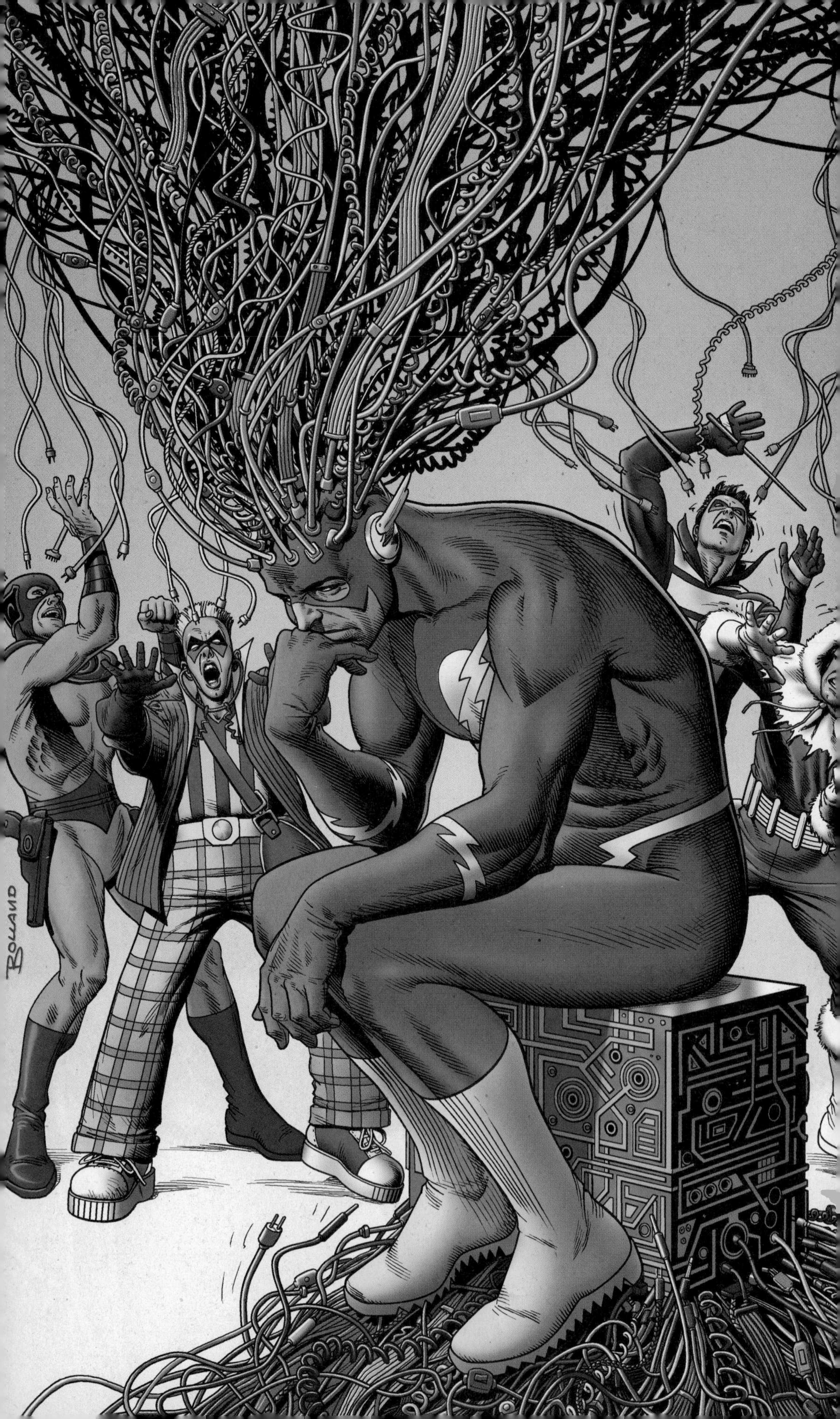
BOLLAND

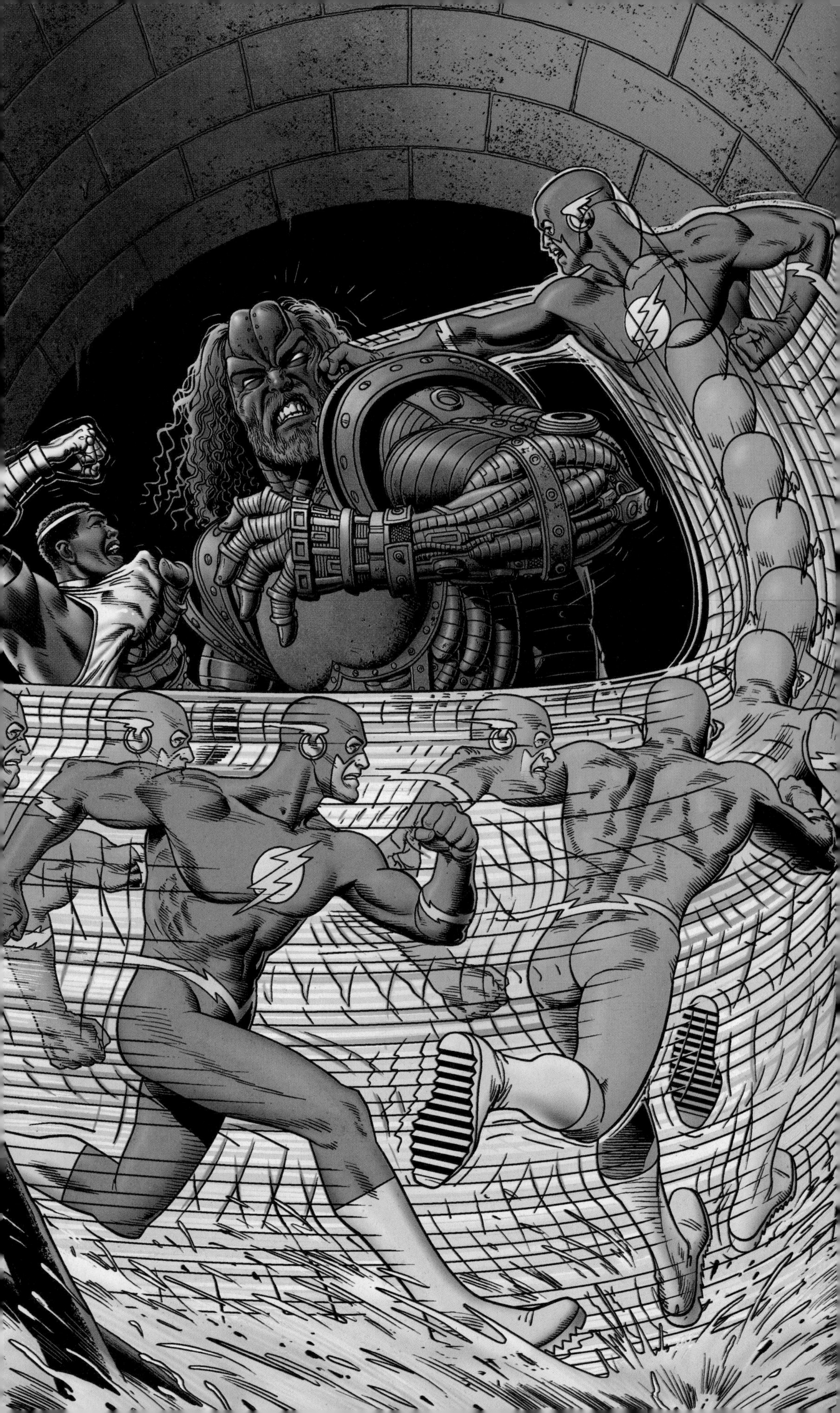

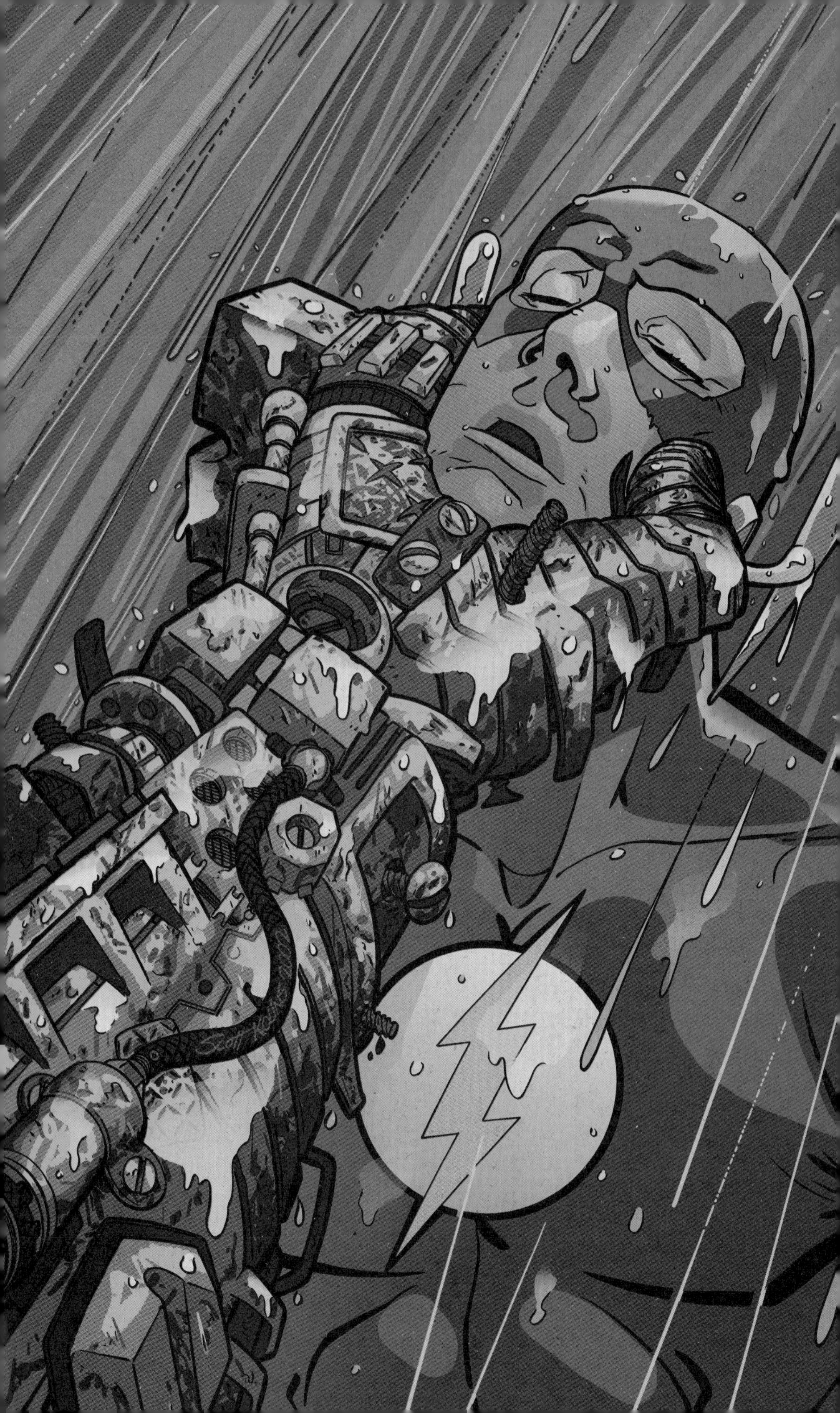

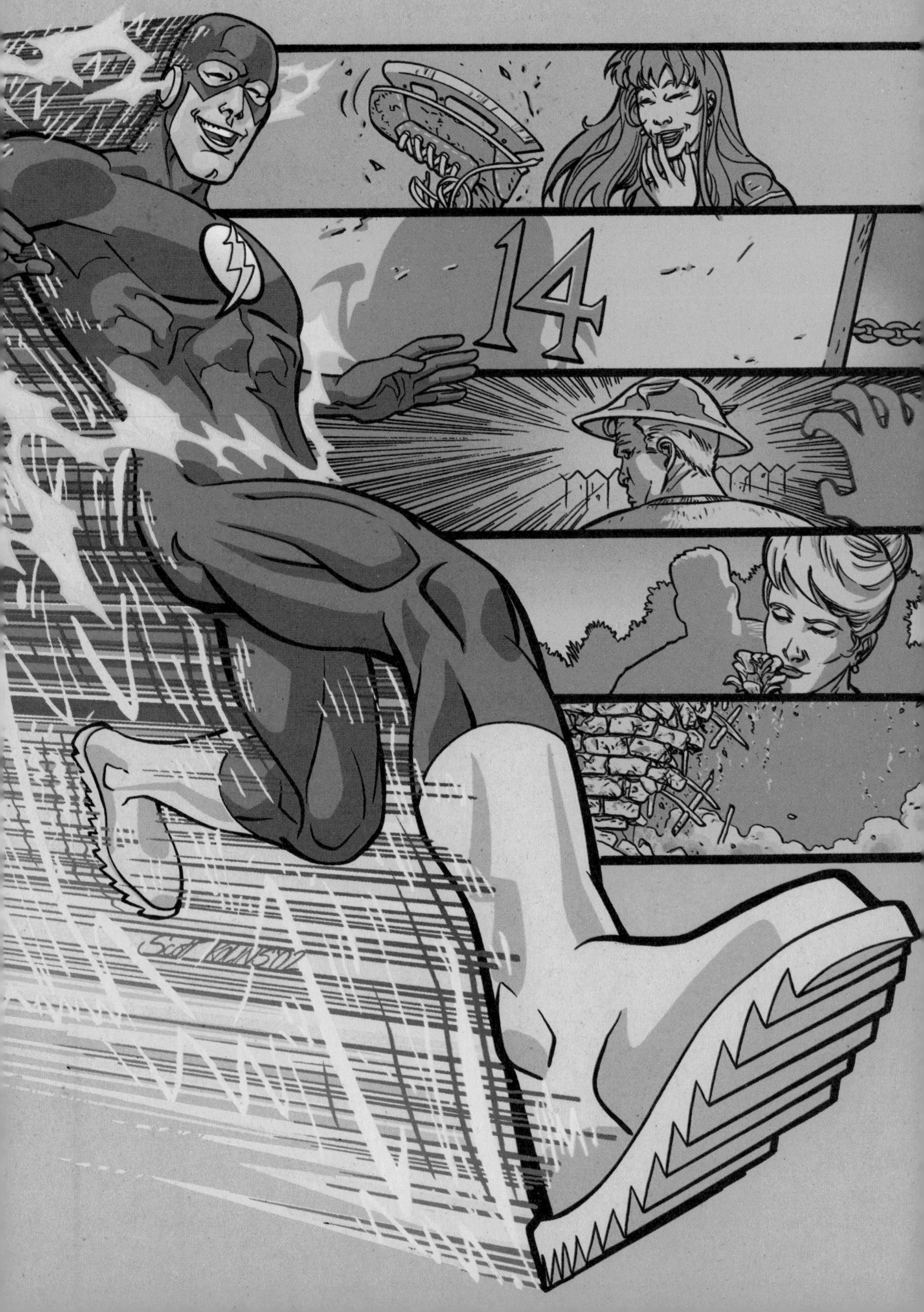
14

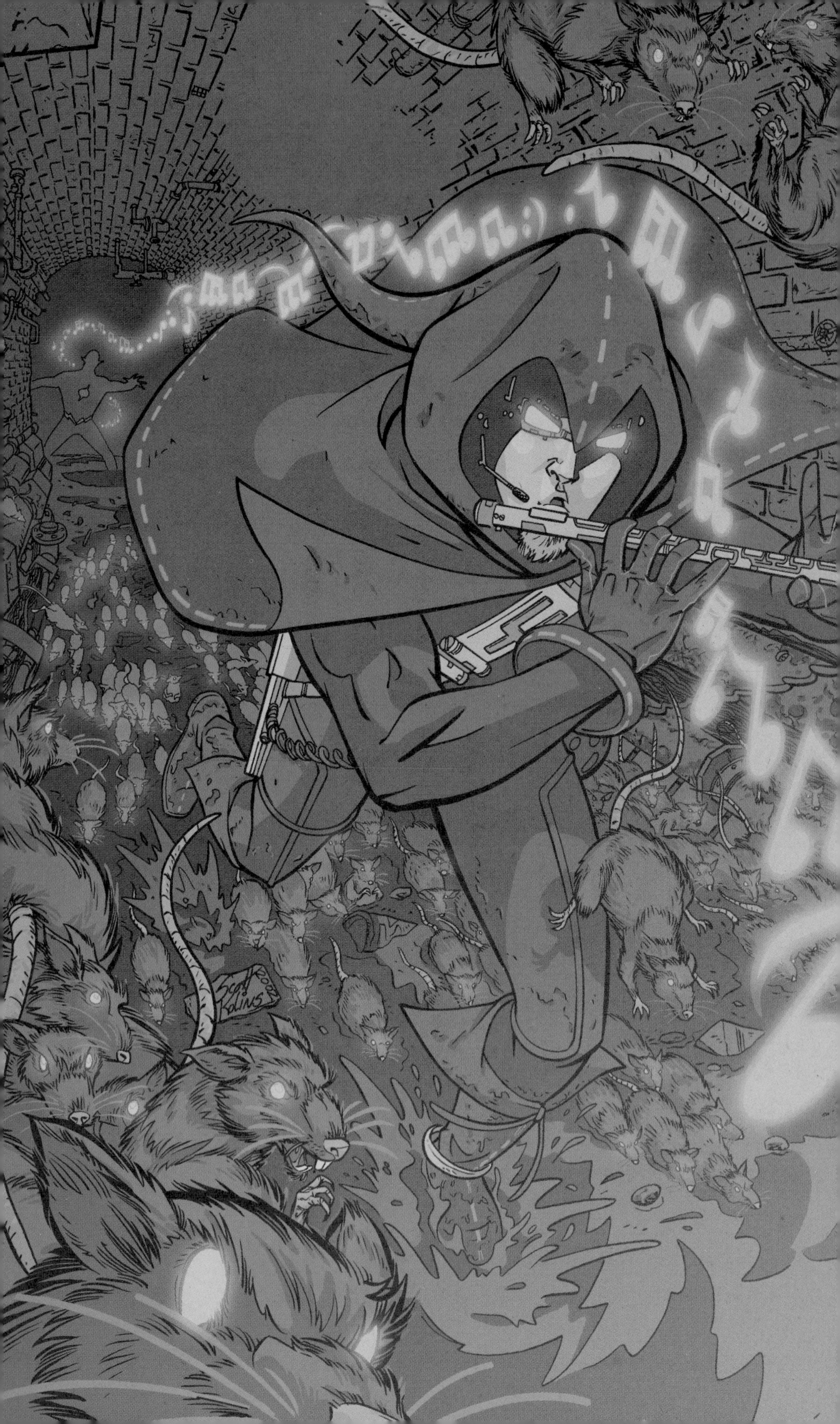

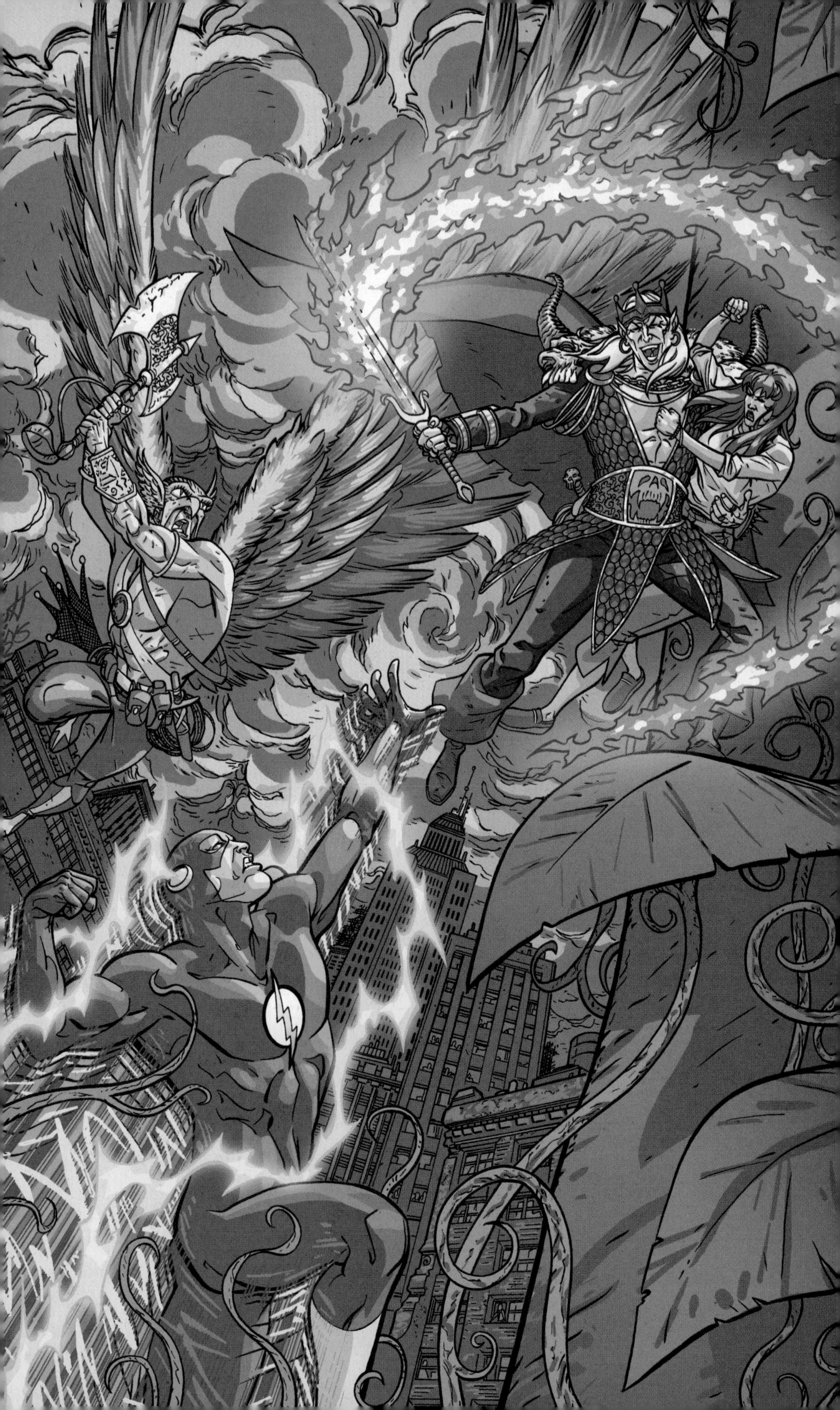

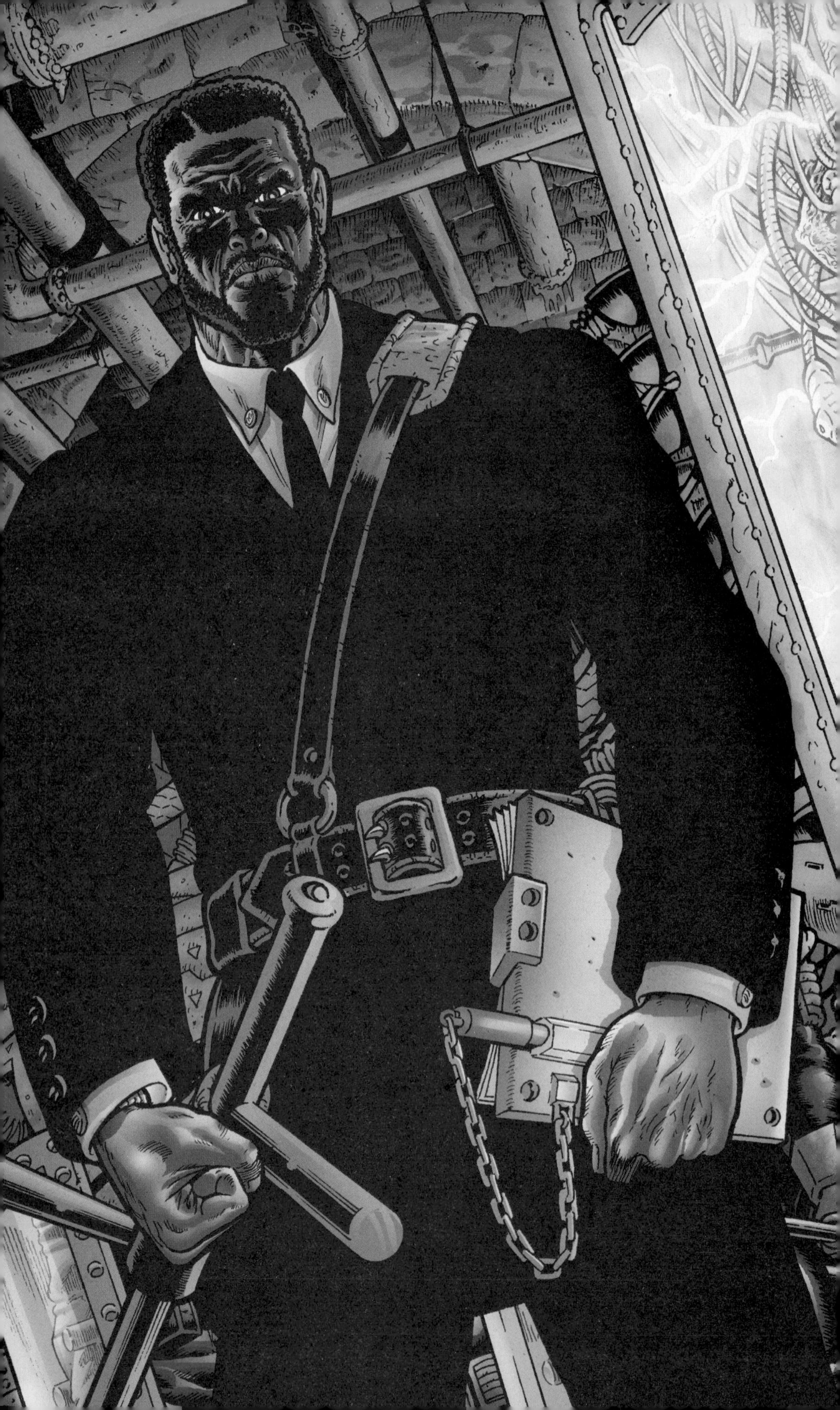

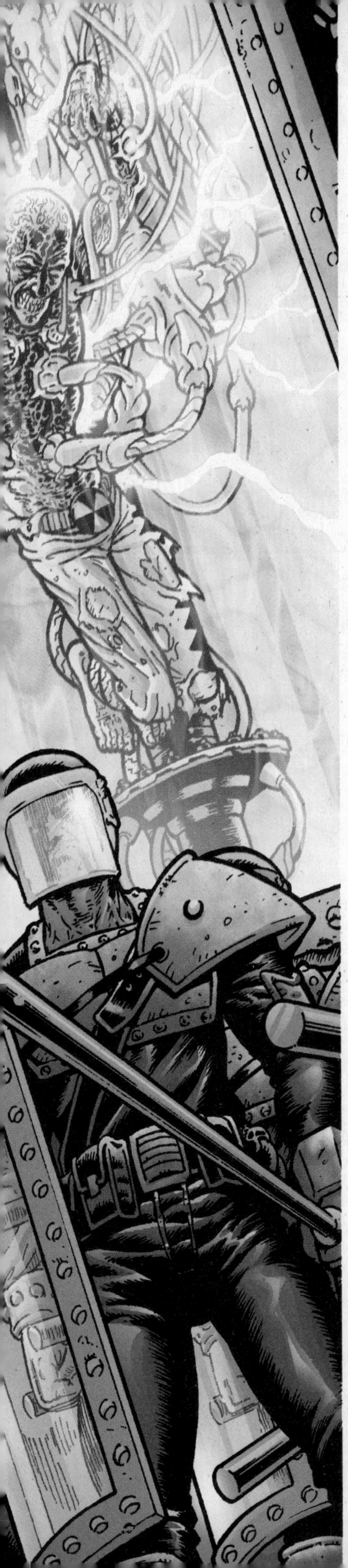

IRON HEIGHTS PENITENTIARY

First Appearance:
THE FLASH: IRON HEIGHTS (October, 2001)

"The only way out of Iron Heights is in a body bag." Up until the recent breakout, this was the motto among Iron Heights' prisoners...and its staff.

Keystone City Penitentiary was a fairly standard institution until Gregory Wolfe took over as warden. Spending a budget of nearly forty million dollars, Wolfe entirely reinvented the prison, transforming it into Iron Heights.

The main structure of the prison houses the worst criminals the surrounding states have to offer, as well as the infirmary – and the Warden's office. Riots are increasingly infrequent, and no guards had ever lost their lives until the recent breakout.

Over forty feet underground, the lower level of Iron Heights is called the Pipeline. Originally just a utility basement, it has since been converted to house metahuman and costumed inmates. The prisoners in the Pipeline are rarely let out of their cells.

Next to the Pipeline is the Power Room. Once, large generators powered the prison. Now, at Warden Wolfe's request, a radioactive rogue named Fallout serves as the power source. The prison saves hundreds of thousands of dollars thanks to his energies.

Currently over one thousand men and women are held within the walls of Iron Heights.

GREGORY WOLFE

Occupation: Warden
Marital Status: Married
Ht: 6' 2" Wt: 195 lbs.
Eyes: Brown
Hair: Black
First Appearance: THE FLASH: IRON HEIGHTS (October, 2001)

Prior to his role as warden, Wolfe was an infamous prosecutor for the city of St. Louis. He earned a reputation for being hard on criminals and seeking somewhat shady help in accumulating evidence. His methods were controversial, but Wolfe almost never lost a case. The only man Wolfe failed to convict was murdered two days after the trial, a case as yet unsolved.

Because of his friendship with the Governor, Wolfe was offered the job of Warden of Keystone City Prison after the previous warden suffered a heart attack and was forced to retire. Looking for a challenge, Wolfe accepted the position.

Wolfe was instrumental in updating and remodeling the institution, renaming it Iron Heights. His frustration with the "revolving door" nature of many prisons with large metahuman populations has driven Wolfe to ensure his building has been outfitted with the latest in containment technology.

Wolfe takes great care in initiating costumed "super-villains" into the prison. He forces them to wear their costumes, so they'll be easily spotted when mingling with the general population.

Although Wolfe held the Flash in high regard, his first encounter with him left him cold. The Flash accused the Warden of excessive cruelty towards prisoners, outraging Wolfe. Unbeknownst to the Flash – as well as to his superiors – Gregory Wolfe has the metahuman ability to control muscular impulses in living beings and, at a thought, can trigger painful spasms within any part of the human body.

WRITTEN BY GEOFF JOHNS. ART BY BRYAN TALBOT. COLOR BY TOM MCCRAW.

THE STARS OF THE
DC UNIVERSE
CAN ALSO BE FOUND IN THESE BOOKS:

GRAPHIC NOVELS

ENEMY ACE: WAR IDYLL
George Pratt

THE FLASH: LIFE STORY OF THE FLASH
M. Waid/B. Augustyn/G. Kane/
J. Staton/T. Palmer

GREEN LANTERN: FEAR ITSELF
Ron Marz/Brad Parker

THE POWER OF SHAZAM!
Jerry Ordway

WONDER WOMAN: AMAZONIA
William Messner-Loebs/
Phil Winslade

COLLECTIONS

THE GREATEST 1950s STORIES EVER TOLD
Various writers and artists

THE GREATEST TEAM-UP STORIES EVER TOLD
Various writers and artists

AQUAMAN: TIME AND TIDE
Peter David/Kirk Jarvinen/
Brad Vancata

DC ONE MILLION
Various writers and artists

THE FINAL NIGHT
K. Kesel/S. Immonen/
J. Marzan/various

THE FLASH: BORN TO RUN
M. Waid/T. Peyer/G. LaRocque/
H. Ramos/various

GREEN LANTERN: A NEW DAWN
R. Marz/D. Banks/R. Tanghal/
various

GREEN LANTERN: BAPTISM OF FIRE
Ron Marz/Darryl Banks/
various

GREEN LANTERN: EMERALD KNIGHTS
Ron Marz/Darryl Banks/
various

HAWK & DOVE
Karl and Barbara Kesel/
Rob Liefeld

HITMAN
Garth Ennis/John McCrea

HITMAN: LOCAL HEROES
G. Ennis/J. McCrea/
C. Ezquerra/S. Pugh

HITMAN: TEN THOUSAND BULLETS
Garth Ennis/John McCrea

IMPULSE: RECKLESS YOUTH
Mark Waid/various

JACK KIRBY'S FOREVER PEOPLE
Jack Kirby/various

JACK KIRBY'S NEW GODS
Jack Kirby/various

JACK KIRBY'S MISTER MIRACLE
Jack Kirby/various

JUSTICE LEAGUE: A NEW BEGINNING
K. Giffen/J.M. DeMatteis/
K. Maguire/various

JUSTICE LEAGUE: A MIDSUMMER'S NIGHTMARE
M. Waid/F. Nicieza/J. Johnson/
D. Robertson/various

JLA: AMERICAN DREAMS
G. Morrison/H. Porter/J. Dell/
various

JLA: JUSTICE FOR ALL
G. Morrison/M. Waid/H. Porter/
J. Dell/various

JUSTICE LEAGUE OF AMERICA: THE NAIL
Alan Davis/Mark Farmer

JLA: NEW WORLD ORDER
Grant Morrison/
Howard Porter/John Dell

JLA: ROCK OF AGES
G. Morrison/H. Porter/J. Dell/
various

JLA: STRENGTH IN NUMBERS
G. Morrison/M. Waid/H. Porter/
J. Dell/various

JLA: WORLD WITHOUT GROWN-UPS
T. Dezago/T. Nauck/H. Ramos/
M. McKone/various

JLA/TITANS: THE TECHNIS IMPERATIVE
D. Grayson/P. Jimenez/
P. Pelletier/various

JLA: YEAR ONE
M. Waid/B. Augustyn/
B. Kitson/various

KINGDOM COME
Mark Waid/Alex Ross

LEGENDS: THE COLLECTED EDITION
J. Ostrander/L. Wein/J. Byrne/
K. Kesel

LOBO'S GREATEST HITS
Various writers and artists

LOBO: THE LAST CZARNIAN
Keith Giffen/Alan Grant/
Simon Bisley

LOBO'S BACK'S BACK
K. Giffen/A. Grant/S. Bisley/
C. Alamy

MANHUNTER: THE SPECIAL EDITION
Archie Goodwin/Walter Simonson

THE RAY: IN A BLAZE OF POWER
Jack C. Harris/Joe Quesada/
Art Nichols

THE SPECTRE: CRIMES AND PUNISHMENTS
John Ostrander/Tom Mandrake

STARMAN: SINS OF THE FATHER
James Robinson/Tony Harris/
Wade von Grawbadger

STARMAN: NIGHT AND DAY
James Robinson/Tony Harris/
Wade von Grawbadger

STARMAN: TIMES PAST
J. Robinson/O. Jimenez/
L. Weeks/various

STARMAN: A WICKED INCLINATION...
J. Robinson/T. Harris/
W. von Grawbadger/various

UNDERWORLD UNLEASHED
M. Waid/H. Porter/
P. Jimenez/various

WONDER WOMAN: THE CONTEST
William Messner-Loebs/
Mike Deodato, Jr.

WONDER WOMAN: SECOND GENESIS
John Byrne

WONDER WOMAN: LIFELINES
John Byrne

DC/MARVEL: CROSSOVER CLASSICS II
Various writers and artists

DC VERSUS MARVEL/ MARVEL VERSUS DC
R. Marz/P. David/D. Jurgens/
C. Castellini/various

THE AMALGAM AGE OF COMICS: THE DC COMICS COLLECTION
Various writers and artists

RETURN TO THE AMALGAM AGE OF COMICS: THE DC COMICS COLLECTION
Various writers and artists

OTHER COLLECTIONS OF INTEREST

CAMELOT 3000
Mike W. Barr/Brian Bolland/
various

RONIN
Frank Miller

WATCHMEN
Alan Moore/Dave Gibbons

ARCHIVE EDITIONS

THE FLASH ARCHIVES Volume 1
(FLASH COMICS 104, SHOWCASE 4, 8, 13, 14, THE FLASH 105-108)
J. Broome/C. Infantino/J. Giella/
various

THE FLASH ARCHIVES Volume 2
(THE FLASH 109-116)
J.Broome/C. Infantino/J. Giella/
various

GREEN LANTERN ARCHIVES Volume 1
(SHOWCASE 22-23, GREEN LANTERN 1-5)

GREEN LANTERN ARCHIVES Volume 2
(GREEN LANTERN 6-13)
All by J. Broome/G. Kane/
J. Giella/various

SHAZAM ARCHIVES Volume 1
(WHIZ COMICS 2-15)

SHAZAM ARCHIVES Volume 2
(SPECIAL EDITION COMICS 1, CAPTAIN MARVEL ADVENTURES 1, WHIZ COMICS 15-20)
All by B. Parker/C.C. Beck/
J. Simon/J. Kirby/various

THE NEW TEEN TITANS Volume 1
(DC COMICS PRESENTS 26, THE NEW TITANS 1-8)
Marv Wolfman/George Pérez/
various

TO FIND MORE COLLECTED EDITIONS AND MONTHLY COMIC BOOKS FROM DC COMICS,
CALL 1-888-COMIC BOOK FOR THE NEAREST COMICS SHOP OR GO TO YOUR LOCAL BOOK STORE.

Visit us at www.dccomics.com